INVENTING CUSTER

The American Crisis Series

Books on the Civil War Era

Steven E. Woodworth, Professor of History,
Texas Christian University
Series Editor

James L. Abrahamson. *The Men of Secession and Civil War, 1859–1861.*

Robert G. Tanner. *Retreat to Victory? Confederate Strategy Reconsidered.*

Stephen Davis. *Atlanta Will Fall: Sherman, Joe Johnston, and the Yankee Heavy Battalions.*

Paul Ashdown and Edward Caudill. *The Mosby Myth: A Confederate Hero in Life and Legend.*

Spencer C. Tucker. *A Short History of the Civil War at Sea.*

Richard Bruce Winders. *Crisis in the Southwest: The United States, Mexico, and the Struggle over Texas.*

Ethan S. Rafuse. *A Single Grand Victory: The First Campaign and Battle of Manassas.*

John G. Selby. *Virginians at War: The Civil War Experiences of Seven Young Confederates.*

Edward K. Spann. *Gotham at War: New York City, 1860–1865.*

Anne J. Bailey. *War and Ruin: William T. Sherman and the Savannah Campaign.*

Gary Dillard Joiner. *One Damn Blunder from Beginning to End: The Red River Campaign of 1864.*

Steven E. Woodworth. *Beneath a Northern Sky: A Short History of the Gettysburg Campaign.*

John C. Waugh. *On the Brink of Civil War: The Compromise of 1850 and How It Changed the Course of American History.*

Eric H. Walther. *The Shattering of the Union: America in the 1850s.*

Mark Thornton and Robert B. Ekelund Jr. *Tariffs, Blockades, and Inflation: The Economics of the Civil War.*

Paul Ashdown and Edward Caudill. *The Myth of Nathan Bedford Forrest.*

Michael B. Ballard. *U. S. Grant: The Making of a General, 1861–1863.*

Donald T. Collins. *The Death and Resurrection of Jefferson Davis.*

David Coffey. *Sheridan's Lieutenants: Phil Sheridan, His Generals, and the Final Year of the Civil War.*

Christopher Waldrep. *Vicksburg's Long Shadow: The Civil War Legacy of Race and Remembrance.*

J. Michael Martinez. *Carpetbaggers, Cavalry, and the Ku Klux Klan: Exposing the Invisible Empire during Reconstruction.*

Steven E. Woodworth. *Beneath a Northern Sky: A Short History of the Gettysburg Campaign, 2nd Edition.*

Edward Caudill and Paul Ashdown. *Sherman's March in Myth and Memory.*

Ethan S. Rafuse. *Robert E. Lee and the Fall of the Confederacy, 1863–1865.*

Alden R. Carter. *The Sea Eagle: The Civil War Memoir of Lt. Cdr. William B. Cushing.*

Edward Caudill and Paul Ashdown. *Inventing Custer: The Making of an American Legend.*

INVENTING CUSTER

The Making of an American Legend

Edward Caudill and Paul Ashdown

ROWMAN & LITTLEFIELD
Lanham • Boulder • New York • London

Published by Rowman & Littlefield
A wholly owned subsidiary of The Rowman & Littlefield Publishing Group, Inc.
4501 Forbes Boulevard, Suite 200, Lanham, Maryland 20706
www.rowman.com

Unit A, Whitacre Mews, 26-34 Stannary Street, London SE11 4AB

British Library Cataloguing in Publication Information Available

Library of Congress Cataloging-in-Publication Data

Caudill, Edward.
Inventing Custer : the making of an American legend / Edward Caudill and Paul Ashdown.
pages cm. — (The American crisis series: books on the Civil War era)
Includes bibliographical references and index.
ISBN 978-1-4422-5186-1 (cloth : alk. paper)— ISBN 978-1-4422-5187-8 (electronic) 1. Custer,
George A. (George Armstrong), 1839–1876. 2. Custer, George A. (George Armstrong),
1839–1876—Influence. 3. Generals—United States—Biography. 4. United States. Army—Biogra-
phy. 5. United States—History—Civil War, 1861–1865—Biography. 6. Indians of North America—
Wars—West (U.S.) I. Ashdown, Paul, 1944– II. Title.
E467.1.C99C38 2015
973.8'2092—dc23
[B]
                                        2015018416

∞ ™ The paper used in this publication meets the minimum requirements of
American National Standard for Information Sciences Permanence of Paper for
Printed Library Materials, ANSI/NISO Z39.48-1992.

Printed in the United States of America

For Robert, Daniel, and Gretchen

For Barbara

CONTENTS

ACKNOWLEDGMENTS

With special thanks to the following for their assistance and advice and for reading all or various parts of the manuscript: Steven E. Woodworth, professor of history, Texas Christian University, and editor of *The American Crisis* series published by Rowman & Littlefield; Ethan S. Rafuse, professor of military history, U.S. Army Command and General Staff College; David Coffey, professor and chair, Department of History and Philosophy, University of Tennessee at Martin; Michael Donahue, chair, Department of Visual Arts at Temple College, and park ranger at the Little Bighorn Battlefield National Monument; Joel Shockley, park ranger at the Washita Battlefield National Historical Site; and John F. Marszalek, William L. Giles Distinguished Professor Emeritus of History, Mississippi State University. And with appreciation to David T. Wright for advice and insight on Custer reenactors; Robert Caudill, for assistance with organizing, editing, and formatting the manuscript; Will Fontanez, director; and Dhara Naik of the University of Tennessee Cartography Laboratory.

INTRODUCTION

Rising high above the Virginia Peninsula in a basket hanging beneath a hydrogen-gas-filled balloon during late April 1862, Second Lieutenant George Armstrong Custer contemplated "a most beautiful landscape" between the York and James rivers, "the theater of operations of armies larger and more formidable than had ever confronted each other on this continent before." To the east, he could see the coruscating expanse of the Chesapeake Bay and the flotillas of naval vessels supplying the Army of the Potomac. Tethered to the ground "by numerous ropes, like a wild and untamable animal," the balloon had risen some one thousand feet, carrying a nervous Custer and an assistant.[1]

Custer wrote about his airborne adventures for *Galaxy* shortly before embarking on the 1876 Montana campaign that made him immortal. The unfinished article, one of a series of Civil War reminiscences he had been writing, was published in the November 1876 issue some four months after his death at the Little Bighorn. Custer recalled that he had accepted the scouting assignment "with no little trepidation, for although I had chosen the mounted service from preference alone, yet I had a choice as to the character of the mount, and the proposed ride was far more elevated than I had ever desired or contemplated."[2]

Observation balloons had been used to identify enemy positions and direct artillery fire. Professional "aeronauts" had been sent up to observe, but their reports were militarily unreliable. Besieging Yorktown during the Peninsula Campaign in 1862, the Army of the Potomac needed better intelligence about Confederate positions. A general had been sent aloft, but when a mooring rope snapped, he had soared into the heavens and drifted over Confederate lines as thousands of astonished soldiers on both sides gaped at the spectacle. After the general crash-landed, narrowly escaping serious injury, a more expendable lieutenant, the twenty-two-year-old Custer, was ordered aloft.[3]

Recalling his initial ascent, the first of many, as he prepared fourteen years later to engage the Sioux and Cheyenne below the Yellowstone, Custer was not just thinking about terrain. He was looking back across the sweep of American history, a story in progress, a narrative in which he might yet play a major part. In the distance, he remembered, was York-town, which had "witnessed the surrender of a disciplined and tired army of veterans" to an army "surely stronger in the justness of the cause for which it contended." Long before the American Revolution, the peninsula had spawned some of the nation's cherished myths about Native Americans, most notably at Jamestown, only a few miles from the clashing armies. There, Custer wrote, had occurred the "incidents upon which is based the familiar story of Pocahontas and her generous conduct toward John Smith."[4]

As a West Point cadet, Custer had read James Fenimore Cooper's *Leatherstocking Tales*. Describing for *Galaxy* his experiences in the American West after the Civil War, he "regretted that the character of the Indian as described in Cooper's interesting novels is not the true one." He likened his changing perspective to coming of age and being "compelled to cast aside many of our earlier illusions and replace them by beliefs less inviting but more real."[5]

The *Galaxy* dispatches reveal a confident young man rising above the territory of his own life, and the life of the expanding nation as he understood it, to see what was real. Above the peninsula, he found it difficult to identify the enemy's pavilions, earthworks, and artillery because they had been well concealed by timberlines. He made several more flights at different times of the day and night and discovered that, by going up just before dawn, he could spot enemy cooking fires and determine the strength of the lines. On the morning of May 4, 1862, he could see by the absence of fires that the Confederates had abandoned their positions and were withdrawing toward Richmond. When Major General George B. McClellan learned this, he ordered the army forward. It was Custer's scouting abilities that first brought the young officer to McClellan's attention and set him on course for rapid promotion, a brevet brigadier general's commission just before the Battle of Gettysburg and promotion to brevet major general by the end of the war.[6]

This Custer largely has been eclipsed by the Little Bighorn, a military disaster on the western frontier brought about largely by Custer's failure to comprehend the territory into which he was leading the 7th Cavalry. There were no observation balloons at the Little Bighorn battlefield, which spread across a meandering valley difficult to assay from the ragged bluffs and ridges of its southeastern approaches. Any misjudgments Custer made in the last hours of his life were shaped by his experiences and expectations of battle formed both in the Civil War and in the West, a story he was writing for posterity even as he rode to his death at the Little Bighorn.

His unfinished memoir is still being written by history, by myth, and by a culture that has never lost its enchantment with Custer, at once both familiar and elusive in popular memory as he rides over the next ridge into collective memory befogged by a cloud of dust. Custer had said he wanted to cast aside illusions about the frontier, but his death multiplied them as nothing else ever has.

"Custer's Last Stand" remains one of the most iconic events in American history and culture. Had Custer prevailed at the Little Bighorn, the victory would have been momentarily notable, worthy of a few newspaper headlines, but only a few among many on the way to the inevitable outcome in the nation's war with the Plains Indians. In defeat, however tactically inconsequential in the larger conflict, he became mythic.

The Little Bighorn Battlefield National Monument receives between three and four hundred thousand visitors each year despite its remote location in southeastern Montana. The visitors are looking for something, perhaps the same thing as nineteenth-century journalists and twenty-first-century historians—an answer certain to elude them, a dramatic tale, perhaps a testament to some greater truth. Or maybe just a souvenir trinket from a nearby convenience store, as the tourists become the modern incarnation of those soldiers who looted tepees and death sites for Indian adornments or moccasins.

From the beginning, the battlefield has attracted journalists in search of a good story. The first, Mark Kellogg, was among Custer's casualties. The story he might have written would have been one of the great "scoops" of military reporting. Just how the story reached the *New York Herald* and beyond in spite of Kellogg's demise is uncertain.

Like Custer's story, the initial news reports have evolved and expanded. Contrary to what has become a cliché, journalism is not the first draft of history but the last draft for tomorrow's audience. Then historians go to work. Later journalists, along with a procession of storytellers ranging from professional and amateur historians to archeologists, ethnographers, biographers, folklorists, novelists, actors, and reenactors, have all wandered across the windy grasslands in search of the real George Armstrong Custer, the 7th Cavalry, and the Native American warriors who fell on that fateful field. Many have been drawn to the event, in part, by the unanswered questions, which are unsettling but alluring.

Hundreds of books, films, articles, broadcasts, reenactments, and public spectacles have resulted—so many, in fact, that the production of more information and interpretation itself becomes part of the story. The reason for the interest, at one level, appears obvious. The Little Bighorn battle ended in a decisive defeat for one side and a decisive, if transitory, victory for the other side. The fight had an element of mystery, with no survivors left among Custer's defeated battalion to tell their story and few credible witnesses among the living to give an objective account.

Moreover, the chief antagonists, Custer, Sitting Bull, and Crazy Horse, were colorful characters easily co-opted by storytellers more interested in sensation than in a careful weighing of the evidence. It was also a love story kept alive by Custer's wife, Libbie, who spent the rest of her life, more than a half century after the Little Bighorn, tending to his memory.

Once the story broke loose from its moorings in mere news columns, it quickly assumed the trappings of the fantastic and became entangled with all sorts of other concerns. It became mythic in all senses of that much abused word, balderdash and hokum as well as transcendent truth grounded in the ideals of the cultural imagination. Myths have utility and may reveal undefined anxieties and aspirations. In the case of the Little Bighorn battlefield, these anxieties and aspirations may be symptomatic of a national neurosis, perhaps merely the sort of enchantment that arises from any conflicted emotions.

The constant in Custer's life and legend is war and conflict. Custer's contentious life and legacy are a matter of his having reveled in battle, in the Civil War and in the Plains Wars. With his death, the verdict was mixed. The only agreement was, implicitly, that he was a great story. Damned or lauded in the popular press, he was a drama and tragedy readers loved. The changing sentiment is apparent from Frederick Whittaker's hero-worshipping biography in 1876 to the scathing biography by Frederic F. Van de Water published in 1934 after Libbie Custer's death. As Custer went from hero to goat, the Indians moved from the ignoble savages of the nineteenth century to the noble red men of the twentieth century. Historians never came to a consensus about Custer, either—bold or reckless, brave or foolish, self-aggrandizing or charismatic?

In this volume, we attempt to look at Custer whole, as a product of the Civil War in which he played an important role, the culture and politics of the Reconstruction era, and the Plains Indian Wars, as well as the battle on the Little Bighorn that made him immortal. Too many books about Custer treat the Civil War period only as a prelude to the Little Bighorn. We see more congruence between the Civil War and the Indian Wars. Understanding the Custer myth that grew out of the Little Bighorn means appreciating the Civil War Custer, whose commendable leadership and impulsive vanity went west with him, along with his confidence in telling a story that found its way into books and magazines.

Insufficient attention has been paid to the journalists and other image manufacturers, including Custer himself, who were inventing what became his myth long before the battle. Journalists, who were gaining authority and readership in a rapidly expanding press system, loved Custer in life and especially death. He was a natural story, whether formally adorned with gold braids and a saber or swathed in fringed buckskin. He looked like the kind of man who could tame the West. That he was writing memoirs before he reached his midthirties is testament both to his vanity and to his deeds.

As he churned out numerous articles for newspapers and magazines, Custer never slighted his own accomplishments. He was composing his own legend, inventing the public persona and what became the historic figure, well before 1876. He was not just a contrivance of his own pen. His Civil War deeds merited praise, as he was a very good field commander and recognized by his superiors as such. But his style—aplomb, boldness, charisma, even good looks—accentuated his command capabilities to make his story a real-life drama—and eventually a tragedy. The timing was perfect, too. Since he died within days of the American centenary, Custer was a natural figure to embody all that was great about, and eventually wrong with, the American character.

As with so many iconic American heroes, we are never quite sure what to make of Custer as he moves through time. Unresolved questions compel further investigation. Each new interpretation is at odds with someone else's views. Partisans in each generation are spoiling for a fight, as were Custer and Crazy Horse.

MYTHIC FIGURES

Inventing Custer: The Making of an American Legend is the fourth in our series of books exploring the lives, myths, and memories of four famous Civil War soldiers. *The Mosby Myth: A Confederate Hero in Life and Legend* traces the long career of Colonel John Singleton Mosby, the partisan ranger called the Gray Ghost of the Confederacy. *The Myth of Nathan Bedford Forrest* tells the story of the Confederate cavalry general whom Major General William Tecumseh Sherman called the most remarkable man either side produced during the war, although his reputation was tarnished by his controversial attack on Fort Pillow and his later association with the Ku Klux Klan. *Sherman's March in Myth and Memory* focuses on Sherman's Atlanta campaign and destructive march through Georgia and the Carolinas.

Our goal in each book has been to explain how an ordinary life becomes extraordinary through circumstance, passing through events filtered by journalism, popular culture, and memory, and is finally reconciled by myth and history to emerge as a usable past. This work is similar in that it, too, ponders the myth. But that myth has been contemplated thoroughly and revealed elsewhere. Instead, we look more at its origins in Custer's Civil War command, his war celebrity, the changing national attitudes about Native Americans, and the shifting sentiments of the journalists, historians, and biographers who tell Custer's story.

The four lives that comprise the subject of our inquiry were shaped by the momentous tragedy of the Civil War, the great crisis of the American experience. Their mythic lives outlive them and reverberate into the twenty-first century. Custer and Mosby were adversaries in northern Virginia and sometimes looked upon each other as war criminals. Sherman and Forrest fought each other hard in the western campaigns of the Civil War, and Sherman considered "that devil Forrest" a formidable opponent. Sherman thought Custer brave but impetuous.

They were soldiers, but their wars did not always begin or end with the Civil War. Custer died first and most famously. Forrest died in 1877, having become something of a national figure during the Reconstruction era. Rediscovered by a new generation of Southerners, he was reconceived as the great agrarian yeoman knight who might have saved the South; a cultural symbol of resistance to Northern industrialism and integration; and finally, to some, an embarrassment whose name has had to be purged from schools and parks.

Sherman, who fought in the Seminole wars and served primarily as a staff officer in the Mexican War, died in 1891, less than two months after the Indian Wars ended tragically at Wounded Knee, his infamous March to the Sea a lingering cultural symbol of the barbarism and effectiveness of total war. Mosby lived on until 1916, a pariah in the South due to his Republican politics, often at war with a government he felt had not given him his due, prickly toward modernism, hostile toward football and automobiles, and unforgiving of his old nemesis Custer.

Custer is among the best-known American soldiers in history. He rides on as a malleable symbol of audacious bravery, his four-year heroics in Virginia, West Virginia, Maryland, and Pennsylvania eclipsed by a few hours in Montana.

Custer, Mosby, and Sherman were fine writers with a talent for publicity. All four had a mythic afterlife as inventions of their apologists, the press, the storytellers, the movies and television, and now the Internet. Some think Custer might have run for president, or at least for high office, had the Little Bighorn battle turned out differently. Sherman said that if nominated, he would not accept; if elected, he would not serve. Mosby was too irascible to hold elected office but might have welcomed a cabinet appointment, a seat on the Supreme Court, or an ambassadorship. Forrest had some behind-the-scenes political instincts and held local offices, but he was more businessman than public figure.

Had the four met for supper after the war, Sherman and Forrest would have been correct but not cozy. Mosby and Forrest would have swapped tales of the saddle service. Custer would have amused Forrest and Sherman, and Mosby would have shot Custer if he had the chance—if Custer didn't get him first. They were not destined to break bread together as a group, however, and that is just as well.

They were, in life, men of many parts, and in memory they have become manticores, mythical beasts with human heads, shark-like teeth, and the bodies of wingéd cinnabar lions with scorpion tails. The manticore was, in legend, a killer that devoured its prey and left no scraps. Our mythic soldiers are, like the manticore, heraldic symbols that can be placed over the door of whatever memory vault we want to enter, there to trouble our dreams and our consciences and remind us from time to time of an age of heroes. Individually and collectively, they were never just one thing, always a composition, with one feature in high definition.

Sherman and Mosby were intellectual soldiers, the brains of the beast. Forrest was a lion, red in tooth and claw and lionhearted. Custer was a scorpion who could sting his victims and in the end wound up stinging himself. Memory, myth, and media have magnified their faults, exaggerated their qualities, redeemed their motives, and reimagined their legacies to fit the agendas of cultures that have had need of them.

Lest the metaphor seem too fantastic, our quartet has a strong presence in fantasy literature, perhaps a sign that the culture encounters its warriors in the deep memory of childhood fears. Sherman in literature has cavorted with vampires, battled evil time travelers, and slithered through Georgia as the head of a mythical invertebrate. Forrest has been cast as a unicorn-riding raider in a pseudomythical Middle Ages, fighting sorcerers and wizards, and as a gigantic living hologram projected by a ray gun. Mosby has been portrayed less as a supernatural paladin and more as a vaguely plausible superhero or villain. He appears in fiction as everything from arsonist, bandit, and spy to Western-style Virginia gunman fighting Custer, who has made his own mark as a sorcerer equipped with magical powers released during the Civil War and as a ghostlike memory tumor inhabiting the brain of a Sioux boy. While history scoffs, myth absorbs the imagined world, which has its own truths to tell.[7]

CUSTER'S WARS

Custer's wars began with his arrival at the War Department in Washington on July 20, 1861, and ended with his death at the Little Bighorn almost fifteen years later. Historian Heather Cox Richardson interpreted the Reconstruction era as "the literal reconstruction of the North, South, and West into a nation in the aftermath of the Civil War. That rebuilding stretched from the end of the Civil War until the start of the twentieth century." Western settlement, supported by subsidies to railroad companies, helped pay down the war debt by stimulating production to generate higher tax revenues. Historian Elliott West explained that the crisis of union the United States faced in the mid-nineteenth century "was far wider than usually described. It was genuinely continental, a challenge both to hold North and South together and to bind West and East into a single nation." The challenge was largely met by 1877, West argued, and achieving the goal had required "both liberation and conquest, both done by a federal government flexing an expanded power and authority from coast to coast."[8]

The Civil War was only part of a larger, continuing conflict, an eruption of domestic discord that had begun with settlement and the first Indian Wars. Under the Articles of Confederation, the Indian presence had threatened to undermine the fragile alliance among the states by which the new nation existed. Congress prior to 1787 provided for an army of only about seven hundred soldiers. Without more help from a central government, hard-pressed state militias were forced to protect settlers from Indian attacks, and if they failed, they looked to stronger powers and new alliances for support, increasing the decentralizing pressures through the threat of secession from the confederation. Ironically, Indian conflicts were one of the incentives for a unified country and federal government from the nation's genesis, through the ensuing century of westward expansion, and even into the twentieth century, when Indians became full citizens.[9]

Fighting between settlers and Indians was matched by brutal tribal wars among the Native Americans. Faced with drought and the disruption of their trading routes to the Atlantic caused by Pontiac's War, the Lakota had, by the time of the Declaration of Independence in 1776, moved from their homelands in what is now Minnesota into the Black Hills. West of the Missouri River the migrating tribes found vast herds of bison, "a roving market on hooves whose various parts provided sustenance, clothing, and shelter, as well as an array of tools and implements," according to historian Claudio Saunt.[10]

By the time of the Little Bighorn in 1876, the Sioux in particular had been almost continuously at war for more than 150 years. Horses and guns brought the Sioux into conflict with other tribes in a struggle for expanded hunting territory. "Peoples who once crept about the periphery of the plains trying to kill the occasional buffalo and growing corn in the river bottoms were suddenly empowered to go where they pleased and

kill buffalo in hundreds. Their populations boomed. Feeding them required vast hunting grounds," according to journalist Thomas Powers. [11]

As the new nation added territories in the Louisiana Purchase and the
Mexican War and the lands were cleared for settlement, the expansion of
slavery precipitated the crisis of the Civil War. But the war exacerbated
the Indian Wars, too, as civil authorities and military adventurers in the
West sought to advance their interests and attain a measure of acclaim
amid the growing turmoil. The expansion of the Union Army and Confederate territorial ambitions in the West emboldened attacks on some
tribes, while others, such as the Apaches in the Arizona Territory, saw the
withdrawal of Federal troops from some areas in 1861 as an opportunity
to pillage outlying settlements. On January 29, 1863, Union volunteer
regiments from California under Colonel Patrick Connor attacked and
destroyed a Shoshone village along the Bear River in the Washington
Territory near what is now Preston, Idaho. On November 29, 1864, two
Colorado militia cavalry regiments and New Mexico infantry under Colonel John Chivington slaughtered Cheyenne and Arapahoe villagers at
Sand Creek in the Colorado Territory, setting off a wave of retaliatory
attacks throughout the region. In the southwest, thousands of Navajo
were driven off their tribal lands in the New Mexico and Arizona territories and marched to Fort Sumner in the Pecos River valley beginning in
1864. [12]

The wars continued for twenty-five years after Appomattox, driven by
the reunited nation's obsession with the West and ending with the
Wounded Knee Massacre in South Dakota in 1890. Sand Creek and
Wounded Knee were "bookends of the Plains Indian Wars, which were
in, in turn, the last sad chapter of the Civil War," according to historian
Ari Kelman. [13]

Sherman, one of the prime instruments of the South's destruction and
humiliation, certainly saw the Civil War and its aftermath, during which
he was commanding general of the postwar army, in terms of the ongoing
chaos that began with the earlier Indian Wars. Commanding troops in
Kentucky in 1861, Sherman had insisted that the state's defense was
crucial to restoring the Union. He was certain that "we must begin at
Kentucky and re-conquer the country from [the Confederates] as we did
from the Indians." His views changed little over time. In a speech to a
West Point graduating class in 1876, just nine days before the Little
Bighorn battle, Sherman told cadets the recalcitrant Indians had to be

brought to heel, as the Confederates had been, in the greater interest of national unity and progress. Nor were Sherman's views unusual among Civil War senior officers who were engaged in the Indian Wars. Historian John Marszalek wrote that most saw the Indian campaigns as "a new phase of securing the nation against anarchic forces."[14]

Custer was just one of many Civil War veterans who fought on after Appomattox to resolve the domestic turmoil in the South and the West. He died alongside other veterans, including his brother Tom. The Civil War never left him, even on the last day of his life, the day Custer's wars ended and Custer's mythic afterlife began. The day Custer's wars ended also was the day his Civil War victories began to fade.

"THAT CHILLING GAZE"

Popular myths are grounded in popular media. As it was for figures we studied in earlier volumes in the series, so it was with Custer. The Little Bighorn and the annihilation of Custer and his men would have been news no matter what. But given the times, circumstances, and primary actors, the event begged for exaggeration and expansion. The national press obliged, creating the foundation for a memory grossly out of proportion to the battle and Custer's impact on the Plains Wars.

Myth matters, in real politics and policy. Custer's decline as hero correlated to changing sentiments about Indians, who became full citizens nearly a decade before Van de Water's condemnatory biography. As media scholar Rita Parks could say of Custer in 1982, perhaps no frontier figure has "undergone such extreme scrutiny by revisionists in the areas of history, sociology, and the arts. . . . Under that chilling gaze, the Custer image has become one of the more fragile of the American Western legends."[15]

Because he is among the most visible and fragile figures in the nineteenth-century story of re-creating and expanding America, he looms large in public memory as the American soldier who led the charge in the war against the Plains Indians. He endures into the twenty-first century as a contested American myth.

We explore how Custer both exemplifies and transcends the memory of the war up to the present. In part I, we look at Custer's early life, his years at West Point, and the Civil War, the defining experience of his life.

We examine his transition to a frontier soldier after the Civil War and the culminating Battle of the Little Bighorn. In part II, we explain how Custer became a legend, shaped by the press and changing sentiments toward American Indians. We consider the extensive historiography of the Custer story, its scrutiny by generations of journalists, historians, biographers, and others, each of whom brought a singular perspective to the task. We conclude by joining the army of visitors who have followed Custer to the Little Bighorn, the millions who have approached the battlefield with awe or scorn, as tourists or storytellers, in search of some séance with the past.

Part I

New Rumley to Appomattox

As scout and commander, Custer won fame on many Civil War battlefields in Virginia, Maryland, West Virginia, and Pennsylvania. He seemed destined for the cavalry, with panache, dash, and bravery. No peril deterred him; no ambition eluded him. (University of Tennessee Cartographic Services)

I

THE DREAM

Custer was dead at the Little Bighorn, and the lanterns of memory and imagination lit the winding path to where it all began, the unlikely hamlet of New Rumley, Ohio, slumbering on the Allegheny Plateau, where timbered knolls and virid pastures rise to meet the Appalachian Mountains. There, George Armstrong Custer was born on December 5, 1839.

As stories about Custer began to be compiled after his death, events little noted at the time were deemed prophetic and contributed to the expanding Custer mythology. Custer was just thirty-six years old when he died. Two brothers, a nephew, and a brother-in-law died with him at the Little Bighorn. Other family members lived a long time. His widow died when she was ninety years old. His father lived to the age of eighty-five, his mother to seventy-four. Two brothers died at seventy-two, and his sisters survived to ages fifty-eight and eighty. Teachers, classmates, soldiers, friends, and enemies remembered him. An abundance of recollection, much of it proffered by those eager to claim close association with the famous general, had to be sorted, weighed, and fitted into a constructed narrative. Because the truth was unknowable, a conflicted and contested memory was bent to suit the needs of the storyteller.

Custer's parents, sturdy, hardworking people without much education and of modest means, had come west to Ohio from Maryland and Pennsylvania. Each previously had married and lost a spouse, and each had two surviving children. Emanuel Custer and Maria Kirkpatrick married in 1836. Emanuel's three-year-old son by his first marriage died soon after, and then the first two children of the second union died in infancy.

George, the third child, soon to be known as Autie or Armstrong, was followed by three brothers and a sister.[1]

Despite its tragedies, the large family seems to have been a fortunate amalgam of personalities. Emanuel was a boisterous, fun-loving black-smith, occasional farmer, and justice of the peace who enjoyed incessant-ly talking politics and joining his children—especially the mischievous Autie—in playing pranks, then restraining them with chores and Sunday piety at the Methodist church. Maria was quiet and industrious, indulging her children's high spirits while tending to their needs. Her oldest daugh-ter, Lydia, usually called Ann, doted on her half-brother Autie and would become one of the strongest influences in his life.[2]

Custer's earliest biographer, Frederick Whittaker, a sometime soldier, journalist, and dime novelist, credited him with a military bloodline dat-ing back to a Hessian officer who fought with the British in the Revolu-tionary War, but later biographers found only a militia sergeant in the family tree. A 1928 biography by journalist Frazier Hunt assumed this Hessian was "a curly-haired blonde giant who was fighting for the fun of it," which seems to anticipate the mythical Autie Custer. Some evidence suggests the family was pacifist Mennonite. The family likely originated in Kaltenkirchen in what is now North Rhine-Westphalia, on the Dutch-German border. A Paulus Küster had arrived in Pennsylvania in the late seventeenth century and may have been Custer's direct link with the Old World. Just where the Custers originated is uncertain, however. Shortly before his death, Custer received a letter tracing his family origins to the Orkney Islands in Scotland, where the name originally was Cusiter. While Custer wore his tartan lightly, jesting with his wife about a possible Orkney inheritance, a romantic bloodline reaching those foggy, wind-swept outcroppings at the top of Britain probably appealed to him.[3]

Whittaker told a story about the four-year-old Autie being given a velvet military suit made by his mother to wear when he accompanied his father to drills of the New Rumley Guards, a small militia unit mockingly known as "The Invincibles" due to the paucity of Indian raids by the 1840s. The little soldier supposedly demonstrated his martial proficiency with a toy gun, foreshadowing his military career. To emphasize the point, Whittaker added a footnote indicating that the very suit Custer wore was, in the year of his death, still in his mother's hands, an authentic Custer relic.[4]

Quentin Reynolds, writing dialogue for his juvenile history and biography *Custer's Last Stand*, has the precocious Autie demanding weapons and a uniform for his birthday and Marie sadly realizing it would "not be long before he'd have to exchange his wooden gun for a real one." Soon, after pointing the toy gun at "imaginary redskins," Autie falls asleep and dreams he is a general riding a white horse into battle against the Indians. It was not unusual for a boy of the time to mimic some form of soldiery, local militias being commonplace, or to imagine leading a sanguinary cavalry charge, especially if encouraged by an exuberant father. Nevertheless, omens suggesting a military destiny for young Custer are inventions. Frazier Hunt embellished the story even further by claiming Custer "dreamed of being a drummer-boy and marching with heroic old General Scott or General Taylor in the Mexican campaigns. Farming was not for him—the saber and the musket were to be his tools."[5]

LEARNING AND TEACHING

Autie did not show much promise as a scholar. He was a sometime indifferent student at the local one-room school, although he enjoyed reading, if not the assigned lessons. Always a prankster, Autie made an impression on his classmates as the class clown and tried hard to live up to his reputation even as he eventually trained to be a soldier. When Autie was about ten, his parents moved the family to a farm a few miles outside New Rumley, and Autie changed schools. He did little better and was apprenticed to a cabinetmaker in Cadiz, the county seat. A larger town than New Rumley, Cadiz had been important enough for Edwin M. Stanton, Abraham Lincoln's future secretary of war, to have joined a law practice there and to have been elected the Harrison County prosecuting attorney.[6]

Young Custer had a chance to be on his own and to see what a small but prosperous commercial and political crossroads community had to offer. For some reason, however, the apprenticeship didn't take. Autie perhaps didn't like living away from his family and may have gotten into mischief as he realized he didn't care for the woodworking trade. His parents then made a decision that was to be an early turning point in the boy's life. In 1842, the family briefly had tried farming near Monroe, Michigan, with unfortunate results, and they returned to New Rumley.

But Ann married David Reed, who lived in Monroe and ran a drayage business, and it was to Monroe, a city of several thousand residents, that young Autie Custer was dispatched. His fondness for his older sister and a chance to trade woodworking for schoolwork may have mitigated whatever reservations he had about leaving New Rumley.[7]

Monroe was a lively little port on the western shore of Lake Erie some fifteen miles north of Toledo, Ohio, and twenty-five miles south of Detroit. In Custer's time the lakefront towns were not yet the industrial metropolises they would become, but they were more cosmopolitan than anything Harrison County, Ohio, had to offer. Monroe, originally called Frenchtown and the site of a famous massacre during the War of 1812, was one of the oldest towns in southern Michigan, and many of the established residents fancied themselves part of a cultural elite. Autie attended the New Dublin School and Alfred Stebbins's Young Men's Academy, returning to New Rumley intermittently and then permanently when the academy closed in 1855. Before he left Monroe, however, Custer may have noticed his future wife, Elizabeth Bacon, the daughter of a prominent judge.[8]

Biographer Jay Monaghan suggested that by growing up in both rural Harrison County and lakeside Monroe, Custer may have developed "a feeling of superiority, a certain youthful maturity," even at the expense of his schoolwork. If so, he was confident enough to continue his education at a boarding school for the training of teachers in Hopedale, some ten miles from New Rumley. When he reached the age of sixteen, he earned a small monthly stipend by teaching at a country school before finishing his own studies. During the summer of 1856, he accepted a position at a larger district school near Cadiz, qualified schoolmasters being in short supply.[9]

Custer found lodgings with a farmer named Alexander Holland, who had a lovely daughter, with predictable results. Custer and Mollie Holland had an infatuation, perhaps something more. The father disapproved and advised Custer to find other lodgings. The evidence for what happened next with the Hollands is suspect; it is more certain that Custer was restless and saw an opportunity to improve himself by getting a free education at the U.S. Military Academy. West Point, he believed, opened up a military career as well as opportunities in business and law and the chance to accumulate wealth. As a military officer he would achieve status. He always had enjoyed reading about battles, but had he seriously entertained ideas about serving in the army? [10]

Reynolds invents a scene with young Autie in conversation about West Point with schoolmaster Alfred Stebbins in Monroe. Autie learns that if he wants to become a general, he must first do his homework, a good object lesson for young readers of heroic biographies. Whether Custer's eventual choice to pursue a military career was more patriotic than pragmatic, however, is grist for the mythmakers. [11]

TO THE POINT

Securing an appointment to West Point presented Custer with a thorny political problem. His father was an outspoken Jacksonian Democrat in what had been a Whig stronghold, and Autie, while not as intense and tending toward jocularity, joined him in criticizing Republican abolitionists and defending Southern rights. The district's congressman was John A. Bingham, friend to Stanton and a strong antislavery Republican familiar with Emanuel Custer's political leanings and Autie's antics. Bingham replied to Autie's letter of application with courtesy, informing him he had made one appointment to the academy already and was considering another, but leaving the door open to future conversations. He met with Custer in Cadiz and was impressed, politics notwithstanding. Alexander Holland, also a Republican, approached his friend Bingham and interceded on Custer's behalf, likely with ulterior motives. Others may also have intervened, but, whatever the case, Custer received a letter from Secretary of War Jefferson Davis offering him an appointment, subject to his passing an entrance examination. [12]

In early June 1857, Custer boarded a train at Scio, Ohio, with connections for the more than five-hundred-mile journey to Albany, New York. He transferred to a steamer that plied the Hudson River waters to the high bluff on the west bank upon which sprawled the barracks, fields, and classrooms of West Point. Custer passed the examination and was mustered in as one of the sixty-eight cadets who comprised the class of 1862. He soon wrote a girlfriend that West Point was "the most romantic spot I ever saw." [13]

Custer's record at West Point was alarming. In his first year alone, he accrued 151 demerits, the highest total of any plebe in his class. In the second year, he received 192 demerits, just 8 short of dismissal. The next year, 191 demerits. The fourth year, 192 demerits. The four-year total was 726 demerits, the worst record in the class. Something of a goat-footed Pan when he could get away with it, he returned from a two-month furlough at the end of his second year with gonorrhea, for which he was treated by army doctors at the post hospital. On another occasion he decamped from the infirmary without permission and was arrested. His academic difficulties presented other temptations. Facing the possibility of failing a course, he entered an instructor's room and, about to be discovered, fled with a page from a remedial examination. In all, he claimed to have spent sixty-six Saturdays over the course of four years assigned to guard duty because of various infractions. [14]

He graduated last in a class of thirty-four. His worst final-year performance was, ironically in view of later events, in cavalry tactics. And for good measure, before he could leave the academy, he was court-martialed for failing to break up a fight, found guilty, and reprimanded, and he might have been dismissed had Bingham and other influential friends not intervened. With war at hand, the army needed officers, even the incorrigible Custer. [15]

For Custer apologists, the West Point years challenged the hero narrative because "last in his class" too easily anticipated "the last stand" that made him immortal. Had the recklessness, the inattention to regulations, and the poor scholarship that he demonstrated at West Point finally caught up with him at the Little Bighorn? Or were the numerous infractions merely high spirits? Whittaker, writing of Custer's "troubles," blamed "the irksomeness of discipline, not the severity of study. Such as he was, a headlong, impulsive, generous lad, full of life and spirits he entered West Point. Would there were hundreds more to-day there, like him." Custer brought "the free, careless air told of the Western man" to the conventions of the East, and his exuberance needed adjustment. [16]

For Reynolds, West Point was where the provincial Custer learned to be an American, helping build the tradition that gave the nation the great generals of World War II. Custer's demerits, test pilfering, and wenching go unmentioned. His low standing is laughed off at the time by the officers, and the court-martial is just the result of a minor mistake Autie owns up to as he learns a valuable lesson. What young Tom Sawyer reading Reynolds's Custer story for a school report wouldn't take comfort in that? [17]

CUSTER'S LUCK

Biographers and historians have taken Custer at his word when he wrote, "My career as a cadet had but little to commend it to the study of those who came after me, unless as an example to be carefully avoided." Frederic F. Van de Water, the journalist and popular novelist who in 1934 published the first critical biography of Custer, claimed, "Few embryo soldiers ever have shown less qualification or ardor for the life they have chosen." Historian James Donovan said that since its founding, West Point "had seen its share of lollygaggers. Armstrong Custer would put them all to shame." Custer dismissed the demerits as "not great in enormity." That they included infractions such as throwing snowballs, card playing, sleeping in class, tardiness, and unkempt hair bears him out. If the accumulation of demerits for such mischief did him no credit, it evidently caused more amusement than censure, demonstrating audacity rather than insolence.[18]

Historian James S. Robbins, in his study of the "goats" of West Point, *Last in Their Class*, claimed that the "same spirit of adventure that led Custer to sneak out of the barracks in the middle of the night to engage in off-post revelries motivated his dramatic cavalry attacks in the Civil War and afterward." Custer scholar Nathaniel Philbrick observed that whenever the accumulated demerits "threatened to end his days at the Point, he'd put a temporary stop to the antics and bring himself back from the brink of expulsion. This four-year flirtation with academic disaster seems to have served him well. By graduation he'd developed a talent for maintaining a rigorous, if unconventional, discipline amid the chaos." Biographer and historian Robert M. Utley just gave the goat his due, noting, "He did not flunk out."[19]

Historian Stephen E. Ambrose would have none of the biographers' contortions about Custer's West Point record, which, in his view, missed the point. Custer made it through the academy by learning "selective obedience" and a sense of timing, which Ambrose compared to a comedian's gift for delivering a punch line. He knew the audience, knew what it wanted and when, and that ability played out throughout his career until the final act. He had all the spit and polish he needed to play the role of soldier. He knew where he stood, how close to the precipice he could stand, and what he could get away with. This timing, Ambrose suggested, was an intuitive gift predictive of creative soldiering. Ambrose also was unconvinced that Custer was a poor student. Given the rigors of West Point, he said, compared to students attending civilian colleges, Custer was "a scholastic monk."[20]

Raising the old school flag this way strains credulity. Within the context of his West Point education, Custer was a poor student, and nothing suggests he would have had any more success at a nonmilitary college. Custer was intelligent but was no man for the cloister. Whatever the explanation for his slipping by, Custer's gift for survival came, in time, to be called by fellow soldiers and journalists "Custer's luck," the aggregation of near misses, fortuitous events, good timing, inconsequential blunders, amazing recoveries, and unexpected successes snatched from the jaws of defeat. A career built on luck raises questions as to what happens when the luck runs out, but that was well in the future when Custer received orders to report to Washington, DC, a newly commissioned second lieutenant in an army in crisis.[21]

"HOW WE ALL LOVED HIM"

Custer always knew where his allegiance lay. He had got on well with cadets from the South, however, and for a time was able to navigate the rising political tensions by helping maintain civility between what he called the "hot-blooded Southron and his more phlegmatic schoolmate from the North." But he saw his Southern friends chasing a romantic ideal, "impatient, enthusiastic, and hopeful. Visions filled their minds of a grand and glorious confederacy, glittering with the pomp and pageantry which usually characterizes imperial power, and supported and surrounded by a mighty army, the officers of which would constitute a special aristocracy." The Northerners, by contrast, "were reserved almost to sullenness; were grave almost to stoicism," temperaments, he said, "as different as the latitudes from which they hailed."[22]

If he truly saw his comrades in this stereotypical way, he nonetheless was able to win their friendship by not pandering to their respective vanities. He was neither elitist nor sanctimoniously democratic or especially moralistic. His brash vitality combined charm, mirth, and merriment with an inchoate, opportunistic cunning and political agility that transcended sectionalism. Many thought him formidable because of, rather than despite, his incorrigibility. They celebrated his abundant contrasts and his unbridled, headstrong courage. One said of him, "West Point has had many a character to deal with, but it may be a question whether it ever had a cadet so exuberant, one who cared so little for its serious attempts to elevate and burnish, or one on whom its tactical officers kept their eyes so constantly and unsympathetically searching as upon Custer. And yet how we all loved him; and to what a height he rose!"[23]

2

THE SUN OF GLORY

Then to the East we bore away, to win a name in story;
And there where dawns the sun of day,
There dawn'd our sun of glory!

—Samuel Lover, "The Girl I Left behind Me," 1872[1]

In 1978, twenty-three-year-old Gregory Urwin was at work on a master's thesis on Custer's Civil War service. The young military historian's research took him to Monroe, Michigan, where he met noted Custer scholar Lawrence Frost, who introduced him to the Custer collections in the Monroe County Library System. With Frost's encouragement, Urwin plunged deeper into the Custer literature. His 1983 book, *Custer Victorious: The Civil War Battles of General George Armstrong Custer*, became the standard work on the period after Custer became a brevet brigadier general just before the Battle of Gettysburg.

Urwin dismissed much of what had been written about Custer as "trivia or trash. His magnetic personality and show-stopping annihilation have attracted the attention of an inordinate number of hacks, cranks, and armchair generals," generating a story "poisoned at its very roots by a curious combination of partisan politics and self-serving individuals, institutions and forces." Urwin attempted "to strike a blow against all those recent flawed and illiberal histories that have been foisted on the reading public, to scrape away the fluff and façade, and to return to the historical grass roots."[2]

He said that while Custer may be the most famous soldier in American history, he is remembered only for "an insignificant Indian battle in southern Montana." Most Americans were only "vaguely aware" Custer was a famously successful Civil War general because Custer failed to finish his war memoirs, while many of his rivals completed theirs and ignored his achievements. He had his supporters, and his heroic reputation grew apace, although their testimony was long forgotten by the time Custer fell victim to the "radical politics and the wave of antimilitarism that swept America in the late 1960s." Custer became a symbol of defeat rather than of success, not yet Custer Victorious but Custer Whipped. [3]

Urwin's youthful project to recover Custer's Civil War renown has not entirely succeeded, eclipsed by the prodigious outpouring of books about the Little Bighorn and the Custer myth. In the midst of all the Little Bighorn history, there are two well-done recent books by Thom Hatch and James Robbins that do justice to the Civil War. Urwin warned of ignoring the Civil War years when he observed,

> Nearly everything written on the "Boy General" has been geared toward that single event—both authors and readers have approached the Custer story with blinders on—and, like impatient mystery buffs who have flipped to the end of the novel to find the solution, they are unable genuinely to appreciate all that had come before. And in history that kind of purposefully constricted vision is the severest kind of handicap. [4]

True, up to a point, but historical and biographical writing usually is burdened with the end of the story known in advance, the question being how and why events happened just that way. Custer historians cannot overcome the burden of the Little Bighorn, nor can they comprehend or reassess it without examining what Custer did throughout the Civil War and even during his early apprenticeship. As one frustrated historian said, "How can you judge a man when you devote your entire attention to the last day of his life, about which you know almost nothing?" [5]

ANIMATED KALEIDOSCOPES

Custer was writing his "War Memoirs" for *Galaxy* during the expedition that would lead to his death. He even sent one installment to *Galaxy* from the field by way of scouts carrying dispatches. While planning the Little

Bighorn campaign, he was thinking about the limitations of Civil War battle reports. He reminded his readers,

> The incidents of a battle are so numerous and changing, and occur over so great an extent of country, often concealed by forests or by inequalities of the surface of the ground, that the entire field may be regarded as an immense series of animated kaleidoscopes, the number of which is only limited by the number of observers, no two of the latter obtaining exactly the same view, and no individual probably obtaining the same view twice.[6]

This perspective came in 1876 as he remembered a war he began as a staff officer with responsibilities that included the gathering and collating of information from multiple sources. The animated kaleidoscopes metaphor is well chosen. He learned early on that a battlefield charges the senses and impairs the memory as a variegated scene of sanguinary carnage unfolds. Custer was a careful observer. His natural literary style was personal, anecdotal, in-the-moment prose combined with confident interpretation and colorful embellishment.

Official reports, in contrast, were formal, self-serving, prolix documents intended to be read as "methodical statements describing the operations of a particular military organization. The officer who submits the report bases it generally on the reports of his subordinates, to which is added such knowledge of facts as he may have so acquired." Such reports typically "are but the hasty, unstudied grouping together of such prominent facts and circumstances of a battle as may up to that particular date have fallen under the personal observation or been brought to the notice of the officer whose duty it may be to record them." Official reports about the same battle, he claimed, were even more inaccurate than multiple newspaper accounts of the same event. Reports passed up the line then became collective interpretations, compilations of elisions "usually so framed as to touch lightly if at all upon the blunders committed and disasters suffered, and to make the most of successes gained, whether these were the result of accident or design."[7]

In preparing his memoirs, Custer knew he was not writing definitive history. He was not limited to what had been written in official reports, which he found less credible than what he saw as "possessing interest." The unstated rule in the reports was *Do not criticize superior officers*. He was confident history eventually would emerge from the collective, flawed recollections of many participants and transcend the time-bound official accounts written in the field. But "history" had not yet emerged a decade after the end of the war. At the time of writing, he was only a few months away from the battle that would define him. He seemed to be foretelling the controversies that came out of the Little Bighorn, a scene of "animated kaleidoscopes" if ever there was one. More important, these articles reveal how he remembered the Civil War and how history might see it differently. [8]

A SPLENDID OPPORTUNITY

Custer's war began with a journey. He arrived in New York on the afternoon of July 18, 1861, having departed that morning from West Point by steamboat for the short voyage down the Hudson River. The vessel churned past Bear Mountain, past the site of the Battle of Stony Point eighty-two years earlier, past Sleepy Hollow and Tarrytown, past the Palisades and finally to the great city, where he stopped to buy a lieutenant's uniform, complete with saber, spurs, and pistol, at Horstmann Brothers military outfitters. He posed for a photograph he sent to his sister in Michigan, then boarded the evening train to Washington. [9]

"At each station we passed on the road at which a halt was made," he recalled, "crowds of citizens were assembled provided bountifully with refreshments, which they distributed in the most lavish manner among the troops. Their enthusiasm knew no bounds; they received us with cheers and cheered us in parting." Some women came forward to kiss their departing heroes, a ritual repeated throughout the nation as young men went off to battle. [10]

He may have slept briefly and fitfully amid the tumult, and with the pale light of dawn, he saw for the first time the capital city, a confusion of soldiers, sutlers, office seekers, and politicians preparing for war. The newly commissioned second lieutenant, assigned to Company G, 2nd U.S. Cavalry, collected his baggage and set off in search of the Ebbitt House, a four-story boarding house at the corner of F and 14th streets, where he expected to find some of his former classmates. [11]

He found James P. Parker, his West Point roommate and partner in mischief, still in bed. Parker, he learned, had been stricken from the army rolls after resigning his brevet commission "in the face of the enemy" and was about to leave for Richmond. There, Custer wrote with disdain, Parker intended to "accept a commission under a flag raised in rebellion against the Government that had educated him, and that he had sworn to defend." However it might have pained him to part from his Southern friends, Custer abhorred what he saw as their disloyalty. He and Parker had been friends. They now were enemies. The reality of the war had become clearer. Parker later rose to the rank of lieutenant colonel, served with a Mississippi artillery unit, and spent much of the war in a Union prison camp. After the war he settled in New Mexico and died in about 1918. If the former roommates ever saw each other again, neither mentioned it. [12]

Custer reported to the War Department and had a surprise audience with Brevet Lieutenant General Winfield Scott. "Old Fuss and Feathers" was an imposing sight to the young lieutenant, who recalled how West Point cadets looked up to Scott "as a leader whose military abilities were scarcely second to those of a Napoleon, and whose patriotism rivaled that of Washington." At seventy-five, Scott had been around longer than the Constitution and had served in the army since 1808. He offered Custer the choice of either drilling troops in Washington or joining Company G in the field with Brigadier General Irvin McDowell, who on July 16 had begun a slow march into Virginia with 35,000 men. The objective was the strategic railroad crossing at Manassas Junction, defended by a smaller army under Brigadier General P. G. T. Beauregard. Despite McDowell's concern that the army was not yet ready, optimistic politicians and newspaper editors anticipated an easy victory, followed by a Confederate retreat to an unsustainable defensive position on the Rappahannock River, a Federal advance to Richmond, and a quick end to the rebellion. [13]

For Custer, eager to get into the fighting as fast as possible, it was no choice, as Scott likely anticipated. But how to reach the battlefield without a horse, which Scott warned Custer would be hard to find in the city, with every soldier and civilian who could ride heading across the Potomac to see the pending battle? As an incentive, Scott told Custer that if he could return by seven o'clock that evening with a mount, he could collect some dispatches for McDowell, whose army was concentrating near Centreville, Virginia, a few miles east of Bull Run. He could ride through the night to deliver them. Custer saluted, shook the corpulent general's buttery hand, and rushed off, like King Richard III, in earnest need of a horse. [14]

The Custer myth is built on a foundation of remarkably improbable, often ironic events, perhaps none packed with more narrative potential than his first full day of active military service in the field. He already had met and conversed with the most famous soldier in the army on the eve of the first major battle of the war. But a frantic search of the city's livery stables turned up nothing.

"I was almost in despair at the idea that I was not to be able to take advantage of the splendid opportunity for distinction opened before me," he later wrote. As he walked along Pennsylvania Avenue, however, he recognized a regular army dragoon he had known at West Point. Captain Charles Griffin, a West Point artillery and tactics instructor, had sent the trooper to collect a horse left behind in Washington when the battery advanced into Virginia. Custer persuaded the soldier to let him ride the horse back to McDowell's camp and then set off to pick up the dispatches. When he returned, he discovered the mount was Wellington, a favorite he had ridden often during cavalry drills. [15]

Quentin Reynolds, in his biography for young readers, found the horse story irresistible. "Autie looked closely at the big horse. 'It's Wellington!' he cried happily. Wellington was a horse which only the best horsemen at West Point were permitted to ride. At mention of his name the horse perked up his ears and whinnied. 'He knows me,' Autie pointed out." [16]

The two riders crossed the Potomac over the Long Bridge as darkness descended upon the embattled capital, rode some twenty-five miles through the night, and reached the awakening army in the early morning hours. Without Wellington, Custer might have missed his first battle. He repeated the journey during the following night when he returned to Washington in the rain with a defeated army.

MAYHEM AT MANASSAS

When he recalled his first engagement, Custer conceded that the seven-company Federal cavalry battalion in which he served at the First Battle of Manassas, or Bull Run, under Major Innis Palmer was "not employed to any considerable extent during the battle except as supports to batteries of artillery." Frederic F. Van de Water, who dismissed Custer as a glory seeker, relegated him to idle spectator, a role "little more than the visiting congressmen's."[17]

He was far more involved than that. Custer witnessed a battle unfolding along a broad front, came under fire, and saw an apparent victory deteriorate into a rout. Not yet one week out of West Point, he saw classroom principles tested by fast-moving events and flying bullets. Palmer had graduated from West Point in 1846 and fought with distinction in the Mexican War. His first impression of his eager young second lieutenant is not recorded. Custer's commanding officer in Company G was First Lieutenant Thomas Drummond, an Iowa state senator and prominent newspaper editor. He was with Custer again at the end of the war when Drummond was killed at the Battle of Five Forks. Throughout the battle, Palmer's cavalry operated sometimes as a single unit and sometimes in detachments at McDowell's direction.[18]

"What boy, whether he is from the North or from the South, doesn't know the story of the Battle of Bull Run?" Reynolds could plausibly ask in 1951. With the battle receding farther into the fog of American history, perhaps the story, if not the name, no longer has the currency for schoolchildren it once may have had. To the extent it is remembered, according to historian Ethan S. Rafuse, it holds a curious and diminished place in Civil War history. "The naive assumptions, rampant hubris, and often silly behavior of the amateur soldiers, officers and political leaders whose actions and decisions shaped the campaign lent an almost comic quality to the war's first military operation." If sometimes comic in execution, especially the Union rout, the battle was no less tragic, with combined causalities of 847 killed, 2,706 wounded, and 1,325 missing.[19]

First Manassas was developing even before Custer was making his hasty departure from West Point. With McDowell on the move, Beauregard looked for reinforcements from the Shenandoah Valley where Brigadier General Joseph Johnston had been concentrating twelve thousand soldiers around Winchester. Opposing Johnston was Robert Patterson, a veteran of the War of 1812 who had left the army in 1848. At the beginning of hostilities, Patterson had been mustered into the volunteer service for three months and commissioned a major general. With some eighteen thousand Federal troops, he had been told to check Johnston while McDowell went after Beauregard. As Patterson dealt with vague orders and expiring enlistments, Johnston eluded him for several weeks. Then Johnston marched his infantry through Ashby's Gap to Piedmont Station, where he took advantage of the Manassas Gap Railroad to move most of his force some thirty-five miles to support Beauregard. That made McDowell's prospects more tenuous and ultimately cost him the battle. Patterson never left the valley.[20]

Led by Colonel Thomas Jackson, soon to be "Stonewall" Jackson, Johnston's brigades began arriving sooner than expected. Beauregard and Johnston drafted an ambitious plan to flank McDowell's left wing, a movement very similar to McDowell's plan to envelop Beauregard's left. But neither movement unfolded quite as anticipated. Orders Beauregard sent to Brigadier General Richard Ewell on the right flank never arrived, which probably was fortunate for the Confederates. With McDowell in motion on the morning of July 21 to move against the left flank, Beauregard shifted forces from his right wing, the intended counterattack against the Union left having been delayed or postponed. As the Federals seized the initiative, the Confederates gained an advantage by fighting on the defensive.[21]

McDowell's flanking divisions started toward Bull Run from Centreville at 2:30 a.m. The banks of the narrow, meandering stream were quite high in places, limiting the number of crossing sites, the most direct being a stone bridge on the turnpike. Three brigades in Brigadier General Daniel Tyler's division, about eight thousand men, reached the bridge about 6 a.m., much later than expected, and skirmished with a small Confederate force commanded by Colonel Nathan G. Evans. Tyler's advance was intended to be diversionary. Behind his regiments marched the divisions of Colonel David Hunter and Colonel Samuel Heintzelman, who turned off the main road onto a cambering trail just beyond the little bridge over a creek called Cub Run.[22]

Custer's cavalry battalion supported the some thirteen-thousand-man flanking maneuver, although McDowell failed to use cavalry effectively to screen the march. Attached to Colonel Andrew Porter's brigade in Hunter's division, the troopers negotiated a "long and tedious movement through an immense forest by which Bull Run was crossed" at Sudley Ford, an eight-mile, seven-and-a-half-hour journey near the east and north banks of the winding stream. Engineers had misinformed the infantry about the feasibility of using the road, which had to be cleared of brush. Detours placed the soldiers some two miles north of the stone bridge. Heintzelman's division was supposed to cross even closer to the bridge at Poplar Ford. The inexperienced troops had lost any element of surprise that might have permitted them to use their numerical advantage to control the field. Their ragged, clumsy, nighttime trudge through the thickets on what was little more than a narrow cart path was slow going, and they had lengthened the march by several miles by getting lost. The Confederates knew they were coming because they could see the gleam of morning sunlight reflecting off the attackers' bayonets. The delay gave the Confederates time to bring up reinforcements to meet the Federals when they emerged from the woods and crossed Bull Run. [23]

Custer recalled halting for "half an hour or more" at Sudley Springs near Sudley Ford and hearing the battle "raging a short distance in our front." The time must have been between 10:10 and 11 a.m., when the fighting was unfolding on Matthews Hill between Hunter and Evans. With the battle then in progress on the Federal right, Palmer's battalion was directed to "move across the stream and up the ridge beyond, where we were to support a battery." All forces had to cross Bull Run at Sudley Ford, then Catharpin Run at Sudley Springs Ford. The elevation was Dogan Ridge. While ascending the crest, Custer heard shellfire directed at Griffin's battery. Griffin had been firing at Confederate positions on Henry Hill and may have been repositioning on higher ground. "Following the battery," Custer recalled, "we also marched within plain hearing of each shot as it passed over Griffin's men. I remember well the strange hissing and exceedingly vicious sound of the first cannon shot I heard as it whirled through the air." He had heard the sound during artillery practice, "but a man listens with changed interest when the direction of the balls is toward instead of away from him." [24]

The battalion took position below the ridge to defend the batteries should they be attacked by infantry. Anticipating such an advance, Custer helped lead his company up the slope to repel a charge that never came, and the battalion withdrew. Custer made light of this action, recalling that he bantered with another green lieutenant, Leicester Walker, about whether they should be holding pistols or sabers. [25]

Just before the ascent, Custer observed a confident officer "of striking appearance, tall, well formed, and handsome" leading another company. The captain rode to the front of his command and shouted, "Now, men, do your duty." This impressed Custer as the kind of soldierly bearing he wanted to emulate. But soon after the battle he learned that the gallant officer had joined the Confederate army. Frank C. Armstrong, commanding the 2nd U.S. Dragoons, ended the war as a brigadier general. Custer's mention of the incident in his memoirs is suggestive. He earlier had recorded with distaste the resignation of his roommate, Parker. Service to the rebellion, however principled, was by definition disloyal. On the other hand, Armstrong had done his duty at Manassas and then honorably resigned. Custer learned to respect his enemies. He bore them no great malice, even as he fought them hard.[26]

From Dogan Ridge, Griffin's and Captain James B. Ricketts's batteries dueled with batteries commanded by Jackson and Captain John Imboden on Henry Hill. Griffin's three 10-pounder Parrott guns and two 12-pounder howitzers and Ricketts's six 10-pounder Parrott guns held the advantage because the guns were rifled and could hit the Confederate lines. Jackson's guns were smoothbore and could not reach Dogan Ridge, where Custer said he heard shells passing over Griffin's position. Despite this edge, McDowell ordered the artillerymen to move off the ridge at about 2 p.m. and reposition on one side of Henry Hill to sweep the Confederate infantry off the slope. This placed them just three hundred yards from Jackson's batteries on the other side of the hill. The Federal gunners were menaced by both infantry and artillery fire. With little infantry support, they were overrun.[27]

There is no indication Palmer's cavalry battalion supported the artillery units at this advanced position. Custer's description of coming under fire from artillery and facing an imminent infantry charge better describes a supporting position on Henry Hill or nearer Matthews Hill rather than Dogan Ridge, but that would have placed him at the center of the battle, while he admitted to being primarily an observer. Palmer's battle reports were not specific as to the battalion's shifting positions, nor did Custer identify positions in his account.[28]

Fighting continued on the Confederate left throughout the day, with both sides pouring in reinforcements. Momentum shifted several times as the ragged, disorganized lines converged. Shortly before 4 p.m., Custer and a West Point classmate were celebrating "the glorious victory which already seemed to have been won, as the Confederates were everywhere giving way," when they saw Colonel Arnold Elzey's brigade, recently arrived from the Shenandoah Valley, emerge from a stand of timber behind them and fire into the backs of the advancing Union regiments. Elzey and Colonel Jubal Early had rolled up Colonel Oliver O. Howard's brigade. Custer recalled that when "the cry of 'We're flanked! We're flanked!' passed from rank to rank, the Union lines, but a moment before so successful and triumphant, threw down their arms, were seized by a panic, and begun [*sic*] a most disordered flight. All this occurred almost in an instant of time." Actually, the Federal position had been deteriorating during the heavy fighting on Henry Hill, and Howard's desperate attempt to turn the Confederate left was unlikely to save the day. Once it failed, the Federal position was untenable.[29]

The army's withdrawal did not turn into a rout until the recrossing of Bull Run. Custer's company was one of the last to cross. Palmer reported that the cavalry "was together and in good condition" during the retreat. Confederate artillery shelled the Cub Run bridge, adding further confusion. Soldiers withdrawing by way of Sudley Ford streamed onto Warrenton Turnpike, which already was cluttered with troops and frightened civilians in buggies who had come out to observe the battle. Custer found a place where Cub Run could be forded, and the cavalrymen rejoined the procession on the pike, halting two miles farther at Centreville at about 8:30 p.m. McDowell formed a ragged defensive line south and west of the town. As darkness settled over his improvised camps, much of the army already was on its way to the Potomac. The exhausted Custer, who had ridden through the previous night, helped cover the retreat, riding at the rear of his company. After arriving at Arlington Heights by early morning, he collapsed under a tree, "where, from fatigue, hunger, and exhaustion, I soon fell asleep, despite the rain and mud, and slept for hours without awakening."[30]

Custer was commended for finding the ford at Cub Run. He said nothing of the incident in his memoirs, but the story must have gotten around. Reynolds gave it prominence, inventing such dialogue as "'Who was that young officer with the golden hair?' some trooper would ask, and another would say, 'Name of Autie Custer.'" Reynolds described bugler Joseph Fought waking Custer the next morning, handing him a newspaper, and telling him he was a hero. It certainly was a moment when heroes were needed. When Custer paid a courtesy call on John A. Bingham, the congressman called him a young Napoleon.[31]

Custer claimed McDowell would have achieved complete victory had Beauregard carried out his plan to counterattack the well-defended Union left wing. Custer contended that despite "a little tardiness in execution, something to be expected perhaps in raw troops, the plan of battle marked out by General McDowell was carried out with remarkable precision up till about half-past three p.m." The late arrival of Johnston's brigades from the Shenandoah Valley turned the tide. Custer's tendentious defense of McDowell may have been justified, given the severity and unfairness of the criticism. Manassas had been a close engagement fought by inexperienced soldiers, most of them operating on unfamiliar ground. Custer's first fight had been a sound defeat, though, no matter how close to victory it might have seemed at the time. He would see many victories before his last battle. But not quite yet. [32]

MISSION AT MIDNIGHT

The failure at Manassas resulted in a change of command for the army and a reorganization. Major General George McClellan was placed in command of the new Army of the Potomac and appointed general in chief on November 1 after Scott resigned. Custer's regiment in the reconfigured scheme became the 5th U.S. Cavalry and temporarily was placed under the aegis of Brigadier General Philip Kearny, who commanded a new volunteer brigade composed of four New Jersey regiments. Kearny needed an aide-de-camp. Seeing that Company G had three officers when it needed two, he asked Drummond if he could have Custer. Drummond assented to the transfer of his most junior subaltern to the general's staff. If Custer had a preference in the matter, he failed to mention it, recording only that he found the staff job "agreeable and beneficial." [33]

Custer said a lot in his memoirs about Kearny, who was with Scott in Mexico and lost an arm after being wounded during the Battle of Churubusco. Custer admired Kearny's bravery and panache but also found him a peculiar officer, strict, haughty, distrustful, restless, and impulsive, characteristics others later ascribed to Custer. Although he did not serve with Kearny for long, he remembered a raid the general ordered to try to capture some high-ranking Confederate officers believed to be meeting at a house near a picket post. Custer was a staff representative on the midnight mission, which was more of a training exercise for the three hundred inexperienced volunteers, "some boyhood scheme involving a movement upon a neighboring orchard or melon patch." At the first sign of trouble, the detachment rushed back to camp. His time with Kearny ended when regular army officers were prohibited from service with volunteer units, and he returned to duty with his regiment. [34]

In early October, Custer went home to Monroe, Michigan. He had received a leave of absence due to an undisclosed illness, and it wasn't until February 1862 that he returned to his unit. He stayed with Ann and visited his parents and brothers, who recently had moved to an eighty-acre farm near Bowling Green, Ohio, about fifty miles south of Monroe. There he learned that his brother Tom, just sixteen years old, had enlisted in the 21st Ohio Volunteer Infantry Regiment.

Custer's activities in Monroe are not well documented. His illness, he told a friend, brought him close to death, but he evidently recovered quickly enough to incur his sister's wrath for excessive drinking. Whether due to embarrassment, the Methodist piety of his youth, or, more likely, the realization that he could not hold his liquor, he promised to give up drink and apparently kept his word for the rest of his life. [35]

"THE GREATEST OF MEN"

When he returned to active duty in February 1862, Custer had little to do for a month and may not have been greatly missed during his leave. The cavalry had been placed under the command of Brigadier General George Stoneman, one of the few officers Custer disparaged in his memoirs. "The record of the cavalry while operating under Stoneman contains nothing to its credit as a separate organization, and worse than nothing if successes are looked for upon which to base its leader's claim to the title of chief of cavalry." [36]

His opportunity for action came shortly after the Confederate forces around Centreville began moving to better defensive positions closer to Richmond. The cavalry trailed slowly behind from Manassas Junction and, on the afternoon of March 14, encountered Confederate pickets at Catlett's Station on the Orange and Alexandria Railroad. Custer temporarily commanded a company in the 5th Cavalry and volunteered to probe the Rebel lines by driving in the videttes arrayed across a hill before them. Moving forward at a slow trot, the fifty horsemen covered the half-mile distance to the base of the hill, charged and opened fire with pistols, then drew sabers. Custer wrote to his parents that "bullets rattled like hail." The pickets, about three hundred according to Custer, retreated across a small stream and set fire to a bridge to inhibit pursuit. There were only a few casualties, including a private who suffered a minor head wound. Custer noted that the journalists who witnessed the skirmish were eager to report the "shedding of the first blood" of the new army and wearied the wounded man with their questions. Custer boasted to his parents that Stoneman was pleased with him, and he was mentioned in the *New York Tribune*.[37]

The reconnaissance confirmed what McClellan suspected about Johnston's movements below the Rappahannock and served as a rather transparent feint as the commanding general began moving his main force, more than 120,000 strong, by some four hundred ships to Fortress Monroe, Virginia, to launch the Peninsula Campaign. The objective was Richmond, and Custer had abundant confidence in his commander. "I would forsake everything and follow him to the ends of the earth. I would lay down my life for him," he wrote his parents. On March 26, he embarked from Alexandria aboard the transport ship *Adèle Felicia*, writing to his sister that the "greatest expedition ever fitted out is going south under the greatest of men." He wrote in the heat of the moment, but years later, recalling the operation not long before he marched to the Little Bighorn, he could still marvel at the scope of the venture, "a stupendous undertaking, the transfer to a new and distant base of an immense army with all its material and accompaniments." In McClellan, Custer had found a new hero, and in his memoirs Custer would vigorously defend him, even when the campaign came to naught.[38]

Custer was among the first to arrive at Fortress Monroe and soon was in action with his company. On April 4 the army began moving up the peninsula, expecting to flank and trap Major General John Magruder's ten thousand troops concentrated around Yorktown. Magruder had stretched his lines some twelve miles from the York River behind the Warwick River and on to the James River. The Warwick, Custer wrote, was "a diminutive stream, undeserving the name of river, and in itself does not constitute a military obstacle; but the Confederates, by a series of dams, constructed at convenient points, and protected by batteries and rifle-pits, had enlarged Warwick river until it had become an almost impassable barrier to the advance of troops."[39]

Custer's regiment moved in a rainstorm with the army's left wing under Major General Erasmus Darwin Keyes, while the right wing under Heintzelman, promoted to major general, moved toward Yorktown. Both columns bogged down. Magruder, one of the war's great thespians, convinced the overly cautious McClellan that he was facing a huge army massed behind substantial entrenchments, when in fact Magruder was shifting his troops along the line. The delay gave Johnston time to move soldiers from Richmond to reinforce Magruder's lines, as McClellan began a siege that continued for almost a month. [40]

In a letter to his sister on April 20, Custer described how he was hunkered down in some woods with sharpshooters during an attack on a fort and was under heavy fire for an hour. The attackers were driven back in the skirmish, which Custer said resulted in several hundred casualties. He was in the burial party and commented on the youth of the dead soldiers. Looking at their faces, he said, he could think only of their brother Tom. [41]

With a siege in progress, the army needed engineers, and although engineering was not a subject he fully mastered at West Point, Custer was ordered to report to Lieutenant Nicholas Bowen, chief engineer on the staff of Brigadier General W. F. "Baldy" Smith in Keyes's 4th Corps. Custer began his service by supervising the construction of a rifle pit in a wooded area on the banks of the flooded Warwick. Confederates across the river had been shooting at working parties, so Custer's group of about one hundred men had to work stealthily to avoid being detected. Once completed, the rifle pit concealed Federal sharpshooters, "a small but most troublesome garrison," who could cover soldiers working on their side of the river. Custer's next assignment, soaring aloft in one of inventor Thaddeus Lowe's observation balloons, was more interesting than wielding a shovel, even if initially it was rather terrifying. [42]

Lowe had been named to head the new Union Army Balloon Corps in July 1861. "Professor" Lowe and other "aeronauts" made regular ascents during the Siege of Yorktown. These scouts were not well regarded because the intelligence they provided was often imprecise. Details such as "clouds of dust" and "great activity along the enemy's works" meant nothing to the army, and the aerial spies also were suspected of embellishing their reports to keep their profitable jobs. Accordingly, army officers began accompanying the aeronauts. One of the most enthusiastic, Brigadier General Fitz-John Porter, the 5th Corps commander, crash-landed on April 11, creating the not entirely welcome opportunity for Custer. He made the most of it, and after a few successful flights, he was reassigned to other staff duties following the Confederate withdrawal. [43]

"IN THE THICK OF THE FIGHT"

Stoneman's cavalry and Federal infantry under Brigadier General Joseph "Fighting Joe" Hooker pursued the Confederates up muddy roads, clashing with Brigadier General James E. B. "Jeb" Stuart's cavalry. They bumped into Major General James Longstreet's division dug in near the old colonial capital of Williamsburg along a defensive line of a dozen earthen redoubts anchored by Fort Magruder. Creeks on either side of the peninsula narrowed the line to only a few miles at that point. Kearny reinforced Hooker, Major General D. H. Hill reinforced Longstreet, and Smith engaged Hill as the battle widened. Attacks and counterattacks spread along the front throughout the afternoon without a Federal breakthrough. Custer put out a fire that had been set to prevent Federal troops from using a bridge. Although he burned his hands badly, he was able to drive off the sniper who had started the blaze. The tactical situation changed when Brigadier General Winfield Scott Hancock, accompanied by Custer, led a flank attack the next day that helped turn the encounter into a victory.[44]

Custer wrote a full account of this engagement, which serves as the final entry in the last installment of his unfinished war memoirs. Informed by Custer that the redoubt on the extreme left of the Confederate line was deserted, Baldy Smith gained approval from the 2nd Corps commander, Brigadier General Edwin "Bull" Sumner, to take the position. Custer guided Hancock's five regiments and eight artillery pieces through some dense woods to a broad, open plain. Across the field, they could see a narrow dam spanning Cub Creek. Once across they were on Longstreet's flank with about thirty-four hundred men behind the Confederate earthworks some four miles northeast of Williamsburg and only about a mile from Fort Magruder. Custer was at the front of the 5th Wisconsin, the lead regiment.

Hancock pushed his command forward, capturing two more redoubts, and shelled the main fort. He thought he could envelop the entire Confederate line if he could get reinforcements, but Sumner thought the position too far extended and ordered Hancock back to the dam. Custer said Hancock was torn between orders and his certainty the orders were wrong. While Hancock was waiting for a reply to his appeal to Sumner, his troops were attacked by D. H. Hill's division led by Brigadier General

Jubal Early's brigade. The attack gave Hancock an excuse to hold the position. He turned to fight it out, his career and reputation on the line.[45]

In 1876, Custer was writing about Hancock's situation as he remembered it, and *Galaxy* would publish his recollections after his death. With a romantically martial flourish, Custer wrote that for Hancock

> the coming contest was destined to become more than an ordinary victory or defeat: if the former, all would be well, and no unhappy criticisms would follow him; if defeat—and defeat under the circumstances implied the loss or capture of most if not all of his command—then death upon the battlefield was far preferable, to the sensitive and high-minded soldier, to the treatment which would be meted out to him, who in violation of positive orders had repeatedly declined to withdraw his command, but had remained until obedience was no longer practicable, and his command was threatened with annihilation.[46]

The Rebel attack had been poorly coordinated. As soldiers unsure of the Federal position rushed out of the woods, they found themselves open to flanking fire as they tried to storm the battery that had been shelling Longstreet's lines. The Confederates took heavy casualties, including the loss of Early to a shoulder wound, and may have been deceived into thinking Hancock was retreating. As the Confederates surged up the high ground, Custer led a counterattack that broke what was left of the Rebel lines. He had rushed to the front, waved his hat, charged on his own, and rallied the brigade. Ten days later Custer told his sister he was "in the thick of the fight from morning till dark." He had captured six men and a large flag, the first Rebel colors captured by the Army of the Potomac. This was Custer at his best—seizing the initiative, acting with alacrity, being where he was needed, and supporting a commander at a moment of crisis.[47]

"GO IN WOLVERINES, GIVE THEM HELL!"

With their Williamsburg flank compromised, the Confederates resumed their slow withdrawal up the peninsula, reaching the flooded Chickahominy River on May 15, burning bridges behind them they as crossed over, and plodding on almost to Richmond. The Chickahominy presented a formidable obstacle to McClellan. The river flows eighty-seven miles, emerging from a hardwood swamp fifteen miles northwest of Richmond and then winding in a southeasterly and southern direction until it drains into the James. Because the Chickahominy bisects the upper peninsula, an army astride the river risks becoming divided. The Federals reached the river on May 20 and began widening their lines along its swollen banks, anchoring the right wing at Mechanicsville a few miles north of Richmond. McClellan had some one hundred thousand soldiers northeast of the Confederate capital, which Johnston defended with about sixty thousand.

Finding suitable river-crossing sites was a job for the engineers and for Custer. The work was risky because likely fords were guarded by Rebel pickets and sharpshooters lurking in the woods along the bank. Accompanying McClellan's chief engineer, Brigadier General John G. Barnard, on a May 22 survey of the river, Custer waded up to his chest through a swift current, crawled through a thicket, mapped Confederate positions, and recrossed the Chickahominy without being detected. [48]

Custer and Bowen found a ford near a burned-out structure at New Bridge. On May 24, as part of a general probe of river crossings at several places, the two lieutenants met two companies of the 4th Michigan Infantry and a cavalry company at the site they had discovered. One of the companies was from Monroe, and Custer knew many of the soldiers. The commander of the expedition sent Custer and the Monroe company across the river. After moving about one hundred yards downstream through the underbrush, the company engaged the Confederates. Custer recrossed the river and, shouting, "Go in Wolverines, give them hell!" guided four reserve companies of the 4th Michigan to the opposite bank, flanking the Rebel position.

The skirmishing continued for several hours. Custer was cited for being the first to cross the river and the first to cross back. The sortie did not lead to a general crossing at that position, but Custer's audacity came to the attention of McClellan, who asked him to serve as his aide-de-camp. Much significance has been attached to this meeting by biographers, from Frederick Whittaker to Jay Monaghan. Just what they said at the meeting or whether McClellan took particular interest in Custer at a critical moment in the campaign is not clear. McClellan later said he became attached to Custer, and Custer idolized the general. Urwin emphasized that McClellan had given Custer his first real chance for advancement. Close to McClellan, "he could bask in the reflected limelight, he could deal with matters more significant than raiding picket posts, and he could demonstrate whatever gifts and talents he possessed where the entire Army of the Potomac could see." The months ahead would show what the ambitious Custer made of his opportunity. [49]

3

THE GENERAL

We are lifted up by circumstance, as by a breaking wave, and dashed we know not how into the future.

—Robert Louis Stevenson, "A Gossip on Romance," 1882[1]

Three days after Custer's staff appointment became official on May 28, 1862, Joseph Johnston's divisions struck George McClellan's extended and divided lines below the rain-swollen Chickahominy River. His primary target was the exposed 4th Corps under Erasmus Keyes at Fair Oaks Station, six miles from the capital on the Richmond and York River Railroad. McClellan expected to be reinforced by forty thousand troops massed at Fredericksburg some fifty miles north of Richmond under Irvin McDowell. Fitz-John Porter's 5th Corps had cleared a path for McDowell's troops by anchoring McClellan's right wing above the Chickahominy at Mechanicsville. All was in readiness to effect a juncture of the two armies prior to a movement on Richmond, where the Confederate government was already packing up essential documents in the event of a hasty exodus. But in the Shenandoah Valley, Stonewall Jackson was making Washington nervous. Lincoln pulled half of McDowell's army back to the valley and tried to get McClellan either to attack or to return to Washington to join in its defense. McClellan was in a vulnerable position, his army stretching some fifteen miles across difficult terrain, and the outnumbered Confederates knew it.[2]

McClellan had his five corps on both sides of the river. On May 30, a thunderstorm of exceptional violence churned up the Chickahominy even more. With its banks and bridges thoroughly awash, the vagrant river impeded the two corps on the south side from corresponding with the three corps to the north. McDowell's movement and the rising waters caused Johnston to scrap his plan to attack McClellan north of the river. Instead, he intended first to destroy the vulnerable Keyes, whose lines extended about one mile from the railroad to a copse of seven loblolly pine trees on the Williamsburg Road from Richmond shortly before it traversed the river at Bottom's Bridge. Johnston then planned to take on Samuel Heintzelman's 3rd Corps.[3]

The subsequent two-day battle, called both Seven Pines and Fair Oaks, was fought to a stalemate in flooded woods with more than eleven thousand casualties. Poor execution and botched orders impeded the Confederate attacks, and fewer than half of Johnston's forces were ever engaged. Some bridges across the Chickahominy withstood the rising waters, enabling Federal reinforcements to reach the embattled corps. The

Figure 3.1. Custer's scouting and engineering duties during the Peninsula Campaign often put him in harm's way. With General John G. Barnard looking on, Custer snuck across the Chickahominy River to locate Rebel positions in May 1862. Sketch by Alfred R. Waud. (Library of Congress)

most important outcome of the battle came as a result of Johnston's wounding and his replacement by General Robert E. Lee, who soon had his Army of Northern Virginia fortifying its lines while simultaneously preparing to go on the offensive. If anything, the carnage rendered McClellan even more cautious. He wrote his wife that he was "tired of the sickening sight of the battlefield, with its mangled corpses & poor suffering wounded! Victory has no charms for me when purchased at such cost." Certain he could expect no help from McDowell, McClellan moved most of his army across the Chickahominy and built fortifications but launched no attacks for several weeks. "The battle," wrote historian Bruce Catton, "was a stalemate and it was followed by a more extended stalemate." The next actions, collectively called the Seven Days Battles, constituted a turning point in the war.[4]

MISSING MAPS AND MUDDY MEN

Before Lee could act, he needed information about the disposition of McClellan's troops and supply lines. On June 12 he had sent Jeb Stuart's cavalry brigade on a reconnaissance north of the Chickahominy. Stuart's main assignment was to find Porter's corps and the right wing of the Federal army. He located Porter's vulnerable position near Hanover Court House, but instead of returning directly to Richmond, he kept going. By June 16, he had completed a one-hundred-mile loop around a more than one-hundred-thousand-man army. As a demonstration of Confederate panache, "Stuart's Ride" was a spectacular success. It made McClellan nervous, as did Jackson's movements east of the Blue Ridge Mountains. It also made McClellan wonder if he should move his base of operations closer to the James River.[5]

Despite Stuart's storied circuit, however, the Federal army had some advantages of its own in gathering intelligence, and Custer was learning the art of military sleuthing. He considered his assignment with the topographical engineers "a most invaluable experience." As a staff officer and cavalryman, Custer was close to McClellan and saw firsthand how logistics, field telegraphy, mapmaking, engineering, and scouting on and above the ground could determine the fate of an army.[6]

Historian Thomas B. Buell called attention to important Confederate deficiencies at the time of the Seven Days Battles. Maps were scarce, out of date, inaccurate, and all but useless, especially when floods had washed away trails and rickety bridges. Lee didn't even have a good map of Henrico County, the crucial field of conflict, until June 21, only four days before fighting commenced, and the one he located was the army's only copy. McClellan's staff knew as much as the enemy in the enemy's backyard. When Brigadier General Richard Taylor came to Richmond, he claimed the Confederate staff "knew no more about the topography of the country than they did about Central Africa. Here was a limited district, the whole of it within a day's march of the city of Richmond . . . and yet we were profoundly ignorant of the country; were without maps, sketches or proper guides, and nearly as helpless as if we had been transferred to the banks of the [Congo]." McClellan had Brigadier General Andrew Humphreys, who directed a staff of topographical engineers and map-makers. "As a consequence," according to Buell, "Northerners knew the Virginia roads and countryside, and the Virginians did not. The maps would time and again determine the outcome of the battles that were to follow in the Seven Days."[7]

Moreover, the Federals had a critical edge in engineering and communication competence. The Confederate armies did not have an engineering corps until May 1863, and engineering units were disbanded in the Army of Northern Virginia a few months later. Few regular army engineers had sided with the Confederacy. Those who did lacked equipment and sources of labor. The Union began the war with two engineering corps, although they lacked much support from Congress. Barnard, McClellan's cantankerous chief engineer who had built the fortifications that protected Washington, and the capable Humphreys gave McClellan an advantage, however. The North also made better use of telegraphy. Edwin M. Stanton, Lincoln's war secretary, had served as a director of the Atlantic and Ohio Telegraph Company. He controlled military use of the telegraph with great efficiency. Confederate systems, limited to begin with, remained private companies, and there was a shortage of copper wire.[8]

Custer's engineering credentials may have been suspect, as he seemed to imply when writing about his appointment as assistant to Nicholas Bowen. Practical knowledge of such engineering tasks as erecting field works and building fortifications, he said, was "supposed" to have been mastered by West Point graduates. If he did not know exactly what he was doing, though, Custer spent enough time up to his armpits in jaspery

Virginia streams and muddy entrenchments to claim a proper field education. Frederick Whittaker said Custer "had a sort of roving commission to go anywhere he could to acquire information, that would aid him in his maps and sketches, and his idea of the duties of an engineer officer as laid down [in his *Galaxy* article] are exacting enough to fill the role of a general officer. There were not many such engineers as Custer." Possibly not, but Custer undoubtedly admired Stuart's bold gallop through the unmapped Virginia landscape and wished he, too, were playing the cavalier rather than the sapper. Although the staff work was a significant aspect of his military career, it played no part in the Custer legend. Custer valued the experience, but for the most part his biographers and historians, as well as Custer himself, found other aspects of his career more consequential. [9]

THE SEVEN DAYS

The battles began on June 25 with a sharp but indecisive engagement launched by McClellan to drive off Confederate pickets in front of his lines and deprive the enemy of an advantageous wooded bog south of the Chickahominy. More than eight hundred combined casualties resulted. The next day Lee advanced north of the river without Jackson, whose three divisions were late arriving to attack the rear of Porter's corps aligned behind Beaver Creek Dam near Mechanicsville. This disrupted Lee's plan to push Porter off the right flank so that he could move down the north bank of the Chickahominy with fifty-five thousand soldiers, link up with his forces south of the river, cut the railroad, and force McClellan away from his base at White House Landing. Tired of waiting for Jackson, Brigadier General A. P. Hill attacked, followed by Longstreet and D. H. Hill, in four brutal frontal assaults. The fighting continued until late evening, with 1,484 Confederate casualties against 361 Federal losses, a tactical failure for Lee's first major assault. [10]

McClellan sent Custer to assess the situation at Mechanicsville. Carrying messages of encouragement from McClellan, Custer rode along the battle lines, rallying the Pennsylvania Reserves division. McClellan next ordered Custer to look for defensive positions farther down the north bank of the Chickahominy. If Porter needed to withdraw from his strong position along Beaver Creek Dam, he had to be able to cross the Chickahominy. Custer found Barnard looking for suitable bridgeheads and told him McClellan wanted to know more about an area along a creek on the north bank several miles from Beaver Creek Dam. Taking Barnard's map, Custer showed the engineer the position that McClellan had in mind, tracing a line along Boatswain's Swamp, a marshy, creek-fed, wandering tributary protected by high ridges. Behind the swamp was a steep, crescent-shaped plateau with an escape route across the Chickahominy at the Grapevine Bridge, should it come to that. [11]

Early on June 27, Porter withdrew his twenty-seven thousand men to the new position. Unable to locate Jackson, Lee again sent A. P. Hill's ten thousand men toward Porter's lines only to see the doughty gray-clad "Light Division" vanish into the swamp and forest and be swept by artillery fire. Elements of Jackson's, James Longstreet's, and D. H. Hill's scattered commands strengthened A. P. Hill's flanks, the whole line pressing forward in uncoordinated, desperate charges until Porter's lines finally broke in the center. Custer guided two brigades across the Grapevine Bridge and up to the plateau to help support Porter's withdrawal across the Chickahominy. The roads were clotted with frightened civilians and lost soldiers. As dusk settled, the relief columns reached Porter, discouraging the weary Confederates from further pursuit. [12]

Porter's men crossed the river through the night, leaving his bridges dismantled and ablaze behind him. The battle, somewhat misleadingly called Gaines's Mill, resulted in sixty-nine hundred Federal casualties and about eight thousand Confederate casualties. McClellan, with his supply lines severed and Lee on the north bank of the Chickahominy, ordered his army south toward Harrison's Landing on the James, where it would be succored by Union gunboats. The engineers had to build the necessary infrastructure to move 100,000 men, some 5,000 wagons, 281 pieces of field artillery, 26 heavy guns, and a herd of 2,500 beef cattle across White Oak Swamp and transfer supplies from the abandoned base at White House Landing. Custer helped guide troops to new positions and assisted with care of the wounded. Lee pursued, still hampered by poor coordination among his commanders and lack of reliable intelligence. Still, Lee smelled victory. If he could overtake McClellan's wagon train, he might be able to smash the Federal army before it reached the James. [13]

McClellan's state of mind at this crucial point has been much debated by historians. With Porter about to cross the river, McClellan "panicked" and reached "a new and heightened level of illogical thinking," according to David J. Eicher. Catton said McClellan "had been whipped into something close to hysteria" and had already given up. Eicher claimed the situation was still in McClellan's favor because four of his five corps barely had been engaged, and Porter had fought well against long odds. McClellan thought he was whipped when he wasn't. Clifford Dowdey noted that by not retreating down the peninsula, McClellan had chosen to "maintain his army in the heart of the enemy's country as a threat to the capital and its communication. . . . In fact, McClellan's army still possessed the potential for defeating Lee when night fell on June 28."[14]

But, if so, Lee still had the potential for defeating McClellan. On June 29, the fighting continued at Savage's Station, with 1,590 Federal casualties, not including 2,500 wounded soldiers captured when a field hospital was abandoned. The Confederate toll was 626. Lee almost trapped McClellan's army at Glendale on June 30, but blunders lost the advantage. The day's fight cost the Federals 3,797 casualties and the Confederates 3,675.[15]

Malvern Hill, the final battle, on July 1 resulted in 3,214 Federal and 5,355 Confederate casualties. Determined to strike yet again before McClellan could reach Harrison's Landing, Lee thundered forward. But this time McClellan had almost his entire army concentrated in an impregnable position. Porter already had occupied Malvern Hill, a slope rising 150 feet above the marshy approaches and about eight miles by road from Harrison's Landing. Some 250 cannons curled around the relatively open crest, providing a lethal field of fire. Lee launched an infantry attack that repeatedly was hurled back and largely cut to pieces by the massed artillery.[16]

At Malvern Hill, according to Whittaker, Custer, Bowen, and two orderlies dashed beyond their lines to reconnoiter a thicket that might conceal an enemy patrol. Out rushed a half dozen cavalrymen firing pistols. The Federal horsemen turned toward their own lines, then reversed course and captured their scattered pursers. With the Confederate line advancing, however, they had to release their captives, but not before they relieved them of their weapons.[17]

The total casualty count for the Seven Days came to about sixteen thousand Federals, half of them from Porter's corps, and some twenty thousand Confederates. That was out of a total of almost two hundred thousand men engaged. Custer had wanted to see a fight, and he had seen a big one. McClellan remained convinced, as did Custer, that Lee's armies outnumbered the Federals two to one and thus overestimated the size of Lee's army by one hundred thousand men. Custer later claimed the Federal army "should have been annihilated without McClellan to lead us." Just what it had all added up to, besides a fantasy, would ever after occupy the thoughts of the participants, journalists, politicians, and then historians. Richmond was, for the moment, redeemed, but at a fearsome cost. McClellan's army had won most of the battles, but had it forfeited the campaign by the "change of base" (or retreat) to the James? For Catton, the issue was less about who won than the fact that the war was going to continue: "The hope that the war could be something less than a revolutionary struggle died somewhere between Mechanicsville and Malvern Hill. And so, for the matter of that, did thousands of young men."[18]

SPOILS OF WAR

For a month after the battles, Custer drowsed with McClellan's army at Harrison's Landing as daytime temperatures climbed above one hundred degrees. More than forty thousand men were reported to be suffering from malaria, typhoid, dysentery, and other diseases. On July 17, Brevet Captain Custer officially was appointed to the rank of first lieutenant in the regular army. He was bored with camp life and looked forward to some more excitement. By the end of the month, however, he learned that Washington was done with McClellan's ossified campaign. McClellan was to bring the Army of the Potomac north to coordinate with the Army of Virginia, a new army under the command of Major General John Pope. Before leaving, Custer would kill his first man in combat.[19]

On August 5 he accompanied Colonel William Averell and several hundred cavalrymen on a twenty-mile raid from Harrison's Landing to White Oak Swamp. At midmorning Custer spotted a detachment of Confederate cavalry, and Averell ordered a charge. Custer captured one Confederate, then chased an officer whose horse cleared a high rail fence and was slowed by some wet ground. Custer's mount barely made the jump and galloped on until Custer pulled within range. He ordered the Rebel to surrender, waited, and then fired his pistol. The shot went astray. Custer again demanded surrender, and when again rebuffed, he fired a second shot. The Confederate tumbled to the ground as Custer rode on with other cavalrymen and captured a Rebel who had fled into the woods. When Custer returned, a lieutenant told him that after the Confederate fell, "he rose to his feet, turned around, threw up his hands and fell to the ground with a stream of blood gushing from his mouth." The wound was mortal. Averell cited Custer for bravery and pluck. [20]

Custer gave a telling account of this action in a letter he wrote to his sister on August 8. He had been at war for more than a year, and if he had killed anyone, he makes no mention of it. Yet in his letter, Custer is more eager to share an adventure than to deal with the brute reality of war in recounting his first kill at close range. Custer's black horse "seemed to enjoy the sport as well as his master." The chase, he wrote, was "exciting in the extreme," culminating in the leap over the fence. The officer he pursued was merely "game." He described at length the captured horse of the officer, "a perfect beauty, a bright bay, as fleet as a deer." He recognized the horse "by a red morocco breast strap which I had noticed during the chase. . . . He is a blooded horse, as is evident by his appearance. I have him yet and intend to keep him. The saddle, which I also retain, is a splendid one, covered with black morocco and ornamented with silver nails. The sword of the officer was fastened to the saddle, so that altogether it was a splendid trophy." Of the man he shot, Custer only wrote, "It was his own fault; I told him twice to surrender, but was compelled to shoot him." [21]

Custer had captured two of the thirty prisoners taken in the engagement. He was not bloodthirsty. Nor was he especially troubled, as McClellan evidently was, by the effusion of blood. Once he got into action, Custer was eager to show off the spoils of war and share the thrill of the chase. He already was creating his own myth. Jay Monaghan commented on the prancing style of the letter: "A youthful big-game hunter might write like this after his first kill." [22]

The zestful adventures continued after Custer left Harrison's Landing with McClellan and "travelled by easy marches" to Williamsburg. The general remained for two nights after arriving on August 18. For the next couple of weeks, Custer lingered in Williamsburg to visit his West Point friend Captain John "Gimlet" Lea, a Mississippian who had been serving with the 5th North Carolina Infantry. Lea had suffered a leg wound at Williamsburg, and Custer helped him after his capture. Lea had been paroled and was being cared for at Bassett Hall by a local family, the Durfeys. As the Army of the Potomac began its departure from the peninsula, McClellan gave Custer permission to visit Lea. His old comrade introduced him to his fiancée, Margaret Durfey, and her cousin, and Custer agreed to stay for the wedding, expedited by several days so he could serve as the best man. Custer wrote his sister about the wedding on September 21, devoting more space to his encounter with Lea, his bride, and her cousin Maggie than to the Battle of Antietam on September 17, still the bloodiest day of battle in American history.[23]

Some biographers have given this incident the full, sentimental "romance of reunion" and "brother against brother" treatment. It is a good story, the centerpiece of which is Custer's dalliance with the beautiful "Cousin Maggie," who trilled Southern songs and coquettishly urged him to stay on and join Lee's army. When Custer telegraphed McClellan for permission to remain in Williamsburg, McClellan was in the midst of extricating his enormous army from the peninsula. He had no time to be pestered by his lovesick aide.

The wedding was a splendid affair, with Custer and Lea standing side by side, each in his respective dress blue and dress gray uniform, the bride and her bridesmaid both "dressed in pure white, with a simple wreath of flowers upon their heads." "I never saw two prettier girls," Custer said. He told his sister he had never heard nor read "of a wedding so romantic throughout." Custer stayed on, playing cards, gamboling on the green lawns, dancing, singing songs, enjoying the hospitality of his secessionist hosts, holding forth with idle palaver, even failing to notice the return of Confederate soldiers as the Federals withdrew. He slipped away after dark, arriving at Yorktown after midnight, only to find that he had missed the last transport vessel. He located a vessel that could take him to Fortress Monroe, where he learned that McClellan had departed with his staff on August 23. "His general and his army had left him behind while he was dancing, eating, and singing at a rebel's wedding," Duane Schultz noted in his *Custer: Lessons in Leadership*. Another general might have summoned him to a court-martial or had him demoted.[24]

By the time he reached Baltimore, Custer had learned of Pope's defeat at the Second Battle of Manassas on August 29–30, opening a path for Lee to invade the North. No sooner had Custer arrived in Washington than he learned Pope's army was to be absorbed into the Army of the Potomac. With the vanguard of Lee's army on the banks of the Potomac on September 3 and the last troops of his own command just departing from Fortress Monroe, McClellan had little time to lose. In what historian

James McPherson described as "perhaps [McClellan's] finest hour," the general "brought order out of chaos and licked the troops into shape in a remarkably short time."[25]

"THE GREATEST BATTLE EVER FOUGHT ON THIS CONTINENT"

McClellan's new army, some eighty-seven thousand men, left Washington in pursuit of Lee on September 7. Lee, who began the campaign with an estimated fifty-five thousand men, less than half the number McClellan imagined, was already in Frederick, Maryland. The next day Custer reached McClellan's headquarters at Rockville and found the general already enjoying a friendly reception from the border state's residents, whom Lee's army had found wanting. As McPherson put it, the first casualty of Lee's invasion was "the anticipation that Marylanders would flock to the Southern banner." The Appalachian and western Piedmont regions of the state were not as enamored of the Confederacy as were the Tidewater counties to the east and south. Nor did the macerated army's bedraggled appearance offer much confidence. A Frederick resident told a newspaper reporter he had "never seen a mass of such filthy, strong-smelling men . . . the roughest set of creatures I ever saw, their features, hair, and clothing matted with dirt and filth; and the scratching they kept up gave warrant of vermin in abundance." Hundreds of Confederates refused to cross the Potomac, claiming they had enlisted only to repel the invader, not encroach upon the North. Thousands deserted or simply fell by the wayside due to illness, hunger, and fatigue.[26]

Custer and the Army of the Potomac, in contrast, were heartened by the joyous reception they received from the Marylanders as they slowly moved north along the Monocacy River, their guidons snapping in the late summer breezes. They were, in effect, "out of the swamp" they had endured on the peninsula. When they reached Frederick on September 13, marching jovially along the brick streets, they were greeted by cheering patriotic crowds waving American flags. Custer, still the youngest aide on the staff, arrived with McClellan. Custer was about seventy-five miles from Cresaptown, the village where his forbearers had lived before setting off for Ohio. He may have felt pride in returning to defend his ancestral homeland.[27]

Figure 3.2. President Lincoln meets with his commanding general, George B. McClellan, and his senior officers on the Antietam battlefield in October 1862. Brevet Captain Custer, at the far right of the photograph, is discreetly peripheral to the staged photograph by Alexander Gardner. (Library of Congress)

Concerned about his supply lines from the Shenandoah Valley as he moved north, Lee had sent Jackson west to seize the Federal garrison at well-stocked, strategic Harpers Ferry and nearby Martinsburg, which were defended by some thirteen thousand Federal troops. Longstreet moved behind the Blue Ridge and waited for Jackson at Boonsboro, leaving D. H. Hill and Stuart to defend the gaps through which McClellan would have to pass if he were to engage Lee. First he would have to find him. The opportunity came when a corporal resting beneath a tree near Frederick found a copy of Lee's battle plan wrapped around three cigars. The plan was delivered to McClellan, who was said to have proclaimed, "Now I know what to do!" If he couldn't defeat Lee with this information, he said, he would go home. And yet McClellan, being McClellan, was in no hurry, and it was another eighteen hours before Federal troops were in motion to capitalize on the orders that had been handed to him. [28]

Custer was sent that evening to find Brigadier General Alfred Pleasonton's cavalry and reached him at Middletown about seven miles from Frederick. The next day and through much of the night, he rode with Pleasonton into Fox's Gap and Turner's Gap, where he discovered D. H. Hill's soldiers spread across a small valley. Behind him, columns under the overall command of Major General Ambrose Burnside were coming up to flank the gap and fight their way up the slopes to control the high ground. By midnight, with a mist settling over the hollows, Hill began pulling back. It had been a costly day for the Southerners, with almost a quarter of those defending the gaps reported as casualties.

The next morning, just before a hazy sun began to rise over the bloody tableau of the previous day's carnage, Pleasonton sent Custer riding forth through creeping tendrils of fog with Colonel Elon J. Farnsworth's 8th Illinois Cavalry regiment to harass the retreating Confederates. At Boonsboro, they encountered Longstreet's rear guard as the army marched away toward Sharpsburg. Custer went forward another two miles, helping collect prisoners and abandoned cannons before being halted by Pleasonton, who cited the eager captain for bravery. Custer reported he had learned from prisoners that Lee had been injured and had lost fifteen thousand men. According to Major General Joseph Hooker, Custer said, the Rebels were demoralized and heading for Shepherdstown across the Potomac. Hooker told Custer to tell McClellan they could capture the entire Rebel army. Everything, Custer reported, was as the Federals might wish.[29]

A few days before the invasion, Lee had fallen while trying to restrain his horse, broken one hand and sprained the other, and arrived in Maryland in an ambulance. The prisoners Custer interrogated had told the truth, but Lee was far from incapacitated. He had been intending to retreat across the Potomac on the morning of September 15 but reconsidered when he learned of the imminent surrender of the Federal garrison at Harpers Ferry. He chose to make a stand in rolling country with his back to the Potomac and his lines extending a few miles north of Sharpsburg to Antietam Creek, a shallow, twisting tributary that could easily be forded or not so easily crossed by concentrations of troops at narrow bridges. The line was forming by noon, and observers near Turner's Gap, about eight miles from Sharpsburg, could see it.

"They are in full view," Custer reported. "Their line is a perfect one about a mile and a half long. We can have equally good position as they now occupy. . . . We can employ all the troops you can send us." Lee had only about fifteen thousand men in line but continued to assemble his army; by September 17 he had some thirty-six thousand men on the field, with A. P. Hill's division still at Harpers Ferry. McClellan had about seventy-five thousand Federals deployed in a six-mile arc in front of Lee, with more troops on the way. Had McClellan not waited two days to attack, he could have faced an army less than half the size of its eventual strength.[30]

Custer spent most of the day of battle close to McClellan's headquarters across Antietam Creek. Rather than sending Pleasonton's cavalrymen to the flanks, McClellan concentrated them in reserve in the center of his lines, leading McPherson to suspect McClellan had "some Napoleonic notion of a grand mounted charge against broken and fleeing Confederates." But there was to be no grand mounted charge on September 17. McClellan's attacks against the Confederate lines were not well coordinated or supported, giving Lee the opportunity to shift his divisions to the most vulnerable sectors. This came at a great cost, with one of Brigadier General John Bell Hood's regiments, the 1st Texas, losing 82 percent of its strength in less than one hour. Nothing was left of Colonel John B. Gordon's 6th Alabama. Lee lost close to a third of his army on the field. By late afternoon, with Lee's right flank in jeopardy, A. P. Hill's timely arrival from Harpers Ferry saved the army from being swept into the Potomac, assuming McClellan would have hurled his army forward. "This war," Bruce Catton wrote, "saw many terrible battles, and to try to make a ranking of them is just to compare horrors, but it may be that the battle of Antietam was the worst of all." With more than twenty-six thousand casualties, the most awful single-day slaughter suffered by American soldiers in any war, it would be hard to disagree.[31]

The memory of the battle carries with it a threnody of lugubrious names—Bloody Lane, Burnside's Bridge, the Dunkard Church, the Cornfield, the East Woods, the West Woods—all evoking American deaths juxtaposed against Lincoln's Emancipation Proclamation and a new meaning for the war.

Custer had no doubt that he had witnessed "the greatest battle ever fought on this continent," that it was a stunning Federal victory, while it exonerated McClellan and even humiliated his critics. Custer threatened to horsewhip a Monroe editor who thought otherwise. Custer's reaction to Lincoln's Emancipation Proclamation was probably much like his father's and his commander's dissent, although he later modulated his views out of either a change of heart or a growing sensitivity to the nuances of Washington politics. McClellan soon was writing letters calling the proclamation "an accursed doctrine" and warning of "despotism," although publicly he kept his own counsel on the matter. On September 26 Custer returned some paroled Confederates, including a colonel, across the Potomac. He joined them for "an hour's social chat, discussing the war in a friendly way," inquiring about his friends from West Point, and praising his classmate John Pelham for his success as an artilleryman. Although Ambrose overstates the point, there is truth in his observation that the Civil War "had some of the aspects of a game about it, at least to Custer; it was as if he were a modern college football player, congratulating his opponents at the end of a hard-fought game." The next day Custer sent his sister a piece of silk he said he had torn from a captured Confederate state flag at Sharpsburg, not mentioning how he had obtained it. [32]

Lincoln's arrival during the first week of October broke the monotony of camp life at McClellan's Harpers Ferry headquarters and the army positions around Sharpsburg. Custer was kept busy with ceremonial duties, while the president again ordered McClellan to take immediate action. But McClellan stalled for several weeks, during which time Major General Jeb Stuart, with eighteen hundred Confederate troopers, again circumvented the Federal army and looted Chambersburg, Pennsylvania. McClellan finally advanced tentatively into Virginia, intending to concentrate the army at Warrenton. But it was too late, and he received word just before midnight on November 7 that Lincoln had fired him. McClellan was gone by November 11. The next day he was in Trenton, New Jersey, where he was to await orders from Washington that never came. [33]

CUSTER AND McCLELLAN

Long after the war Custer wrote that even as McClellan was about to fight his next battle on the Rappahannock, "serious changes tending to weaken the army" were being made. He attributed McClellan's failure to end the war to "dominating spirits who at that time were largely in control of the Federal Government." Custer was certain McClellan could have suppressed the rebellion, restored peace to the country, and brought back the seceding States in such time and manner as would have shortened the struggle, saved to the country, both North and South, the blood of thousands of its best and bravest citizens, and spared the nation a large if not the greatest part of the heavy debt now borne as one of the inheritances of the war.[34]

Many in the army at the time agreed with Custer, some evidently, as McClellan said in his memoirs, "in favor of my refusing to obey the order and of marching upon Washington to take possession of the government." Was Custer among them? Whittaker implied that he was. With "plenty of wild talk going on," the youthful Custer "joined in with the rest. Boy-like, he was wild with indignation." In 1912, James H. Wilson, whom Custer knew at West Point, published a memoir in which he recalled a group of McClellan's aides denouncing the Emancipation Proclamation and defending McClellan. "One of the number, in a loud and resonant voice," declared he would resign should McClellan be dismissed, according to Wilson. Frederic F. Van de Water claimed none "had raged more violently or adorned potent personages with more reckless defamation than Custer . . . the yellow-haired firebrand." Jay Monaghan embellished the story further to include boozing aides "swaggering around the headquarters tents. Slapping their holsters, they advocated resistance," a march on Washington, and the induction of McClellan as dictator. The soldier with the loud and resonant voice became "a thick-tongued braggart—and it may have been Custer, although he didn't drink." It may have been Custer, but it probably wasn't, based on this account.[35]

Stephen E. Ambrose picked up the story, claiming Custer "felt himself a patriot when he joined in campfire talk about marching on Washington and putting Little Mac at the head of the government." Custer joined in the "drinking and swaggering" in Ambrose's account. Robert M. Utley, the dean of Custer historians, names Custer as one of the blustering hotheads making "wild threats to mutiny." Just what really happened is difficult to say, although a conspiracy pointing toward a coup d'état ensuing from a few bottles of whiskey seems unlikely. It's a good story for the Custer mythmakers, however, because Custer can be seen as a soldier admirably loyal to his commander, a contrarian patriot, a hotheaded schemer, a traitor—whatever fits the intent of the writer.[36]

Custer's adulatory relationship with McClellan often is explained in terms of its political symmetry. Both were Democrats, the argument goes, so Custer naturally became "a McClellan man." Political affinity does not explain the hero worship, however. Even after the war he continued to praise McClellan "as a military leader whose mental training and abilities were of a higher order." But what could Custer learn from this military giant whom he so admired if the historical consensus, according to historian Thomas J. Rowland, is that McClellan "became the Civil War's biggest dud"? Perpetually perplexed and obsessively cautious, McClellan was anything but audacious, hardly much of a role model for the Custer he remembered as "a reckless, gallant boy." McClellan's failing, according to McPherson, was that he was "a perfectionist in a profession where nothing could ever be perfect." Accordingly, he was "afraid to risk failure, so he risked nothing." Custer, by contrast, became a great improviser who risked everything. Risking failure, he failed in the end at the Little Bighorn in such a grand style as to become even more a symbol of failure than his mentor. Unlike his mentor, however, Custer also became a symbol of boldness and dash.[37]

McClellan, like many professional soldiers of his time, came out of the Enlightenment tradition of "scientific" management in military affairs with an emphasis on rational planning, engineering, logistics, technology, calibration of risk, and operational control mechanisms. The science of war had begun to take root in the American army as early as 1775 with the ascendence of Henry Knox to George Washington's staff.[38]

From this tradition McClellan extracted his Fabian strategy of limited engagement in battle. His elaborate plan to march his well-supplied army up the peninsula was a means of demonstrating rational action and control. The problem was that military leaders like McClellan thought warfare was best left to the professionals, especially at a time when so many amateurs had been given army commissions and served in local militias and volunteer units. Professionalism differed from the Jacksonian belief that military talent was innate, an idea bolstered by the fact that some high-ranking officers in both armies had left civilian occupations and become competent soldiers.

Inevitably, the "misunderstanding between McClellan and the government, as well as the public, arose partly over the contradiction between his deliberate methods and the impression he gave of the man of action," wrote historian Clifford Dowdey. McClellan embodied the prevailing romantic spirit, so much so that no soldier "ever glimpsed in Washington so suggested the heroic dream of assault" as McClellan did, nor was any soldier so self-deluded about his image and the reality of his actions. Acculturated "to embrace a romantic and melodramatic image of war as a test of strength—moral and physical—on the battlefield, the North expected its generals to seek a decisive battle with the rebels," according to historian Ethan S. Rafuse. [39]

Custer and much of the rest of McClellan's army, if Whittaker is to be believed, approved of the "scientific warfare" that characterized the Seven Days Battles and Antietam, not realizing that the prosecution of the war was going to change. Custer, while tutored in McClellan's logic, instinctively was a romantic. For a time he balanced both tendencies and benefited from the cross-referencing. But in the absence of McClellan's steadying influence and away from his staff and engineering duties, he became much more the romantic knight than the scientific soldier. [40]

Custer, out of a job and soon to be relieved of his brevet captaincy, was given leave, and he gladly took a train home to Monroe to await his next assignment. He did not stay long but was there long enough to formally meet and woo the alluring Libbie Bacon, whom he would marry some fourteen months later. He met Libbie at a holiday party at Boyd's Seminary, from which she had graduated that June with the distinction of being the class valedictorian. While courting Libbie, he also was attempting to secure the colonelcy of the newly organized 7th Michigan Cavalry. He briefly returned to Virginia, probably to try to gain an advantageous staff appointment for a Michigan junior infantry regiment officer, Henry Clay Christiancy, the son of Isaac Peckham Christiancy, a prominent state supreme court justice and Republican Party stalwart who lived in Monroe. [41]

The army was in a state of confusion after the Federal defeat at Fredericksburg under Burnside, McClellan's successor, on December 13. But young Christiancy received a staff appointment, and Custer may have put the word out that he wanted a cavalry job for himself as well. His interest in helping Christiancy may have had something to do with the assistance he sought from his father. Custer was trying to use whatever influence he could muster to help persuade Republican governor Austin Blair that he was the best-qualified man to command the volunteer regiment. He again had the support of his old friend Congressman John A. Bingham, who once before had overlooked Custer's politics to secure his appointment to West Point. Despite support from Christiancy and Bingham, Custer was turned down flat. The governor reminded Christiancy he was obliged to make a patronage appointment for the regimental command, and Custer was "a McClellan man."[42]

Custer must have taken this snub very hard because several months later he was still attempting to get Blair to appoint him to the command of a cavalry regiment, forwarding letters of endorsement from five generals. This time the governor was more encouraging but said he had no vacancies to fill with the 5th Michigan Cavalry. Custer persisted, and to improve his chances, he solicited signatures on a petition he circulated among 5th Michigan officers at a time when their colonel was on leave. They declined the impetuous request. One lieutenant later wrote that Custer had the "cheek" of a government mule and was too young to command the regiment.[43]

In December, Custer's leave in Monroe was cut short when he was summoned to Trenton to help McClellan prepare his official report about the Maryland campaign. He returned to Monroe for a time and was back in Washington on April 10, 1863. From there he joined McClellan in New York, where the general was writing a defense of his leadership as the commander of the Army of the Potomac. Custer stayed in the Metropolitan Hotel, a plush, brownstone edifice on Broadway and Prince Street. For a few days he worked with McClellan at the general's residence. Custer was not just writing reports. He was shaping history and giving thought to what posterity would say about events he had witnessed and people he had known. He was learning that history was a tenuous story compiled through variegated perspectives. Ordered back to Washington, he spent his time doing less interesting staff jobs and going to the theater—in "genteel idleness," as Whittaker called it—a plum assignment except that Custer was bored and wanted to rejoin his old regiment, or any regiment, in the field. The opportunity came on May 6, when he accepted Pleasonton's offer to become his aide-de-camp in a reorganized cavalry division just two days after the Union defeat at Chancellorsville.[44]

BEAU SABREUR

The reorganization had begun under Hooker, Burnside's successor, to rectify weaknesses in the way cavalry units had been used under McClellan, who, although he had published a manual of cavalry tactics in 1861, had placed cavalry regiments with infantry rather than giving them independent commands. It took some time for the Federals to figure out how to use cavalry effectively. According to Whittaker,

> A great jealousy existed between the horse and foot of the Army of the Potomac, and the former had been so badly handled that it had fallen into contempt with the infantry. Cut up into small detachments and placed under control of infantry generals, who disliked it, the few unfortunate charges it had made confirmed the general impression that was trumpeted through the press, that "the days of cavalry were over" as a fighting body.[45]

Cavalry units came out of antiquity, achieving romantic distinction in the Middle Ages and the Napoleonic Wars. Called dragoons, hussars, chasseurs, chevaliers, uhlans, knights, beau sabreurs, lancers, cavaliers, troopers, or just horse soldiers, cavalrymen were used for scouting, raiding, skirmishing, flanking, guarding artillery batteries and supply wagons, and protecting staff officers. They might screen the movement of infantry; harass retreating armies; serve as mounted videttes, sentinels, pickets, and escorts; burn bridges; steal horses; cut telegraph lines; or just provide some dash and panache during military parades and maneuvers. Occasionally they crossed swords with opposing cavalry units in sensational single combat. Less frequently they rode headlong into the jaws of death inspired by the famous cavalry charges of legend at Eylau-Preussisch and Balaclava or William Henry Harrison's charge into the British lines at the Battle of the Thames in 1813. Artillery and the rifled musket came to render such charges bloodily unavailing. In the United States, regular army cavalry, or dragoons, were used sparingly and primarily as a constabulary on borders and frontiers until about 1855. They had limited use before the Mexican War but were widely used during the Indian Wars, probably more as a matter of chasing nomadic tribes than the result of any tactical insights by military brass.[46]

Hooker had reshaped the Army of the Potomac's cavalry by consolidating disparate units and creating a ten-thousand-man-strong corps with three divisions, temporarily commanded by Pleasonton at Falmouth, Virginia, after George Stoneman's removal on May 20.

Although Custer had a high opinion of Pleasonton, and he of Custer, many historians have found little to admire in the general. "A gifted schemer," according to Gregory Urwin, Pleasonton "strove to weasel his way into Hooker's good graces, disparage Stoneman, and grab control of the Cavalry Corps." He deceived journalists by giving them bogus accounts of battles, puffing up modest achievements into sensational victories. Historian Charles Francis Adams Jr., who attained a brevet generalship at the end of the war, called Pleasonton "a newspaper humbug" and "a bully and a toady." Jeffry D. Wert noted his "reputation for untruthfulness and shameless ingratiation with superiors," while Urwin saw "an aversion to risking his life in battle." Ambrose, however, thought Pleasonton was better described as "a tough old regular" who enthralled the eager Custer with colorful stories about fighting the Sioux and may have been Custer's "first close contact with a real Indian fighter." Custer indulged in a bit of humbuggery himself later when he reached the frontier.[47]

Pleasonton immediately sent Custer off on a raiding expedition with a detachment of the 3rd Indiana Cavalry under the command of Captain George H. Thompson and Lieutenant Abner L. Shannon. Information had reached Pleasonton that a party of civilians was carrying a large amount of Confederate money, valuable mail, and other potential plunder from Richmond to Urbanna and thence by boat down the Rappahannock to the Chesapeake Bay. Just who these civilians were, where they were going, and why was never made clear. Custer's party boarded the steam ferries *Tallaca* and the larger *Manhattan* at Aquia Creek. Under cover of darkness, they plied their way slowly down the Potomac and were delayed by running aground on a shoal before reaching the Yeocomico Inlet, a filigree of coves and creeks near the site of a naval battle during the War of 1812. They slipped several miles into the tidewater estuary, disembarked at Moon's Landing, mounted their horses, and raced thirty-seven miles across Virginia's Northern Neck to the north bank of the Rappahannock opposite Urbanna at Chowning's Ferry, where they hid in the piney woods until morning.[48]

They found several boats Custer called canoes, although they were probably skiffs or scoop-hulled longboats. The boats had to be caulked before they could be used to cross the river. The riparian raiders rowed out from the marshy shore in two boats, each carrying ten men, Thompson commanding one and Shannon the other. They saw a sailboat coming toward then and gave chase after it turned toward the south bank. Custer estimated the pursuit went on for some ten miles before the cavalrymen were able to drive the vessel aground. The passengers, a family of six carrying $132 in Confederate money, claimed they were trying to escape from Virginia. Thompson concluded they were only part of the group the squadron had been sent to intercept, the rest having left Urbanna the previous day.[49]

Custer, Shannon, and three enlisted men waded ashore to visit a manor house. Recumbent on the veranda, Lieutenant William B. Hardy was on leave from an artillery battery with the 55th Virginia Infantry and was reading *Hamlet*. According to Custer's account of the raid, Hardy had just read the first words of Hamlet's soliloquy, "To be or not to be," when Custer took him prisoner. Custer claimed that as they marched back to the river, he and Hardy "had many a hearty laugh over his literary habits." Plucked from his home and subsequently transported to the Union prison at Johnson's Island in Sandusky Bay, Ohio, where he almost was "not to be" due to illness, Hardy may have been more melancholy about his fate than Custer imagined. Custer said the party recrossed the river, burned two schooners and a bridge, and chased pickets out of Urbanna. By the time they arrived back at Yeocomico Inlet, the detachment had collected a few more prisoners—mostly Confederate deserters—shoes, fifteen horses, Confederate money, and two barrels of whiskey. On May 24, the raiders were back in camp, and Custer received personal congratulations from Hooker.[50]

Custer's account of this expedition, written in a letter to Nettie Humphrey, a friend of Libbie's from Monroe, takes some liberties with Thompson's report. Custer gave the impression he was commanding one of the boats and that he took Hardy prisoner. Thompson's report attributed the officer's capture to Shannon. Custer implied he led the raid back across the river to Urbanna, while Thompson's report does not mention a separate action or Custer's role in one. Custer said thirty horses were captured, and Thompson said fifteen, two of which were captured by Custer—one he kept and the other he gave to Pleasonton. Another difference was that Custer mentioned gallantly apologizing to Hardy's sisters for capturing their brother. "I could not but feel sorry that they were to be made unhappy through any act of mine," he wrote. He also noted that two young ladies were in the captured boat and that he was compelled to make them his prisoners, providing them with horses, a carriage, and a driver for the return journey back to Yeocomico Inlet.[51]

Some of this embroidery can be attributed to his wish to impress Libbie. Very little actually was accomplished, and Pleasonton may have intended nothing more momentous than boosting the morale of his new cavalry corps and giving his new aide-de-camp a chance to play the corsair. For his efforts, Custer scuttled a family outing, liberated some horses, made some poppets swoon, and dragged a drowsy soldier from the mists of Elsinore to a prison camp. But at least he was back in action, and Pleasonton loved him, or so he imagined.

CAVALRY CLASH AT BRANDY STATION

On June 3, the Army of Northern Virginia began to budge. Hooker sent Major General John Sedgwick's 6th Corps across the Rappahannock to find out if Lee was adjusting his lines or pulling out from Fredericksburg. A. P. Hill's Confederate 3rd Corps was waiting for Sedgwick south of Fredericksburg. Sedgwick could not determine if he was facing the entire Army of Northern Virginia or just the tail end of it. Until he had better information, Hooker had to stay put, which gave Lee time to move the bulk of his army west once he ascertained Sedgwick's intentions. Hooker knew Stuart's cavalry was at Brandy Station on the Orange and Alexandria Railroad guarding the fords across the Rappahannock some thirty miles west of Fredericksburg, so he ordered Pleasonton to break up the Rebel force, its provisions, and its supply lines, before it could flank the Federal right or ride off on another raid. While harassing Stuart, Pleasonton might also learn if Lee was moving his army. The mission would test whether the reorganized cavalry corps could hold its own against Stuart's Invincibles. But Hooker didn't know that Lieutenant Generals Richard Ewell and James Longstreet were encamped near Culpeper Court House, too. Pleasonton could be facing two corps of the same army that had thrashed Hooker at Chancellorsville.[52]

Pleasonton split his eight-thousand-man corps into two columns. Brigadier General John Buford's division was to cross at Beverly's Ford some two miles northeast of the railroad bridge just above Brandy Station. At Kelly's Ford, six miles to the southeast, the divisions commanded by Brigadier General David M. Gregg and Colonel Alfred Duffié would splash across. Some three thousand infantrymen supported the cavalry. Once on the south side of the river, the two wings would converge on Stuart, who had almost ten thousand troopers. Custer was to accompany

Buford's division, riding in first with Colonel Benjamin "Grimes" Davis's regiment.[53]

Stuart was not expecting visitors. The ebony-plumed cockerel had been in a celebratory mood since June 4, when he had hosted a dress ball at the courthouse. The crowd, intoxicated by the martial pageantry, moved outside and danced around robust bonfires, "the ruddy glare of which . . . gave the whole scene a wild and romantic effect," according to Major Heros von Borcke, a Prussian aristocrat who was a special favorite of Stuart's. This Wagnerian tableau was followed the next day by a grand review at Brandy Station with mock combat, jousts, artillery fire, and another gala promenade, the social event of the year for the prosperous wheat farmers of Culpeper County, their ladies, and their guests, who came from as far away as Richmond.[54]

The grand review was repeated at Fleetwood Hill above Brandy Station on June 8 for Lee and the ten thousand men of Hood's hard-fighting division, who traded insults with the preening cavalrymen. Hood had staged his own review on May 27 and perhaps thought Stuart, with all his foppery, was trying to upstage him. Brigadier General Fitzhugh Lee, a brigade commander with Stuart and once Custer's instructor at West Point, had proffered an invitation to Stuart and his "people," presumably meaning his staff, and Hood had showed up with his entire command. But the day had been a great success, and the evening was pleasantly warm. Stuart's brigades were spread out in all directions, ready to pack up and cross the Rappahannock the next day but not in good position to fight. Robert E. Lee, tired from the day's festivities, was close by, writing his wife about the splendid cavalry review with Stuart "in all his glory." Stuart sent his wagons and baggage back to Culpeper and stretched out beneath two tent flaps on the slope of the hill, perhaps gazing before he fell asleep at the glimmery Rappahannock three miles away and chuckling about how Hood had crashed the party.[55]

At about 4:30 the next morning, Custer crashed the party as well. He came out of the woods with his orderly, Private Joseph Fought, and approached Beverly's Ford as the river's aspiring vapors formed a dense fogbank. Close by, Custer could hear the dirge of a clanking and churning waterwheel, which may have subsumed the sound of hoofbeats. Behind him galloped Grimes Davis and the 8th New York, 8th Illinois, and 3rd Indiana. Exchanging shots with startled pickets as they splashed through the shallows, Custer and Fought led the column up Beverly's

Ford Road, across Ruffans Run, toward the slumbering camp of Brigadier General William E. "Grumble" Jones, a hard-nosed, profane fighter who only recently had joined in a destructive monthlong, seven-hundred-mile raid through the western Virginia mountains almost to the Ohio River. Jones and Stuart despised one another, but on this morning Jones, riding barefoot and hatless, took the brunt of Buford's strike as the vanguard of Stuart's awakening dragoons. Fighting soon spread for three miles along the river. Suddenly, Custer was, in the words of historian Steven E. Woodworth, in "the biggest cavalry battle the continent had yet seen." Eicher called it "an antiquated cavalry battle, with mounted saber attacks along with firing guns." Cavalry usually dismounted in such engagements, but the "surprise and chaos" at Brandy Station, a battle that lasted more than twelve hours, were unprecedented. [56]

Davis's regiments smashed into a hastily assembled company of the 6th Virginia Cavalry under Major Cabell E. Flournoy during the initial surge of the battle, giving the embattled Confederates time to move horse artillery to a high ridge near Jones's camp about two miles from the ford. Custer grew uneasy as he saw butternut soldiers, probably from Brigadier General W. H. F. "Rooney" Lee's brigade, dismounted behind a stone wall on Buford's right flank. Davis's men charged across the field and swarmed through a fringe of trees and into a clearing. Custer's horse failed to clear the stone wall cleanly, tossing its rider. He quickly remounted and sped down a rutted road after a fleeing battery. Gray horsemen, probably from Fitz Lee's brigade, approached him from the left. Before Custer could turn, a Federal rider told him Davis was dead, shot in the forehead at close range by Lieutenant Robert Owen Allen, who had been at the rear of Flournoy's retreating company. Davis had slashed at Allen, who avoided the blow by ducking behind the neck of his horse. Allen fired three times, and the colonel fell to the ground, mortally wounded. [57]

Monaghan, Urwin, and Ambrose all say Custer took command after Davis was killed. Jeffry D. Wert, however, found evidence that Colonel Thomas C. Devin took command after Major William McClure, not Custer, had temporarily taken charge. The correction is important because it shows Custer was still well down the chain of command less than a month before Gettysburg and had not yet commanded a brigade. It does not, however, diminish his heroism in the fight, during which he led or joined in several charges and later carried the captured flag of the 12th Virginia Cavalry to Pleasonton, who cited him for gallantry. [58]

Stuart rallied his command and threw fifteen regiments into the fight. Charges and countercharges continued all day before Pleasonton left the field and crossed to the north side of the river. Federal casualties numbered 69 killed, 352 wounded, and 486 taken prisoner. The Confederates reported 523 casualties. Custer had been at the front of a surprise attack and had seen its initial shock effect on a somnolent enemy. He never forgot the lesson. The fight at Brandy Station gave him confidence and a precedent. He might well have concluded after the war that if he could hold his own against Grumble Jones, the Lees, and Jeb Stuart, he had little to fear in the West from disorganized "savages" fighting under Red Cloud, Crazy Horse, and Sitting Bull. [59]

Stuart claimed he had won a victory. Pleasonton had gotten the worst of the battle and failed to fulfill his orders to the degree he intended. Although Lee praised Stuart, the cavalry general was widely criticized by many soldiers in the Army of Northern Virginia as well as in newspapers throughout the South. Pleasonton had shown that if the Federal cavalry couldn't quite defeat Stuart, it could fight him hard and not be underestimated. Stuart was embarrassed at Brandy Station and sought something bold to restore his tarnished reputation. [60]

ECHOES OF EXCALIBUR

One of Pleasonton's objectives was to find Lee's infantry if it was in the area. He may have seen some infantry in Major General Robert Rodes's division, which had marched to within two miles of Fleetwood Hill but was not engaged. Pleasonton collected a lot of rumors about the infantry and tried to pass this information off as solid intelligence, but his sources were suspect. Hooker, therefore, learned little more about Lee's movements than he had known before Pleasonton's clash with Stuart and remained cautious. Lee's plan was to bring his army north by crossing the Blue Ridge and moving up the Shenandoah Valley to the Potomac. By crossing the river, he intended to draw Union forces away from embattled areas elsewhere in the Confederacy, resupply his army, and let the North experience the cudgel of war on its own soil. More important, he wanted to win a battle on Northern soil to encourage a political settlement that would work to the South's advantage. [61]

Stuart crossed the Rappahannock on June 16, screening Lee's advance as he moved behind the mountains. Rodes's division had begun crossing the Potomac on June 15, and Brigadier General Albert Jenkins's cavalry brigade was already in Chambersburg, Pennsylvania. Hooker began to follow, sending Pleasonton ahead to locate Lee east of the mountains where Stuart was protecting the gaps. Hooker still had no idea where Lee was going and was concentrating his forces at Centreville. Custer rode with Gregg's division on June 17 as it encountered Fitz Lee's brigade, under the command of Colonel Thomas T. Munford, covering Longstreet's flank at Aldie. Brigadier General Judson Kilpatrick had Gregg's lead brigade. When the 2nd New York faltered during a punishing assault, Custer joined Kilpatrick in leading the 1st Maine Cavalry in a counterattack. At the end of a scorching day, Munford had pulled back toward Middleburg, having lost 119 men. The Federals lost 305. [62]

Accounts published in Michigan newspapers embellished Custer's role in the battle, but they were nothing compared to what Whittaker did with the story later. In five pages of spectacularly bad writing, Whittaker has Custer rushing into the fight "wearing a plantation straw hat, from under which bright curls flowed over his shoulders," and wielding a sword that sounds more like Excalibur than a cavalry saber. Years later Whittaker claimed, "Men said that hardly an arm in the service could be found strong enough to wield that blade, save Custer alone." He may have been reading *Le Morte d' Arthur*. Whittaker quotes from a letter Custer wrote to his sister claiming the plantation hat saved him from being killed when he was surrounded by Rebels because he looked like one of them and was able to escape. [63]

A SUIT OF BLACK VELVET

The skirmishing continued, but Stuart still held the gaps and kept the Federals away from the Blue Ridge. The Confederate partisan ranger and scout John Mosby arrived in Middlesboro to tell him Hooker was still moving northward roughly parallel to Lee while east of the mountains. His army, keeping between Lee and Washington, was spread out more than thirty miles, with the 12th Corps under Major General Henry Slocum arriving at Leesburg on the Potomac on June 19. More important for Stuart, he was facing more Federals coming through the gaps than he had imagined. He slowly pulled back toward the Blue Ridge after a sharp fight at Upperville, then moved back toward Aldie after Pleasonton withdrew on June 21. Pleasonton's signalmen had spotted the Army of Northern Virginia in the Shenandoah Valley from the Blue Ridge. Hooker knew elements of the army were in Pennsylvania, but the sighting confirmed an all-out invasion was in progress, and he had to move quickly. Stuart, meanwhile, began on June 25 to swing around Hooker's army on an extended raid before he was to find Ewell's corps somewhere in Pennsylvania.[64]

Custer was with Pleasonton in Frederick, Maryland, where he learned on June 28 that Hooker had been replaced by Major General George Meade. Unbeknownst to Custer, Pleasonton had reorganized the cavalry and gained approval to appoint three new generals: Captains Wesley Merritt, Elon Farnsworth, and George Armstrong Custer. Each had been a staff aide. Each would now command a brigade, serving as a brigadier general of volunteers. Custer would be in Kilpatrick's 3rd Cavalry Division as commander of the 2nd Brigade, composed of the 1st, 5th, 6th, and 7th Michigan cavalry regiments and an artillery battery. Custer had asked Blair for command of the 5th Michigan. Now the regiment and the brigade were his. Farnsworth also would serve under Kilpatrick, and Merritt would join Buford.[65]

It often is asserted that Custer was the youngest man to serve as a general in the Civil War, and Ambrose claims he was the youngest to serve at that rank in the U.S. Armed Forces. That distinction usually goes to Galusha Pennypacker, a Medal of Honor winner who became a brigadier in 1865 at the age of twenty, although his true age has been questioned. Purists might claim that the Marquis de Lafayette should be considered the youngest because he was appointed a major general in the Continental Army in 1777 at the age of nineteen. But at twenty-three, Custer was, briefly, the youngest U.S. general, and he claimed in a letter to his sister that he was the youngest by more than two years. Charles Cleveland Dodge had been appointed a brigadier general at age twenty-one in 1862 but then resigned before Gettysburg and later served with the New York militia. Edmund Kirby, a few months younger than Custer, was nominated for a commission by Lincoln on the day he died from wounds suffered at Chancellorsville, but he was not confirmed by the

Senate. The youngest Confederate general, also twenty-three, was William Paul Roberts, promoted to the rank in 1865 and slightly older than Custer at the time of appointment. [66]

Custer's youth was part of the foundation for his myth. Yet he isn't remembered just because he was the "boy general" of the Civil War. That designation is a creation of the press and the early biographers, as well as Custer himself. Pennypacker and Roberts long ago faded from public memory. Half the soldiers in the Federal army were under twenty-five. Many officers in both armies were advanced in rank, especially toward the end of the war, through attrition, and so it has been in many wars. Custer expressed his thoughts on rapid promotion when he wrote about McClellan long after the war. His mentor's disadvantage, according to Custer, was that he had been vaulted into a leadership position "without having first had an opportunity to prepare himself" by advancing gradually through intermediate grades and gaining self-confidence. Custer was commanding a brigade, not an army. Perhaps Custer also was remembering his own struggle to turn bravado into poise and assurance. [67]

All that happened immediately after Custer became a brigadier general became vital to the way he was remembered. First Whittaker and then most subsequent biographers told a story about how Custer came to learn of his promotion. Quentin Reynolds's juvenile biography jumps immediately from Bull Run to just before Gettysburg. "The war dragged on," and then Custer's oft-heard claim that he would be a general before the end of the war suddenly came true. Custer finds an envelope addressed to Brigadier General Custer. Suspecting a prank, he opens the envelope and learns from an official-looking document that he now commands the Michigan Brigade. With tears in his eyes he realizes his childhood "dream" has come true. Published at a time when the Korean War was dominating the news and a general was running for president, *Custer's Last Stand* delivered a powerful moral. Custer's boyish whoop had been emphasized throughout the story. If a real American boy could become a boy general in the Civil War, maybe any boy could become a Cold War military hero. He didn't even have to stop being a boy. What he needed, like Autie Custer, was patriotism, courage, and a dream. Van de Water's revisionist biography gave the story a very different interpretation. Custer learns "his miraculous attainment of each soldier's dream was not enough." Having won his miraculous star, according to Van de Water, Custer would be all but driven mad in his quest for glory. [68]

Custer's first priority after getting his instructions from Pleasonton was to join his brigade. He learned that the 5th and 6th Michigan cavalry regiments had passed through Gettysburg and were now scouting south and east of the town. He ran into some elements of the 1st and 7th near Frederick on the morning of June 29. His attire drew attention, and his image as a peacock has endured, perhaps unjustly. Custer knew he had to strike a pose if he were to establish credibility with the troopers he would command, and he had little time to put together a suitable ensemble for his part. His aide, Private Fought, recalled how he found silver stars and sewed them on a navy blue "sailor shirt" Custer had been given. This was covered by "a velveteen jacket with five gold loops on each sleeve." Captain James H. Kidd of the 6th Michigan met Custer the next day at Hanover, Pennsylvania, and later described the black velvet suit as

> elaborately trimmed with gold lace, which ran down the outer seams of his trousers, and almost covered the sleeves of his cavalry jacket. The wide collar of a blue navy shirt was turned down over the collar of his velvet jacket, and a necktie of brilliant crimson was tied in a graceful knot at the throat, the long ends falling carelessly in front. The double rows of buttons on his breast were arranged in groups of twos, indicating the rank of brigadier general. A soft, black hat with wide brim adorned with a gilt cord, and rosette encircling a silver star, was worn turned down on one side giving him a rakish air.

Could such a foppish costume have been produced so quickly? Wert doubted its provenance, speculating that Custer likely had the uniform secretly made to order well in advance, carefully folded, and stored in his trunk.[69]

This seems unlikely. Living in close quarters with other soldiers, Custer would have risked an embarrassing exposure and certain ridicule. This, too, assumes he had some reasonable expectation of rising in rank from brevet captain to general. The ensemble would have appeared even more outlandish had he worn it as a major or a colonel. Fought's improvisational haberdashery is the more probable explanation.

And it served a purpose. As biographer D. A. Kinsley observed, Custer already had "proven himself a good actor—a *grand poseur*—the first characteristic of a good or popular officer." He no longer was playing a supporting role, however, so he needed all the dash he could muster.[70]

Custer's new division commander, Judson Kilpatrick, had been an acquaintance at the academy. Kilpatrick was almost four years older than Custer, although they were only a class apart, and both graduated early due to the war. The diminutive Kilpatrick had been something of a brawler at West Point, unwilling to be bullied, not shy about voicing opinions, and quick with his fists. He had achieved rapid promotion in the army while earning notoriety as a self-promoter whose battle reports exaggerated his achievements and shifted blame for his losses. Kidd described him as "brave to rashness, capricious, ambitious, reckless in rushing into scrapes, and generally full of expedients in getting out, though at times he seemed to lose his head entirely when beset by perils which he, himself, had invited. He was prodigal of human life, though to do him justice he rarely spared himself." His men called him "Kill-Cavalry" "for the reason that so many lives were sacrificed by him for no good reason."[71]

Few generals have been described more variously. Kidd said he had "a countenance that once seen, was never forgotten." Others noted eyes "cold and lusterless" and called him "imp-faced," "hunchbacked," "insignificant looking," "ugly," "vain, conceited, egotistical," and "a frothy braggart without brains, who gets . . . his reputation by newspapers." A general said Kilpatrick's "memory and imagination were often in conflict." Still others remarked on his agility, enthusiasm, energy, and natty appearance. He was, a biographer claimed, competing with Custer for glory and determined to win the contest.[72]

Custer had to look for his scattered brigade because Kilpatrick's division was strewn across the Maryland and Pennsylvania countryside, clashing at times with Stuart's cavalry and delaying the Rebel horsemen as they sought to find Lee and deliver booty captured during Stuart's circuit around the Army of the Potomac. Custer found elements of two of his regiments, the 1st and 7th, near the Pennsylvania line on June 29 and went right to work. His manner was brusque with his new subordinates, who seemed amused by Custer's youth and appearance, muttering about "the boy General of the Golden Lock." Skeptical or not, they fell in behind their new commander, crossed into Pennsylvania, and reached Littlestown, where they joined Farnsworth's 1st Brigade. The next morning, Custer's brigade, accompanied by Kilpatrick, cantered seven miles northeast to Hanover, about fifteen miles east of Gettysburg, with Farnsworth following. The riders remained about two hours, receiving provisions and garlands from the anxious townsfolk, who already had seen

Confederates. They were on their way north toward Abbottstown by mid-morning. [73]

Farnsworth's trailing regiment was attacked by the lead elements of Stuart's cavalry moving north from Union Mills, Maryland. Stuart had been trying to get around the Federals and rejoin the rest of Lee's army, so he was in a fight he did not want. When Farnsworth brought another regiment into the skirmish and drove the Confederates back, Stuart got into position on a ridge to await the arrival of two of his brigades. Kilpatrick and Custer, hearing the sound of the guns, turned their horsemen back to Hanover. Custer set up a battery north of town, while Farnsworth's regiments spread out in front of Stuart's columns as they came into line. South and west of town, Custer's two other regiments had encountered Fitz Lee's brigade, which was holding Stuart's flank. When these Federals rode into Hanover, Custer's brigade, about twenty-three hundred strong, was assembled for the first time under his command. The brigade also had the firepower of six 3-inch rifled guns of Battery M, 2nd U.S. Artillery, which had fought in all of the Army of the Potomac's major battles. Lieutenant Alexander C. M. Pennington, whom Custer knew at West Point, commanded the formidable unit. [74]

A cannonade continued through the afternoon. The dismounted 6th and 7th Michigan advanced in waves across a wheat field toward the Confederate batteries until Stuart withdrew, riding east to Dover and then north to Carlisle to skirt the Federal flank. Stuart had fought well enough but had further delayed his rendezvous with the main body of Lee's army. Custer and his men then encamped for the night just outside Hanover. In the fields all around them, they could see the twinkling campfires of Major General George Sykes's 5th Corps as the weary infantry regiments settled in after their long march north. Earlier that day, Buford's division had ridden into Gettysburg with orders from Pleasonton to secure the town. Buford looked around, studied his maps, and marked Lee's known concentrations to the northwest based on reports from his scouts. When one of his colonels boasted he could brush aside any Confederate regiments that might show up on the morrow, Buford corrected him. "No, you won't," he promised. "They will attack you in the morning, and they will come booming." [75]

4

GETTYSBURG

[Custer] looks like a circus rider gone mad!

—Colonel Theodore Lyman, 1863 [1]

When Custer awoke on the morning of July 1, he knew from the previous day's action that the Michigan Cavalry Brigade could fight. The 1st Michigan had been in the field since September 1861 and had been tested in the Shenandoah Valley and at Second Manassas. The 5th and 6th were newer regiments, recently armed with Spencer repeating rifles that held seven rounds. The 1st and 7th were equipped with single-shot carbines. The brigade also had experienced artillerymen with the firepower of six 3-inch rifled guns. The 5th, 6th, and 7th Michigan, the newest regiment, had been skirmishing with Mosby's Rangers in the vicinity of Fairfax Court House in Virginia. [2]

Custer got his brigade moving northeast of Gettysburg to find Jeb Stuart and protect the flank of the Army of the Potomac with Judson Kilpatrick and David M. Gregg, commander of the 2nd Cavalry Division. Stuart was at Carlisle skirmishing with Pennsylvania militia. Confederate infantry regiments were reported all over the area, their destination unknown. As their horses galloped along dusty roads past the plenteous fields, bright meadows, and rolling pastures, the Wolverines could hear the distant thunder that had erupted west of Gettysburg when John Buford's cavalry encountered Major General Henry Heth's division. By midmorning the fight had enlarged with the arrival of Major General John Reynolds's 1st Corps. About noon Major General Oliver O. Howard took command after Reynolds was killed as more Confederate divisions arrived from the north. The fighting intensified along a crescent north of the town until some Federal brigades broke and raced back through Gettysburg. More Federal troops streamed onto the field as the famous "Fishhook" began to form on Culp's Hill and Cemetery Hill, then south about a mile and a half along Cemetery Ridge to the unoccupied rocky summits of Little Round Top and the more densely wooded Big Round Top. The Federals secured a defensive line Major General Winfield Scott Hancock called "the strongest position by nature upon which to fight a battle that I ever saw."[3]

That night an observer noted "a scene of weird, almost spectral impressiveness. The roads south and southeast of the town flowed with unceasing, unbroken rivers of armed men, marching swiftly, stolidly, silently." On Cemetery Hill, soldiers "lay down, wrapt in cloaks, with the troops among the grave stones," recalled Major General Carl Schurz. "There was profound stillness in the graveyard, broken by no sound but the breathing of the men and here and there the tramp of a horse's foot; and sullen rumblings mysteriously floating on the air from a distance all around."[4]

SULLEN RUMBLINGS

If things were quiet in the cemetery, there was plenty of activity elsewhere during the morning hours of July 2. Kilpatrick brought the division closer to Gettysburg, covering the flank of the converging infantry as the battle shifted to the south. Custer's brigade took the lead, halting at two o'clock northeast of Culp's Hill, and then skirting the eastern edge of the battlefield to help prevent Confederate cavalry and infantry from slipping around the Fishhook. The division was ordered to get behind Richard Ewell's 2nd Corps and disrupt his assault on Culp's Hill. Again, Custer took the lead, with the 6th Michigan at the front of the brigade. At about four o'clock, as they passed through Hunterstown four miles northeast of Gettysburg on a narrow dirt road bordered by rail fences, cornfields, and wheat fields, the 6th Michigan encountered Confederate cavalry.[5]

Stuart, thirty miles away, had learned of the developing engagement shortly after midnight and ridden through the night well ahead of his lost legions to reach Robert E. Lee at Gettysburg. Lee was perturbed with

Stuart for keeping him without most of his cavalry, according to most authorities, but put aside his displeasure to direct attacks on both flanks. Brigadier General Wade Hampton's brigade was coming from Dillsburg with captured wagons and was protecting the rear of Stuart's cavalry. It was Hampton's pickets, part of Cobb's Legion, a Georgia regiment of about three hundred men commanded by Custer's West Point friend Colonel Pierce Young, that Custer first saw at Hunterstown. [6]

In his memoirs Custer recalled a conversation he had with Young when they were still cadets during the winter of 1861. Young had predicted they would both be colonels in the cavalry during the coming war and might have to fight each other. Although the Federals would have the initial advantage, he predicted, "we'll get the best of the fight in the end, because we will fight for a principle, a cause, while you will fight only to perpetuate the abuse of power." [7]

Hampton had moved through Hunterstown and was talking with some of his officers when he was shot by a cavalryman from the 6th Michigan who was scouting the area. Hampton was not seriously wounded and drove off his assailant with a well-aimed pistol shot to the wrist. Shortly thereafter, a rider charged out of the woods and whacked Hampton on the back of the head with the broad side of a sword, the force of the blow cushioned somewhat by a felt hat possibly stuffed with dispatches. Hampton bellowed, then pursued, but his pistol misfired, and the rider raced back to Hunterstown. Pickets told Hampton that Federal cavalry was in the village in force. He ordered Young to spread his regiment across the road, then positioned the 1st South Carolina Cavalry and the Phillips Legion on the flanks. [8]

Kilpatrick ordered Custer to drive the Confederates back. Custer took up a position at a farm south of town, concealing some companies from the 6th Michigan in a barn and placing other units in the fields as skirmishers, with batteries on both sides of the road. He was setting a trap. Brandishing sabers, Captain Henry E. Thompson's company, with Custer at the front, charged down the road to stir up the Confederates and was cut to pieces by Hampton's cavalrymen concealed in the fields as well as by "friendly fire" from their own troopers covering the advance. Thompson was among the forty-four casualties, and Custer was thrown to the ground when his horse was shot. Rebels took aim as Custer struggled to his feet, but he was rescued by an alert private who shot one dragoon, hoisted his general up on his own mount, and rode back to Hunterstown. [9]

Gregory Urwin concluded that Custer had "led his company into a deathtrap, got half of it wiped out, and [come] within a second of having his brains blown away. It was the most reckless and thoughtless stunt he had ever pulled in his life." It was no stunt, but Custer rashly had led a charge at the head of about sixty men, no place for a brigadier general, against a waiting force of at least six hundred. The charge was Kilpatrick's idea. The execution was Custer's. Perhaps he rushed into action because he remembered Young's boast and was determined to prove him wrong. [10]

If Custer was reckless, Young was no wiser. His Cobb's Legion pursued the fleeing Michigan cavalrymen but fell into the same trap as had Custer. The narrow roadbed compressed the attacking forces, and the fields and fences offered too many sites of concealment. Dismounted cavalrymen fired at the Confederates as the batteries opened up, resulting in sixty-six killed, wounded, or captured. Custer and Kilpatrick both claimed victory, as did Stuart. "The actual outcome," according to historian Stephen Z. Starr, "was that both sides—less the casualties—retained their original positions and settled down for the night, in ignorance of the bitter and far more costly fighting that had taken place a few miles to the west, at the Round Tops." [11]

Historian Tom Carhart contended that other historians incorrectly have attributed a great blunder to Custer, who, he claimed, drew a lesson from the Battle of Cowpens in the Revolutionary War and cleverly lured the Confederates into a trap. Carhart's point was that a smaller force can defeat a larger force, and deception sometimes wins a battle. West Point cadets studied historical battles and learned to apply the lessons. Whether or not Custer was thinking about Continental Army brigadier general Daniel Morgan's defeat of a slightly larger British force under Colonel Banastre Tarleton near Cowpens, South Carolina, on January 17, 1781, is speculation. With Kilpatrick on the field, it is more likely Custer acted impulsively. [12]

The 3rd Cavalry Division had a chance for a few hours of rest at Hunterstown. But before midnight, George Meade, concerned about a possible move against his left flank, neither flank being protected by a significant cavalry presence, ordered the division to ride south six miles to Two Taverns, a crossroads inn about five miles southeast of Gettysburg on the Baltimore Pike, the main Federal supply route. Custer's brigade, about two thousand strong, arrived after 3 a.m. on July 3 and sprawled out by the side of the road. Elon J. Farnsworth's brigade was just a few miles west on the pike. Gregg's 2nd Cavalry Division, which had been heavily engaged in action at Brinkerhoff Ridge, the true end of the Federal right, was bivouacked about a mile closer to Gettysburg on Baltimore Pike.[13]

At 6 a.m., Alfred Pleasonton ordered Gregg farther up the Baltimore Pike to help defend Culp's Hill against Ewell's continuing attacks and interpose his division between Culp's Hill and Cemetery Ridge should Ewell strike toward the Federal rear. Gregg favored redeployment with reinforcements farther east at the intersection of Low Dutch and Hanover roads, not far from Brinkerhoff Ridge. Gregg had observed an elevation called Cress Ridge from which Stuart's cavalry might descend virtually undetected, then sweep into the Federal lines on Cemetery Ridge. Pulling the cavalry screen in closer to Culp's Hill, he reasoned, might invite a wider Rebel envelopment of the Federal position along the unprotected Bonaughton Road. But Pleasonton reiterated the order, conceding to Gregg only the addition of a brigade from the 3rd Division to replace his absent 2nd Brigade. He ordered Kilpatrick to move across the Emmitsburg Road beyond the Round Tops, where he would be joined by Brigadier General Wesley Merritt's Reserve Brigade. They were to hold the southernmost flank, still considered vulnerable after the withdrawal of Buford's division, and strike the Confederate left, unprotected by Stuart's cavalry.[14]

Kilpatrick moved out immediately with Farnsworth's brigade, summoning Custer to follow. Soon after Custer left, one of Gregg's aides, unable to locate Kilpatrick, asked Custer to take a position near the Rummel farm three miles north and several hundred yards below Cress Ridge. Thus, Custer had contradictory orders. But Gregg's orders had Pleasonton's endorsement, so Custer detached the command and moved toward the farm, arriving about 10 a.m., just as the attack on Culp's Hill was winding down. By the time Kilpatrick found out Custer was gone, it was noon, and Kilpatrick assumed a mistake had been made. In the confusion, no one had told him of Custer's position. By then Kilpatrick's dismounted cavalrymen had been engaged with John Bell Hood's division across Emmitsburg Road. At midafternoon, Kilpatrick launched an all-out mounted attack against fortified lines. His battalions were slaughtered. Farnsworth, leading the charge and refusing to surrender, was shot and killed. Had Custer followed the division into battle, he might well have suffered the same fate, or he might have made a difference. But he was at the other end of the battlefield. [15]

Custer got his troopers in place, with Cress Ridge about one mile toward the northeast. He sent two squadrons of fifty men to search the woods to the north and set up a skirmish line along a creek that flowed from a springhouse on Rummel's farm to the Hanover Road. He dismounted the 5th Michigan and moved the regiment into the fields to the northeast. Gregg had positioned his 3rd Brigade below the Hanover Road, extending the 16th Pennsylvania Cavalry as a picket line for several hundred yards while remaining in correspondence with Federal infantry two miles to the southwest. Gregg was protecting the flank against Stuart, wherever he might try to break through. To reinforce Custer farther to the east, Gregg moved Colonel John McIntosh's 1st Brigade between the Baltimore Pike and Hanover Road. Custer's regimental strength on the field was 1st Michigan, 427; 5th Michigan, an estimated 500; 6th Michigan, 477; and 7th Michigan, 383. McIntosh had between 600 and 800 men on the field. [16]

"COME ON, YOU WOLVERINES!"

On Cemetery Hill, during the calescent late-morning hours, Federal soldiers saw in the distance a stunning sight. Thousands of horsemen were riding northeast out of Gettysburg on the York Pike toward Cress Ridge, two and a half miles away. These troopers comprised brigades commanded by Colonel Milton J. Ferguson and Colonel John R. Chambliss Jr. Each brigade had slightly more than 1,000 men. Hampton, with 1,740 men, and Fitz Lee, with just under 2,000, were to follow later, along with several batteries with a strength of about 250 men. The Virginia Battery, with about 50 men, accompanied the first brigades. Stuart rode at the head of the column. [17]

On Cress Ridge the Confederate cavalrymen tried to conceal themselves in the dappled woods on the north slope. It was, said Stuart's adjutant, Major Henry B. McClellan, "as peaceful as if no war existed . . . and not a living creature was visible on the plain below." At about noon Stuart moved an artillery piece out from the woods into open ground, ordered a few random blasts from a Parrott rifle in several directions, then ceased firing. He ordered Lieutenant Colonel Vincent Witcher's 34th

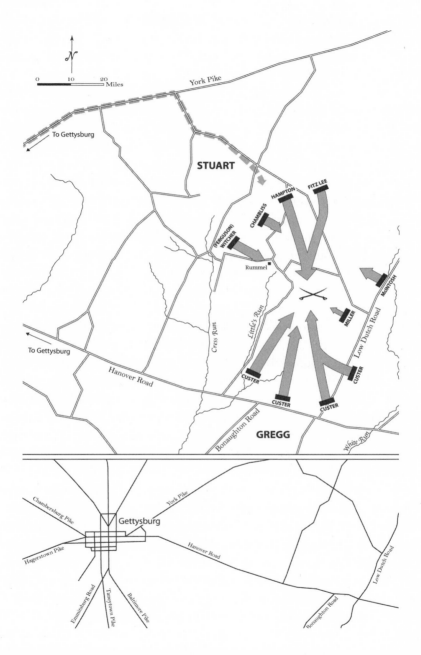

Map 4.1. The Gettysburg campaign, East Cavalry Field. The battle made Custer famous, as he led several important cavalry charges and may have kept General Stuart from supporting George Pickett's charge on July 3. (University of Tennessee Cartographic Services)

Virginia Battalion—332 men plus about an additional 100 men from two regiments in Ferguson's brigade—to dismount and move forward to the large frame barn on Rummel's 135-acre farm, there to spread out behind a stone fence crossing the property. [18]

Custer was still sweltering on Hanover Road. He had heard reports that Confederate cavalry units were on Cress Ridge, but he did not know their size or purpose, nor did he know why the battery was firing. Orders soon came from Pleasonton to send Custer to rejoin Kilpatrick and move McIntosh forward to replace Custer across Hanover Road. Custer sent some of the 6th and 7th Michigan riding away, but removing the rest of his brigade from the emergent battle was proving difficult. The Virginia Battery had been "pouring shot and shell into my command with great accuracy," Custer stated in his report. Alexander Pennington's batteries swept the ridge, putting some of the Rebel guns out of action. Around the farm the fighting intensified as Colonel Russell A. Alger's 5th Michigan got into action. Dismounted skirmish lines swept across the field to try to rescue eight companies pinned down behind a line of fences by the 34th Virginia. The Virginians were behind a longer, parallel fence line and got around the Federal flank, driving the skirmishers back. McIntosh put more men on the vulnerable flank. Stuart countered with nine Virginia companies from Ferguson's brigade and more troopers from Chambliss's brigade and Hampton's 2nd South Carolina as it arrived on the field. Seeing the skirmish was turning into a larger battle, Gregg brought up four 3-inch guns to support Pennington, and the combined firepower drove the Rebels back to Cress Ridge, where batteries directed more fire on the Federals. [19]

For a second time, Custer had conflicting orders. Kilpatrick wanted him back, and the outnumbered Gregg wanted him to stay. Whatever course he took potentially involved disobeying orders, although Gregg assumed the responsibility. Custer and Gregg realized they were facing most of Stuart's division, and with guns blasting in full timbre to the west, they may have suspected the dénouement of the Battle of Gettysburg was at hand. Custer wisely stayed with Gregg and sent riders to intercept the troopers who had hastened to join Kilpatrick. [20]

Near Pennington's battery, James H. Kidd's squadron of the 6th Michigan was stationed on a rise from which he could see "every phase of the magnificent contest that followed. It was like a spectacle arranged for us to see. We were in the position of spectators at joust or tournament where the knights, advancing from their respective sides, charge full tilt upon each other in the middle of the field."[21]

On Seminary Ridge, another spectacle was underway. At 1:07 p.m. the first of 164 Confederate cannons had opened fire on the Federal lines. After a brief intentional delay, the Federal guns on Cemetery Ridge replied. Shortly before 2 p.m. the firing slackened, and at about 2:30 some 12,500 Confederate infantrymen moved toward the Federal lines. Major General George Pickett shouted, "Up, men, and to your posts. Don't forget today that you are from old Virginia!" Federal artillery fire swept the field as the Confederates advanced. It was a charge for the ages, but Custer would have his moment of glory in due course, and with better results.[22]

Back at the East Cavalry Field, as it came to be known, Fitz Lee's regiments began moving off Cress Ridge. Custer sent several 6th Michigan squadrons to shore up the embattled line along the creek, then spurred the rest of the 5th Michigan forward, about four hundred men. As they were attacked by the dismounted 9th and 13th Virginia in Chambliss's brigade, followed by the 1st and 3rd Virginia, McIntosh rushed in what units he could find but had no reserves. The 5th Michigan's retreat prompted Custer to lead Colonel William D. Mann's 7th Michigan in the first mounted attack of the afternoon. Custer's smallest regiment, and the greenest, was just returning. He shouted, "Come on, you Wolverines!" and the 7th Michigan thundered diagonally across the field toward the 1st Virginia. Dismounted regiments fired at the horsemen, forcing a change in direction that caused the 7th to bunch up against a fence. Cavalrymen fought hand to hand, slashing with sabers and firing pistols, "a state of indescribable confusion," according to Kidd. The 1st Virginia's desperate charge forced Custer to retreat. From the ridge Hampton sent in two regiments that hit the 7th from behind. The 9th and 13th Virginia fired into the flank as the Federals raced by. A charge by a mounted battalion of the 5th Michigan may have saved the regiment. When the 7th drew nearer to Hanover Road, the artillery opened up with canister and drove the Confederates back. Once again the Federal artillery had shown its superiority.[23]

STUART'S INTENTIONS

At about three o'clock, the guns beyond the western ridges had gone silent. Although no one on the cavalry field yet knew it, the Confederates had been repulsed at Cemetery Ridge. Looking toward Cress Ridge, Custer thought he saw some movement through the dark trees just beyond the crest. Others saw a solitary officer on a burly bay warhorse riding down the ridge. Kidd sensed "the supreme moment" was at hand. The wily Stuart was about to throw his two best brigades into the fray and "sweep the field with one grand, resistless charge."[24]

Just what was Stuart doing on Cress Ridge to begin with? And why had he fired his cannon to alert Custer of his position? Although many theories have been advanced, Stuart biographer Emory M. Thomas concluded, "Stuart's intentions on July 3 are not at all clear." In 2005 Carhart provoked controversy with the publication of *Lost Triumph: Lee's Real Plan at Gettysburg and Why It Failed*. He argued that Lee had formulated a plan when Stuart returned on July 2 and Custer ruined it. He contended that Lee would not have risked everything on July 3 by striking the center of the Federal line while fifty thousand Confederate troops did nothing. Accordingly, there must have been other elements to the plan that did not come together. Stuart was not all the way out on Cress Ridge to guard Ewell's flank but to follow a back road into the Fishhook. The cannon shots that opened the battle were a coded signal to Lee that Stuart was on Cress Ridge and the road ahead was clear all the way to Meade's back door. In about twenty minutes, Stuart would join Pickett at the point of penetration and sweep north to join the Confederate attack on Culp's Hill as James Longstreet attacked the other end of the line. Stuart would begin as soon as Lee halted the artillery barrage against Cemetery Ridge.[25]

Historian Eric J. Wittenberg, among others, discredited Carhart's argument, stating, "There is not a scintilla of reliable evidence to support the theory that Stuart's cavalry thrust was coordinated with the grand Southern attack against Cemetery Ridge." The cannon shots, he claimed, were intended to induce Gregg to attack, a "reconnaissance by fire." Stuart's mission was to guard the flank and, if he broke through at some point, to cause confusion in the Federal rear. Wittenberg said Custer, still inexperienced, had less to do with the success of the charges than did Gregg. Carhart, in contrast, thought little of Gregg and concluded, "At Gettysburg, Custer truly saved the Union."[26]

THE FATEFUL CHARGE

Hampton came out of the woods on Cress Ridge, most of his brigade behind him. He later said he was trying to retrieve two of his regiments that had followed the retreating 7th Michigan too far when he realized most of the rest of his brigade was already behind him, assuming he was leading a charge. Stuart then sent in parts of Chambliss's and Fitz Lee's brigades to cover Hampton. Carhart was skeptical of their reports and believed that Stuart threw all available men into a time-sensitive, gallant rush to reach the main battlefield. When the charge failed, those writing the postbattle reports had a vested interest in keeping the number involved in the attack smaller than it was. The grand Napoleonic charge didn't fail, in other words, because in their reports it had never occurred. Instead, there was an impromptu battle appropriate to a flank guard, with perhaps nine regiments, or about twenty-eight hundred men, engaged and not Stuart's entire remaining force.[27]

Carhart estimated that four thousand Confederate cavalrymen made the charge. Stuart saw what looked like five to six hundred blue cavalry (McIntosh's brigade, including the intrepid Captain William Miller's company) about halfway down the field and mostly on the eastern side. About one hundred of them were across the middle of the field and in the woods to the west. At the southwestern corner, about one thousand troopers (5th, 6th, and 7th Michigan), many dismounted, were scattered about. Custer was in the southeast corner, with four hundred men of the 1st Michigan who had been held in reserve. It looked easy, and it was now or never. "Stuart had no choice but to initiate his own version of Pickett's charge on horseback and force the Yankees from the pathway to his objective," in the words of historian Thom Hatch.[28]

On came Stuart's Invincibles, raked by percussion shells and canister from the artillery and scattered bursts of enfilading fire from McIntosh's men in the woods. Gregg ordered the 1st Michigan into the jaws of Stuart's charge. Custer mounted his black horse, Roanoke, rushed well to the front of the regiment, his pennon fluttering behind, and shouted for his Wolverines to come on. The trailing horses cantered and then galloped forward, their advance arrested until the onrushing Confederates had been stunned by a storm of canister. The Michigan men burst into the gray swarm. The concussion threw riders to the ground, where they were trampled, shot, or skewered unless they could find another mount. When

Roanoke was shot in the foreleg, Custer pulled himself up on a riderless horse and continued dueling with embattled Confederates. A captain from the 3rd Pennsylvania said the clash of riders reverberated "like the falling of timber." McIntosh and Gregg sent in more detachments to support the 1st Michigan. On the other side of the Rebel columns came troopers from the 5th and battered 7th Michigan and 1st New Jersey, one of whom gave Hampton two more gashes to the head and drove him from the field. The Confederates soon pulled back to Cress Ridge.[29]

In the first few minutes of combat, the outnumbered Wolverines lost 86 men but blunted the charge. The final tally for the brigade was 29 killed, 123 wounded, and 67 missing. The Federals reported 254 casualties overall, and Confederates losses have been estimated to be as high as 450. "For a moment, but only for a moment, that long, heavy column stood its ground; then, unable to withstand the impetuosity of our attack, it gave way to a disorderly rout, leaving vast numbers of dead in our possession," Custer boasted in his report. "I challenge the annals of warfare to produce a more brilliant or successful charge of cavalry." If Stuart was supposed to ride to glory on Cemetery Ridge to meet the fifty infantry regiments Lee had sent to break the Federal line, Stuart had failed, and Custer had been at the head of the charge that stopped him.[30]

Custer acted boldly, but Carhart gives him too much credit in victory, just as he is given too much blame in defeat. Even without Custer, Stuart was not going to ride unmolested all the way to Cemetery Ridge. Stuart's part of Lee's plan, if indeed there was such a plan, already was coming apart with or without Custer. Custer did provide the spark at key moments in the East Cavalry Field fight. His bravery and audacity inspired others, all the more remarkable in that he was so new to command. It is wrong to claim, however, as Carhart does, that Custer saved the Union at Gettysburg. Nor would his having done so removed the burden of defeat at the Little Bighorn. If Carhart's book stimulates further reassessment of Custer's role at Gettysburg, the debate will surely add more fuel to the Custer myth, which inevitably polarizes him as either hero or goat, savior or destroyer.[31]

PURSUIT

The next day Lee began to pull out of Gettysburg, sending a seventeen-mile-long caravan of wagons and ambulances toward the Potomac crossing at Williamsport, Maryland, in a steady rain. The column was accompanied by cavalry under Brigadier General John Imboden, followed by Hampton and Fitz Lee. A second train on an alternate route consisted of Ewell's plunder and ambulances carrying wounded soldiers. Once Lee began to move his infantry, Meade ordered his cavalry to pursue. By noon Custer already had moved his brigade to Emmitsburg, Maryland, ahead of the rest of the division. Scouts spotted Ewell's wagon train as it moved through Fairfield Gap protected by Grumble Jones's cavalry brigade. Kilpatrick ordered the 1st Michigan to attack the rear wagons while he and Custer moved to cut off the rest of the train below Monterey Pass. This required a treacherous climb up South Mountain on a foul night. [32]

Near the top of the mountain, the Federals ran into cannon fire and sharpshooters. Custer dismounted the 5th and 6th Michigan and sent a skirmish line scrambling aloft while two squadrons remained ready to charge, as did the 1st and 7th, held in reserve. It was a large force but strung out along the narrow defile. After some skirmishing, the troopers pushed the Confederates across a plank bridge over a flooded creek. Custer and his men could hear wagons going down the mountain. The crossing secured, the 640-man 1st West Virginia, assigned to Custer from Farnsworth's brigade, hastened after the fleeing train, the 2nd Michigan trailing behind. The regiments secured the prize—wagons, carriages, and ambulances—that stretched down the road for ten miles, along with a reported 1,360 prisoners, most of them wounded. At Ringgold, Maryland, the Federals halted and rested. *New York Times* reporter E. A. Paul, who had ridden with the division over the mountain, spotted Custer sprawled under the dripping eaves of a chapel "enjoying in the mud one of those sound sleeps only obtained through fatigue, his golden locks matted with the soil of Pennsylvania." Even asleep, Custer was an imposing figure to the journalist. [33]

The next day, July 6, Custer found Buford's thirty-five hundred troopers facing Imboden's twenty-five hundred trying to get the Confederate wagons across the flooded Potomac by hauling them aboard a cable ferry. Imboden was in a bad spot because a pontoon bridge downstream had been destroyed by Pennsylvania cavalry. He had to hold the crossing, or else Lee would be trapped north of the river until the flooding abated. Imboden held long enough to be supported by Hampton and Fitz Lee after Kilpatrick pulled Custer out to fight Stuart. At Hagerstown, Stuart had opened a corridor for Lee to move troops down to the river. At Falling Waters, Lee's engineers set about building an eight-hundred-foot floating bridge, while the infantry set up a strong defensive position. Meade, meanwhile, was approaching the Confederate lines cautiously from the east and did not order a reconnaissance in force until July 14. By then the bridge was complete, and the Potomac had fallen to four feet at the ford. Infantrymen waded across the river, hastening the evacuation. By morning, most of Lee's army was across, except for Heth's division, the first Confederate force to be engaged at Gettysburg.[34]

On July 14 Kilpatrick's division reached Falling Waters, where Custer had dismounted two companies of the 6th Michigan and sent them to determine the strength of the Rebel works. Kilpatrick told Custer to mount a battalion and charge the lines. At first, the Confederates covering the withdrawal of Heth's division thought the fifty-eight riders were their own cavalry. When the men in blue entered the lines, they were set upon at close range. Fifteen Federals were killed, and twenty-five others were wounded or captured. A Confederate counterattack drove the rest of the 6th Michigan back, until the 1st Michigan and some additional troopers from Buford's brigade gained the advantage. Custer led the dismounted 1st and 7th Michigan into the works before all of the remaining regiments could cross the river, impaling a Rebel who was about to shoot him. The brigade collected some four hundred prisoners, while Buford and Kilpatrick reported a combined and likely inflated total of some two thousand captives for the cavalry units engaged, bringing the Gettysburg campaign to an end. Federal casualties at Gettysburg were about 23,000, including more than 3,000 dead. The totals for the entire campaign exceeded 30,000. Confederate casualties were estimated at about 23,000, including 4,536 dead, with an additional 4,500 casualties for the campaign as a whole.[35]

On July 15, Custer took command while Kilpatrick was on sick leave. He led the division across the river on a pontoon bridge into Virginia, then moved south fifteen miles along the Blue Ridge. On July 17 and 18, the Michigan Brigade moved into Snicker's Gap, while Buford held Manassas Gap to keep Lee in the Shenandoah Valley, where he was vulnerable to flank attacks by pursuing infantry. After skirmishing at Ashby's

Gap and Upperville, the division crossed the Rappahannock and moved on to Amissville on July 23 as Lee moved down the Shenandoah Valley. The 5th and 6th Michigan briefly became cut off and had to fight their way back through the lines. Custer called for reinforcements, but when Meade denied the request, Custer pulled farther back across the Rappahannock to Warrenton Junction, where he stayed until Kilpatrick returned.[36]

Custer's first month as a general had been eventful. He had won the respect and confidence of his brigade and his superiors even when confronted with conflicting orders. Many of his troopers were now wearing the red necktie Custer had adopted. He had led and survived several cavalry charges. He contributed to the Federal victory at Gettysburg, arguably preventing Stuart from breaking the Fishhook on July 3. Custer had commanded a division for several weeks and led it eighty-five miles into Virginia. Gettysburg and its aftermath gave rise to his initial fame, which Frederick Whittaker attributed to E. A. Paul's battle reports. "It must be remembered," Whittaker wrote, "that the young general was then entirely unknown to the public, but these letters [in the *New York Times*] opened people's eyes. At the same time they marked the brilliant commencement of that career which henceforth never knew a serious disaster."[37]

Paul, however, gave Custer relatively little attention in his July 21 summary of cavalry activities in the campaign. He cited Kilpatrick frequently. Paul mentioned the fight at Rummel farm almost as an afterthought, saying only, "Gen. Gregg's division, assisted by Gen. Custer's brigade of Gen. Kilpatrick's division, rendered an important service here." If Custer truly was the hero of the largely overlooked East Cavalry Field fight, that "important service" was not yet evident to a reporter inclined to boost Custer's achievements. Custer's real buildup in the press would come later.[38]

MISCHIEF BY MOSBY

August began quietly with staff work to resupply the brigade and find replacements for its casualties. Some relief arrived when the 1st Vermont Cavalry became part of Custer's brigade. These "Green Mountain Boys" fit in well, proudly wearing red neckties and calling themselves the "8th

Michigan." One of the reconstituted brigade's first challenges was to do something about Major John Mosby, the twenty-nine-year-old lawyer who had been operating as an independent guerilla under the provisions of the Partisan Ranger Act enacted by the Confederate Congress. The act authorized independent companies that were part of the army but could keep or sell the plunder taken during their raids. Early in 1863, Stuart had set Mosby up as ranger in an area between the Bull Run and the Blue Ridge Mountains, including portions of Loudoun and Fauquier counties. The increasing size and audacity of Mosby's command forced the Federals to assign more men to try to capture the rangers or at least keep them at bay. Mosby's irregular tactics tested the abilities of the Federal cavalry, however. His men raced through enemy cavalry in unorthodox formations that imitated Indian attacks. Rather than fighting with sabers, rangers favored Colt revolvers and were crack shots. [39]

As Lee moved south to the Rapidan, the Army of the Potomac spread out along the Rappahannock to the north to await Lee's next move. Meade needed to keep the Alexandria and Orange Railroad cars rolling in order to provision his one-hundred thousand-man army, and he wanted to repair the Manassas Gap Railroad so it could support operations from the Piedmont toward the mountains. Mosby's Rangers attacked the railroads and robbed the passengers, cut telegraph wires, burned bridges and trestles, raided Federal camps, hijacked sutler and army wagons, and captured soldiers and occasionally even a general. They rustled cattle and stole horses, uniforms, boots, coffee, ice cream, ammunition, bolts of calico, a pair of red slippers, and anything else they could haul away before disappearing into the countryside. Pleasonton ordered his cavalrymen to shoot armed civilians found with the partisans. Rangers sometimes wore blue uniforms and rode among Federal squadrons, stealthily picking off straggling riders. Custer hunted for Mosby with three hundred men but was unable to catch him. Custer resumed the chase later in the war. [40]

On August 17 the division moved down the Rappahannock to a camp near Falmouth for picket duty. A week later Custer's men clashed with an infantry regiment farther down the river near King George Court House. Brigadier General Evander Law's brigade and artillery guarded the ferry crossing opposite Port Conway in order to transport supplies and conscripts from the Northern Neck. Outgunned, Kilpatrick ordered a withdrawal and told Pleasonton he needed infantry to drive the Rebels from the Neck. Observing the fight was nineteen-year-old Lieutenant James Christiancy, whom Custer recently had appointed to his staff, likely as a favor to Christiancy's father in Monroe. Young Christiancy wrote Judge Daniel S. Bacon that Custer was cool under fire, giving orders "as though conducting a parade or review" and from the most exposed position on the field. Custer must have known the letter could only strengthen his position with Libbie's father.[41]

"A VERY MERRY BLUE EYE"

After learning that Longstreet's 1st Corps had embarked for Ringgold, Georgia, to support the Army of Tennessee, Meade sent ten thousand cavalry under Pleasonton across the Rappahannock on September 13 to do battle with Stuart, who was at Culpeper Court House. Kilpatrick's division forded the Hazel River and returned to Brandy Station, scene of the June 9 engagement. The Federals attempted to dislodge the Rebel guns on Fleetwood Hill but were driven back below the railroad. Joining Gregg and Buford, the 3rd Division moved forward in a five-mile front along the Orange and Alexandria Railroad, brushing aside pickets and halting within a mile of Culpeper in a crescent-shaped envelopment.[42]

Stuart knew the Federals were coming. He moved some of his wagons and put Brigadier General Lunsford Lomax's brigade in and around the town, along with three pieces of horse artillery. Cavalry under Buford and Gregg charged Lomax's brigade but were repulsed by artillery firing from a ridge. Kilpatrick sent the 2nd New York Cavalry rushing toward town, while the dismounted 6th Michigan fired from the hills. At the far left of the Federal line, Custer tried to turn Stuart's flank and support the other assaulting regiments. But he saw a train arriving and moved to capture the prize before it fled from Culpeper Station.[43]

While Pennington shelled the train, Confederate batteries shelled Custer's regiments. He set off with portions of the 1st Michigan and 1st Vermont, but the battalion became mired in swampy ground. Custer made his way to higher ground under heavy fire while leaving most of the battalion behind to struggle on. Instead of waiting, he improvised another attack force and headed directly for the guns. His regiments silenced the batteries and stormed into town with the 2nd New York, scattering the remaining Rebels from Lomax's dismounted 11th Virginia and other units, firing on the escaping train, overrunning Stuart's headquarters, and appropriating his dinner, stores, weapons, and provender. Stuart put additional artillery on Greenwood Hill southwest of town, shredded the attacking 5th New York with canister, and counterattacked. The 2nd New York and 1st West Virginia joined in as Custer charged with the 1st Vermont and 7th Michigan before canister killed his horse, ripped Custer's boot, and bloodied his leg. Stuart abandoned the position and pulled back to the Rapidan.[44]

Colonel Theodore Lyman from Meade's staff had been watching the train pull out when his attention was diverted by the "really handsome charge." He was even more impressed by the whimsical, flaxen-curled harlequin general who reported to Pleasonton at Lyman's side. Lyman thought his appearance, however strange, was also agreeable, "as he has a very merry blue eye, and a devil-may-care style." Pleasonton told Custer, "Well, boy, I am glad to see you back. I was anxious about you." Custer replied, "How are you, 15-days'-leave of absence? They have spoiled my boots but they didn't gain much there, for I stole 'em from a Reb." Custer was soon aboard a train and on his way to Monroe. He got a good deal of credit for the success and national notice. The *New York Times* and *Harper's Weekly* praised him.[45]

Figure 4.1. Custer's cavalry charge against Stuart's men near Culpeper Court House in September 1863 brought him more national attention in the press and the admiration of a staff officer who liked Custer's "devil-may-care style." Artist Edwin Forbes sketched some of the action. (Library of Congress)

Kilpatrick may have been offended by Custer's going directly to Pleasonton with a leave request, and the publicity his subordinate was receiving likely rankled. There had been tension between the two since Gettysburg, when Custer had stayed with Gregg rather than reporting to Kilpatrick as ordered. Kilpatrick probably blamed Custer for the failure of Farnsworth's charge. Other incidents of what Kilpatrick considered insubordination followed. As Kilpatrick's biographer Samuel J. Martin put it, the two were "competing for glory, and Kilpatrick was determined to win that contest."[46]

MASQUERADE

Custer arrived in Michigan on September 16 to a hero's welcome. Fittingly, on September 28 he escorted Libbie to a masquerade party dressed as Louis XVI. His regal appearance must have melted whatever resistance remained, and after a night of dancing not seen since Custer twirled Cousin Maggie around at Bassett Hall in Williamsburg, Libbie accepted his marriage proposal rather than sending him to the romantic guillotine. But the wedding would have to wait. By October 7 Custer was back with his brigade a few miles west of Culpeper and near the Robertson River.[47]

Two days later Lee began to move around Meade's right flank toward Culpeper. Near James City, Custer's brigade skirmished with Hampton's cavalry, while Confederate infantry moved west of the line Kilpatrick was holding. Custer was ordered to pull back beyond the Rappahannock, following the railroad while screening the retreating Federal infantry. Pressed hard by Fitz Lee and Stuart, and with Brigadier General Thomas Rosser blocking his path just outside Brandy Station while Buford supported him from Fleetwood Hill, Kilpatrick charged ahead with Colonel Henry E. Davies and the 1st Brigade on his right and Custer on his left. The 3rd Division fought its way through, with Custer leading the 1st and 5th Michigan in a saber charge that cost Custer another two horses. After uniting with Buford and fighting several rear guard actions, Custer and Davies crossed the Rappahannock, with Stuart following.[48]

Louis N. Boudrye, chaplain of the 5th New York Cavalry, provided a colorful description of Custer in action at the Third Battle of Brandy Station: "Gen. Custer, pulling off his cap, gave it to his orderly, and thus led on the charge, while his yellow locks floated on the breeze." It is significant that he did not witness the action but either heard about or imagined it. Custer's "yellow locks" by this point were an essential part of his image. In press dispatches and letters, Custer's locks were floating on the breeze even when he cut his hair short. As Custer became better known to the Confederates, these golden locks made him an inviting target.[49]

Lee, meanwhile, was marching northeast toward Manassas to try to hit Meade in the open. At Bristoe Station Meade routed A. P. Hill's division, and Lee withdrew toward the Rappahannock. Custer led Kilpatrick's two-thousand-man pursuit of Stuart's rear guard in heavy rainfall and skirmished with the Rebels at Gainesville on October 18. The next day Kilpatrick found Hampton's twenty-eight hundred troopers, commanded by Stuart, at Buckland across the west bank of Broad Run, a swollen stream running deeply through dark woods and traversed by a stone bridge.[50]

Custer dismounted three regiments and deployed them above and below the bridge, holding two regiments in reserve. After several attempts to take the bridge, Custer asked Kilpatrick for support. Instead, Kilpatrick told Custer to ford the stream and flank Stuart's lines. The 7th Michigan found a ford a mile below the bridge and struck Stuart's flank. When he heard the 7th engaging Stuart, Kilpatrick ordered Custer to take the bridge, ostensibly prompting Stuart to withdraw to the west. Kilpatrick sent Davies's brigade after Stuart, but when he ordered Custer to join the pursuit, Custer begged off. He wanted his men to eat breakfast, make coffee, and feed their horses. He was annoyed with Kilpatrick, who tried to coax his recalcitrant subordinate into following orders rather than relieve him of command. He had, after all, just stormed the bridge. Custer also may have suspected Stuart gave up the fight too easily. The two men compromised: Custer's men would have their breakfast. He would send his wagons ahead and fall in later. As Kilpatrick and his staff rode off after Davies shortly after noon, the Wolverines tarried, finishing their meal on a warm day, with a few taking naps on the late-season grass near the stream. Hours later, Custer had his men moving across the bridge in the direction of New Baltimore, Warrenton, and the Rappahannock.[51]

Stuart and Fitz Lee were leading Kilpatrick into a trap. Lee's fifty-two-hundred-strong division was at nearby Auburn, and he suggested Stuart withdraw so Lee could get between Broad Run and Warrenton, trapping Kilpatrick in the middle. Kilpatrick thought troops in the area were part of Merritt's cavalry. Kidd wrote later that Kilpatrick fell into the trap "with eyes wide shut." Just three hundred yards across the creek, Kidd's 6th Michigan was attacked and flanked. Custer retreated across the bridge before Lee could trap him. Some of Lee's riders pursued the outnumbered Michigan brigade halfway to Gainesville, while the rest waited to ambush Kilpatrick when he returned. Hearing the fighting behind him, Kilpatrick alerted Davies, who headed his regiments back toward the bridge, with Stuart right behind him. Kilpatrick then learned Custer was across the creek and Stuart's men had blocked Davies's retreat. The Federals fled until the 43rd Pennsylvania Infantry came to their rescue. Kilpatrick's casualties numbered about 150, and he lost his wagons.[52]

In one of the wagons, Stuart's men found Custer's desk, reports, and a passel of personal letters written to a woman. According to Captain William W. Blackford, one of Stuart's aides, the letters "afforded some spicy reading" and found their way into the Richmond newspapers, although "the spicy parts did not appear." Stuart called the rout the "Buckland Races."[53]

Kilpatrick was not much troubled by the fiasco, throwing a victory party for officers that night at his headquarters. His less-than-forthright report continued the military masquerade, further stoking Custer's enmity. By delaying the pursuit, Custer still stepped into the snare but saved his battalion without being hurt too badly. Had he followed Davies quickly, the 3rd Division would have been farther along the road, trapped between two divisions without an escape route. Kidd said Custer's men felt they had "saved their bacon and their battery." More likely, bacon and a late breakfast had saved their division.[54]

The entire breakfast incident, however, is curious. One explanation might be gleaned from Custer's after-action report, in which he states that when his men first arrived at Buckland, Stuart "was seated at the dinner-table eating, but owing to my successful advance, he was compelled to leave his dinner untouched, a circumstance not regretted by that portion of my command into whose hands it fell." If so, some of Custer's men ate for the first time since the previous evening, and most did not, which was bad for morale. He also had captured Stuart's dinner on September 13 at Culpeper, suggesting that the meal left on the headquarters table was meant to taunt Kilpatrick and Custer, a sign the Confederates knew they were coming. Or the mock seriousness with which Custer records the incident is another of his inside jokes. His low regard for his division commander was no joke, however. "All would have been well had General K. been content to let well enough alone," he wrote a friend in Monroe. "My consolation is that I am in no way responsible for the mishap, but on the contrary urged General K. not to take the step which brought it upon us, and the only success gained by us was gained by me."[55]

"EVEN THE DOGS WELCOMED HIM"

Little happened for a month until the Army of the Potomac crossed the Rapidan on November 26. Custer again commanded the division in the absence of Kilpatrick, whose wife had died on November 23. Custer did nothing more than skirmish for a week. As the weather turned seasonably cooler, the armies began to ossify in their winter encampments. The division set up quarters near Brandy Station and awaited Kilpatrick's return on December 21.[56]

Assuming his young readers were more interested in battles than romance, Quentin Reynolds covered the next part of Custer's story rather briefly: "He went to Monroe to find that Elizabeth Bacon, whom everyone called Libbie, was waiting for him, and now that Autie was a general her father wasn't so stern. They were married, and then Autie went back to fight the Civil War. It was a long war, and he saw plenty of action." That is a fair capsule summary of what happened.[57]

Custer secured a leave and traveled to Ohio to visit his family and friends, then proceeded north to Monroe. The wedding took place on February 9. The newlyweds traveled to New York, stopping at West Point. "When we got out of the train we found the river frozen, and the ferry not running," Libbie wrote her father. "I was drawn by a man, in a sled, Armstrong pushing behind. I never dreamed there was so lovely a place in the United States. Everyone was delighted to see Autie. Even the dogs welcomed him." After a few days in Washington, Custer returned to his brigade at Stevenson, Virginia. He and Libbie took up residence at Clover Hill, a farmhouse that served as brigade headquarters and the general's residence, which he soon called "Camp Libbie." On February 28 Custer left camp on a risky mission that almost ended the honeymoon prematurely.[58]

5

SHINING STAR

I served with him in the army,
In the darkest days of the war;
And I recken ye know his record,
For he was our shining star.

—Captain Jack Crawford, "The Death of Custer," 1876[1]

Eager for redemption after the failure of the "Buckland Races," Judson Kilpatrick volunteered to lead a spectacular raid to free Federal captives in lightly defended Richmond. On February 12, 1864, Lincoln approved the raid so long as Kilpatrick distributed leaflets announcing the president's amnesty proclamation along his route. In December, Lincoln had offered amnesty to Confederates who swore allegiance to the Union, but few had come forward. Alfred Pleasonton, angered by Kilpatrick's political maneuvering, opposed the raid, but George Meade overruled him, not wishing to strain his relationship with the president further.[2]

Kilpatrick's first volunteer was Colonel Ulric Dahlgren, the son of a Union admiral who was a friend of the president. Just twenty-one years old, Dahlgren had lost his lower right leg to amputation soon after Gettysburg while serving with Kilpatrick at Hagerstown. He only recently had rejoined the army, his truncated limb augmented by a prosthesis.[3]

The plan called for Dahlgren to lead 460 troopers into Richmond from the south. Kilpatrick would come in from the north and pass Robert E. Lee's right flank with four thousand handpicked raiders, many from Custer's brigade. They would tear up railroad track and cut telegraph wires along the way. Kilpatrick, still rankled by Custer's insubordination, excluded him from the Richmond raid. Instead, Custer was to lead a diversionary raid toward Charlottesville with about fifteen hundred troopers from David M. Gregg's division and Wesley Merritt's reserves. Their nominal mission was to destroy the Lynchburg Railroad bridge over the Rivanna River. John Sedgwick's 6th Corps would advance to Madison Court House to support Custer, who was uncharacteristically pessimistic, doubting many in his command would return. He had heard that the bridge was heavily guarded and that he would have to contend with Jeb Stuart deep within his own domain. He told Sedgwick that if he did not return in three days, he would either try to cross behind Lee and join Kilpatrick or, failing that, try to find William Tecumseh Sherman in Tennessee. Custer may have suspected he was being set up as a sacrifice to Kilpatrick's vanity.[4]

On February 28 Custer left camp to join Sedgwick, arriving about suppertime. Departing early the next morning, the battalion was across the Rapidan at daylight after some light skirmishing. Accompanying the column was London-born journalist and artist Alfred R. Waud, reporting for *Harper's Weekly*. Waud knew the flamboyant Custer interested readers, and Custer welcomed the publicity. Three hours later, Custer was in Stanardsville, just below the Blue Ridge, and then turned toward Charlottesville. Prisoners told him Fitz Lee was in the city in force, and Jubal Early's infantry division was arriving imminently on trains, thousands more men in gray than Custer's bluecoats could handle if the information were correct, which it wasn't. He faced only about 450 men from a mounted artillery battalion.[5]

Custer cautiously ordered sixty-five men to ford the Rivanna and head downstream to investigate, while he turned the main column two miles to the north. In dense woodlands below Rio Hill, they found the artillery battalion's winter encampment. A detachment set fire to stables and cabins, then came under artillery fire. In the ensuing confusion, Custer was not sure what or whom he was dealing with. He assumed the mounted artillerists approaching were the vanguard of a major cavalry attack by Fitz Lee's men and withdrew. Custer could hear the sound of approaching train whistles and thought he would have to fight his way past four batteries, two cavalry brigades, and an unknown number of arriving infantry before he could torch the railroad bridge two miles away. Instead, he recrossed the wooden Rio Bridge and burned it, set fire to three grain-filled flour mills, and headed back toward Stanardsville with captured horses and a wagonload of bacon. [6]

A heavy rainfall began that afternoon and turned to sleet. The raiders had a miserable few hours trying to stay warm and dry in the blustery weather. When they resumed marching toward the Rapidan, they discovered Colonel William Stedman's 6th Ohio Cavalry was gone. He had ridden through the night after becoming separated from Custer during the storm and crossed the Rapidan before daybreak. In his report, Custer called this exodus a misunderstanding while avoiding the more probable excuse that the units assigned to him were not from his beloved Michigan cavalry. North of Stanardsville Custer encountered cavalry regiments under Brigadier General Williams C. Wickham blocking his path to the Rapidan. Custer said Stuart was present and led a charge that was repulsed, with the Confederates being driven back "in great disorder." Custer counterattacked and drove past Stuart with some artillery fire and skirmishing. He confused the Confederates by staging a diversionary attack while the main column escaped. The raiders crossed the river before Stuart could overtake them, reuniting with Stedman and reaching Madison Court House by late afternoon. Custer said he had ridden more than 150 miles without losing a man. He was given favorable notice in the *New York Times* and *Harper's Weekly*, which published Waud's sketches, one on the cover. [7]

The Kilpatrick-Dahlgren raid had been a disaster. Kilpatrick was within a mile of the city, shelling a fort at 3 p.m. on March 1, when he decided to turn back. He changed his mind about 10 p.m., but by then he was in a fight with Wade Hampton. The next day Kilpatrick reached Tunstall's Station about twenty miles east of Richmond on the peninsula, where he was joined by the remnants of Dahlgren's command. He had divided his force and run into heavy resistance. Dahlgren had been killed and most of his command either slain or captured. Kilpatrick reached Yorktown on March 4, and his brigades began departing by ship the next day. Among the raid's 340 casualties, 176 came from the Michigan Brigade. The raid became infamous after a boy discovered papers on Dahlgren's body allegedly ordering the burning of Richmond and the assassination of Jefferson Davis and his cabinet. Kilpatrick denied knowledge of some of the papers, which may have been forgeries, but Meade and others suspected he was complicit if there was a plot. Kilpatrick tried to shift the blame to

Dahlgren, but Theodore Lyman, on Meade's staff, probably spoke for the commanding general when he said, "Kill has rather dished himself."[8]

James H. Kidd, who commanded the 6th Michigan during the Richmond raid, claimed Custer achieved his purpose by creating enough commotion for Kilpatrick to be well beyond the Rapidan before he was discovered. It was, however, "a fatal mistake" to leave Custer behind, for "the Michigan brigade without Custer, at that time, was like the play of *Hamlet* with the melancholy Dane left out. With him the expedition might well have been successful; without him it was foredoomed to failure."[9]

By the time he published his war memoirs in 1908, Kidd had decided that Kilpatrick committed "a fatal error of judgment" when he divided his command and that Custer "made the same mistake when he went to his death" at the Little Bighorn. Custer uncharacteristically was cautious at Charlottesville. With little credible evidence as to what he was riding into, he probed the flank "to satisfy myself concerning the enemy's strength and position" and then withdrew upon learning "the vast superiority of the numbers of the enemy, compared with my own, and the strength of his position." He followed the most conservative interpretation of his orders and went home. If he later learned he had been duped about the enemy's strength, he likely regretted that he had not followed a bolder course.[10]

Did he learn a lesson at Charlottesville that he remembered at the Little Bighorn twelve years later? Or, by following Kilpatrick's precedent, did he fail to heed a lesson? A rooted memory may blossom when least expected. Custer may have feared being outwitted at the Little Bighorn, as he was at Charlottesville, more than he feared being confronted by a larger force. At Charlottesville, he was fighting a force he respected. At the Little Bighorn, he was fighting those he considered savages. He was confident he could prevail in a fight, but he could not countenance the embarrassment that came from backing away from a fight he might have won or allowing his prey to escape into the mountains.

Once he committed himself to attack an enemy of uncertain strength at the Little Bighorn, dividing his command was one of several rational options, and it had worked for him often enough in the Civil War when he knew what he was up against. At the Little Bighorn, he did not know but acted as if he did. At Charlottesville, he said he did know ("the vast superiority of the numbers of the enemy") but in fact did not. At the Little Bighorn, would a unified command have prevailed, as Kidd thought it might, or would the lack of information have led to the same result? All commanders make mistakes. The great commanders learn the right lessons from the wrong decisions.

CHANGES

On March 24, the Custers boarded a train for Washington. The general had been granted a twenty-day furlough to recover from a tumble from a carriage. The cavalryman who had been thrown from a number of wounded war horses in battle after battle had been riding with Libbie when the carriage horses bolted. Custer suffered a concussion and needed time to collect his wits. Aboard the special train was Ulysses S. Grant, who had been promoted to lieutenant general and given overall command of all the Federal armies on March 9. Libbie found Grant not much to look at but "unassuming" and "funny." In deference to Libbie, Grant withdrew to a platform to smoke a cigar, but Custer, at Libbie's request, implored him to return. By Libbie's count, Grant smoked five cigars in the one hour and fifty-two minutes she said it took the train to reach Washington, or one cigar every twenty-two and a half minutes, a combustion rate worthy of a tobacco bonfire. [11]

Libbie wrote her parents about Custer's warm reception in Washington. "It astonishes me to see the attention with which he is treated everywhere," she noted. "One day at the House he was invited to go to the floor, and the members came flocking round to be presented. . . . None of the other generals receive half the attention, and their arrivals are scarcely noticed in the papers. . . . I wonder his head is not turned." She said Lincoln "knew all about" Custer when they were introduced. On another occasion when she met the president, he said, "So this is the young woman whose husband goes into a charge with a whoop and a shout." [12]

Leaving Libbie in Washington, Custer returned to his brigade on April 14, ready to sort out the reorganization of the Army of the Potomac. Grant retained Meade as commander but sent Pleasonton to Missouri and appointed Major General Philip H. Sheridan as chief of cavalry to replace him. Kilpatrick was sent to Georgia to serve under Sherman and replaced as 3rd Division commander by Brigadier General James H. Wilson. Custer did not like Wilson and wanted the job himself. But he was pleased to learn he and the Michigan Brigade would be moved to the 1st Cavalry

Division under Brigadier General Alfred Torbert, along with the 2nd
Brigade under Colonel Thomas Devin. An experienced infantry commander, Torbert had replaced John Buford, who had died from typhoid
fever in December. Custer wrote Libbie that Torbert was "an old and
intimate friend of mine, and a very worthy gentleman." Gregg would
command Sheridan's 2nd Division, and Merritt would direct the regulars
in the Reserve Brigade. Custer's first meeting with Sheridan commenced
on the evening of April 15 and continued until almost 4 a.m. Custer told
Libbie that Sheridan impressed him "very favorably."[13]

The two were compatible in temperament and had grown up eighty
miles apart in small Ohio villages. Both were energetic, courageous, magnetic, confident, and impulsive. As their relationship evolved, Sheridan
learned how to get the most out of Custer and knew his subordinate's
limitations, among them a lack of deliberation. Sheridan was combustible
but seldom hasty. Both were inclined to action over thought, but Sheridan, the more calculating of the two, sometimes played the solid schoolmaster to Custer's pupil, the alert, precocious boy without much discipline who needed an occasional ear twisting.

The thirty-three-year-old Sheridan's West Point conduct record was
worse than Custer's, including a one-year suspension for insubordination
and brawling. The bantam Irishman fought in the Indian Wars in the West
before serving as a captain in the 13th Infantry in Missouri at the beginning of the Civil War. He was named colonel of the 2nd Michigan Cavalry in May 1862 and became a major general of volunteers by the end of
the year. He came to Grant's attention during the Battle of Stones River
and won Grant's acclaim after he stormed Missionary Ridge at Chatta-
nooga.[14]

As the new cavalry commander, the pugnacious Sheridan inherited a
saddle-sore fighting corps with hardly more than 5,000 men ready for
active duty out of a total force of some 12,500 troopers and 860 horse
artillerymen. He told Meade that holding what amounted to a sixty-mile
picket line stretched the cavalry too thin. Sheridan proposed concentrating the cavalry in a single force that could defeat Stuart. Meade agreed to
relieve the cavalry of some of its picket duty but still insisted the cavalry's main function was to guard supply trains and the army's flanks.[15]

INTO THE WILDERNESS

Grant's strategy was to apply relentless pressure on all fronts. The United States had a continental army of some 533,000 men in the field, and these Federal forces, properly coordinated, could leverage their numerical and matériel advantage to win the war. In the East, Grant would remain with the Army of the Potomac and lead from the front lines, with Meade in nominal command. In the fertile Shenandoah Valley, Major General Franz Sigel would occupy troops that might otherwise reinforce Lee. Major General Benjamin Butler, commanding the newly formed Army of the James, would move up the peninsula to attack Richmond from the east. [16]

On May 4 Grant launched the Overland campaign by crossing the Rapidan and entering the labyrinth known for centuries as the Wilderness, a dense forest of scrub oak, cedar, dogwood, pine, and thickly coiled vines. Its hazel and briar thickets concealed small glades, low ridges, wandering creeks, marshes, and bad roads. The Wilderness was no place for cavalry operations, and both sides had difficulty screening the movement of their own armies and locating the flanks of the enemy.

The seventy-five-square-mile patchwork of woodlands had been settled in the eighteenth century by German miners who extracted iron ore from the ground near the Rapidan. Timber from old-growth forests had been cleared to fire furnaces and foundries, creating poor soil and dense shrub land. Sawmills, charcoaling operations, and plank-road construction had contributed to the wasting process. Chancellorsville, a ravaged clearing near a three-way intersection, had been at the center of a Wilderness battle that had resulted in thirty thousand casualties a year earlier. Now, in the greening of spring, deep in the hollows, thickets, and craters, more men would die among the ossuaries of partially uncovered graves. [17]

Two days earlier, from a signal station atop the six-hundred-foot elevation of Clark's Mountain several miles east of the Wilderness, Robert E. Lee and his lieutenants had observed the Federal troops approaching the fords across the river and were ready for them. Grant and Meade hoped to pass through the Wilderness unmolested to more open ground in forty-eight hours, moving around Lee's right flank and forcing the Army of Northern Virginia to move south to protect its communications. [18]

Sheridan's 2nd and 3rd divisions had crossed the river ahead of three infantry corps, while Custer's 1st Brigade helped guard four thousand supply wagons, a job Sheridan thought should be given to the infantry. The brigade crossed over before dawn the next day. About noon Custer was at Chancellorsville behind the left flank of the Union lines. During the night, the brigade made it to the Brock Road between Winfield Scott Hancock's 2nd Corps and Gregg's 2nd Division at Todd's Tavern to strengthen the Federal left flank. On the way, the Michigan troopers encountered the 1st Vermont, the "Green Mountain Boys," now part of Wilson's 3rd Cavalry, which had been bloodied in a fight with Thomas Rosser's cavalrymen. Meade's headquarters was convinced George Pickett's division from James Longstreet's corps was creeping around the Federal flank and might find one of the hidden roads that would lead him into the rear of the extended Union position. But Pickett was nearer Richmond than the Wilderness. Told to look for Pickett in the wide gap between Hancock's divisions, Custer concealed his troopers in the woods around a wide field divided diagonally by a sloping ravine. [19]

It soon became evident no infantry was in the vicinity. His orders, as historian Gordon C. Rhea put it, "called upon Custer to attack a body of Confederates he knew did not exist." Nevertheless, the 1st and 6th regiments held the right side of the line, and the 5th and 7th held the left along with Devin's brigade, while two companies extended down the Brock Road as a picket line. [20]

Suddenly Rosser's 35th Virginia Cavalry Battalion came rushing toward the field along the west side of the Brock Road, "charging full tilt toward our position," as Kidd recalled the scene. "He did not stop to skirmish with the pickets but, charging headlong, drove them pell-mell into the reserves, closely following, with intent to stampede the whole command." Custer, yelling and squalling, bolted to the woods concealing his troopers and ordered the 1st Michigan to force Rosser's men back. Custer threw his entire line into the ravine, where the men opened fire with their Spencer rifles. A battery shelled the field, but the Wolverines held, Custer riding conspicuously behind the bloody swale. When Rosser flanked Kidd's 6th, Custer shifted Russell A. Alger's 5th Michigan to the right and sent the 7th to the ravine. Devin's brigade hit Rosser's left flank with the 17th Pennsylvania as the 1st and 7th Michigan surged out of the ravine, routing the Confederates with help from Gregg's artillery. The engagement turned into a gory artillery duel punctuated by wild charges. Custer prevented Rosser from flanking Brigadier General Francis C. Barlow's division holding the extreme left flank of the Union line. Ironically, the racket from the cavalry fight confused Hancock and caused him to weaken his lines by moving soldiers where he did not need them.[21]

Custer was ordered to remain on the field until dark, when the brigade withdrew. The next morning it advanced toward Todd's Tavern, with the 1st Michigan dismounted and moving through the woods to cover the troopers riding on the road. After pushing back Stuart's skirmishers, the brigade made contact with Gregg, and on the next day the entire corps massed on the Plank Road. Only then did the cavalrymen begin to understand the scope of the confusing battle.[22]

Lee had moved three infantry corps to counter the slow movement of Meade's three corps through the Wilderness. Meade ordered Major General Gouverneur Warren's 5th Corps, heading south, to strike what he thought was a division moving in from the east on the Orange Turnpike soon after 7 a.m. The division turned out to be Richard Ewell's corps, and soon the fighting spread along a broad front. A. P. Hill's corps came in below Ewell and briefly was stalled by Wilson's 3rd Cavalry. Meade moved forces to the Brock Road to push Hill back. By noon, as reinforcements poured in from both sides, the entire front became a slaughter pen as units battled the Wilderness as much as each other. Visibility, already poor, became worse from smoke, and the integrity of military organizational structures began to collapse as clusters of men from different units fought side by side in improvised detachments. Attacks and counterattacks continued into the evening. Fires set off by exploding shells spread across the battlefield, a macabre immolation of dying men and horses.[23]

Meade and Grant resumed the attack at dawn. Lee was awaiting the arrival of Longstreet's 1st Corps, rushing to the battlefield from Mechanicsville. Just as Lee's right flank began to fold as Hancock pushed forward against A. P. Hill, Longstreet launched a counterattack that stabilized the line. Hancock was told his extended left wing, held by Barlow, was in jeopardy from Rosser, which it wasn't because of Custer's attack. Hancock had held back, missing a chance to strike Longstreet's flank. Fighting continued through the morning, with Longstreet's troops beginning to push the Federals back. But while organizing a flank attack on the Federal left, Longstreet was shot and carried from the field. Lee delayed the attack, but by then Hancock had fortified the vulnerable position, and the attacks broke off. By evening on May 7, Grant had the army moving south toward Spotsylvania Court House. There would be no turning back, although two days of fighting in the Wilderness had cost the Federals

17,666 casualties out of about 100,000 engaged. Confederate losses were at least 7,750 out of about 60,000 engaged.[24]

SUNDOWN AT YELLOW TAVERN

Sheridan continued to argue with Meade about the way he had been using his cavalry. He said Meade had erred in abandoning the crossroads at Todd's Tavern and other positions because he thought the flank had been turned, giving up ground that the cavalry had won in heavy fighting. Frustrated by trying to direct piecemeal cavalry operations, Sheridan wanted to mass his entire force and eliminate Stuart entirely. Grant told him to go ahead and try, and before dawn on May 9, "Little Phil" left Aldrich's Station near Fredericksburg with ten thousand horsemen riding four abreast in a thirteen-mile-long column heading around Lee's right toward Richmond. Kidd's 6th Michigan led the way, with Custer following behind the regiment with his staff and in front of the rest of the brigade. Stuart followed with only three of his six brigades. Because he wanted to reach the Richmond defenses before Sheridan, Stuart pushed his riders and his horses hard, while Sheridan intentionally kept a slower place. His target was Stuart, not Richmond, and he wanted his men rested and ready to fight.[25]

At Chilesburg, Custer paused to help assemble the 1st Cavalry Division, temporarily under Merritt's command, then turned toward Beaver Dam Station on the Virginia Central Railroad. About sunset, soon after crossing the North Anna River, the horsemen spotted some four hundred Union prisoners from the Wilderness being marched to the station. Driving off or capturing the guards, the 1st and 6th Michigan galloped into the station and seized the trains waiting to transport the prisoners. The plunder included two locomotives, with one hundred boxcars loaded with rifles, tents, medical stores, one hundred tons of bacon, and enough foodstuffs to feed the Army of Northern Virginia for weeks. After arming the prisoners, replenishing their rations, tearing up track, and cutting telegraph wires, the Wolverines set everything in sight ablaze.[26]

On May 10, the Federals reached the South Anna River and rested, giving Stuart a chance to get around them. The bold dragoon was appalled at the destruction at Beaver Dam Station, reminiscent of his own mayhem in Pennsylvania, and remained convinced Sheridan was striking for Richmond. Stuart divided his command and accompanied Fitz Lee's two brigades on a shortcut, reaching Hanover Junction after sundown on a hot day. After a short rest, the gray riders resumed the race, traveling through the night. The exhausted Rebels arrived at Yellow Tavern, an abandoned inn at the intersection of Telegraph Road and Brock Turnpike six miles from Richmond, about 10 a.m. on May 11. The roads formed a *V*, with the inn just below the point of intersection. [27]

Stuart had only about three thousand mostly dismounted men arrayed to fight Sheridan, who was supported by artillery. Brigadier General James Gordon's brigade was coming up behind Sheridan from the northwest on the Mountain Road, which intersected with Brock Turnpike about a mile from the inn. Had Sheridan raced past the intersection and headed for Richmond, Stuart and Gordon could have attacked the rear of the Federal column as it penetrated the Richmond defenses. The Union cavalry arrived about noon. Merritt, the ranking officer on the field, sent Devin's dismounted 2nd Brigade to the right flank at the intersection, put Colonel Alfred Gibbs's Reserve Brigade in the middle, and sent the Michigan Brigade, mounted in battalions, to a field further left. Stretched out along the Mountain Road, the Federal riders streamed onto the battlefield in segments, giving the initial advantage to the Confederates, who were already in position. [28]

Facing Custer across the field to the north was a thin line of woods, behind which six artillery pieces were firing from a bluff, while dismounted cavalrymen from Wickham's brigade poured fire into Custer's lines. Between the lines were five fences, a shallow creek called Turner's Run, and a smaller tributary flowing to the south and southeast. To Custer's right along the Telegraph Road, Stuart had lined up Lunsford Lomax's brigade. To avoid being penned up under artillery fire, Custer sent the dismounted 5th and 6th Michigan springing forward to drive away Lomax's pickets. When Alger's 5th Michigan came under heavy flanking fire from the ridge to the left, Custer steadied the troopers and adjusted his lines, while Kidd and the 6th drove the Confederates back to the bluff. Fighting continued for two hours, each side gaining a temporary advantage, and tapered off about 2 p.m. The outnumbered Confederates fought well and thought they could drive Sheridan from the field when reinforcements arrived from Richmond. [29]

Shortly before 4 p.m., fighting resumed. Sheridan had Wilson's division lined up next to Merritt's, with Custer approximately in the middle of the line. Stuart's brigades held the ridge. Sheridan ordered a mounted charge with Custer striking for the troublesome Baltimore Light Artillery Battery. The Wolverines were joined by the 1st Vermont. Custer sent the 5th and 6th Michigan marching toward Wickham's position on the heights east of Telegraph Road, while the 1st and 7th Michigan and the Green Mountain Boys charged up Telegraph Road aiming for the battery. Other units supported the attack. Just as the artillery opened up, the sky darkened into a smoky gray, and a thunderstorm exploded over the battlefield. Eruptions of cannon fire were matched by bolts of lightning "so terrific, that sometimes we couldn't tell the flash of one from the other," a Virginia cavalryman recalled. [30]

Custer's men splashed across Turner's Run and charged uphill toward the guns, met by the 6th Virginia. Sheridan sent Wilson's regiments racing up the ridge toward Wickham on the left, while the Wolverines climbed fences and barricades, raced across a narrow bridge, and began to overrun the battery, defended by the 1st Virginia. Stuart was on horseback behind a fence in an isolated position on the field, waving his saber and encouraging the 1st Virginia. Charging Federal riders swept past him as the Virginians launched a mounted counterattack. Stuart fired his Whitney Navy revolver at Federals who were caught within the Rebel lines. A dismounted cavalryman running by shot the general from close range. Stuart rose up in the saddle, grasping the pommel as soldiers rushed to help him. The line began to collapse as stunned Confederates under Fitz Lee rallied briefly, then began to scatter. Stuart's wound was mortal. He was carried from the field and died in Richmond the following day. [31]

Custer received much of the credit for the victory, which cost his brigade 113 casualties. *New York Herald* reporter Solomon T. Bulkley wrote that Custer "placed himself at the head of his command, and with drawn sabers and deafening cheers charged directly in the face of a withering fire. . . . It was, without exception, the most gallant charge of the raid, and when it became known among the corps cheer after cheer rent the air." Custer's yell during a charge was "equal to that of any of the Rocky Mountain aborigines." After the war, Wilson, Custer's rival, grumbled that sensational newspapers gave the impression that Custer and his brigade did most of the fighting. Custer was a good story for the press, so Wilson's complaint was justified. Before the campaign concluded, however, Custer said Wilson "proved himself an imbecile and nearly ruined the corps by his blunders."[32]

By 11 p.m., Sheridan had the corps mounted and on its way around Richmond. The foul weather continued, and the winds in the city were so strong they blew down a church belfry. Sheridan's purpose was not to cause havoc in the Confederate capital, although he briefly relished the opportunity, but to reach Butler's lines on the James River. Getting there was proving difficult because the Confederates had mined and booby-trapped the road. Wilson, who was in the van of the column, was duped by a devious guide and led into the city's outer defensive lines manned by home guards. Jefferson Davis himself was rumored to be in the front lines. With Gordon's cavalry behind him, the guns of Richmond in front of him, the weather against him, and his flank on the turbid Chickaho-miny, Sheridan was in a tight spot. He sent Custer and Merritt to lead the way east across the Meadow Bridge used by the Virginia Central Rail-road, but when they arrived, they found the bridge had been partially burned and some of its planking removed. Fitz Lee had set up artillery on the bluffs across the river, and dismounted cavalry and infantry held the crossing behind breastworks, ready to fire on Federals approaching the railroad span.[33]

Kidd noted, no doubt with sarcasm, that although the Michigan men had not yet had their coffee or breakfast, "they rode cheerfully forward for the performance of the duty assigned to them." Custer sent squadrons of men swinging and leaping across the bridge scaffolding like acrobats, while Confederates shelled the structure, one of the projectiles landing close enough to splatter Custer with mud. When enough troopers were across, they began skirmishing, while sappers wedged whatever pieces of wood they could find between the tracks to provide planking for horses. When all were across and the Confederates driven into the woods, the division raced on to the James and reached Butler at Haxall's Landing. Federal casualties for the entire raid came to 715. The Rebel losses were estimated at about 800.

The loss of Stuart demoralized the Confederacy as much as it bol-stered the spirits of Sheridan and the Army of the Potomac. But the cost was high for the Federals, too. According to Rhea, the raid

> proved to be a costly mistake. Chasing Stuart was another sideshow
> for the campaign, which would be decided by what the armies did at

> Spotsylvania. By abandoning the main theater of conflict to pursue his whimsical raid south, Sheridan deprived Grant of an important re- source. . . . Sheridan's absence hurt Grant at Spotsylvania in much the same way that Stuart's absence from Gettysburg had handicapped Lee.

Nevertheless, Grant advanced thirty miles south without the cavalry. [34]

TRIAL AT TREVILIAN STATION

By the time Custer rejoined the army near Chesterfield Station on the North Anna River on May 25, Grant had lost another 17,500 men of some 110,000 engaged and Lee at least 10,000 out of about 50,000 at Spotsyl- vania. Grant again had slipped around the Confederate right and soon was facing Lee across the North Anna River. On May 26 Custer's brigade led the way south to the Pamunkey River. Custer helped the 1st Michigan construct a pontoon bridge, and on May 28 the infantry crossed the river while Gregg scrapped with two divisions of Hampton's cavalry dis- mounted behind breastworks at Haw's Shop. Custer's charge to relieve the battered Gregg checked the Rebels but cost the lives of forty-one Michigan troopers. [35]

Sheridan, ahead of Grant, pushed toward the key crossroads at Cold Harbor, only ten miles northeast of Richmond. Devin, Custer, and Merritt beat back enemy assaults at Matadequin Creek on May 30. The next day Torbert's 1st Cavalry Division (Torbert had been on leave) came in con- tact with Rebel artillery, infantry, and Hampton's cavalry at Cold Harbor. After a flank attack under Merritt began to find success, the 1st Michigan stormed the Rebel line. Sheridan wanted to pull his three thousand caval- rymen out because Lee was just six miles away at Mechanicsville, but Meade ordered him to hold the position. [36]

The next morning two infantry brigades under Major General Joseph Kershaw attacked the 1st Michigan while Custer rode along the line, encouraging his dismounted men. They repulsed two attacks until re- lieved by the 6th Corps. Two days later Grant ordered the great charge at Cold Harbor he always regretted. In less than an hour, seven thousand Federal soldiers were cut down, followed by ten days of trench-like war- fare, with Sheridan guarding the flanks. [37]

Grant next moved the army south of Richmond to Petersburg to con- trol the railroad hub sustaining Lee and the capital. On the night of June

12, Meade secretly began moving the Army of the Potomac out of its trenches toward the James while screened by Wilson's cavalry. Sheridan, meanwhile, had embarked on a raid toward Charlottesville on June 7 to draw Hampton's cavalry away from Lee. His mission was to tear up Virginia Central Railroad track and wreck the James River canal, impeding the flow of supplies coming to Lee from the Shenandoah Valley. His six thousand horsemen were to connect with Major General David Hunter's troops near Charlottesville. Hampton and Fitz Lee, with about five thousand cavalrymen, were dispatched to protect the railroad. The ensuing battle of Trevilian Station reprised Yellow Tavern, albeit with much better odds for the Confederates.[38]

Sheridan planned to follow the north bank of the North Anna River until the cavalry was above Trevilian Station, a freight and water stop on the railroad twenty-eight miles east of Charlottesville, then cross the river, capture the station, and destroy everything between Louisa Court House and Gordonsville. The raid had little chance of success because Hampton's cavalry beat Sheridan's to the station, Major General John Breckinridge's infantry corps had been alerted and moved to Gordonsville, and Hunter never made it to Charlottesville. Sheridan camped on the night of June 10 at Clayton's Store, a strategic crossing several miles north of the station.

Early on the morning of June 11, Merritt and Devin struck two advancing brigades before the Confederates could get far from the railroad. Custer's brigade was east of the station working its way through dense woodlands on the extended flank north of Louisa Court House. He was moving around Hampton's right when Wickham's brigade attacked the 7th Michigan. Custer sent the 1st Michigan to help fight it off. Fitz Lee was not where Custer expected him to be, nor was Custer where Lee expected him to be. For the moment, that presented Custer with an opportunity. An advance battalion had spotted Hampton's battery, supply wagons, and ambulances moving toward Gordonsville near the station. Alger's 5th Michigan stormed through the wagon train, rounding up fifteen hundred horses and fifty wagons and taking eight hundred prisoners, but overran the station during the pursuit. Fitz Lee, coming up from Louisa Court House, moved in behind Alger, separating him from the rest of Custer's brigade. Hampton pulled Rosser's brigade off his left flank and sent it dashing into the 5th Michigan from the front, recapturing the wagons and horses.[39]

Isolated with only his staff around him and about to come under attack from several directions, Custer hastily sent some companies from Kidd's 6th regiment to relieve Alger. "Custer never lost his nerve under any circumstances," recalled Kidd. "He was, however, unmistakably excited. 'Charge them' was his laconic command; and it was repeated with emphasis." Kidd led a wild charge on a runaway black horse but had no real idea what or whom he was charging. Soon he found himself within enemy lines surrounded by Confederates and surrendered, as did many of his men. As they were being led away, a battalion from the 6th Michigan rescued them by driving off their captors. [40]

Custer led the 7th Michigan to the station and placed the 1st and 6th Michigan to guard the road behind him. Close to the station he battled Rosser in his front and on his right flank and Fitz Lee on his left flank and soon was surrounded in an area devoid of cover. One of Alexander Pennington's guns was dragged off, and Custer led a charge to recover it. He was stung by spent balls on the arm and shoulder. Kidd said this fight "was a melee which had no parallel. . . . Custer was everywhere present giving directions to his subordinate commanders," and he led desperate mounted charges with more horses shot out from under him. When other Federals finally pushed back Hampton's brigades and reached Custer and his gritty Wolverines, a last stand was averted. "Never has the Brigade fought so long or so desperately," Custer wrote Libbie. He lost 416 men in the fight, including 41 killed and 309 taken prisoner. [41]

As historian David Coffey summarized the action, "In a scene that anticipated the events on the Little Bighorn in 1876, Custer found himself trapped behind enemy lines and badly outnumbered." Having survived such a trap once, Custer had good reason to think he could do it again—until he couldn't. [42]

More hard fighting occurred the next day. Torbert tore up some track and tried to dislodge Hampton's and Fitz Lee's troopers from a strong position at Mallory's Cross Roads on the Gordonsville Road. In unrelenting heat, Custer fought off a counterattack and sent in all his battered regiments and part of Torbert's reserves before Sheridan began a general withdrawal with more heavy losses. Sheridan lost more than one thousand raiders at Trevilian, including one hundred dead. Confederate losses were about six hundred. The column took seventeen days to fight its way back across the James. It reached White House on the Pamunkey on June 21 and found the army removed to City Point on the James. Sheridan brought more than nine hundred supply wagons to the new base with Gregg and Devin covering the flanks and fighting off Hampton. Custer was back with the main body of the Army of the Potomac besieging Petersburg by the end of the month. He had been a general for one year.[43]

"THE SIDE OF HUMANITY"

For three weeks the cavalry refitted and rested. Sheridan's attention next was turned toward the Shenandoah Valley. On May 15, Breckinridge had defeated Sigel at New Market. Early had defeated Hunter, who had replaced Sigel, at Lynchburg in June and driven him out of the valley. Early had his 2nd Corps before the ramparts of Washington on July 11. On July 31, Brigadier General John McCausland, under orders from Early, burned Chambersburg, Pennsylvania.[44]

Grant realized the political implications of these actions in a presidential election year at a time when the army was stalled at Petersburg and smarting from the disastrous Battle of the Crater. Because the Federal armies had so little success in the valley going back to Robert Patterson's sluggish deployments in 1861, Grant consolidated departments, named Sheridan as commander of the Middle Military Division as well as field commander of the Army of the Shenandoah on August 7, and ordered him to raze the fertile corridor with a force of about fifty thousand men. Sheridan was to march 120 miles from the Potomac to Staunton and create such a tumult that Lee would have to deplete his ranks at Petersburg to fight on a second front.[45]

Grant had been using explosive language about the valley for weeks, telling Hunter to create a "desert" and to clear out the countryside so thoroughly that "crows flying over it for the balance of the season will have to carry their provender with them." He told Sheridan, "Nothing should be left to invite the enemy to return. Take all provisions, forage, and stock wanted for the use of your command. Such as cannot be consumed destroy." Sheridan weighed in on his assignment after the war when he wrote that the populace "did not care how many were killed or maimed, so long as war did not come to their doors, but as soon as it did come in the shape of loss of property, they earnestly prayed for its termination. As war is a punishment, and death the maximum punishment, if we can, by reducing its advocates to poverty, end it quick, we are on the side of humanity."[46]

Custer had been in Michigan with Libbie while on leave from July 13 until July 30. On August 4, his brigade left City Point on transports and arrived with the 1st and 3rd cavalry divisions near Harpers Ferry on August 9. Torbert was given overall command of the cavalry. His chief of staff was Brevet Major Marcus Reno, who, with Custer, would find immortality at the Little Bighorn. Merritt took command of the 1st Cavalry Division. Gregg was still with Meade and Grant, and a new 2nd Cavalry Division under Brigadier General William Averell was formed. Wilson remained in command of the 3rd Cavalry Division. James E. Taylor, an artist whose work appeared in *Frank Leslie's Illustrated Newspaper*, witnessed Custer's arrival. He found Custer a "picturesque presence" and sketched the general riding a black horse at the head of his column in front of the Harpers Ferry arsenal.[47]

On August 10, the Army of the Shenandoah began moving south—up the valley—looking for Early near Bunker Hill, some twelve miles distant. Early's strength generally was overestimated by the Federal forces. The Rebel general may have had between fifteen and twenty-three thousand soldiers, depending on how quickly his scattered units had concentrated. Sheridan's reconnaissance in force swung east toward Berryville to pass beyond Early's anticipated right flank and get behind him. Moving west toward Winchester the next day, Custer had a hard skirmish that left five of his men dead. This was a rear guard action, however, as Early had moved farther south to Fisher's Hill and was behind substantial earthworks spanning a narrow valley between Strasburg and Cedar Creek. Operating without Wilson's cavalry, Sheridan paused, his position complicated by reports that Lee might be sending Early reinforcements through the Blue Ridge.[48]

Sheridan sent Devin and Custer to Chester Gap and Front Royal to take a look. Initially finding no enemy activity in the immediate area, Devin positioned the 9th New York to protect the fords and Guard Hill, a citadel that dominated the landscape and presented an imposing barrier to attacking troops. Behind the hill was a tributary of the Shenandoah called Crooked Run. The main body of Federal troops was encamped about one mile north of Guard Hill. Custer sent about 150 troopers from the 6th Michigan out as pickets and put the rest of his brigade on the east side of Front Royal Pike. Soon they spotted Fitz Lee's cavalry and Kershaw's

infantry division approaching a Shenandoah River ford. They were followed by more infantry under the overall command of Lieutenant General Richard H. Anderson, a total of about six thousand men. Anderson
needed to secure the fords to cross the Shenandoah River to join Early or
hit Sheridan's flank.[49]

The Confederates pursued pickets from the 6th Michigan down Front
Royal Pike, then pushed Custer and Devin off the slopes of Guard Hill,
blasted by artillery and a counterattack as they gained the crest. Custer
dismounted and concealed the 5th Michigan, then charged Brigadier General William T. Wofford's Georgians of Kershaw's division, who were
trying to wade across Crooked Run unobserved and scale the heights.
Custer threw in a battalion of the 1st Michigan to cut them off, forcing
many to surrender, while the rest of the 1st and 7th Michigan drove off
Wickham's cavalry brigade trying to cut a way out for the infantry.[50]

According to Kidd, who had been promoted to colonel on July 1,
Custer "caught Kershaw astride the river and trapped him completely,"
and all who crossed were killed or captured. Had Custer first charged the
cavalry, the infantry would have crossed unmolested and overwhelmed
the Michigan brigade. Kidd said such quick thinking in the face of overwhelming odds made Custer a formidable commander. Custer had initiat-
ed and survived a charge unequaled in the war, according to Kidd, who
was prone to exaggeration where Custer was concerned. Gregory Urwin
concurred, calling the battle "one of the most brilliant actions George
Custer ever directed, and one that is scarcely paralleled by the annals of
the war."[51] Custer reported 8 men killed and fewer than 40 wounded,
while Confederate casualties were at least 350.[52]

E. A. Paul's festive account of the battle in the *New York Times* again
gave Custer top billing. Paul reported that Custer "dashed upon an inter-
vening crest overlooking the situation. He saw at a glance, with a practiced eye" a column of Rebel infantry approaching. As Custer "rode
rapidly along the crest under a withering fire . . . he was observed to put
his hand to the side of his head, and for an instant it was feared he had
been wounded; subsequently it was ascertained that a bullet had cut off
some of his hair and it fell upon his shoulder." Even a curl sheared off by
a bullet added to Custer's daring reputation.[53]

Custer returned to Sheridan's main body, operating as part of the rear
guard in the redeployment from Front Royal, as the Army of the Shenandoah withdrew to Halltown, West Virginia, a few miles from Harpers

Ferry. Sheridan had Anderson on his flank, was still not at full strength, and had trouble protecting his supply wagons from the depredations of irregulars. As a former army quartermaster, he knew the importance of wagons. Grant and Lincoln wanted Sheridan to be aggressive but cautious. If he could not gain a decisive victory, he was to avoid anything that looked like a defeat. As the army pulled back, shortening its line of communications, the cavalry screened its retreat and began its harvest of fire, torching granaries and gristmills, despoiling crops, and confiscating livestock. Custer and the Michigan Brigade were near Berryville. Their main antagonist was John Mosby.[54]

THE GRAY GHOST

On August 13, several hundred of Mosby's Rangers had shelled, looted, and burned a portion of Sheridan's 525-wagon train near Berryville. The plunder included seven hundred horses and mules and seventy-five wagons loaded with rations. Three days later, Grant angrily told Sheridan to hang any of Mosby's men he caught, locate families of the rest, and hold them as hostages. As an afterthought, he urged Sheridan to send cavalry into Mosby's lair, arrest all men under fifty, hold them as prisoners of war, and plunder their homesteads. Sheridan told Grant on August 17 he already had shot six of Mosby's men and hung another, although there is doubt this occurred. On the night of August 18, Lieutenant Colonel William Chapman, Mosby's second in command, shot a vidette from the 5th Michigan whom he was trying to capture. When Michigan men found the body, Custer presumed the vidette had been bushwhacked. The next morning fifty men from Alger's regiment under the command of Captain George Drake were burning a building when Chapman and about 150 rangers charged them. About twenty-five surrendered, and Chapman's men shot them all. One private survived and told his comrades what had happened. Custer soon had the 5th and 6th Michigan burning the farms of well-known Rebels.[55]

Sheridan tried to quiet things down by banning house burnings, but by rounding up twenty wagonloads of adult males below the age of sixty from around Berryville, he could hardly have provoked Mosby any more. Further outrages of all kinds were attributed to both sides, but just who did what to whom was difficult to document. Bands of irregulars were in the area, and bushwhacking and lynching occurred. Riders disguised themselves in garments of blue and butternut to wreak havoc as the leaven of malice expanded the violence.[56]

On August 25, Torbert moved Merritt's and Wilson's divisions toward Williamsport, Maryland, to see if reports that Early and Fitz Lee were moving across the Potomac were correct. The horsemen found cavalry at Kearneysville, West Virginia, and drove them toward Leetown, West Virginia, where a dismounted picket line from the 51st Virginia Infantry appeared. Custer and Devin drove the 51st back, then pulled up short when they realized they had run into Breckinridge's two divisions moving north. Early brought up two more divisions, and Torbert retreated toward Harpers Ferry. Near the Potomac, Confederate infantry attacked his rear guard. Custer, sent to relieve the embattled cavalrymen, was almost cut off from Torbert's column by John Gordon's division. Custer formed the brigade and parts of other regiments in a horseshoe with his back to the Potomac, fired some artillery rounds, and created the impression the brigade was ready to attack. This bought some time. While Gordon prepared to drive the Federals into the river, Custer moved his men and his battery across at a ford he had located. Alger was among the last to cross in what would be his final military action of the war.[57]

Custer's most dependable regimental commander resigned from the army due to ill health in September. He served after the war as governor of Michigan, a U.S. senator, and secretary of war. He despised Mosby and thwarted the old partisan's advancement in government. When they met on the streets of Washington, Alger would remove his top hat and give Mosby a mocking bow.[58]

"GO IN"

Grant had grown tired of what appeared to be a stalemate in the valley and left City Point to meet with Sheridan at Charlestown, West Virginia, on September 16. He came bearing battle plans, but Sheridan preempted him with a plan of his own. Sheridan proposed moving the army to Newtown, fighting Early's scattered divisions one at a time, and cutting off his line of retreat. Anderson returned to lead Lee's 4th Corps, leaving Early with about twelve thousand infantry and Fitz Lee's sixty-five hun-

dred cavalry. Grant, satisfied that Little Phil's Irish was up and he had a
workable plan, told him, "Go in."[59]

Early learned of the meeting and deduced that Sheridan's army would
soon be on the move. Early intended to concentrate his army at Winchester, but Sheridan moved quickly to strike the two divisions there first,
then fight those that would be coming from Martinsburg. On September
19 Sheridan began to advance westward down Winchester-Berryville
Pike. Wilson's cavalry was in front of the 6th Corps under Major General
Horatio G. Wright and the 19th Corps under Brigadier General William
H. Emory, with Brigadier General George Crook's 8th Corps in reserve.
The first obstacle was Opequon Creek, which divided the armies. Wilson
crossed the creek at Spout Springs and ran into hard fighting in Berryville
Canyon, a narrow two-mile-long ravine through which the army had to
pass before reaching the plateau east of Winchester. Behind the cavalry,
Wright's infantry and wagons had bunched up, and it wasn't until about
ten o'clock that Emory's corps had passed through the canyon.[60]

Merritt's division was to cross at the northern fords, join Averell at
Stephenson's Depot above Winchester, scatter the defenders, and sweep
south to cut off Early's retreat. Colonel Charles Russell Lowell, commanding the Reserve Brigade, and Devin crossed the creek at Seiver's
Ford. Downstream, Custer found Locke's Ford defended by dismounted
cavalry and battled across at dawn with several charges and a flanking
movement. He then combined with Merritt's other brigades to battle infantry from Brigadier General Gabriel Wharton's division. Wharton soon
was pulled back to Winchester, leaving only cavalry to hold the northern
approaches. At about 2 p.m., five Federal cavalry brigades, including
Averell's, drove through Stephenson's Depot and advanced toward Winchester, clashing with a smaller force of Fitz Lee's cavalry. Custer said
they charged as "one moving mass of glittering sabers." Lee's regiments
retreated, pursued by Custer's brigade until the Federals ran into infantry
and artillery.[61]

East of Winchester, Wright and Emory had advanced on the Confederate lines but faced resistance from Gordon, Robert Rodes, and Major
General Stephen Ramseur. A gap opened between the Federal lines just
as Gordon and Rodes counterattacked, halting the advance and menacing
Sheridan's right until he threw in Brigadier General David A. Russell's
division. Brigadier General Emory Upton's brigade broke the Confederate thrust. Both Rodes and Russell were killed, and Upton was wounded

later in the day. Sheridan put Crook's two divisions on his right as the cavalry advanced.[62]

At 4 p.m. the entire Federal line was in motion, pushing the Confederates back to Winchester. When Early moved troops to strengthen his lines, Custer led about five hundred Wolverines directly into an infantry concentration three times the size of his depleted brigade. Custer, an observer wrote, was "in the midst of a throng of the enemy, slashing right and left." About to be shot at close range, Custer "causes his horse to rear upon its haunches, and the ball passes, just grazing the General's leg below the thigh. Then a terrible sword stroke descends upon the infantryman's head, and he sinks to the ground a lifeless corpse." The brigade charged over the enemy's earthworks, and the Rebel line "broke into a thousand fragments after the shock," according to Merritt.[63]

Coffey said the engagement "represented the first fully realized employment of mounted cavalry as a major strike force against infantry in a large battle during the war, and it confirmed long-held beliefs among horsemen that they were good for much more than scouting and raiding and flank protection, that they could in fact decide battles." Even Confederate newspapers praised Sheridan's cavalry. The Petersburg *Daily Express* acknowledged the "splendid condition" of the horsemen, while the *Mobile Daily Advertiser and Register* claimed the Confederate cavalry was "utterly worthless." The *Richmond Whig* noted the "disgraceful stampede" of the Rebel riders through the streets of Winchester. Credit for the strategic victory, according to Coffey, belonged to Sheridan, who had "an abiding confidence in his cavalry. . . . [N]o other army commander on either side had thus far so effectively employed all branches of his force in a single major battle."[64]

Custer was ecstatic. He claimed in his report, "Considering the relative numbers engaged and the comparative advantage held on each side, the charge . . . stands unequaled, valued according to its daring and success, in the history of this war." Considering the qualifiers, that may well have been true. Custer also said his five hundred men had collected seven hundred prisoners, including fifty-two officers, and would have captured more if the Federal infantry had not arrived.[65]

The Battle of Opequon, also called the Third Battle of Winchester, was costly to both sides. The Federals reported 697 men killed, 3,983 wounded, and 338 missing. The Confederates reported 276 killed, 1,827 wounded, and 1,818 missing.[66]

INCIDENT AT FRONT ROYAL

Early retreated up the valley to Strasburg, Front Royal, and Fisher's Hill with Sheridan in pursuit. Rather than launching a frontal assault on the entrenchments at Fisher's Hill, Sheridan outflanked Early by sending Crook's two divisions to advance on his left flank. Early lost another tenth of his rapidly diminishing force, which scattered into the Blue Ridge to await reinforcements while Sheridan rampaged up the valley. Custer had been sent circling eastward to Front Royal with the Michigan Brigade and Lowell's brigade to cut off Early's army. Wilson's two brigades had led the pursuit of Early out of Winchester on September 20, then turned off toward Front Royal to deal with Wickham's two brigades. Once Wickham had been contained, Torbert was to rush up the Luray Valley, cross the mountains at New Market, and block Early's expected retreat. Caught between the infantry and the cavalry, Early would have to surrender.[67]

Custer, Merritt, Lowell, and Torbert arrived in Front Royal on September 21. Wilson by then had pushed Wickham six miles south of the town to Gooney Run, a tributary of the south fork of the Shenandoah. When Wickham learned Torbert was on the way, he abandoned his strong position and withdrew farther south to Milford. That was crucial to the failure of Sheridan's plan. Torbert sent Custer to cross the river west of where he thought Wickham was, circle behind him, and strike his right flank. Wilson was to send two brigades across the run. Torbert spurred his whole force to Milford. Wickham, meanwhile, had turned his command over to Thomas T. Munford while he consulted with Early. At about 7 a.m., Torbert found Wickham's men holding high ground and wedged into a formidable niche between the river and a mountain spur. Seemingly befuddled, Torbert ordered some shelling and a halfhearted late-afternoon flanking maneuver around the 2nd Virginia Cavalry. Munford tried some theatrics—moving buglers around at regimental intervals and sounding the charge—and Torbert, his own envelopment of the reinforced 2nd Virginia parried, lost his nerve and retreated. "Torbert made a fiasco of it," Kidd said. Sheridan was livid.[68]

Torbert's retreat involved removing his ambulances and supply wagons in a long procession on the Luray Road through Front Royal to Cedarville on September 23. The train's two-hundred-man escort was commanded by First Lieutenant Charles McMaster of the 2nd U.S. Cavalry, who was with Lowell's brigade in Merritt's division. Lowell's regulars rode behind the wagons, followed by Custer's Michigan Brigade guarding the rear. Wilson's two brigades covered the flanks. Attacks from Munford were expected to come from behind. The head of the column, accordingly, was lightly guarded. Captain Samuel F. Chapman, searching for a Federal picket post at Chester Gap with about 120 of Mosby's Rangers, spotted the wagon train as it approached Front Royal and moved to attack. He divided his force, sent forty-five men under Captain Walter E. Frankland to strike the train from the front, and personally led about eighty rangers to the rear. Coming over a rise, Chapman ran into Lowell's brigade, sent his rangers back to Chester Gap, and rode to warn Frankland, who already was in trouble. Chapman and Frankland fought their way out, leaving a dozen or more Federal escorts dead, and raced for the gap, with Lowell's men in pursuit.[69]

At Chester Gap, the Confederates met other cavalrymen from the train who had cut them off. Most of the rangers were able to gain the shelter of the mountains. Accounts of all that happened during this melee are wildly different, and the differences led to a long controversy involving Custer and Mosby. McMaster was mortally wounded, the Confederates claiming he was a fair casualty of war during their escape. Merritt reported that McMaster first surrendered, then was shot in the head and robbed. Some rangers, between six and thirteen, were taken prisoner. In some accounts, four of the men, including seventeen-year-old Henry Rhodes, were taken back to Front Royal and shot. Rhodes, who was not a ranger, had gotten caught up in the excitement of the morning, mounted a borrowed horse, and joined in the attack; he was chased down by Custer's men, tied up and dragged behind a horse, then shot to death in front of his pleading, widowed mother. In other accounts, Custer's band struck up a tune. Two rangers were hanged from a walnut tree, and placards were placed around their necks bearing the inscription "Hung in retaliation for the Union officer killed after he had surrendered—the fate of Mosby's men" or "Such is the fate of all Mosby's Men." On October 13, Colonel William H. Powell, who had been appointed to command the 2nd Cavalry Division, hanged another of Mosby's men by snapping him into the air at the end of a rope tied to a bent sapling, and he threatened to execute more at a 1:21 ratio if necessary. Mosby added this seventh execution to the Front Royal total.[70]

THE CASE AGAINST CUSTER

Mosby, who was recovering from a gunshot wound, said he did not learn about the Front Royal executions until September 29, when he returned to duty and ordered an investigation. It is not known if Mosby personally interviewed witnesses, of whom there reportedly were many, or if others did so and reported to Mosby. In 1869, in response to charges against him appearing in the *New York Sun*, Mosby stated, "In September, 1864, General Custer captured and hanged seven of my men in the streets of Front Royal, Va." In his memoirs, published in 1917, Mosby included newspaper articles from the *Richmond Examiner* and an unidentified paper based on information provided by "informants" and an anonymous eyewitness reporter. One article identified Custer as responsible. That apparently persuaded Mosby of Custer's culpability. On November 11, Mosby wrote Sheridan that the executions occurred "by order and in the immediate presence of Brigadier-General Custer."[71]

The accuracy of newspaper accounts is questionable. The Confederate press, especially late in the war, published under difficult conditions. Sources were unreliable. Stories reporting alleged outrages, such as those that occurred in the wake of the Kilpatrick-Dahlgren raid or the Front Royal killings, often were sensationalized for propaganda value.[72]

Custer, Torbert, and Merritt made no mention of the executions in their reports, which prompted the lawyerly Mosby to write, "It was their duty to report the fact, and, if justifiable, to report the circumstances that justified it; but none of them were willing to assume the responsibility, and admit or to go on record about the hanging. No matter whether they were active or merely passive in the business, this silence gives it a dark complexion." Mosby again was on the defensive after one of his former rangers, Major Adolphus E. "Dolly" Richards, spoke on September 23, 1899, at the unveiling of a monument to the men executed at Front Royal. After the war, Richards was elected to a superior court judgeship in Kentucky.[73]

Richards acknowledged the rangers had believed Custer gave the orders because Front Royal residents had told them they had seen him riding through the town. Reflecting on the "official record of the war," however, he had changed his mind and was convinced Custer was not responsible. McMaster and the other Federals killed were in Lowell's command, so "we may reasonably conclude that it was under his immediate supervision, and not Custer's, that our men were executed," he reasoned. The ultimate responsibility, moreover, was Grant's because he impulsively had advised Sheridan to hang any of Mosby's band that he caught.[74]

Mosby was outraged when he read Richards's remarks. He wrote a letter to the editor of the *Richmond Times*, owned by Joseph Bryan, a former ranger, defending Grant and indicting Custer. Whether Torbert, Merritt, and Lowell were equally to blame was, he argued, irrelevant: "It is no concern of mine whether only one or all the generals participated in the crime; they may all have been *in pari delicto*. They can settle that question among themselves. The people of Front Royal considered Custer the most conspicuous actor in the tragedy, and so I stated in my [November 11, 1864] letter to Sheridan. Custer never denied it."[75]

Richards wrote to the newspaper in response, restating his position and suggesting Custer's fame was the cause of his indictment. He was "a conspicuous figure, in his velvet uniform, with long golden curls. The citizens of Front Royal had learned to recognize him. Seeing him in the streets at the time, it is not surprising that they should have reported him in command." As additional proof, Richards quoted a letter from Rosser, Custer's longtime friend and wartime adversary. Rosser said he had seen a great deal of Custer after the war, and in their talks "he stated that he was in no way responsible for the execution or murder of those men. I have no doubt of Custer's innocence, for he was not in command, and his superior officer was present." On December 12, 1899, Mosby wrote another former ranger about the exchange. He was inclined, he said, to reply to Richards and "tear him to tatters," but thought better of it, although he would not "acquiesce in his indictment of General Grant." Referring to William Chapman's August 19, 1864, killing of Custer's men, Mosby said a man "who will burn houses from revenge over the heads of women and children as Custer did would commit murder—a murderer generally denies it. So I attach no importance to what Rosser says Custer said."[76]

"A LARGE BRANCH OF DAMSONS"

Mosby and Custer biographers and other Civil War writers examined the evidence and came to different conclusions about the assignment of guilt. These can be summarized as follows:

Frederic F. Van de Water: "Their execution was ordered by George Armstrong Custer, and carried out under his eyes. He apparently suffered no qualms then or later."[77]

Jay Monaghan: "The important thing is that Custer's brigade was not in Front Royal on September 23. Instead, it was following the retreating Confederates through New Market and on to Harrisonburg. . . . Custer might possibly have ridden through Front Royal September 23 but if so he took a 10-mile detour on a 40-mile march. . . . Custer must be deemed innocent until proved guilty."[78]

D. A. Kinsley: "Aggravated by McMaster's death, and by the fact that Mosby held several captive Michiganders to ransom, Custer ordered four of the Rebels shot and the other two hanged."[79]

Lawrence A. Frost: "The evidence is quite clear that Custer had nothing to do with the hanging or shooting of Mosby's men. . . . The real victim is the person whose character is smeared unfairly with a charge of murder, the charge being perpetuated by writers who have neither the time, interest nor opportunity to search for the facts."[80]

Jeffry D. Wert: "Torbert and/or Merritt gave the orders. Custer was present and undoubtedly concurred with the decision. There is no evidence, however, that he issued a direct order for the execution of any of the prisoners."[81]

Thom Hatch: "The men hanged at Fort [sic] Royal, however, had not been executed by Custer, who had in fact taken a ten-mile detour around that particular city."[82]

David Coffey: "Mosby later blamed Custer, whose men participated in the execution, but Merritt or Torbert gave the order."[83]

Virgil Carrington Jones: "But decades later some folks awakened to the fact that perhaps Torbert, who was chief of cavalry, had been instrumental in bringing about the killings. . . . However, regardless of who was to blame, the action would certainly seem to bear the approval of the Union high command."[84]

James A. Ramage: "Torbert ordered the hangings, and nobody ordered the four shootings."[85]

David J. Eicher: "The executions had been approved by Torbert. Custer and Merritt were also involved with the decision."[86]

Kevin H. Siepel: "While the two [prisoners] had been held in the wagon lot, Custer and his staff had ridden past. Custer was occu-

pied, in the words of an eyewitness, with 'a large branch of dam-
sons, which he picked and ate as he rode along.'"[87]

Joseph Wheelan: "[Mosby] mistakenly believed that Custer had ordered the Front Royal executions, when Merritt and Torbert had
done so."[88]

Edward G. Longacre: "Wesley Merritt avenged his subordinate by
shooting four of the prisoners and hanging the others."[89]

Jay W. Simson: "There can be no other conclusion than that the orders
for the executions were either issued at the instigation of Torbert or
with his full and complete approval."[90]

If history's verdict on the charge that Custer was a war criminal in connection with the Front Royal killings remains open, the jury of historians
leans toward acquittal. The episode is a microcosm of the larger debate
about Custer's entire career, especially the "last stand." The verdict is
mixed, the testimony self-interested, and the subtext expansive, while the
sources are inconclusive and the feelings intense. It becomes a matter of
Custer myth replacing Custer history, or history challenging myth, an
endless debate questioning the presumptions of history and picking at it
when it bleeds into myth.

Custer and Mosby both profited by their heroic reputations when it
suited them and faced censure and reproach when fame turned to infamy.
Custer, according to Mosby, was "the most conspicuous" participant, *in
pari delicto*, in the eyes of the Front Royal witnesses. Because he burned
houses in the Shenandoah Valley, he was capable of murder. He did not
deny it, so he must have done it. By that logic, Mosby might stand
condemned for the outrages his own men committed, as well as those
attributed to him even when they were committed by other guerrillas and
outright bandits not under his command. Judge Richards's conclusion
that Custer's fame was the cause of his indictment rings true and could
also be applied to Mosby.

6

CHECKMATE

[Custer] always gathered the fruit, as well as shook the tree of battle. He regarded his real work as only beginning, when the enemy was broken and flying.

—Colonel Alvred Bayard Nettleton, 1876[1]

In the aftermath of the Winchester and Fisher's Hill battles, Philip Sheridan appointed Custer as commander of the 3rd Cavalry Division, replacing James Wilson. James Kidd succeeded Custer at the head of the Michigan Brigade, which Custer had commanded for fifteen months. He had seen 350 men killed and almost 1,300 wounded or missing, but his surviving troopers did not want to lose him. Custer wrote Libbie that his bandleader wept and some of his musicians were so upset they "threatened to break their horns." Custer soon joined his new command at Harrisonburg, Virginia, and within a month he had his second star. He told Libbie his new field headquarters was "almost as large as a circus tent."[2]

The mayhem in the Shenandoah Valley continued, however, and the Front Royal incident would come back to haunt Custer. Lieutenant John R. Meigs was killed near Dayton while returning with two orderlies to Sheridan's headquarters. Meigs, a topographical engineer, was the son of the army's quartermaster general and one of Sheridan's favorites. His party had approached three riders wearing similar waterproof ponchos in the rain. Each group realized the other was hostile, calls for surrender were ignored, and Meigs was shot. Sheridan assumed the Rebels were partisans from Dayton and ordered the town and the area around it burned. He partially rescinded the order the next day, sparing the town but not the surrounding countryside, and took some prisoners in Dayton. Many of the farmers in the area were pacifist Mennonites. Years later, the Confederates involved claimed they were not with John Mosby but served in Thomas Rosser's cavalry brigade. They claimed Meigs had fired on them first with a concealed weapon and had been shot in self-defense. Following Sheridan's orders, Custer burned buildings throughout Rockingham County as violence spread during what came to be known as "the Burning." *Harper's Weekly* said the order to turn the Shenandoah Valley into a wasteland "was carried out with unsparing severity."[3]

On October 6, the army started a slow regression toward Winchester, immolating anything not already burned as it went and leaving some four hundred square miles of ruined farmland. Lunsford Lomax returned to harry the Wolverines in Wesley Merritt's division, while the persistent Rosser pursued his old friend Custer's new division to a stream near Woodstock called Tom's Brook.[4]

Before their coming fight, Custer rode to the front of his lines, looked toward Rosser's position on Wiseman's Hill, and swept his broad-brimmed hat across his body in salute. Both sides cheered. "That's General Custer the Yanks are so proud of," Rosser told a subordinate. "I intend to give him the best whipping today that he ever got." After the two commanders took each other's measure through the midmorning hours, Custer sent the 18th Pennsylvania and the 8th and 22nd New York into Rosser's flank, then led the 1st and 2nd brigades across Tom's Creek and up the hill, shattering the Confederate line and sending Rosser's men rushing off in "headlong flight." Merritt, meanwhile, was smashing Lomax's line, and a general twenty-five-mile rout resulted that came to be known as the "Woodstock Races."[5]

Custer got carried away in his battle report, writing no doubt for Rosser's benefit. "Vainly did the most gallant of this affrighted herd endeavor to rally a few supports around their standards and stay the advance of their eager and exulting pursuers, who, in one overwhelming current, were bearing down everything before them." Custer plundered one of Rosser's wagons and came away wearing his larger friend's capacious uniform coat and hat, to the great amusement of the men of his new command.[6]

CRISIS AT CEDAR CREEK

From his aerie at Fisher's Hill on October 18, Early listened to John Gordon's proposal to strike the somnolent Federals at Cedar Creek four miles north. Gordon had climbed to a signal station and observed the Federal camps spread out across the attenuated valley. Several days earlier, Sheridan had departed for a brief meeting with Stanton and army chief of staff Henry W. Halleck, leaving 6th Corps commander Horatio G. Wright in charge. George Crook's Army of West Virginia and William H. Emory's 19th Corps were camped north of Cedar Creek, and Merritt's and Custer's cavalry divisions were west and north of the infantry. Gordon had discerned a path between Massanutten Mountain and the swollen river that might permit covert transit for the three divisions of his corps to deploy astride the Federal army's flank. This "dim and narrow pathway" was so constricted that "but one man could pass at a time," according to Gordon. The rugged mountain spur abutted the river so closely as to make any potential movement by the Confederates from that direction an unreasonable concern. These divisions would march by night, creep along the railroad cut, and twice pass through the chilled waters of the Shenandoah before effecting their ambuscade. Joseph Kershaw would advance upon Colonel Joseph Thoburn's isolated division across the coiling creek while Gabriel Wharton brought his division down the Valley Pike with the artillery. Rosser was to occupy Custer and Merritt on the western side of the valley some two miles out on the far-right flank, the direction from which any attack by Jubal Early was expected, to create a diversion.[7]

Gordon forded the Shenandoah south of Strasburg and skirted the base of the fog-draped mountain, the men clinging to bushes and outcroppings as they negotiated the steep trails. Kidd said the Michigan Brigade was near Custer on that "perfect night, bright and clear." On a nearby hilltop he could see the white tents of Custer's camp illuminated "like weird specters in the moonlight." At about four o'clock, tendrils of fog rising from the creek, Rosser skirmished with Federal pickets, alerting Custer, Merritt, and Kidd that riders were active. Custer sent a regiment to investigate, while troopers prepared breakfast. Unexpected firing from the direction of Middletown and Rosser's dismounted cavalry and artillery by the creek roused the division. When it appeared Rosser would not press his attack and the shelling from the infantry positions to the left increased in intensity, Custer sent a brigade toward Middletown. He found Merritt's

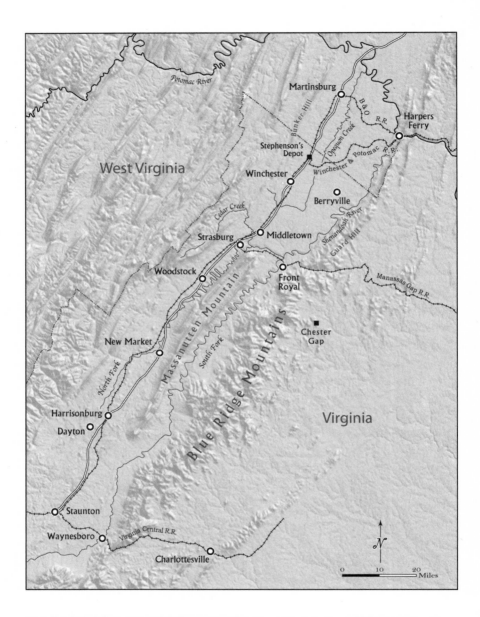

Map 6.1. The Shenandoah Valley campaign. Custer's talent as a field commander became evident. He won praise in the North and from superiors. But his burning raids provoked condemnation in the South. (University of Tennessee Cartographic Services)

1st Cavalry Division formed in a line of battle on a ridge confronting advancing Confederate infantry. Custer sent the brigade across the pike to support Merritt, leaving a contingent force behind to stop Rosser from gaining the Federal rear.[8]

Kidd, with Merritt in front of and to the left of Custer, recalled the moment when the "full scope of the calamity which had befallen our arms burst suddenly into view." Entire infantry regiments were in full flight, a "disorganized mass that had simply lost the power of cohesion," their withdrawal hardly arrested by 5th U.S. Cavalry skirmishers who were "making ineffectual efforts to stop the stream of fugitives who had stolidly and stubbornly, set their faces to the rear."[9]

What Kidd witnessed through the early morning was the aftermath of the attack on the left flank. Kershaw's men swarmed out of the fog to drive Crook's exposed 1st Cavalry Division toward the 19th Corps across the Valley Pike as the jubilant Confederates turned abandoned artillery on the Federals. Thoburn was mortally wounded while trying to rally his troops. Gordon's attack had picked apart the left flank, crushing Rutherford B. Hayes's 2nd Division. The future president dislocated his ankle when he was thrown from his horse. Taking another mount he was knocked senseless by a spent round and almost captured as he tried to restore his fractured lines. Another future president, Major William McKinley, also was on the field. Stephen Ramseur easily disposed of Crook's Provisional Division, whose commander was mortally wounded. As Gordon and Kershaw tried to overrun the 19th Corps, Emory sent the 2nd Brigade from behind earthworks to high ground across the pike to hold back the charging Rebels. In hand-to-hand fighting, the brigade slowed the Confederate advance for thirty minutes before giving way. The 8th Vermont Regiment lost 106 out of 159 men engaged.[10]

As the Confederates swarmed around its flanks, the 19th Corps decamped and joined the frenzied retreat. Some fifteen hundred Federals had been captured in two hours, and hundreds more had been killed or wounded. With the army's back to the wall, Wright, dripping blood from a face wound, turned to 6th Corps commander Major General James Ricketts to hold the high ground behind Meadow Brook. Ricketts soon was wounded and replaced by Brigadier General George W. Getty. The division beat back repeated charges by Kershaw but was battered in a counterattack. When joined by Gordon's men, Kershaw pushed Getty's crippled corps back beyond Middletown, where, abetted by cavalry, it held off attacks for an hour until artillery drove the corps back another mile. Getty was still on the field, and the fragmented Federal lines began to coalesce. Although Gordon wanted to attack, Early hesitated, anxious about the presence of Federal cavalry on his flanks. Gordon had executed one of the most brilliant flanking maneuvers of the war, but his men were spent. Exhausted and famished Confederate soldiers had looted the Federal camps they had overrun, eating whatever rations they could find and stripping the wool uniforms from the dead. They would do no more without respite. [11]

Sheridan arrived on the field after completing the epic ride that became an American myth second only to "the midnight ride of Paul Revere." Generations of schoolchildren, along with a good many barroom balladeers, learned to recite Thomas Buchanan Read's poem "Sheridan's Ride," extolling the glories of the stalwart Rienzi, the "steed as black as the steeds of night," the "steed that saved the day / By carrying Sheridan into the fight, / From Winchester—twenty miles away!" Read's poem, gleaned from newspaper accounts and, in turn, widely published in newspapers, was written shortly after the battle. [12]

The national publicity, if not the poem, may have helped Lincoln carry the hotly contested Connecticut and New York states in the November election. Rienzi's ride was closer to a dozen miles than twenty. Some two hundred thousand copies of the *New York Tribune* containing the poem were distributed on Election Day. Lincoln carried New York by fewer than seven thousand votes and Connecticut by fewer than two thousand. Rienzi died in 1878 and now resides—stuffed for posterity—in the Smithsonian Museum. [13]

Sheridan learned of the disaster only after he had finished a leisurely breakfast and mounted Rienzi about nine o'clock to return to Cedar Creek. As he drew closer he encountered frightened and haggard troops streaming toward Winchester. He spurred the great horse forward, shouting, "Come on back, boys!" as he went. When he reached the battlefield about 10:30, Alfred Torbert greeted him by saying, "My God, I'm glad you've come!" Rienzi, although ridden hard and lathered, bolted forward and vaulted a barricade, while the revived and heartened soldiers cheered the return of their confidant commander. Sheridan quickly fortified Getty's line, sent Custer's division around the 19th Corps and back to the right flank, and then rode across the entire front to rouse the troops. When Custer saw Sheridan, he hugged and kissed him. The little Irishman blustered, flushed, and gawped, then rode on. Custer might be incorrigible, but he was a fighter, and Sheridan needed fighters. Five hours passed without a Confederate assault. Then the 19th Corps wheeled forward from the right flank and swept Gordon's men from the two hills they held nine hundred yards away. Wright moved slowly forward in the center, ready to press Gordon's right as the wheel turned. On the left, Merritt's cavalry surged ahead, inspired, no doubt, by the death of Charles Russell Lowell "in the thickest of the fray," according to his commander. Custer found Ramseur in an ambulance after the battle, took him to Sheridan's headquarters, and was with him the next day near the time of his death. [14]

"YOU HAVE DONE IT FOR ME THIS TIME, CUSTER!"

After further skirmishing with Rosser's cavalry, Custer's troopers exploded out of the west and turned Gordon's flank as the Federal infantry swept forward. "Realizing the necessity of at once gaining the bridge, the disordered masses of the enemy, now completely panic-stricken, threw away their arms, and in a headlong and disgraceful manner sought safety in ignominious flight," Custer wrote in his report, overlooking the flight of his own army during the morning. Gordon recalled that there "came from the north side of the plain a dull, heavy swelling sound like the roaring of a distant cyclone, the omen of additional disaster. It was unmistakable. Sheridan's horsemen were sweeping across the open fields to intercept the Confederates before they crossed Cedar Creek." [15]

Some Confederates managed to rush across the Cedar Creek bridge while Custer, leading the Green Mountain Boys and the 5th New York, located a ford and crossed to the south bank. Charging skirmishers firing from behind a stone wall, the Northerners broke through to the clattering baggage wagons, chased the Confederates beyond Strasburg to Fisher's Hill, and collected prisoners by the hundreds, with entire companies happy to surrender, according to Custer. Encroaching darkness probably saved Early's army from complete destruction. Although a great victory, the battle had cost Sheridan 5,665 casualties out of about 32,000 engaged. Early lost 2,910 men out of about 21,000. [16]

At about 9 p.m. Custer arrived at Sheridan's headquarters near Middletown at the Belle Grove plantation home partially designed by Thomas Jefferson in 1794. As he saw Custer riding up to the limestone mansion,

Figure 6.1. This wood engraving from a photograph by Alexander Gardner appeared in *Harper's Weekly* soon after the war. Custer is seated at far right next to generals George Crook (center) and Wesley Merritt (left). Standing behind are generals Philip Sheridan (left) and James Forsyth. (Library of Congress)

Sheridan rushed out, pulled Custer from his mount, and shouted, "You have done it for me this time, Custer!" Sheridan and his staff started a bonfire on the lawn and danced around it in a sort of conga line. Custer lifted Sheridan up in a bear hug and swung him around, then grabbed Torbert and gave him a spin as well. All was elation, but after the battle a minor contretemps arose among Custer, Merritt, and Thomas C. Devin, fed by reports in the *New York Times*, as to who did what, when, and where. Custer's version of events prevailed. Sheridan sent him with captured battle flags to attend a War Department ceremony in Washington on October 25 and recommended him for promotion to major general. He returned to duty on October 28, and the 3rd Cavalry Division moved into its winter encampment near Kernstown. [17]

On November 7, Mosby had his revenge for the Front Royal executions. He had written Robert E. Lee on October 29 stating his intention "to hang an equal number of Custer's men whenever I capture them." Lee endorsed the request on November 3 and forwarded his instructions to Richmond. On November 6, Mosby took twenty-seven of his Federal captives from a makeshift storehouse jail in Rectorstown. Not all of the prisoners were part of Custer's command at the time of the Front Royal killings. The prisoners were forced to draw lots out of a hat. Seven slips of paper were marked with a number corresponding to the seven executed men. An eight-man execution detachment took the condemned men to some woods near Berryville, where the executions took place at 4 a.m. the next morning, but some were botched. One man got loose and hid in a ditch. Two men were shot and left for dead but survived. A fourth man ran into the woods and hid after a gun misfired. Three others were hanged. Mosby later said he was glad some of the prisoners escaped "as they carried the story to Sheridan's army which was the best way to stop the business."[18]

"WE MUST DIE TOGETHER"

Custer moved Libbie into Long Meadow, a charming Virginia mansion owned by Quakers outside Winchester. The Custers had the accommodations and time to enjoy a bit of domestic life and do some entertaining with their hosts, "delightful people" who treated the Custers "as special guests," according to Libbie. She told a friend their hosts were "glad to have an officer in the house. It protects them from the rough element found in every army. We have such gay times." Life settled into a routine, including attendance at Sunday services at Christ Episcopal Church in Winchester. One regular guest was Lieutenant Tom Custer. The general's nineteen-year-old brother had been discharged from the 21st Ohio, briefly served on Kidd's staff with the 6th Michigan, and had been transferred, at Custer's request, to the 3rd Cavalry. At the end of November, the brothers rode off together with some cavalry in pursuit of Rosser, who was raiding in West Virginia, but returned five days later, cold, tired, and empty-handed.[19]

On December 19, Custer accompanied Torbert on a raid Ulysses S. Grant had been urging to wreck the Orange and Alexandria Railroad. Merritt and William H. Powell, who had replaced William Averell at the head of the 2nd Cavalry Division, moved east of the mountains while Custer took two brigades slogging south toward Staunton on the muddy Valley Pike. His principal assignment was to worry Early in his winter encampment. Custer would keep Early in the valley, giving the rest of the cavalry a freer hand. The column reached Lacey's Springs, nine miles north of Harrisonburg, on December 20 after some skirmishing. Custer set up a headquarters at an inn and arranged his evening deployments. Colonel Alexander Pennington, the Michigan Brigade's former artillery commander, led his own brigade, which was stationed east of the thoroughfare and below the inn. Brigadier General George H. Chapman's brigade was placed to the west. Pickets were posted, and the brigades settled in for the night. A snow-covered landscape greeted the earliest risers when Rosser's cavalry charged into Chapman's camp. Hearing shots and seeing Rebel riders outside, Custer ran bootless from the inn, possibly wearing Rosser's captured coat as a disguise, mounted a horse, and sent the 2nd Ohio galloping toward the Confederates. [20]

In his battle report, Custer claimed that after their first attack, Rosser's men seemed "completely bewildered" and scattered. He estimated his losses at one or two killed, twenty-two wounded, and twenty missing. He estimated Rosser's losses at about one hundred. He also claimed Rosser had three brigades and that an infantry division was on its way. The information came from prisoners, however, and was unreliable. The worsening weather, lack of rations, and "large body of wounded" convinced Custer to scratch the mission. The column struggled back to Winchester, with some of the riders suffering from frostbite. The tone of Custer's report suggests he may have been under some pressure to explain to Sheridan why he was caught off guard. [21]

Custer celebrated Christmas at Long Meadow with Libbie and Tom. He was on court-martial duty until January 13, 1865, then left for a furlough in Michigan. On February 6, the Custers left for Winchester, arriving on February 10 after a brief stopover in Washington. While they were away, Custer's headquarters had been moved to Elmwood, an even grander mansion, where the general and Libbie took up residence, with her parents soon arriving as guests. [22]

Before the spring offensive began, Sheridan sent Torbert off on extended leave, never to return, and put Merritt in charge of the cavalry. Devin, promoted to brigadier general, replaced Merritt at the head of the 1st Cavalry Division. Powell had resigned, and Colonel Henry Capehart's 2nd Division brigade, four crack regiments, was transferred to Custer's command, bringing his division's strength to forty-six hundred men. Wright's 6th Corps and one of Crook's divisions had been sent to Petersburg. Crook, hauled out of bed by raiders, was in a Confederate prison, awaiting exchange. One of Emory's divisions was in Savannah, and Chapman remained in the Shenandoah Valley with a cavalry brigade. [23]

Most of what remained of Early's army had been sent to Lee. Early remained at Waynesboro guarding the Virginia Central Railroad with about two thousand troops under Rosser and Wharton. Sheridan had vague orders from Grant to reach Lynchburg, tear up the railroad and the James River canal, and then find his way to North Carolina to join William Tecumseh Sherman. He had the option of returning to Winchester. With the end of the war at hand, however, Sheridan wanted to be near Grant, and he wanted one more chance to destroy Early. [24]

On February 27, Sheridan began to move south on the Valley Pike with artillery and cavalry, about ten thousand in all, heading for Early, who, with Wharton, was holding Rockfish Gap through the Blue Ridge and protecting Charlottesville. At Mount Crawford, Rosser's dismounted cavalry tried to burn the covered bridge over the North River. Custer sent two regiments swimming across the river to flank the Confederates out of their position while a column charged across the burning span and extinguished the flames. [25]

On March 2, Custer's division reached Staunton and then turned east toward Waynesboro, where they found Early's infantry and artillery spread out on a ridge northwest of the town. Custer might have waited for Devin and Merritt to come up in support but instead decided to attack immediately, foreshadowing his advance at the Little Bighorn. Unlike at the Little Bighorn, however, he had a numerical advantage and faced a wounded opponent. Seeing a gap between Early's left flank and the south fork of the Shenandoah, Custer sent Colonel William Wells's brigade to test the strength of the position, while Pennington sent three dismounted regiments armed with Spencer carbines sneaking into some dense woods near the river. At a signal, Custer's artillery opened fire, Wells and Capehart assaulted the line, and the 8th New York and the Green Mountain Boys charged over the breastworks, while Pennington's men rushed up the ridge, guns blazing. Wharton's line collapsed, and Custer sent in two more mounted regiments to chase the Rebels twelve miles through Rockfish Gap and round up sixteen hundred prisoners, eleven cannon, seventeen battle flags, and two hundred wagons and ambulances. It was checkmate for Early, who narrowly escaped capture by riding through the icy Blue Ridge north of Rockfish Gap. [26]

After the battle, Custer wrote Libbie that he read scripture and prayed with Theodore J. Holmes, chaplain of the 1st Connecticut Calvary. "He and I alone with God gave thanks for our victory. He has vouchsafed our arms." A few weeks later, Holmes left the army. He wrote Custer,

> I cannot express my gratefulness to the Almighty that He should have made you such a General and such a man. I rejoice with the 3rd Division, with the army, with the whole country in the splendid military genius that has made your name glorious in the history of War. But even more I rejoice in the position you have taken deliberately, and, I believe, finally, in regard to a moral and religious life. You cannot know what a great power you are exercising in this way upon your staff, your command and upon the whole army.

Custer's letters, for a time, became considerably more pious.[27]

The next day Custer arrived in Charlottesville, whose mayor and councilmen surrendered the town like medieval burghers by turning over a set of keys to the conquerors and pleading for sanctuary. Faculty of the University of Virginia, Mosby's alma mater, waved a white flag as the cavalrymen passed. After brushing aside a cavalry remnant, the division made camp near Thomas Jefferson's mountaintop neoclassical villa, the fabled Monticello, its octagonal dome gleaming in the late-winter sunlight. The riders left the town and the campus undamaged, save for quartering some troops in abandoned dormitories, as they ripped up Virginia Central Railroad track and razed bridges to the north and south.[28]

They left Charlottesville on March 6 and, bypassing Lynchburg, continued raiding north of the James River while turning toward Richmond. On March 15, Custer skirmished with James Longstreet's infantry and Fitz Lee's cavalry at Ashland. Pennington's brigade held the Confederates in check until the rest of the cavalry could cross the South Anna River. Longstreet, drawn away from Lee's defenses, did not follow.[29]

During the engagement, Custer was riding with his staff when his horse, Jack Rucker, stepped into a hole and fell, "turning a complete somersault, rolling over, then lying with his full weight upon my back. Had he struggled I should have been crushed to death." The animal remained still until Custer's staff could pull it off the general. Custer told Libbie his "preservation from death, or being maimed, crippled, for life, was miraculous, and strengthens my grateful dependence on the Merciful Being Who has so often shielded me."[30]

Figure 6.2. This iconic image of Custer as a major general near the end of the war captures his spunk, mettle, and flamboyance. But his folded arms and weary countenance reveal the burden of battle as well. (Library of Congress)

With the war coming to a close, he may have been contemplating how close he had come to death and wondering how long "Custer's luck" was going to hold. Libbie captured this mood as well, urging Custer "not to expose yourself so much in battle. Just do your duty, and don't rush out so daringly. Oh, Autie, we must die together."[31]

FIVE FORKS

On March 18, Sheridan's cavalrymen reached the Pamunkey River and the Federal supply base at White House Landing. The gunboats and transports in the harbor were a welcome sight. Custer found a temporary residence, where he displayed his captured battle flags. One regular visitor was *New York Times* correspondent E. A. Paul, who again was lavish in his praise of Custer's command. Paul had been following the division since Staunton, and his reports boosted Custer's fighting reputation. But there was to be little time to savor past glories. The "mud march" from Staunton had taken its toll on man and beast. More than two thousand horses needed attention, and one in three cavalrymen needed a new mount. Some had been forced to ride in on captured mules. A cacophony of hammers meeting iron rang through the night as farriers and blacksmiths labored by their glowing forges to refit the herd. There was no time to waste. On March 25, Sheridan's cavalry crossed the peninsula and rejoined the Army of the Potomac at the makeshift river port at City Point, where Grant, Sherman, and Lincoln were discussing how to end the war.[32]

Grant wanted to force Lee to extend his lines to the west to draw him out and defeat him before he could leave Petersburg to unite with Joseph Johnston in North Carolina. Lee, in turn, had tried to force Grant to move reinforcements from his left to his right to give Lee room to get by him. Sheridan and two infantry corps were to advance to Dinwiddie Court House, a crossroads about thirteen miles southwest of Lee's flank at Hatcher's Run, there to tear up the Southside Railroad and the Richmond and Danville Railroad, Lee's primary supply lines. Or, if some of Lee's force came out to meet him, Sheridan could try to separate it from the main body of Lee's army and destroy it.[33]

On March 29, Sheridan, with the addition of six thousand cavalry from Crook's 2nd Division leading the way, a total of up to fifteen thousand cavalry and horse artillery, moved out in a rainstorm before dawn. Next came Devin. Custer trailed behind, struggling with the teamsters to pry braying mules out of the mud and keep the wagon train rolling. He also had the unenviable job of corduroying roads so supplies could be moved from the railroad. The 2nd Infantry Corps under Andrew Humphreys and the 5th under Gouverneur Warren marched closer to Hatcher's Run and Gravelly Run, with continuous skirmishing. By nightfall, three army corps moving through a fogbank toward a final reckoning were on Lee's flank. When Grant realized this, he changed his mind about wrecking railroads and told Sheridan, "I now feel like ending the matter. In the morning push round the enemy if you can and get onto his right rear." The next morning, the entire battleground having turned into a quagmire due to heavy rains, Grant changed his mind again. [34]

Sheridan told Grant he was making a serious mistake not to press the attack. Grant gave in and told him to go ahead but would not give him the 6th Corps he wanted. Meanwhile, George Pickett had led five infantry brigades to the crossroads at Five Forks, six miles north of Dinwiddie Court House, to reinforce Fitz Lee's cavalry spread out behind breastworks, a total of about ten thousand men. Five Forks was a crucial junction for the Army of Northern Virginia because it was where the road to the railroad crossed the road to the army's flank and rear. Robert E. Lee ordered it held "at all hazards." Sheridan began his attack on the morning of March 31 by sending Devin and Crook toward Five Forks. Pickett, however, found a road through dense woods and swung some brigades around the Federal left, isolating Devin from Sheridan's other divisions. Sheridan sent Merritt to extricate Devin from the trap, pulled back Crook's division, and rushed Custer forward with two brigades, his troopers thrilled to be out of the mud. [35]

Custer moved Capehart's brigade to a ridge above the Dinwiddie Court House road and Pennington's brigade to the right. Pickett drove Pennington back, but the Federals held and counterattacked before combat was halted by nightfall. Custer had helped rally the troops and set up breastworks. Grant told Warren to move his twelve-thousand-man infantry corps to Dinwiddie Court House to reinforce the cavalry and had Brigadier General Randall Mackenzie's one-thousand-man cavalry division brought up from the Army of the James. Pickett might have won the day but was sawing off the branch he was sitting on by cutting himself off from the rest of the embattled army. Warren tarried, however, and Pickett had time to move back to his fortified lines along White Oak Road.[36]

On April 1, Custer spread out a dismounted skirmish line on Pickett's right flank. Warren, however, did not begin to move until 4:15 p.m. Pennington's brigade charged forward twice but was repulsed, and on the third try the troopers broke through Pickett's lines. Custer led Wells's brigade around the Rebel right flank and twice charged a battery without success. He moved Capehart farther out on the flank and tangled with Rooney Lee's cavalry, then chased the butternut riders for six miles and rounded up prisoners. Warren's slow attack on the Confederate left flank bogged down when some divisions got lost. An enraged Sheridan took charge, spurring Rienzi along the battle line and over the breastworks. Sheridan personally captured several prisoners, who joined forty-five hundred others of the ten-thousand-man Confederate force as captives. Pickett, famously absent for a shad-bake lunch with Rosser and Fitz Lee, arrived in time to see his left flank collapse, with total Confederate casualties of about six thousand, most of them prisoners. Sheridan fired Warren on the spot and gave his command to Brigadier General Charles Griffin, whose battery horse, Wellington, had previously carried Custer to Manassas.[37]

Two days later, the Federals took Richmond and Petersburg, and most of the Army of Northern Virginia was across the Appomattox River and fleeing west. On his way toward Amelia Court House to help intercept Lee, Custer found the wagon bridge burned at fifty-foot-wide Namozine Creek and Brigadier General William Paul Roberts's brigade behind breastworks across the stream. Custer shelled the position with canister and sent the 1st Vermont to flank the enemy out of the position. Once across the stream, Custer's brigades pressed on to Namozine Church, where they ran into about eight hundred troopers of Brigadier General Rufus Barringer's brigade. The Green Mountain Boys once again advanced, while the 8th New York turned the flank and charged, forcing the Confederates back. The 15th New York joined the pursuit, and the Federals captured about half of Barringer's brigade, while the rest fled into the woods. Tom Custer won the Medal of Honor during the action after he took the colors of the 2nd North Carolina and captured fourteen prisoners.[38]

The Rebels were on the run from Petersburg and Five Forks, and Custer joined the chase. Lee was north of the Appomattox, moving west while trying to concentrate what remained of his scattered forces. If he could get to the Richmond and Danville Railroad at Amelia Court House thirty-five miles away and then reach the junction near Burkeville, where the railroad intersected with the Southside Railroad, before the Federals did, he had a slim chance of getting his army south to join Johnston or west to Lynchburg. Wells's brigade, accompanied by Custer, rushed after Rosser, Thomas Munford, and Fitz Lee, while Capehart chased Richard Anderson's infantry and Roberts's cavalry. Custer called it a "running fight . . . the enemy being driven at the gallop before a vastly inferior force. Prisoners, guns, and battle-flags were captured all along the line of retreat."[39]

Lee's columns found none of the supplies they expected to be awaiting them at Amelia Court House. Some of Sheridan's cavalry, meanwhile, had reached the railroad depot at Jetersville, eight miles southwest of Amelia Court House, and were blocking the railroad. By the time Lee began to move on April 5, Sheridan had his infantry at Jetersville choking off any means of escape by that route. Lee turned toward Farmville, twenty-three miles to the west, to try to break through the cavalry screen ahead of the infantry.[40]

AN ACCOUNTING AT APPOMATTOX

Custer attacked part of Lee's wagon train, exploiting a gap between Major General William Mahone's and Anderson's divisions in the bottom-lands near Sayler's Creek. When Longstreet's artillery moved into the gap, Custer's men sabered the battery crews and seized ten guns before Anderson's infantry chased them off. Trailing Anderson, Richard S. Ewell's corps, reduced to a few thousand men, including Kershaw's division, crossed the creek pursued by Wright's corps, about twelve thousand men. Merritt swung the cavalry about two miles west of the infantry, with Custer's two brigades on the right. John Gordon, meanwhile, had turned off the road and followed Ewell's wagon train closer to the Appomattox River. The Confederates were being chivied from two directions and were fighting back to back. Pennington's mounted brigade charged Anderson's supply train but was driven back by artillery fire until it changed course and flanked the train guard. Capehart's mounted West Virginians attacked in double lines at a right angle to Kershaw's line, surging over the breastworks. Custer was all over the field and lost another horse in the fray. Tom Custer, riding with Capehart, won his second Medal of Honor, suffering a facial wound. Crook and Devin, meanwhile, broke up the rest of Anderson's column, while Wright crushed Ewell's corps. [41]

The Confederates surrendered en masse, including Ewell, a lieutenant general and corps commander, and five other generals. Another seventeen hundred prisoners and several hundred wagons were captured from Gordon's corps as it brought up the rear on another road. A third of the Army of Northern Virginia was gone, at least eight thousand casualties. When Robert E. Lee saw his magnificent army in ruins, he said, "My God! Has the army been dissolved?" [42]

But he kept on going, reaching Farmville on April 7, and was feeding his troops on the north side of the river when he learned Crook was approaching from the south, tailing Longstreet's column, and Humphreys's 2nd Corps was coming in from the northeast. Lee set fire to the bridges, then concentrated on a ridge north of Farmville, where the Confederates battled the 2nd Corps. A regiment from Crook's lead brigade forded the river and chased after a wagon train but was driven off and briefly trapped on a narrow road by Munford and Rosser. Crook pulled his pummeled regiment back to Farmville before turning west on the Southside Railroad and advancing to Prospect Station. [43]

Custer had been leading his division south of the Appomattox River to block any attempt Lee might make to head toward North Carolina. When Lee left Farmville, however, it seemed likely he was making for Lynchburg by way of Appomattox Station, where he hoped to find rations. Late on the afternoon of April 7, Sheridan sent Mackenzie's cavalrymen to join Crook at Prospect Station, then followed with Merritt's troopers. The next morning Sheridan learned that four trainloads of rations were moving on the Southside Railroad near Appomattox Station fourteen miles away. He directed Custer toward the station first, with Devin and Crook moving on the flanks. The two infantry corps of the Army of the James under Major General Edward O. C. Ord followed the cavalry, marching for almost twenty straight hours to reach Appomattox Station. [44]

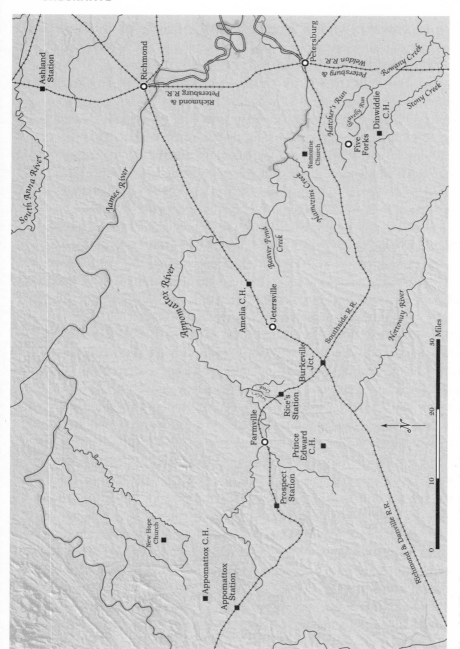

Map 6.2. The Appomattox Campaign brought the fighting in Virginia to an end on April 9, 1865, while leaving the once serene landscape soaked in blood. (University of Tennessee Cartographic Services)

Custer's division reached the station shortly after 2 p.m. and captured three of the trains, while another fired up and chugged off toward Lynchburg. Brigadier General Reuben Lindsay Walker's artillery, a wagon train, and Brigadier General Martin W. Gary's depleted cavalry brigade were north of the station on a ridge along a stage road to Appomattox. About four hundred of Custer's troopers scattered the startled Confederates and ransacked the wagons before the cannons rumbled and canister sliced through the attackers. A Confederate artilleryman recalled seeing Custer "on a white horse in the center of a long line of cavalry . . . urging his men to charge. . . . I urged my men to take good aim and shoot at General Custer, and I shot at him a number of times myself."[45]

Repeated charges failed to dislodge the Confederates even as more of Custer's division and Devin's joined in the attack, which continued well into the evening. Finally, Wells's brigade got around the left flank and turned eastward, overtook Gary's cavalrymen after an uphill ride through dense woods, and ran into skirmishers from the main body of Lee's infantry just west of Appomattox Court House. About a dozen cavalrymen from the 15th New York dashed into the village and were repulsed, their lieutenant colonel shot dead in the street in front of the courthouse. Custer finally overran Walker's defensive ring and captured the heavy guns, the remaining wagons, and the rear guard defenders.[46]

In his battle report, Custer imagined he was facing two infantry divisions and neglected to mention how many guns, wagons, and soldiers were withdrawn during the protracted attack. Nor did he mention his casualties, which a surgeon said had piled up quickly. "Our loss was slight," Custer reported. His claim that his riders "charged into the camp of the rebel army" that night was equally misleading. Eager to claim a rousing victory, he had taken a tough position against a formidable foe, but the undermanned Confederates had fought it out and saved almost as much as they gave away. Custer, however, had deprived Lee of his desperately needed supplies, blocked an escape route, and shortened the war by at least a few days.[47]

Sheridan's main concern was keeping the Rebels in place with his cavalry until the infantry could come up and finish the war. The commander moved Crook's division behind Custer's and along his left flank. Brigadier General Charles H. Smith's brigade relieved Custer's advance guard in front of Appomattox Court House, deployed across the stage road to Lynchburg, and constructed breastworks. The next morning, Palm

Sunday, the Confederates lined up along a three-mile diagonal line running from the northwest to southeast in front of Appomattox Court House, with Munford, Rosser, and Rooney Lee on the right, then Gordon's infantrymen. At about 6:30, Gordon's gray line and Rooney Lee's cavalrymen moved forward toward Smith's right flank, pushing the Federals back and capturing a few pieces of artillery. When both their flanks were turned, the brigade withdrew to a second defensive line established by Crook and Mackenzie, supported by Devin, then Custer and the 3rd Cavalry Division.[48]

Kept out of action during the early hours of the battle due to their exertions of the previous day, Custer's division moved to the right of Devin's flank in some woods as Ord and Griffin arrived with their infantry corps. When Gary's brigade approached from the east, Custer sent Pennington's brigade in pursuit until the riders encountered a dozen guns on a hillside and cautiously turned back to seek shelter. While the 8th and 15th New York skirmished with Gary's men, the more important action of the morning was taking place on the Lynchburg Road, where Crook's dismounted troopers were being driven back by the Confederates. Just as a breakout seemed likely, the Confederates saw an awesome sight—the oncoming legions of the Army of the James moving up the ridges on both sides of the road. Soon after 10 a.m., the Federals began seeing white flags moving toward them from the Confederate lines.[49]

A messenger from Gordon's lines was brought to Custer, who apparently was provoked by what he saw as a presumptuous call, or demand, for a cease-fire at Lee's behest. By one account, Custer cut off the discussion and replied, "We will listen to no terms but that of unconditional surrender. We are behind your army now and it is at our mercy." When the rider galloped off, Custer followed with his own flag and found Gordon and then Longstreet. "In the name of General Sheridan I demand the unconditional surrender of this army," the twenty-five-year-old Custer told Lee's "Old War Horse," an 1842 West Point graduate and Lee's senior commander. Longstreet ignored Custer until the younger man repeated his demand, then reddened and shouted, "I am not the commander of this army, and if I were, I would not surrender it to General Sheridan." He added that if the truce did not hold, it would be Custer's division that would be annihilated. Longstreet told Custer that Lee and Grant would soon determine the next course of action. Briefly chagrined, or perhaps appeased, Custer was escorted back to his own lines.[50]

David Coffey thought the incident did Custer no credit. "On a day when men on both sides of the lines displayed great magnanimity, Custer showed none," he wrote. Just what Custer thought he was doing is not clear, and the accounts differ. He had no authority to negotiate on behalf of Sheridan, who was elsewhere on the field talking with Gordon. Perhaps Custer expected to capture his second corps commander in a week. Other ad hoc negotiations among generals were occurring throughout the line, while some units, including Gary's, kept up sporadic firing. Tensions, understandably, were high as exhausted men, thousands facing imminent defeat and others a costly victory, looked each other in the eye on soil soaked in blood.[51]

For the next few hours Custer chatted amiably with old friends in the Army of Northern Virginia. Grant came through the lines about 1 p.m. and met Sheridan and Ord at Appomattox Court House; then he met Lee about thirty minutes later in the front parlor of the home of Wilmer McLean. Negotiations continued until about 3:45. Sheridan bought the little table on which the surrender document had been signed for the price

Figure 6.3. A flag of truce borne by a Confederate rider is brought to Custer at Appomattox. In high spirits, Custer drew a rebuke from Confederate general James Longstreet, but with characteristic bonhomie, Custer soon was reunited with the West Point comrades from whom he had been separated by the war. Sketch by Alfred R. Waud. (Library of Congress)

of two $10 gold pieces. He gave Custer the table as a gift for Libbie along with a note praising her husband's service. Custer continued greeting old friends, including Gimlet Lea, whom he had not seen since the wedding at Williamsburg. One of Custer's staff officers wrote that he saw Custer and Fitz Lee embracing each other and then rolling on the ground like schoolboys.[52]

"EXTERMINATION IS THE ONLY TRUE POLICY"

The cavalry did not linger at Appomattox Court House but began a slow movement to Petersburg, arriving on April 18. While resting in Petersburg after Libbie's arrival from Washington, Custer wrote Justice Isaac Peckham Christiancy a letter, which he apparently expected to be published, stating his views about the course of action that should be followed. The letter soon appeared in the *Detroit Advertiser* and was reprinted in the *New York Times*. He began by acknowledging the "deepest gloom" throughout the army in the wake of the Lincoln assassination and expressed his "unconditional" support for the former president. He expressed confidence that President Andrew Johnson would pursue the wisest policy toward the defeated South, indeed the only policy that could secure a safe future. Although he conceded that he might be mistaken, he based his optimism on Johnson's past political actions, his "superior knowledge of the rebel leaders and their plans" as a border state Southerner, and his April 18 speech to the Illinois delegation in Washington, in which he had said that "treason is the blackest of crimes and . . . traitors must be punished."

Americans, according to Custer, were an "impulsive people," inclined to be "carried away with the good feeling consequent upon our glorious success, and thereby inclined to pardon and overlook all crimes committed by Southern traitors." Such misguided magnanimity, he insisted, would be but little better than self-murder. The nation's future welfare, its very existence, its standing among other nations, depended on just recompense for the crime of aggravated treason. He said he believed he expressed the universal view of the army. "Extermination is the only true policy we can adopt toward the political leaders of the rebellion, and at the same time do justice to ourselves and to our posterity." Those who supported the rebellion, including newspaper editors, were to face "retribution," and government was to be purged of "every disloyal traitor." Then and only then could the "avenging angel sheathe his sword" and the country emerge regenerated. [53]

The extraordinary letter reflected none of Lincoln's magnanimity and was a balm to the radical Republicans in Congress. The audacity of the letter is astounding. Custer was putting Johnson, a fellow Democrat, on notice ("I may be mistaken") that his actions must live up to his words. While he did not specify the punishment he had in mind, "extermination" leaves little to the imagination. He cited "those who have occupied prominent positions in the rebel State Governments or the so-called Confederate Government" as among those who should be "punished with unrelenting vigor." Presumably that would, at a minimum, have included the entire Confederate cabinet, the president and vice president, all state governors, and dozens of newspaper editors, all bound for the scaffold or the dungeon. Presuming to speak for the army, Custer had put himself at risk of censure by his military superiors, and by seeking to influence the political leadership, he spoke out of turn as a military officer.

But he was not censured (at least not publicly) and may successfully have gauged the temper of the times, as well as the opinion of his fellow soldiers. His motivation in writing the letter is not clear, however. When he described Americans as impulsive, he was explaining himself. He may have been thinking about resigning from the army and going into politics. Perhaps he was just tired and angry. Johnston's army was still fighting in North Carolina, Jefferson Davis was still at large, and Lincoln's assassin had not been found at the time Custer wrote the letter. The letter publicly affirmed his support for Lincoln's war policies, perhaps because his loyalty to the Republican president had been questioned when he was perceived as a "McClellan man."

Custer's guarded confidence in Johnson was not shared by his father-in-law, who, after learning of Lincoln's assassination, wrote Libbie, "The thought that a man, such as Andy Johnson, lunatic, drunkard, is to be at the head of the government at this, the most critical period of our national existence is *awful* beyond words."[54]

On April 24, the cavalry left Petersburg along with the 6th Corps to support Sherman in North Carolina but turned back on April 28 at South Boston, Virginia. Sheridan had learned of Johnston's surrender at Bennett Place, North Carolina, effectively ending the war in the East, save for some remnants in Alabama and Mississippi. Custer remained in Petersburg until May 10 and was camped with his division near Washington on May 21.[55]

On May 23, the Army of the Potomac marched from the Capitol to the White House down Pennsylvania Avenue. First came George Meade and his staff, then Merritt leading the cavalry, followed by Custer, "vociferously cheered at various points of the line, and . . . somewhat encumbered by wreaths and bouquets which had been presented to him, and which he appreciatingly carried with his left arm," according to a *New York Times* account. He was not alone in receiving the floral tributes, but the press singled him out. Custer's dark bay stallion, Don Juan, suddenly bolted in front of the grandstand and sprinted forward. Custer, curls flying, lived up to his reputation as a mad circus rider after losing his hat and sword. A reporter for the *Daily National Intelligencer* noted that Custer's "golden locks were displayed to great advantage as the frightened war-steed glided by to the amazement of the beholders." The spectacle drew gasps and applause from the crowd, along with some knowing glances between military men. Once again, Custer had stolen the show.[56]

In his address to the 3rd Cavalry Division, written on the evening of April 9 at Appomattox Court House, Custer had thanked and praised his soldiers. With the end of the war at hand, he told them, "The task of the historian begins." When their daring deeds were recorded in the history books, he said, he asked only that his name might be recorded as commander of the 3rd Cavalry Division. Custer's name, however, would forever be linked to another unit, another time, and another war.[57]

"A BEAUTIFUL GAME"

Custer ended the Civil War a great hero with a well-deserved reputation as a bold fighter. Given opportunities, he acted resolutely. He was fortunate in his mentors and learned quickly, first as a staff officer, then as a field commander. Impelled by circumstances, he rose in rank from brevet captain to brevet brigadier general just before Gettysburg. His temperament was suited to the cavalry, which required courage, dash, intuition, and a talent for improvising under fire. His legendary panache inspired his men, most of whom were volunteers, not professional soldiers. He led by example from the front and never asked his subordinates to go where he would not. He inspired loyalty, even devotion, in others and usually was loyal to his superiors.

He grew fond of publicity and was given to boasting in his reports and letters, especially later in the war. He was envied by many officers and grew envious of others in turn. Given specific orders and fighting in concert with other units, he usually achieved the desired results and won the praise of his commanders. Left to his own devices, he could, on occasion, overreach and falter.

Long after the war, and long after Custer's death, Lieutenant Colonel Charles Capehart gave his own assessment of Custer after he had read one too many memoirs by Sheridan and other officers who he thought had neglected to give his old commander his due:

> I have seen [Custer] under the most varying and critical circumstances, and never without ample resources of mind and body to meet the most trying contingency. He was counted by some rash; it was because he dared, while they dared not. There can be no doubt that he had a positive genius for war, while Merritt, Devin, Wilson, Crook, etc., were comparatively but mediocrities. If I were to begin giving instances of his daring, brilliancy and skill, I should never stop.[58]

Custer confiscated a chess set from one of Jubal Early's headquarters wagons after the Battle of Waynesboro and sent it to Libbie. "I am learning to play," he told her in a letter. "It is a beautiful game, much like a battle. If you will learn, it will be a great source of pleasure to us hereafter." It is revealing that Custer had not learned to play the cerebral game until the end of the war and looked forward to continuing the "battle" on a domestic field for pleasure.[59]

Assessing Custer's virtues as a cavalry commander, historian Gregory Urwin pointed out that an "effective cavalry commander could not operate like a chess master. He did not enjoy the luxury of time to frame his tactics or reactions before his enemy would strike, and perhaps strike again." Custer did take up chess after the war and is known to have played it with a judge while he and Libbie were living in Elizabethtown, Kentucky, in the early 1870s. In time, Custer might have become a parlor "chess master," but, as a field commander, chess was not his game.[60]

Part II

Requiem and Resurrection

7

FROM CIVIL WAR TO
INDIAN WARS

1865–1876

After the end of the Civil War, Ulysses S. Grant ordered Philip Sheridan to Louisiana to quell any lingering Rebel resistance in Texas. This also would send a message to the French, who had invaded Mexico two years earlier and had thousands of occupying troops there. Sheridan would provide a show of force to dissuade empire ambitions in North America via Mexico. When Sheridan assembled his command, he named Custer to lead about four thousand cavalry. In June 1865, Custer arrived in Alexandria, where he would begin training troops. Although hardened by four years of war, the youthful Custer still was inclined to pranks and silliness, which did not help with ill-disciplined soldiers, among whom desertion and alcoholism were chronic. His troops also were in a sour mood because they had expected to be mustered out with the end of the Civil War, as had other army units. The idea of heading into Texas, perhaps even Mexico, sharpened resentment.

Custer made matters worse with his determination to show his authority and by doing so with such excessive measures as ordering flogging for foraging. In Alexandria, he even had a deserter executed. In November, Custer set up headquarters in Austin, Texas, where he mainly headed a police force in the rather lawless region. In what became standard practice for Custer, he turned the assignment into a lark—hunting, horse racing, and dancing. But the Texas stint was short, with the state reentering the Union and the French threat disappearing rather quickly. Custer and his cavalry mustered out in January 1866. [1]

During the next few months, Custer toyed with the idea of leaving the army for the chance to make money in mining and railroads, and he had an extended visit to New York City with an eye toward that goal. After Libbie's father died in May, she and Custer spent the next several months visiting family and settling her father's estate. In early 1866, Congress authorized military reconstruction, which meant reorganization and adjustments in ranks. Sheridan became commander of the Fifth Military District, which included Texas and Louisiana. In July 1866, Congress authorized four new cavalry regiments, which included the 7th Cavalry. Custer was now a captain in the regular army, after having been a major general of volunteers.

The brevet system had inflated ranks during the war. In many cases, the promotions were deserved, given for outstanding performance, but not necessarily on the battlefield. One could receive a brevet promotion for staff work or simply as a means of promoting a junior officer who performed well. So those who had been generals might now be captains or majors. With Sheridan backing him again, Custer was appointed lieutenant colonel and became second in command of the 7th Cavalry under Colonel A. J. Smith. Custer reported for duty to Fort Riley, Kansas, in October. His job was to protect the westward-moving railroad and settlers from the Indians. His troops were inexperienced with Indian fighting and lived under very tough conditions in the winter plains. Desertion and alcoholism were rampant. When Smith left in February 1867 for an assignment in Arkansas, Custer became field commander of the 7th Cavalry, a position he held until June 25, 1876. [2]

A NEW KIND OF WAR

He had been a saber-slinging cavalryman, adorned in a red necktie, and now would be a buckskin-clad, Indian-fighting frontiersman. Indian fighting and big-game hunting were the primary subjects of his earliest journalism, articles in *Turf, Field and Farm* and *Galaxy* magazines. His Civil War memoirs came later. Custer found that battling Indians was not easy. The father of "hard war" in America, William Tecumseh Sherman, called fighting Indians the "hardest kind of war." Troops often were far from their base camps, traveling for days, even months, into unknown, unmapped territory. They often were not sure where they were going or where the enemy might be. The troops were poorly trained and sometimes ill prepared when battle commenced. Climate extremes exacerbated the misery, ranging from dusty, scorching heat to blizzards, in which the soldiers had nominal shelter and provisions. It was a new kind of war, too, not just because it lacked a front or conventional tactics but because the Indians were mobile, which brought a new set of frustrations for the army. Because some of the tribes depended on buffalo for subsistence, they were nomadic and freed from the constraints of a base of operation. Many of the army's resources were spent simply trying to find the Indians. If all that were not enough, commanders and soldiers were well aware that the same government telling them to subdue the Indians was feeding the enemy and supplying them with modern weapons, ostensibly for hunting. Humanitarians in the East deepened the chagrin by accusing the army and the government of being the real barbarians. [3]

An 1867 expedition under Winfield Scott Hancock, whom Custer had so capably served at Williamsburg, gave Custer his first taste of Indian fighting. In one respect, the Hancock expedition started well for Custer, whom a prominent reporter praised for his potential. Correspondent Henry M. Stanley accompanied the expedition, but it was more than four years before his mythic "Dr. Livingstone, I presume" moment in Africa. As for fighting Indians, Stanley wrote, "Custer is precisely the man for that job. A certain impetuosity and undoubted courage are his principal characteristics." Not everyone agreed. One of the officers reporting for duty was Captain Frederick Benteen, whom Jeffry D. Wert described as having "a backbone of steel . . . a soul of vinegar." Benteen was a capable officer but the antithesis of the jovial, extroverted Custer. Benteen later said he disliked Custer upon first meeting him. Things never got better. [4]

In April 1867, a meeting at Fort Larned, Kansas, with Cheyenne and Sioux chiefs failed to win assurances the Indians would be peaceful. The meeting included Hancock, commander of the Department of the Missouri, Custer, and other officers. Hancock ordered a march on a village west of the fort, but Custer and about six hundred troopers found only an abandoned encampment when they arrived. Hancock, certain that the tribes were hostiles, ordered pursuit, which proved futile. In the meantime, Custer concluded that the Indians they were after were innocent of the killings of which they were accused. During the cold and rainy April, desertions climbed while Custer and the troops were at Fort Hays, Kansas, to resupply. Ninety men had deserted by the end of the month. Frustrated with the lack of progress in the war, Hancock visited Fort Hays from May 3 to 5. He castigated Custer for being at the fort instead of chasing Indians.

One officer, in a letter to his wife, noted a changed Custer, who was angry about something, apparently a result of the dressing down by Hancock. Other officers also saw the change. As Custer became more critical, his officers became less cooperative, even dodging the duty of being his officer of the day. Custer became extremely demanding, in one instance ordering a fifty-mile march to check out a rumor of an Indian attack. As desertions increased, the punishment of deserters escalated. A *Harper's Weekly* correspondent visited the fort and wrote that Custer was depressed, attributing his moodiness to his having been outwitted by the Indians. Others have noted that Custer often was a defensive personality, suffering mood swings, and at the same time an impulsive show-off. Poor living conditions and rations at the fort only darkened his melancholy. As if all that were not enough, he was without Libbie.[5]

Custer finally got his first real Indian fight, which was more a skirmish than a battle. In June 1867, after arriving at Fort McPherson, Nebraska, Custer met with Sioux chief Pawnee Killer, who told Custer he and his tribe were peaceful. In return, Custer, lacking experience with Indians, believed the chief and gave him some rations. Custer did not know that Pawnee Killer was among those he had been looking for in Kansas. When Sherman arrived to review campaign plans, Custer recounted the Indians' peaceful intentions, which Sherman dismissed as unlikely. Sherman then ordered Custer to search for Sioux along the Republican River and the South Platte. On June 18, Custer left for the Republican River area under orders from Sherman to drive the Indians out. Six days later, a small band headed by Pawnee Killer attacked Custer's camp a few miles north of the river, trying to drive off the cavalry's horses. After a brief parley that brought no results, the troops pursued the Indians, who eventually surrounded Custer's small detachment. The cavalrymen held the Indians off for several hours, suffered no casualties, and reported killing a few Indians.[6]

In addition to pursuing Indians that summer, Custer spent much of July chasing Libbie. After the fight near the Republican River, Custer headed south toward Fort Wallace, Kansas, but on the way found the bodies of First Lieutenant Lyman Kidder and ten of his men, who were on their way from the Colorado Territory to deliver orders to Custer. Instead of finding Custer, they ran into Sioux, probably Pawnee Killer and some of his warriors. Custer found the bodies on July 12, scalped and so severely mutilated that Kidder's body could not be sent home for proper burial, as was customary for officers. Custer and his troopers arrived exhausted at Fort Wallace on July 13, having covered about 180 miles in a week. Custer was hoping to find Libbie at the fort but did not. His concern for Libbie sharpened, and his command judgment dulled. In *My Life on the Plains*, Custer said he made the march in order to get supplies at Fort Harker, Kansas, because those at Fort Wallace were nearly exhausted. That was not true.[7]

Custer set out for Fort Hays with more than seventy soldiers. He apparently was not breaking any orders, which had been only to report to Fort Wallace. His concern for Libbie could have reflected legitimate fear for her safety, fresh after he had seen the results of the Kidder massacre, or worries about a recent cholera outbreak. On July 15, he left for Fort Hays, which was another 150 miles away. He arrived there on July 18, then went on to Fort Harker, another sixty miles, and arrived there the afternoon of July 19. It had been a nearly nonstop march. She was already gone. So he hopped a train for her destination, Fort Riley, Kansas, where he finally caught up to her. Smith put a damper on the reunion when he ordered Custer to return to Fort Harker and had him arrested for deserting his post at Fort Wallace. He was found guilty of the principal charge of leaving his command and suspended for a year with a loss of pay. It had been a pretty lousy year or so for Custer. The court-martial and suspension were the culmination of a period in which the Indians had eluded him, the marches had been miserable, his troops had grown to despise him, and desertions and drunkenness had been rampant. The failed Hancock campaign had diminished Custer's stock as an Indian fighter and only emboldened the Indians, who, having seen the soldiers' inability to catch them, became more contemptuous of army authority.[8]

CUSTER AS JOURNALIST

Perhaps lacking the adventure of battle or having no troops to whip into shape, Custer began his journalistic endeavors about this time. The writing—a common income supplement for officers, especially those posted to remote areas—filled the extra time, and he made some money at it. It was a natural extension of that part of his duties requiring report writing. For Custer, it also was an opportunity to tout his own accomplishments, the recounting of which would be required in official reports and the embellishment of which would attract readers and earn dollars. He wrote under the pseudonym "Nomad," conjuring up the image of the wanderer, the adventurer, the individual loosed from civilization. This fed the public appetite for frontier romance. And he was a good writer.[9]

While at Fort Leavenworth in 1867 and 1868 and serving his suspension, Custer started his Civil War memoirs. A few years later, while stationed in Kentucky and during another less adventurous time, he started writing for *Galaxy*. The publisher, Sheldon and Company, not only ran the series in the magazine but eventually published a selection as *My Life on the Plains*, which covered 1867 to 1869. *Galaxy* later began publishing his memoirs in a series of articles. Custer wrote a total of fifteen "letters" for *Turf, Field and Farm* from 1867 to 1875, mostly about hunting and horses, as appropriate to the magazine's focus. Only three articles concerned Indian fighting, and those were about the Hancock expedition. In addition to passing time productively in a remote outpost and earning extra income, the writing enhanced his reputation, as he regaled his audience with tales of pursuing beasts, horsemanship, marksmanship, and endurance.[10]

As Custer wrote in 1867 and 1868 of his exploits, his constant champion, Sheridan, planned a winter campaign in the southern plains, where the previous summer had seen numerous attacks by Cheyenne, Arapaho, and Kiowa upon settlers, railroads, stage lines, and soldiers. In July 1868, a band of Cheyenne attacked settlers on the Saline and Solomon rivers in Kansas, killing fifteen men, raping five women, burning their cabins, and stealing their livestock. Sheridan had assumed command of the Department of the Missouri in March. He faced pressure from politicians, businessmen, and settlers to punish the Indians. From his Fort Hays headquarters, Sheridan had sent out the 7th Cavalry and the "buffalo soldiers" of the 10th Cavalry to little effect. He created an elite unit of frontiersmen, which lost half its force in a fight with Sioux, Cheyenne, and Arapaho in eastern Colorado. So he ordered all friendly bands to use Fort Cobb as their agency. Otherwise, they would be considered hostiles. This forced government action and suspended wavering on how to approach the Indian problem.

Easterners and the Indian Bureau tended toward a humanitarian approach and believed the Indians could be brought peacefully to reservations or even assimilated into the white, Christian culture. Westerners, conversely, demanded forceful retribution, which was in concert with Sheridan's, Sherman's, and the army's views. Easterners, they believed, were naive in their isolation from the reality of the problem. Sherman and Sheridan, not too surprisingly, determined total war was a solution, rather like their campaigns a few years earlier in Virginia's Shenandoah Valley and from Atlanta to the sea. On the plains, it would mean not just fighting the warriors but subjecting the whole Indian populace to the suffering and hardship of war. A winter campaign would be better because the nomadic Indians were hard to catch on the vast, open expanse in the summer. Of course, a winter campaign would be tough and would require a leader who was tough. Sheridan telegraphed Custer, then in Monroe, on September 24: "Generals Sherman, Sully, and myself, and nearly all the officers of your regiment have asked for you, and I hope the application can be successful. Can you come at once?" Custer was on a train for Kansas the next day. [11]

THE WASHITA CONTROVERSY

Custer put their idea of total war into practice at the Battle of the Washita. In July 1865, Sherman had assumed command of the Military Division of the Mississippi, with the name changed later to Military Division of the Missouri. His Civil War ideas about the effectiveness of total war carried over to the Plains Wars. Well before he was named commanding general of the entire army in 1869, he advocated dealing severely with the Indians. After two frustrating summers in 1867 and 1868 of chasing the Indians around the southern plains, both Sherman and Sheridan believed a winter campaign against Indians was the way to find them, pinned down and immobilized by severe winter weather. The generals had no qualms about killing the warriors; destroying villages, foodstuffs, and horses; and wreaking havoc on and impoverishing the Indians as punishment. Raids on white settlers in spring and summer 1868 gave Sheridan justification for dealing harshly with those responsible—though it often was difficult to sort out the friendly and hostile individuals, let alone tribes. Upon receiving reports in late summer of Cheyenne attacks, Sherman wrote Sheridan to "compel their removal south of the Kansas line, and in pursuing kill if necessary. This amounts to war; but I hope on a small scale, confined to that locality." Sheridan wrote, "These Indians require to be soundly whipped, and the ringleaders in the present trouble hung, their ponies killed, and such destruction of their property as will make them very poor."[12]

Subsequent events showed Sheridan had picked the right man. On November 21, he visited Camp Supply, indicating the importance of the campaign. The next day, Sheridan ordered the march toward the Washita River and the village that was presumed to be there. He directed Custer to "destroy their villages and ponies, to kill or hang all warriors, and bring back all women and children." A string of encampments along a ten- to fifteen-mile stretch of the river included Cheyenne, Arapaho, Kiowa, Comanche, and Apache. More than six thousand Indians were in the winter camps in the area.[13]

Custer and about eight hundred troopers of the 7th Cavalry left Camp Supply at dawn on November 23 in a foot of snow from an overnight blizzard. They traveled toward the Washita River, where the village included the Cheyenne tribe of Chief Black Kettle, who had sought peace with the settlers and the army. But not all of his warriors were peaceful. Soldiers discovered the village four days later, and Custer found what he wanted—a fight and a chance for redemption and new glory. About 110 men remained behind with the supply train, near the Canadian River, leaving Custer with nearly 690 troopers when the fight commenced. Custer himself led the charge across the Washita River and into the village, which the 7th overran in only about twenty minutes. The fight was short but wild. Custer made one of the first kills, by his own account, as he charged into the village and shot a warrior who was taking aim at him. The Indians had been taken by surprise, pouring out of their tepees as the troops fired and slashed through the mayhem. Overwhelmingly outnumbered and outgunned, many Indians fled for the river and into nearby woods. A few bands, about seventeen warriors, made it to nearby ravines from which they could return fire, keeping Custer's force at bay for several hours. But 7th Cavalry sharpshooters eventually found positions from which to pick them off.[14]

Major Joel H. Elliott and seventeen cavalrymen chased some of those fleeing villagers downstream while Custer finished the village conquest. There are a number of versions as to what transpired next, whether Custer and his cavalry spent the rest of the day destroying the village and eliminating pockets of resistance. There was armed resistance, and soldiers found evidence of attacks on settlers, such as clothing, mail, and other items. Custer did report stopping one officer who was firing into a group of women and children. He reported 102 Indians killed and 53 women and children taken prisoner. Custer's count of the warriors killed came from a gathering of officers in camp on the way back to Camp Supply, at which each officer gave an accounting. The casualty count did not come from counting the dead on the battlefield, as Custer implied in his report. The village was burned and, along with food and other supplies, a herd of about 600 ponies was destroyed after Custer took 225 for scouts, captives, and his soldiers.[15]

In his report, Custer listed eighteen of his men killed, including Elliott, even though Custer did not know what had happened to all of them. Randolph Keim, a correspondent with the *New York Herald*, later wrote from Camp Supply that Elliott had left the village fight of his own accord to pursue fleeing Indians. As the battle subsided, the question of Elliott's whereabouts arose. Keim reported, "There is no doubt that he and his party struck the approaching Kiowas and Arapahoes coming to the rescue of the Cheyennes and were cut off by them. . . . For these unfortunate men there was no possibility of escape. Their alternative was death by some friendly bullet or death by the horrible fortune which the hellish ingenuity of the savages alone can invent."[16]

Custer sent out a search party, which returned after going only about two miles, though there is some debate over how far Captain Edward Myers went with his search party. That nominal effort roused ire among the officers of the 7th Cavalry, and Elliott's fate became a black mark on Custer's triumph. Officers accused Custer of abandoning Elliott, of leaving the field without determining what had happened to Elliott and his men. Custer apparently was concerned with getting out of the area once he determined more Indians camps were in the vicinity. His pack train, casualties, and lack of supplies, together with the number of Indians, made his concern a reasonable one. Part of the reason for slaughtering the ponies had been to expedite leaving the area, since the herd would have slowed him down. On December 11, Sheridan, Custer, and more than one thousand cavalry returned to the battle site. They found the bodies, all severely mutilated, several beheaded. Keim had accompanied the search party and, in recounting Sheridan's and Custer's reconstruction of events, reported that Elliott had been surrounded and outnumbered. Sheridan and Custer, as they worked their way back to the main camp, also found the bodies of a white woman and small child. The woman had been shot in the head. The child's head, they surmised, had been smashed against a tree.[17]

The Elliott episode inflamed the anti-Custer faction of the 7th, Benteen in particular. His contempt for Custer was such that he even asked Ben Clark, who was Custer's chief of scouts for the march, to provide a statement that Custer knowingly allowed Elliott to lead the risky pursuit without trying to save him. Clark declined to do so. The incident provoked an initially anonymous letter to the *St. Louis Post-Dispatch* that assailed Custer's performance at the Washita. When Custer found out about the letter and got a copy of it in January 1869, he called his officers together, demanded to know its author, and threatened to thrash the guilty party. Benteen, the story goes, stepped forward, read a few lines of the letter, and recognized it as one he had sent to friends in St. Louis, not intending its publication. He invited Custer to have at it because he, Benteen, was the author. Custer stomped away, thrashing unadministered. The Elliott episode was the only stain on the victory.[18]

The battle also illustrated the virtues and flaws of Custer as frontier commander. He gambled on the village being isolated, but he did not know the strength of the enemy. The unknown terrain only heightened the gamble. Conversely, he succeeded where all others had failed the past two summers—finding and destroying a hostile village and doing so with minimal casualties. The Washita also meant fame for Custer. He became a national figure, a celebrity Indian fighter.[19]

Though the battle often has been characterized as a massacre, it was not a clear case of armed aggression against a peaceful tribe. Some warriors in Black Kettle's village had conducted raids against settlers and fought soldiers. Black Kettle himself advocated peace, but his village was divided, with both war and peace advocates. As noted, Custer and his men did find evidence of raids on settlers and even some army mules in the village. Also, Black Kettle had been warned about the hostile actions and told that if he and his tribe did not surrender, they would suffer the consequences. Sherman, Sheridan, and Custer defended the attack. First, they said, Cheyenne raids and killings the previous summer justified the military response. Second, Black Kettle's family had been offered sanctuary at Fort Cobb and warned of possible consequences of not coming in. Third, there was evidence of attacks on settlers. Finally, they noted, it was necessary to use force against the savages, who were immune to more civilized courses of action. [20]

Continuing the winter campaign, Sheridan and Custer split up. The former caught up to a large band of Kiowa and forced most of them to return to the reservation. In January 1869, Custer and a group of forty-five sharpshooters convinced a village of Arapaho to surrender. A few months later, in mid-March, he found several Cheyenne villages of about 260 lodges. Believing the Indians were holding two white women captive, Custer decided not to attack; instead, he convinced the Indians to release the hostages and won the Indians' assurance they would go back to the reservation. Moving out of Fort Sill, Oklahoma, and into Texas, Custer found the villages of Cheyenne chiefs Medicine Arrow and Little Robe. Another inconsequential point in fact became large in myth when Custer met with Medicine Arrow, who reportedly put a curse on Custer. According to Cheyenne oral tradition, during the smoking of a ceremonial pipe, Custer and the chief talked of peace. Before Custer left, Medicine Arrow tamped the pipe's ashes on one of Custer's boots, proclaiming that if Custer was dishonest with the Cheyenne, then the soldiers would die. The campaign was over by the end of March, all the Cheyenne having returned or agreed to return to reservations. [21]

The winter campaign, and the Elliott episode in particular, resulted in even more tension between Custer and Benteen, who had managed to work together in spite of their dislike for one another. They first met at Fort Riley, and Custer wrote in a letter to Libbie before the Washita battle that Benteen could be counted on, that he was a "superior" officer. Benteen's letter accusing Custer of abandoning Elliott and performing poorly sealed their enmity, which has spawned more than a century of historical speculation about Benteen's reasons at the Little Bighorn not to "be quick [and] bring packs." [22]

The campaign became the foundation of Custer's reputation not only as an Indian fighter but also for having intimate knowledge of Indian culture—and of one Indian in particular. Meotzi was among the captured at the Washita and served as an interpreter for Custer for the balance of campaign. In addition, legend and rumor have it that she also bore him a son. Cheyenne oral history holds that she gave birth to the child in the fall of 1869, and he was named either Yellow Tail or Yellow Swallow. There is no documentation of the birth. The only other sources for the story are Benteen, who despised Custer, and scout Ben Clark, who held a grudge against Custer for dismissing him. So the only three sources for the story are unreliable.[23]

DANCING, DUKES, AND DOLLARS

After winning fame as an Indian fighter, Custer next became a hunting celebrity. Summer 1869 saw decreased Indian raids in Kansas. Custer and Libbie were at Fort Hays, and he had the chance to indulge his passion for hunting. He resumed writing for *Turf, Field and Farm*, creating a popular series about hunting and the adventurous life on the plains. The series, in turn, enhanced his frontiersman image and drew other celebrities to him for hunts, including a variety of politicians and even P. T. Barnum. Libbie wrote that Custer had more than two hundred visitors for such hunts in summer 1870. All of this was a great step removed from his ignominious first buffalo hunt, which took place in 1867 during the Hancock expedition. When Custer saw his first buffalo, he gave chase on his horse. As he pulled out his pistol and prepared to shoot, the buffalo turned and charged. The horse reared. Custer fired and felled his horse with a head shot. The buffalo ambled off, and Custer was left stranded on the plains. A detail of the 7th later came along and rescued him.[24]

The Custers were nomadic during the next few years, leaving Fort Hays for Fort Leavenworth in October 1869. Custer took a brief leave to return east, visiting Sheridan in Chicago, the mayor of Detroit, and family in Michigan. When he rejoined Libbie at Fort Leavenworth in January, they enjoyed a social life of dances, dinners, and parlor games at the outpost. A bloody summer intruded on the revelry, and Custer moved troops between Forts Hays and Harker, oversaw patrols, and even led a detachment in mid-July. But the raids continued.[25]

That fall, the couple returned to Fort Leavenworth, but Custer soon was on the move again, turning a sixty-day furlough in January 1870 into a nearly six-month leave, during which he chased dollars instead of Indians or buffalo. He traveled to New York and spent time among the financial elite, trying to find investors for a Colorado mining venture. The fiscal dignitaries included John Jacob Astor, who invested $10,000. Custer and a partner offered two thousand shares at $50 per share, Custer himself subscribing $35,000 that he did not have. After several years of mining and assaying, the enterprise collapsed. But it had provided Custer the chance to court the Eastern elite, including *New York Tribune* publisher Horace Greeley and *New York Times* editor Whitlaw Reid. In September 1871, he returned to duty, reporting to Elizabethtown, Kentucky, where with Company A of the 7th Cavalry he was assigned to inspect and buy horses, duty the adventurous Custer surely loathed. He and Libbie were there for about a year and a half, during which Custer wrote for *Galaxy*, the first article appearing in May 1872.[26]

In a break from the Kentucky drudgery, in January 1872, Custer went on his best-known buffalo hunt. He and Buffalo Bill Cody were guides to Grand Duke Alexei Alexandrovich of Russia. The hunting party killed twenty to thirty buffalo on the duke's January 14 birthday hunt. They killed fifteen more the next day, which ended with an Indian dance and powwow, provided by Custer's scouts for the duke's entertainment. The vacation itinerary next included a hunt near Denver. On the morning of January 20, Custer escorted the duke ahead of the hunt party, and the duke killed another buffalo. Then, on to Topeka, Kansas. When they spotted buffalo from the train, they started firing. After the hunt ended, Custer continued to accompany the duke, posing for photographs in St. Louis, where Libbie joined them as they headed south, ending what was probably the most famous buffalo hunt in the history of the plains. The press again had found a great story in Custer, covering the hunt extensively and gilding the Custer image.[27]

DAKOTA TERRITORY

In February 1873, Sheridan assigned the 7th Cavalry to the Dakota Territory, where the Northern Pacific rail line was to run through land belonging to the Sioux, Cheyenne, and Arapaho. Custer, who found Reconstruction duty in the South rather dull, was ready for action. He and the 7th arrived in April 1873 at Camp Sturgis. In May, they headed for Fort Sully on the Missouri River, traveling over difficult terrain in a remote area with numerous stream crossings. After arriving at Fort Sully, Custer court-martialed several soldiers for desertion and other crimes. This sparked new conflict between Custer and Benteen, whom Custer accused of violating orders concerning alertness and efficiency. Benteen successfully defended himself but effectively took himself out of any substantive role in an upcoming Yellowstone expedition. The incident only exacerbated the ill will between them. On May 30, Custer and his command continued up the Missouri River.[28]

The court-martial of the cavalrymen probably was a matter of several things—the hard life of the frontier, the difficult march in particular, alcohol as a common outlet for the dullness of the days, and the fact that recruits often were uneducated, poorly trained, and ill disciplined. On June 9, Custer and the 7th arrived at the small outpost of Fort Rice. Life was no more interesting there, and discipline problems continued. Perhaps to impress upon the men the gravity of the mission, Custer even had his brother Tom and another officer arrested for disobeying orders. After they were confined to quarters, they were assigned to the rear of troops for the rest of the expedition. That would have been especially uncomfortable on the dry, dusty march because they would have been in the thick of the dust cloud kicked up by mules, wagons, and horses. They were released from the onerous spot later in the march. The expedition left Fort Rice on June 20 with nineteen infantry companies, ten companies of the 7th Cavalry, six hundred cattle, almost three hundred wagons, and nearly two thousand horses and mules, stretching for miles across the prairie. The sizable expedition also included more than three hundred civilians, including teamsters, scientists, and engineers.[29]

The first Yellowstone expedition in 1871 was to help determine the route of the Northern Pacific Railroad from Bismarck, Dakota Territory, to Bozeman, Montana Territory. The 1873 expedition would follow roughly the same route but go farther into Montana Territory, with Colonel David Stanley in command of the 79 officers and 1,451 men, including Custer and his 7th Cavalry. It was an important expedition, and Custer had a good time, as he led daily hunts for buffalo, deer, and other big game and rode ahead to scout the route. Custer's tendency to be gone for many hours away from Stanley's authority caused tension between the two. A little more than a week into the expedition, Stanley wrote to his wife that so far he had no trouble from Custer, "but I have seen enough of him to convince me that he is a cold-blooded, untruthful and unprincipled man." Stanley's alcoholism also flavored his assessment of Custer, who wrote Libbie that Stanley was "acting very badly, drinking." Custer was not easy to work with, either, and Stanley eventually left Custer alone to a near-independent command. Custer seemed to presume that as commander of the cavalry, he was free to come and go from the main column as he pleased, whether to hunt or scout. That rankled Stanley. A few days after he wrote his wife about the "unprincipled" cavalryman, he confronted Custer for leaving the main column, which had become bogged down after a week of rain. While the command attempted to fashion a crossing of a flooded stream, Custer took the cavalry miles into the country, then sent a message back to Stanley asking for food and forage. Stanley ordered Custer's return and told him "never to presume to make another movement without orders." He wrote his wife that it had to be done, as Custer was presuming to take command and Stanley had to deal with the arrogance.[30]

A week later, a drunken Stanley again accosted Custer, this time over a civilian's use of a government horse. That civilian was a brother-in-law of Lieutenant James Calhoun, who was Custer's brother-in-law. Custer did not back down. Instead, he asked Stanley how it was that he allowed a *New York Times* reporter a mount. Stanley ordered Custer arrested and put at the rear of the column for the next day. A few days later, Stanley sobered up and released Custer from arrest. The two apparently made up. Stanley was not the only one with whom Custer had difficulties. The expedition also highlighted Custer's dark side—as he was harsh, demanding, impulsive, and arrogant in his command, to the point that on occasion officers even excused themselves from the evening campfire when Custer showed up.[31]

Other than the run-in with Stanley, Custer enjoyed the expedition, complementing his scouting and hunting with new hobbies of taxidermy and paleontology. They reached the Yellowstone River on July 15. A few weeks later, Custer and about ninety soldiers were attacked. Only about a half dozen warriors were trying to drive off the cavalrymen's horses, so Custer, brother Tom, and about twenty soldiers took off in pursuit. After a few miles, they found they had been drawn into an ambush and were surrounded by about three hundred Sioux. The balance of the cavalry force arrived a few minutes later. Custer and the men took cover in timber and a dry riverbank, exchanging fire with the Indians for about three hours. With ammunition running low, Custer charged, surprising the Sioux, who fled. Three soldiers were killed. It was Custer's biggest fight since the Washita. On August 11, the battle erupted anew, involving about 450 cavalrymen and 500 Sioux, who were firing from bluffs across the Yellowstone onto the encamped troops. Some Indians swam their ponies across the flooded stream to flank the camp from both sides, and Custer counterattacked.[32]

Much in keeping with the tactics that had worked in the previous fight, Custer took the initiative, did the unexpected, and thwarted the Sioux, who quit the attack with the arrival of infantry. Custer figured Indian casualties at forty in the two battles. He lost four killed and four wounded. Newspapers picked up on the story, maintaining Custer's celebrity. Though Custer came through in each case, he made some missteps. In the first, he was moving on his own, with a concealed enemy nearby, and was nearly cut off from escape. In the second battle, Custer had ignored a scout's warning of Sioux gathering for an attack. Custer's rendition naturally turned both events into a sporting adventure. He wrote that some civilians in the command "enjoyed themselves immensely" in the August 11 skirmish and pronounced Indian fighting "the best sport in the world," which indicates that Custer failed to take the Sioux seriously. In his report, Custer wrote, "The Indians were made up of different bands of Sioux, principally Uncpapas [*sic*], the whole under the command of 'Sitting Bull,' who participated in the fight, and who for once has been taught a lesson he will not soon forget." Later histories also said Crazy Horse may have been in the fight, though the evidence is inconclusive. Either way, it was nice fertilizer for the mythology that sprouted after June 1876.[33]

The expedition returned to Fort Abraham Lincoln on September 21, 1873. Custer received orders that he would command the fort, still under construction, near Bismarck, Dakota Territory. Sherman telegraphed a welcome-back message to Custer, who was lauded by the Northern Pacific, the public, and the press. The *New York Times* and the *Army and Navy Journal* published Custer's expedition report, which the public loved. *Galaxy* asked for new articles. Though Custer had won his Indian-fighter reputation, the 1873 Yellowstone expedition was only his second direct fight with Indians. It may speak more to the lack of experience generally in the army in dealing with the Indians that Custer had gained such an outsize reputation from less than a decade of intermittent actions, only two of any substantial size, with some of the acclaim coming from his own hand, including *My Life on the Plains*, published while he was at Fort Abraham Lincoln. His postmortem reputation rose with his account titled "Battling the Sioux on the Yellowstone," another adventure story about the 1873 expedition, published in *Galaxy* in July 1876, shortly after Custer's death.[34]

Shortly after his return to Fort Abraham Lincoln, Custer journeyed to Monroe and in November brought Libbie back to the fort. It was a dull and cold winter, with little excitement until April 1874, when Indians drove off a herd of mules. Custer took all six companies in pursuit, leaving the fort undefended. After dark, Custer and his cavalry returned with the mules but no Indians. Sheridan, meanwhile, had been making plans for an outpost near the Black Hills in order to discourage Sioux raids into Nebraska and along travel routes in the region. The Black Hills were in territory granted the Sioux in the Fort Laramie Treaty of 1868, which permitted building railroads across the reservation if the Indians were consulted and paid. Neither side, though, worried about legal details. In June, Sheridan informed Custer that he would lead an expedition into the Black Hills to look for a fort site and check rumors of a gold strike.[35]

ON SACRED SOIL

Settlers and mining and lumber interests were pressuring the government to open up the Black Hills of the Dakota Territory. To the Sioux, it was sacred ground. To Sheridan, it was a center of Sioux power, so the army needed to control it. Sherman agreed, and Sheridan immediately selected Custer to head an expedition into the region. Custer probably had as much experience as anyone in Indian warfare, and he was well known to the public, which meant he would be good press for the military. The force included ten companies of the 7th Cavalry, two infantry companies, and seventy-five Indian scouts. In addition, the expedition included topographers and engineers for mapping the land and identifying a fort site. The inclusion of journalists from Chicago, New York, and Bismarck in the mission must have influenced the nature of the expedition. An Indian menace—which never materialized—was more appealing reading than agronomy and geography. Not surprisingly, the coverage became overwrought on occasion, with incessant anticipation of Indian fights, the discovery of a new Eden, and the possibility of finding gold. The coverage was akin to the modern-day hokum of celebrity outdoorsmen taking fellow celebrities to exotic locales to hunt and fish, scale mountains, and put themselves on the brink of mortal existence in the wilds, all in range of a regiment of camera and audio crews. [36]

The expedition left Fort Abraham Lincoln on July 2, 1874, for the two-month-long, nearly nine-hundred-mile trek. Custer expected Indian trouble, but not until the end of July did he come across a village of five lodges and twenty-seven Indians. Prospectors discovered flecks of gold, which set off a frenzy of panning among the troops. No fortunes were made, but it was enough gold to generate headlines. By the end of 1875, an estimated fifteen thousand miners had descended on the Black Hills, in spite of a geologist with the expedition declaring that he had seen no gold. Custer reported that the discoveries were small but in "paying quantities." With his return from the Black Hills, Custer resumed command at Fort Abraham Lincoln, where he and Libbie spent the next winter. In September 1875, Custer and Libbie took leave, during which she visited relatives in Michigan and he went to New York, where he again pursued speculative investments in mining and railroads. They returned to Fort Abraham Lincoln in March 1876. [37]

TOWARD THE LITTLE BIGHORN

In December 1875, Interior Secretary Zachariah Chandler decreed that tribes were to report to reservations by the end of January 1876. Custer was east at the time, and his departmental commander, Brigadier General Alfred H. Terry, postponed preparations for a campaign until Custer's return. Weather and politics delayed things, with a blizzard in March and Custer's foray into Washington politics. That brief but telling chapter in Custer's life in 1876 showed he was a better soldier than politician.

In March, Congressman Heister Clymer asked Custer to appear before the House Committee on Expenditures to testify about corruption and kickbacks from Indian-post traders. Custer was testifying against not only Secretary of War William Belknap but also the Grant administration. Belknap was accused of selling post traderships. With evidence of guilt accumulating, he resigned on March 2, nearly a month before Custer arrived. But Clymer wanted to indict more Grant administration figures. Custer already had criticized the corruption and, in earlier activities, had created ties with leading Democratic voices, including the *New York*

Herald and the *New York World*. Both newspapers were critical of Grant. With his Democratic ties and knowledge of the military outposts, Custer would be a good witness against the Republican administration.

As though that were not enough, Custer even testified against the president's brother, Orvil Grant, regarding the sales of post traderships. Though notable, his testimony was more gossip than fact. The *New York Times*, a Republican newspaper, said Custer was as "full of information as an egg is of meat, but somehow it is only hearsay and gossip, and no witnesses appear to corroborate it. If this sort of thing goes too far, the Democrats, if they should have the next Administration, may not, after all, make him a Brigadier-General." Grant relieved Custer of command of the upcoming Yellowstone campaign, a move that apparently surprised Custer. Despite Custer's entreaties and loitering in the White House for hours, Grant refused to meet with him. Custer's mentor, Sheridan, also was infuriated by the testimony. But he knew Custer was the man for the Yellowstone job. Pressured by Sheridan, Sherman, and Terry, Grant finally reinstated Custer but gave him command only of the 7th Cavalry, not the expedition, which went to Terry.[38]

They were heading into nearly unmapped territory with poorly trained troopers, some having never been on a horse and many having had very little practice with their rifles. So they were, in many cases, ill-disciplined, untrained cavalrymen who were lousy shots and poor horsemen. Even the horses were suspect, many having never been used in battle. On May 10, Terry and Custer arrived at Fort Abraham Lincoln and left with the column a week later. Benteen commanded the 7th Cavalry's left wing and Major Marcus Reno the right. Custer was with the advance guard, and Terry was with two battalions for building bridges and roads. A freak snowstorm hit the force on June 1, and they made it into Montana Territory two days later.

Two weeks later, at the mouth of the Tongue River, the force found the remains of a cavalryman, perhaps from the 1873 expedition, who had been tortured and burned. On June 18, Reno reported from near the Rosebud and Yellowstone rivers that he had found an Indian trail. Terry, Custer, Reno, and Colonel John Gibbon met downstream from the mouth of the Rosebud, where Custer criticized Reno for not pursuing the Indians. But Reno provided important information: The Indians were up the Rosebud or in the Little Bighorn valley. They did not know that, as they spoke, General George Crook was fighting the Indians farther up the

Rosebud. The next morning, Terry ordered Custer to go all the way up the Rosebud and cross the Wolf Mountains to the Little Bighorn in pursuit of the Indians whose trail Reno had found. Terry expected the escape route for the Indians would be in the vicinity of the Bighorn River, so he and Gibbon moved west to that area. Custer had more than six hundred men, including civilians and scouts, in his column when he moved out on June 22. For three days, the column moved up the Rosebud, finding abandoned campsites along the way and evidence of a sun-dance ceremony. On June 24, Crow scouts told Custer the Sioux had gone east over the Wolf Mountains. Custer did not go further south. Having found the trail, he cut over the mountains. [39]

8

CROSSING THE RIVER

The war horse is a vain hope for victory, and by its great might it cannot save.

—Psalm 33:17[1]

On the morning of June 26, 1876, the Montana Column, led by Colonel John Gibbon and accompanied by General Alfred H. Terry and a portion of his Dakota Column, crossed a divide and turned southeast into the valley of the Little Bighorn River. The column had begun moving south from the Yellowstone on the afternoon of June 24. After advancing up Tullock's Creek, where Terry and Gibbon had expected to hear from Custer, the column turned west into the Bighorn River valley, coming near the river about midnight after a hard march. During the night they had seen a distant light described as "so faint that it was looked upon as atmospheric phenomena of some kind. In the morning the place of the light was taken as a column of smoke." They might have been the Children of Israel on their way through the desert following a beckoning pillar of fire ascending from a flaming cresset beyond the dry brown hills. Moving upstream, the column crossed to the east bank of the Little Bighorn at about noon and rested in the early summer torpor.[2]

From the high bluffs above the river later that afternoon, horsemen under the command of Second Lieutenant Charles F. Roe of the 2nd U.S. Cavalry spotted mounted Indians almost motionless on a ridge across the valley in what looked like a skirmish line. Some distance behind the Indians, guidons snapped in the wind as about sixty cavalrymen aligned in a smart formation. This puzzled Roe and another trooper, who later recalled, "There was an indefinable something in their movements that did not appear altogether natural." Were these Custer's men from the 7th Cavalry, or George Crook's column, bringing in prisoners from what appeared to be a village in retreat, or were the blue-clad horsemen an army of phantoms? A sergeant and two soldiers moved forward cautiously to investigate and, with rising horror, realized the troopers were no mirage but corporeal Indians in blue uniforms, who commenced firing. Roe's party withdrew and reported to Terry, who already was uneasy because of reports from Crow scouts under First Lieutenant James H. Bradley that Custer's men had been killed. Although some still thought Roe must have seen elements of Custer's command, Terry ordered the column to bivouac and braced for a possible attack. The night was quiet, however, and the troopers awoke the next morning to find the blue riders, whether friends or imposters, had departed. [3]

As the column resumed its march along the west bank of the river, it came to the smoldering remains of a recently abandoned village littered with cavalry debris, dead and dying horses, the bodies of several Indian warriors, and the badly burned severed heads of three white men hanging from a pole. Each subsequent bend of the river revealed more bodies among the gutted Sioux and Cheyenne encampments that had stretched for several miles. On the bluffs across the river, they saw what appeared to be the carcasses of a slaughtered herd of buffalo. Bradley and a squadron of mounted infantry rode down from the bluffs to confirm what the Crow scouts had told them the previous day. The lieutenant approached Gibbon and Terry and told them he had counted what was left of almost two hundred corpses, the carnage spread across more than a mile of rolling and rutted terrain. One of them, he thought, was Custer. [4]

THE SCENE OF THE CRIME

A reader new to a study of the Battle of the Little Bighorn can expect to be overwhelmed by speculative hypotheses and unanswered questions. Like the battlefield landscape itself, the information is alternately barren and lush, the view expansive and limited. The crime scene has proven fertile ground for the imaginations of historians, journalists, novelists, filmmakers, and tourists. There never has been, nor will be, a final harvest of evidence. Much of it is gone. On the other hand, as Robert M. Utley declared, "One problem is not too little evidence but too much."[5]

Questions arose from the beginning. The possible answers have multiplied ever since Bradley came down from the hills to make his report. As with any mystery, the answers largely must remain conjectural, reflecting the spirit of the time in which they were proffered. In 1951, Quentin Reynolds could conclude his account of the Little Bighorn for young readers with the story of the wounded claybank gelding Comanche found wandering on the battlefield. "Only Comanche knew the real story of Custer's Last Stand," Reynolds wrote. "But Comanche never said a word." Of course, "the real story" could not have been told by a talking horse any more than it could have been told by the hundreds of human witnesses who saw some portion of the battle, or claimed they had, and lived to tell the tale, or their version of it. And, unlike Comanche, many talked to anyone willing to listen.[6]

The modern mind-set brings to the story expectations conditioned by the language and narrative tropes of criminal forensic investigations made popular by mass media. Terry, Gibbon, and the men of the Montana Column had come upon something very much like a historical crime scene but with few scientific tools at their disposal. There was no yellow police barricade tape to delineate and secure this scene, so the first investigators had to deal with a corrupted environment. As Bradley reported, the corpses already were mutilated and would be further disturbed by natural predators. The soldiers attempted to bury the bloated bodies of their comrades as best they could, but the dry soil yielded little to the few entrenching tools that could be located.

The sergeant in charge of the burial detail recalled that arms and legs often protruded from the makeshift graves. The dead, like the news and the myth, would not be buried easily or completely accounted for—ever. A total of 204 bodies, many of them unidentified, were interred in the area where Custer's battalion had fought. Other remains were located years later, and some never were found. Any attempt to examine the battle site for clues as to what had happened was further compromised by soldiers and horses tramping across the fields, along with the removal of artifacts and evidence. A detachment of the 2nd Cavalry looked for Indians in the Bighorn Mountains but found the suspects had evaded them. The soldiers were not even sure who or how many they were looking for.

Estimates of the number of Indian warriors engaged expanded from fifteen hundred to nine thousand within a few years.[7]

The testimony of witnesses was suspect from the start. Custer's two primary subordinates had something to protect, if not to cover up, and they had not been on good terms with their commander. In 1879, Marcus Reno appeared before an army court of inquiry in Chicago, which functioned as something like a grand jury. Twenty-three witnesses, including Reno and Frederick Benteen, were called to give testimony, after which the court took no action against Reno. Nor were Custer's superiors keen to assume responsibility for the disaster. Indians, when questioned later by journalists, told contradictory stories. They had no immunity and had every incentive to shape their memory of events, which in any case reflected an oral culture with its own standards of truth. "Indian testimony is difficult to use," according to Utley. "It is personal, episodic, and maddeningly detached from time and space, or sequence and topography. It also suffers from a language barrier often aggravated by incompetent interpreters, from the cultural gulf between questioner and respondent, and from assumptions of the interviewer not always in accord with reality." Early in the twentieth century, scholars began to revisit what the Indians had to say, but the popular culture was slow to respond to accounts that challenged the heroic narrative. As late as 1951, Reynolds could get away with forgetting there were Indian witnesses. The biggest piece of physical evidence was a stuffed war horse.[8]

The "crime" remained a cold case until 1934, when Frederic F. Van de Water's indictment of Custer was published a year after Libbie Custer's death. With assistance from influential friends, Libbie had so controlled the memory of her husband that her death broke the seal on the Custer files and reopened the debate. "Elizabeth Custer would be blamed for keeping the truth about her husband and the Little Bighorn hidden or obscured during her lengthy lifetime," wrote journalist David Hardin. "But what was the truth?" That was yet to be decided. Van de Water had revived a counternarrative, prompting new evaluations of the evidence beginning in the 1930s and 1940s. Professional historians and geographers entered the debate by sifting evidence and broadening the investigation. New archeological, anthropological, ethnological, and psychological voices were introduced. The Indian perspective was reevaluated. The axis of the story shifted. If something like a crime had been committed, it no longer was clear who was the perpetrator and who was the victim. The idea seemed to take hold that the mystery eventually could be "solved" through more intensive crime scene investigations, an accretion of facts, and new evidence that would turn up, inspiring a flood of Little Bighorn books and articles, each claiming new insights and affirming there was still more to be learned. [9]

THE VALLEY OF DEATH

With the first intimations of dawn threading through the swelling clouds behind him, Second Lieutenant Charles Varnum climbed to a double-peaked ridge in the Wolf Mountains and strained to see anything to the northwest in the shallow Little Bighorn valley slowly becoming visible in the receding night shadows. The vantage point, near a sheltered pocket where Custer's chief of scouts had slept for no more than an hour after arriving in deepest darkness, faintly reminded Varnum of the Crow's Nest, a mountain aerie at the northern edge of West Point overlooking the Hudson River. The name fit this mountain venue, as Crow raiding parties concealed their horses in a hidden fissure when scouting the Sioux villages that had violated the tribe's ancient lands. Now the Crow, Arikara, and civilian scouts who had accompanied Varnum told him to look for a pony herd moving about on a distant plateau. He still saw nothing in the diminishing shadows but trusted the eyes of his scouts and sent two Arikara messengers to alert Custer at his encampment on Davis Creek some five miles away that the Sioux encampment had been found. [10]

Custer, a blithe spirit fulsome in mirth on the last morning of his life, mounted a horse bereft of a saddle after he received Varnum's report and rode through the camp to alert his troopers of an imminent departure. He reached the mountains sometime after 9 a.m., riding ahead of the column, which was sequestered in a nearby ravine while Varnum led Custer to the Crow's Nest. At first he could see nothing of the huge Indian camp his scouts claimed was hidden behind the distant bluffs. Later, by some accounts, Custer, with the aid of borrowed field glasses, thought he saw the pony herd and some tepees that indicated the presence of a village. Perhaps he convinced himself he saw something. He expected to find an encampment on the lower Little Bighorn, the river the Indians called the Greasy Grass, so there it must be, less than fifteen miles away. His discretionary orders from Terry had been to follow the Rosebud farther south, as much as 125 miles, before crossing the Wolf Mountains toward the upper Little Bighorn, where Terry thought the Indians most likely would be found. By attacking from the south, Custer could then drive the Indians against Gibbon's infantry column advancing up the Bighorn and the Little Bighorn from the Yellowstone. Gibbon's last words were, "Now Custer, don't be greedy, but wait for us." Custer laughed and replied, "No, I will not." A perplexing answer in view of subsequent events. [11]

The orders presumed the Indians were on the Little Bighorn and had not turned in another direction. That was still a possibility, but Custer had followed the converging Indian trails after marching about sixty miles down the Rosebud and was about to cross the mountain divide to drop into the Little Bighorn valley. He had expected to wait another day before attacking the camp, but first scouts and then his brother Tom persuaded him that Indians had spotted the advancing column. He feared the Indians would scatter if he waited. He intended to attack on June 25. There was no point in sending a scout down Tullock's Creek, barely visible in the distance from the Crow's Nest, to look for Indians and report to Terry now that Custer had left the Rosebud, nor were the Indians in that direction. The Indians were in front of Custer, not closer to the Yellowstone. And he was certain the 7th Cavalry alone could handle them. [12]

Custer mounted a sorrel thoroughbred called Vic, sparing his favorite war horse Dandy, which he had ridden hard during the morning. Benteen's company, having affirmed its readiness, won the honor of leading the column's ascent to the divide, Custer trailing behind. Finding Benteen's pace too rapid, however, Custer galloped ahead with his staff to arrest the column's progress as it crossed the spine of the hills, then halted it shortly after noon in a narrow canyon along the middle fork of Sundance (later Reno) Creek to map out his plan of attack. [13]

Three companies comprised Reno's battalion: A, under Captain Myles Moylan; G, under First Lieutenant Donald McIntosh; and M, under Captain Thomas H. French. Benteen's battalion also consisted of three companies: H, under Benteen; D, under Captain Thomas B. Weir; and K, under First Lieutenant Edward S. Godfrey.

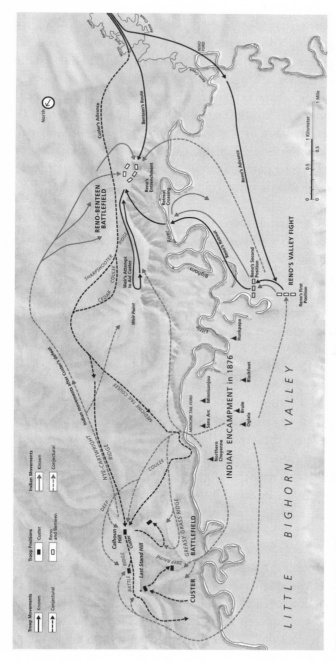

Map 8.1. The Little Bighorn battlefield. The general contours of the battle are among the best known in American history. But many details are a mystery and probably will remain so. (University of Tennessee Cartographic Services, based on map from National Park Service)

Custer's battalion had two wings. Captain Myles W. Keogh commanded the right wing's three companies: I, under Keogh; C, under Second Lieutenant Henry M. Harrington; and L, under First Lieutenant James Calhoun, Custer's brother-in-law. Captain George Yates commanded the left wing's two companies: F, under Yates, and E, under First Lieutenant Algernon E. Smith. Captain Tom Custer served as aide-de-camp to his older brother. Their younger brother Boston and nephew Autie Reed came along as civilians. Custer's adjutant was First Lieutenant William Cooke. The pack train was commanded by First Lieutenant Edward G. Mathey and escorted by Company B under Captain Thomas M. McDougall.

The approximate strength was Custer's battalion, 220; Reno's battalion, 140, plus some 35 scouts, guides, and interpreters; Benteen's battalion, 118; and the pack train, 131, including civilian packers. [14]

Benteen was to take his battalion off to the left across a series of bluffs to prevent any Indians he might find from escaping to the southeast. If the bluffs were clear, Benteen was to return to the main column quickly. Reno was to proceed down the left bank of the meandering creek while Custer's battalion moved along the right bank, both wings expecting to converge on one of the outlying villages that had been spotted from the Crow's Nest. Soon the three battalions were in motion through the sagebrush hills under an unforgiving sun. Some four miles from the Little Bighorn, Custer's scouts came upon a hastily evacuated compound with a single remaining tepee containing the body of a Sans Arc warrior mortally wounded a week earlier during the fight with Crook at the Rosebud. A party of mourners, who apparently had just left the area, was returning to the main camp. Custer, angered by the possibility that the Indians had begun to scatter, ordered the lodge burned as Reno's column approached. Benteen, meanwhile, had been following Custer's orders to extend his reconnaissance farther down the bluffs and had yet to rejoin the main column. Seen through the refulgent blue eyes of Benteen, the scouting mission was pointless, and he dawdled. Custer may have sent him off as a small accommodation to Terry's discretionary orders, however. [15]

Just then a rider on an ebony steed was seen waving his hat from atop a hill not far from the Lone Tepee. The interpreter Fred Gerard had seen for himself the dust clouds the Crow scouts had been reporting and shouted, "Here are your Indians, running like devils." Perhaps his fervor outweighed the limitations of his observation, for he could have seen from that vantage no more than the fleeing Sans Arcs, not the larger encampment.[16]

Custer next sent Reno and the recalcitrant Arikara scouts, hesitant to move without cavalry support, in pursuit of whatever was in front of them, "on the jump," as he put it, some two and a half miles away. Varnum, too, had been on high ground. Reporting to Custer as he saw Reno riding off, Varnum said the entire valley was "full of Indians." Custer sent Varnum to join Reno, as Custer's own battalion trotted behind. As Custer came within two miles of the Little Bighorn, he learned that about fifty warriors had been spotted on the bluffs to Custer's right. Reno, farther ahead, was not going to catch them. He was near where Sundance Creek met its north fork, no more than a mile from the Little Bighorn, in position to engage the main village across the river. Accordingly, Cooke and Keogh brought word to Reno of Custer's instructions to do just that, assuring the major he would be supported by the entire command. Just before three o'clock, Reno's scouts and troopers splashed across the winding river, which was about fifty feet wide and fairly shallow, climbed the west bank, passed through stands of cottonwoods and clusters of bullberry bushes, and moved toward the village in columns of four.[17]

Reno advanced across a broad grassy plateau toward a dust cloud some two miles from a village he could not see. Indians, in considerable numbers, were barely visible to his scouts, and Reno assumed they were coming toward his battalion. He sent messages to report the situation to Custer, whose troopers continued advancing slowly toward the bluffs in columns of four above the eastern bank of the river. Custer still was unable to see the village until he reached the high ridgeline.[18]

When more of the valley did come into view from what later was called Sharpshooter Ridge, Custer and his men must have been awestruck. Across the river below them and stretching about two miles to the northwest was part of an immense village. Hundreds of blanched tepees were clustered along the river, beyond which was a herd of ponies so thickly covering the grassy hills that guessing their number was like counting buffalo on the open range. Custer, lynx-eyed with predatory anticipation, ascended a higher precipice for an even better look through his borrowed binoculars. Trumpeter John Martin, who survived the subsequent battle, was near. Custer saw a dry valley striated with deep ravines, dry gullies, and the ephemeral watercourses gouged into coulees over centuries by the river's vagrancy. In the village, however, all was torpor. Instead of warriors rushing to the defense of the village, Custer could see only women and children about, along with a few dogs and ponies, and thought the warriors must be sleeping in the tents. Custer muttered "Got them this time," then waved his hat and shouted the news to his men. [19]

The size of the village Custer saw from the ridge is contested. As in the Civil War, commanders in the Indian Wars tended to exaggerate the forces arrayed against them. Estimating the scope of an Indian encampment spread out along a twisting river and obscured by timber and undergrowth was especially difficult. Each Lakota band within the encampment had its own village circle. Nearest Reno were the Hunkpapa, Minneconjous, Sans Arc, and Oglala, with smaller groups of Brulé, Blackfoot, Yankton, and Santee, each with their own leaders, customs, and councils. The Northern Cheyenne were at the opposite, or west, end of the camp. The population of the camp might have reached seven thousand, including two thousand warriors, with perhaps twelve hundred tepees and hundreds of wickiups, the temporary shelters used by young men. [20]

Utley noted that everyone on the expedition "worried not about how to defeat the Indians but how to catch them before they discovered the soldiers and fled in all directions." [21] By remaining concentrated rather than scattering, according to historian Larry Sklenar, the Indians gained a huge numerical advantage, as much as ten to one, over each of Custer's three battalions. Custer knew he had faced down larger Confederate forces during the Civil War but never anything like ten-to-one odds with a divided command, so little military intelligence, and a decidedly feeble communications system. Custer may even have anticipated problems with corralling his opponent. When he fought John Mosby's men, Custer also usually had the numerical advantage but was frustrated with being unable to catch the rangers, whose guerilla-style hit-and-run tactics were standard warfare for the plains tribes. At the Little Bighorn, as at the Washita, however, the warriors had to defend a village of women and children, who could be rounded up as hostages. Custer had boasted that his 7th Cavalry could defeat any number of Indians. He liked his chances. [22]

RENO'S RETREAT

The three companies that comprised Reno's attacking force began to deploy in a battle line across the plateau, horsemen riding nearly abreast and building speed to a full gallop. In the Hunkpapa and Blackfoot camps, women, children, and the elderly began to flee toward the other end of the camp, while hastily mounted warriors scrambled to meet the attackers. A small number of riders crisscrossing the perimeter of the village stirred up a protective cloud of dust, concealing the dispersal of the noncombatants. The dust cloud also concealed other warriors rushing up a coulee to higher ground on Reno's left flank. Ahead of the column, warriors emerged from Shoulder Blade Creek, a declivity about five feet deep. If some of the onrushing cavalry horses tumbled into the creek, the charge would be broken. As it was, some horses already were causing problems. About a half mile from the village, Reno called for the battalion to dismount and form a skirmish line. "Our horses were scenting danger before we dismounted, and several at this point became unmanageable and started straight for the open among the Indians, carrying their helpless riders with them," Private William C. Slaper recalled in 1920.[23]

Dismounting effectively reduced the size of the attacking column by 25 percent. One man designated as horse holder among every four riders took charge of three additional mounts and led them to a glade in a loop of the winding river to the right while the remaining troopers marched ahead, then knelt or lay down to fire their carbines. At first the firing by the newer recruits was "wild and at random," as Moylan described it, while Varnum recalled many soldiers "shooting right up in the air." Most of the Sioux had been riding well out of range, but after about fifteen minutes some five hundred charged the skirmish line and were repulsed. Yet more of the warriors creeping around the flanks had worked their way to the rear of the skirmishers. When Reno learned of the apparent movement, he ordered the troopers to move toward the woods along the river, where they would find an improvised defensive line, ammunition in saddlebags, and their horses. Reno and his men fought on, as more Indians from the village moved through the riparian glade.[24]

Warriors rallied by Crazy Horse, by some accounts, charged across the field from the hills to the west. At some point, almost surrounded, the troopers began to scatter. Reno, with no sign of aid from either Custer or Benteen and his skirmish line crumbling, began looking for an escape route while shouting orders most of the men never heard. The Arikara scout Bloody Knife was near Reno when Indians from the rear fired a volley of shots, blowing off the back of the scout's head and spraying bone, brain matter, and blood into Reno's face. The major, unnerved and well lubricated with the liquor he had been swigging from a flask during the afternoon, was heard to yell, "Any of you men who wish to make your escape, draw your revolvers and follow me!"[25]

Reno reformed what was left of the three companies and led them back to the prairie while wounded men and those without horses did what they could to get away or find concealment. The warriors on the flanks cut down the retreating riders in a crossfire with bullets, arrows, and war clubs or flailed them with pony whips when they could get close enough, then set prairie fires to smoke out or engulf those hiding in the woods. Moving through the trees along the riverbank, warriors forced the column upriver over cratered terrain, burrowed and aerated by prairie dogs. When their horses stumbled on the uneven ground, troopers were pitched from their mounts and slain. One ghostly rider, an arrow protruding from the back of his head, was borne flaccid and senseless across the prairie before a second projectile finally knocked him from his runaway horse. Near the river, Lieutenant McIntosh was circled by two dozen riders, pulled from his mount, and riddled with bullets. His G Company nearly was wiped out. Unable to reach the original crossing point because of increasing concentrations of warriors from his right, Reno swung left toward a buffalo crossing cut through a steep embankment about a half mile from the wooded glade.[26]

The Little Bighorn at the improvised ford ran at a depth of four feet. Horses and men pinched through the gap and plunged into the stream while warriors on the bluffs fired into their massed ranks or set upon them with knives as the soldiers flailed in the water. The bodies of cavalrymen floated off in the fast-flowing current through eddies of blood. Those who managed to ride across or swim the forty-foot-wide river had to wedge through a yard-wide V-shaped gorge and then face a daunting, slippery ascent up a high bank. Varnum and French tried to rally the men, but it was too late as retreat gave way to panic. Reno splashed across, covered a margin of flat ground, and climbed a ravine to a bluff some two hundred feet above the river. Thirty-five soldiers, three scouts, and two civilians were dead, and about twenty were missing. Seven wounded men rode, climbed, or were dragged to the summit clinging to their horses' stirrups.

Neither Reno nor Moylan seemed capable of bringing order out of the confusion on the ridge until Second Lieutenant Luther Hare shouted, "If we've got to die, let's die like men!"[27]

BENTEEN'S ARRIVAL

As he neared the junction of the two forks of Sundance Creek about a mile from the Little Bighorn, Benteen saw smoke rising from the valley, raising the probability that Custer and Reno were burning the village, the battle effectively over, while Benteen's column had been on its feckless six-mile quest for fleeing Indians on the southern bluffs. Returning to the Sundance Creek trail, Benteen had seen the dust from the pack train approaching. The weary horses and men needed water, and Benteen obliged, taking his time at the swampy oasis the men called the Morass. Chided by Custer earlier in the day for setting too fast a pace, Benteen had been in no hurry to return to the main trail and tarried at the Morass beyond what the impatient Captain Weir could countenance. As thirsty mules from the train approached the watering hole, Weir, eager to find out what had befallen his friend Custer, had his company on the move, with Benteen falling in behind him and quickening the pace.[28]

Soon after the column passed the still-smoldering Lone Tepee, Sergeant Daniel Kanipe galloped by, bearing Custer's order to McDougall to bring the pack train to the high ground without stopping to fix loose packs. The sergeant told Benteen that Custer wanted him to come up as fast as he could. Custer then rode down the line shouting, "We've got them, boys!"[29]

Soon Martin rode up to Benteen, who was at that point ahead of Weir's company, and handed him instructions from Custer that Cooke had copied in a notebook: "Benteen. Come on. Big Village. Be Quick. Bring Packs. WW. Cooke. PS bring pacs." Martin told Benteen that when he last had seen Custer, the battalion was galloping down a ravine toward the Little Bighorn. On his way to find Benteen, the trumpeter had passed Boston Custer, on a fresh horse, riding to join his brothers, and farther along the trail he had seen Reno's command fighting in the valley. Benteen later said Martin told him the Indians were "skedaddling" in front of Custer. When Weir rode up, Benteen handed him Cooke's note, professing perplexity. How, he asked, was he to be quick while waiting for, and then bringing, the packs? Did he mean ammunition boxes? And why were they urgently needed if, as Martin affirmed, the Indians were in flight? [30]

When the reproachful, ruminative, and sometimes phlegmatic Benteen saw the smoke and clouds of dust, then the panicky soldiers in the valley running for their lives in front of hundreds of mounted Indians and Reno, his skull wrapped in a red bandana, riding desperately toward him, he anticipated unwelcome news ahead and soon had it. "For God's sake, Benteen, halt your command and help me," Reno sputtered. "I've lost half my men. We are whipped." [31]

The spare hilltop where Reno's demoralized command had gathered, although poorly situated for defense and exposed to snipers, at least offered a reprieve from the carnage along the river. Nevertheless, a kind of madness seemed to be afflicting many, beginning with the crapulous Reno, who was firing a revolver at Indians one thousand yards away, and the exhausted and blubbering Varnum, who took random shots with a borrowed Springfield rifle. Horrified troopers peering into the valley below could see their comrades being scalped and mutilated. Some few survivors still were clawing their way up the hill. Benteen and others grumbled that Custer had abandoned them, reprising the Major Elliott affair at the Washita. But down in the valley they could see warriors rushing toward the other end of the village. Some, like Weir, Varnum, and McDougall, heard the distant sound of what Varnum called "fearful firing." Reno and Benteen testified they heard intermittent volleys, and neither was interested in leading troops in that direction while fending off attacks on the hill. [32]

During a lull in the fighting, Reno set off with a platoon to try to find his adjutant, Second Lieutenant Benjamin H. Hodgson, leaving Benteen in command of the remaining 350 men on hill. Hodgson had been killed on the riverbank. Reno's party found his body but scurried back up the bluff when Indians fired on them. By the time Reno had returned about thirty minutes later, Weir and his second in command, Second Lieutenant Winfield Scott Edgerly, had determined to go to Custer's aid or at least find out what was going on at the other end of the valley. Reno, Benteen, and Moylan, however, told him he should remain on the hill with the command. If this was an order from Reno, Weir ignored it and headed off to the high ground to the north, later known as Sharpshooter Ridge. Edgerly, seeing Weir depart, assumed the captain had received permission from Reno and ordered D Company to mount up and follow. After the arrival of the pack train, Benteen led his companies and one of Reno's after Weir, soon followed by the rest of Reno's men, the pack train, and the more severely wounded being carried in horse blankets.[33]

From a vista between two peaks on a ridge, subsequently known as Weir Point, about a mile from Reno Hill, Weir and Sergeant James Flanagan could see part of the village and clouds of smoke and dust several miles distant. Weir saw indistinctly something that looked like cavalry guidons and what he thought were cavalrymen. Flanagan handed him binoculars. Weir saw Indians, and they were coming toward the ridge he was standing on. Edgerly and D Company were heading into a valley, unable to see the Indians advancing, and Weir waved them up to the ridge. From there, Edgerly could see many Indians riding around and firing at objects on the ground to the northwest. Varnum thought these objects were white rocks. He later learned he had seen naked bodies. Indians spotted and engaged D Company, which returned fire at long distance. About that time, Benteen reached the area and ordered a withdrawal. He deployed his companies in a skirmish line to support Weir and Edgerly and sent Godfrey's dismounted troops about three-quarters of a mile to the south to cover any assault coming up from the river. Under heavy fire, the cavalrymen on the ridges began to withdraw back toward Reno Hill before they were enveloped.[34]

Benteen had found slightly better defensive ground on Reno Hill within a shallow basin devoid of cover between two low ridges and steep bluffs to the west falling away to the river. Godfrey's twenty-two-man company covered the perimeter for vital minutes while the other troops moved into position. They reached the basin just before being overrun by hundreds of warriors. Heavy fighting continued until the protracted dusk yielded to darkness and brought a respite. The troopers did what they could to dig in and build up breastworks out of anything they could find. Given the overwhelming odds against them, the cavalrymen had suffered comparatively few casualties, a dozen dead and twenty-one wounded. Even with Springfield rifles, the Indians were poor shots. Benteen's company held the southernmost end of the line on a low ridge about a quarter mile from the northern perimeter. Assuming the Indians had broken off the attacks and withdrawn, he left the southern position exposed while his men rested.[35]

During the night, according to Benteen, Reno approached him about abandoning the wounded and marching the battalion to the Yellowstone.

Benteen claimed he told Reno he could not do that. Reno, by many accounts, was drunk, nursing grudges and ranting during the night. Some troopers managed to sleep, while the rest could see fires in the valley and hear drums, chanting, and a chorus of howling dogs. "We were terribly alone on that dangerous hilltop," recalled Private Charles Windolph, who lived until 1950. "We were a million miles from nowhere. And death was all around us."[36]

At first light the warriors resumed the attack. Benteen's exposed position drew fire from a ridge at the north end of the line, and his company took heavy casualties. The trooper lying next to Windolph was shot through the heart. Mounted troopers appeared in the faint light, raising hopes that Custer had returned save them. The abridgement of hope arrived with the dawn, as the cloaked riders were revealed to be Cheyenne and Lakota warriors. Fearing he might be overrun, Benteen persuaded Reno to move some men from French's troop to shore up Benteen's lines. Benteen also led a charge down a ravine filled with Indians, taking the offensive to keep the attackers off balance. Then Benteen sent four companies charging about fifty yards up the north ridge, scattering warriors who had been massing for an attack on Reno's lines. The companies returned without serious casualties. Reno pulled himself out of the rifle pit in which he had been cowering and led the foot charge.[37]

By late afternoon, combat had ended, and the Indians were on their way out of the valley in a column more than a half mile wide stretching for almost three miles. Behind them a screen of dust and smoke from grass fires rose over the prairie. "It was like some Biblical exodus; the Israelites moving into Egypt; a mighty tribe on the march," recalled Windolph. The cavalrymen moved cautiously down to the river, where man and beast could drink of the life-giving water that had been in such short supply on the ridge. Under the cover of darkness, a few men who had been concealed since the previous day's fighting crawled out of their hiding places among the trees along the river and rejoined their comrades.[38]

The next morning, scouts saw dust rising to the north. Fear that the Indians were returning gave way to cautious optimism when officers with field glasses identified what appeared to be a cavalry troop and not a faux column this time. Was it Custer? Crook? Terry and Gibbon? Two Arikara scouts accompanied by Hare and Second Lieutenant George D. Wallace rode bareback down the bluff to investigate. Terry told them Custer and his battalion had been found.[39]

CUSTER'S LAST FIGHT

By the time of Boston Custer's return two days earlier, Autie Custer had, by some accounts, moved down Medicine Tail Coulee to the Little Bighorn. His brother's report likely gave Custer hope tempered with concern. The mules were moving slowly over the rough terrain, and Benteen was still several miles away. Warriors were rushing toward the other end of village. Weighing many options, Custer may have decided to attack in order to support Reno or split the village and take hostages, which had worked at the Washita.[40]

One interpretation of what happened is that Custer sent Yates's left wing down the Medicine Tail Coulee to the river. Yates was to make a noisy, trumpet-blaring demonstration at the river, presumably to deceive the Indians about the size of the attacking force, a difficult gambit considering the left wing consisted of only about seventy-five men. Keogh's larger right wing, meanwhile, would remain with Custer higher in the coulee and then keep a path open for Benteen's battalion on the bluffs. If Benteen did not arrive in due course, Yates would rejoin the rest of the battalion on a ridge. Opinions differ here, too. Based on archeological evidence, Richard Allan Fox concluded that Custer accompanied Yates and the left wing down Medicine Tail Coulee rather than Keogh's right wing on Nye-Cartwright Ridge.[41]

The battalion headed down into the ravine, with Smith's company in the lead and Yates right behind. The river crossing point was near the Sans Arc encampment and apparently was at first lightly defended as the cavalrymen approached. But not many warriors were needed to disrupt a crossing, if one was intended. The main column halted, and some men dismounted and exchanged fire with Indians across the river. Several troopers were killed, one of them an officer in a buckskin jacket at the Minneconjou Ford where the coulee met the river. Some historians and Indian witnesses have speculated this might have been Custer or Smith. The more probable victim was Second Lieutenant James G. Sturgis, the son of Colonel Samuel Sturgis, the nominal commander of the 7th Cavalry. The firing had continued for about twenty minutes when Yates pulled back and withdrew north up Deep Coulee and across Greasy Grass Ridge, followed by warriors under the Hunkpapa Gall crossing the river in force and also climbing up Medicine Tail Coulee.[42]

Keogh's companies had withdrawn from the top of the Medicine Tail Coulee to Battle Ridge, where they skirmished with advancing warriors before being joined by Yates's companies and Custer on Calhoun Hill. The hill takes its name from Custer's brother-in-law, left to hold the position with Company L. Keogh, his commander, remained on the ridge with C and I companies to cover the rear, hold off more incursions, and look for any approach by Benteen. Custer likely saw his best chance was to stay on the attack. Custer and Yates, with only about eighty men, probably swept down the ridge along a buffalo trail to locate a ford and may have tried to cross the river to take hostages fleeing toward a ravine called Squaw Creek. Just what happened will never be known. Oglalas were coming up Deep Ravine and Deep Coulee to threaten both Custer's flank and Keogh's, while Cheyenne were attacking Custer near the ford. With no hope of taking hostages without reinforcements, Custer withdrew toward Battle Ridge as Calhoun and Keogh were being overrun.[43]

The demise of the entire right wing had been slow but inevitable. The attacking warriors had chipped away at the defenders by sending a hail of metal-tipped arrows arcing toward the troopers while moving up the defilements and then springing at them from hidden draws. Many of the arrows killed or wounded horses, causing stampedes and spreading panic. Distant rifle fire was less effective but caused some casualties. When mounted attacks from the river threatened to sweep the ridgeline, Harrington advanced with forty troopers from C Company down one ravine to push the Lakota back from Greasy Grass Ridge, but they returned in greater numbers, engulfing the platoon. Harrington's body was never found.[44]

PHANTOMS ON A HILL

Crazy Horse led his Oglala and Cheyenne warriors to a ford about a mile north of the Cheyenne village, swept around behind the ridges to the east, and charged through Keogh's perimeter. The Cheyenne leader Lame White Man was killed nearby. Some soldiers left alive from Keogh's battalion struggled north along the ridgeline to reach Custer. Only a few made it. Farther up the ridge, attackers were slowly encroaching on Custer's temporary sanctuary. Custer took his staff, his brothers, his nephew, and Yates's F Company to higher ground on the western slope of Battle Ridge. History would know it as Custer Hill or Last Stand Hill. Perhaps fifty men were with Custer to fight it out. Some troopers may have tried to reach the river along a deep ravine the warriors were using as a concealed conduit. Almost all were cut down before they could reach the river. A few may have tried to rejoin Custer on the hill. [45]

Where the facts end, myth begins to substitute for history. So how did Custer die?

According to biographer D. A. Kinsley, it happened like this: "That ragged band of fifty troopers and civilians huddled around Custer's headquarters flag, which was firmly planted in the ashy soil. Their sweat-soaked togs were caked with alkali dust, so that they looked like a cluster of phantoms on the hilltop." For Quentin Reynolds, it must have been even more poetic: "They were ten now, and finally only two. Autie Custer and his brother Tom knelt side by side, pouring lead into the screaming braves. Two bullets hit Autie at the same time. He wheeled toward Tom and reached out a hand. Tom was hit at the same moment. He swerved toward Autie. They died as they had lived—together." [46]

Returning to the historical "crime scene" analogy, two broad questions arise: What happened? And why did it happen? In a criminal investigation, facts are collected, but facts alone do not always resolve the case. Evidence may be suggestive but not conclusive. Evidence may go missing or be reinterpreted later with new forensic tools. The Custer case file is bulging with evidence, much of it unavailable until long after the battle. Some important evidence, for example, turned up in 1983 after a fire on the battlefield revealed the location of shell casings and weaponry useful in determining the position of combatants during the engagement. In a court of law, the "why" of the case is established, in part, through motive. Establishing motive usually involves speculation that might take into consideration the previous behavior of the principal characters involved and a psychological profile developed by qualified experts, who typically disagree.

The Custer file is full of possible answers to both these questions. It took several years before many of the preliminary "facts" of the case came to light in the Reno court of inquiry, during which a lineup of colorful characters presented their versions of what happened, just about all of which have been challenged since the court adjourned. But from the beginning, public interest, fanned by the press and the political actors, focused on Custer as the key personality in the drama. Custer was tried, in absentia, in the court of public opinion.[47]

CUSTER ON THE COUCH

To properly understand the battle, the public was told, one had to understand Custer as a personality. Frederick Whittaker's hasty biography was only the first of many attempts to explain him. Later biographers and historians gathered recollections of Custer from those who knew him or claimed to have known him. These impressions, over time, were blurred by fictional images of Custer and the Little Bighorn that came from spectacles like *Buffalo Bill's Wild West*, in which "performance and history were hopelessly intertwined," according to historian Richard White. In time, dime novels, movies, television, art, and literary works all shaped a mythic Custer, a man of myriad parts. Inevitably, those who wrote and read about Custer and the Little Bighorn were influenced by the increasing interest in psychoanalytical theories developed by Sigmund Freud and others at the end of the nineteenth century.[48]

Custer was not alone as a Civil War–era subject of interest. Historian Merrill D. Peterson, a Lincoln scholar, has identified a 1922 biography, *Lincoln: An Account of His Personal Life*, by journalist and historian Nathanial Wright Stephenson, as one of the earliest psychological interpretations. This was followed in 1931 by L. Pierce Clark's *Lincoln, a Psycho-biography*, of particular interest because Clark was a practicing psychiatrist who had been studying Lincoln's personality since 1919. The Lincoln literature is replete with such studies. The mental state of William Tecumseh Sherman, the commanding general of the U.S. Army at the time of the Little Bighorn, predictably has been of interest to psychiatrists and historians, including Stephen Ambrose. During the Civil War, his eccentric behavior in Kentucky in 1861 prompted the assistant secretary of war to say, "Sherman's gone in the head, he's luny [*sic*]." A Cincinnati newspaper headline declared, "General William T. Sherman Insane."[49]

Did Custer have some kind of psychological problem that foredoomed the Little Bighorn expedition? The Freudian analysis of Custer began with Van de Water's biography in 1934 and was continued by other writers. In 1971, Dr. Charles K. Hofling, a professor of psychiatry, published in a medical journal a psychoanalytical profile of Custer drawn from biographical sources. He incorporated his findings in a book, *Custer and the Little Big Horn: A Psychobiographical Inquiry*, ten years later. [50]

By temperament, according to Hofling, Custer was "something of a show-off and quite impulsive." He was strongly loyal to friends and certain superiors. As a cavalry officer, he showed "dash, drive, imagination and unflagging energy." He often was restless. While not without character flaws, "he was clearly on the side of honesty and decency." At the same time, he had a "decidedly immature personality" and was a "phallic narcissist" with "phobic tendencies." He had inclinations, such as carelessness and messiness, against which he threw up defenses. He felt the need to prove himself, to hunt glory, to seek status, and to overcome unconscious guilt, often rationalizing his failings by blaming others. He was subject to mood swings, "unconscious hostility" toward his mother, and "displacement onto the father and other authority figures of some of the hostility," revealed in a "definite ambivalence toward older men," especially those junior to him in rank. [51]

During the Little Bighorn campaign, he was suffering from an "intensification of conflict," oscillations in mood, and guilt, perhaps connected to his conflict with Ulysses Grant during the Belknap affair and his subsequent relationship with Terry. In this somewhat muddled state of mind, vacillating between the aggressive and the passive, between guilt and glory, Custer marched to the Little Bighorn. Or so the psychiatrist might have testified in a courtroom. [52]

The value of such analysis of an historical figure is questionable. Some would see it as akin to a recent mania for digging up bodies of famous people to determine if forensic evidence supports historical supposition. While this might be important in actual criminal investigations, it serves little purpose as an attempt to appease public curiosity. Moreover, turning Custer's actions at the Little Bighorn into manifestations of a kind of pathology increases the burden of defeat. The classic hero fails, in this case, not because of a moral flaw, but rather due to a psychological weakness, some childhood trauma begetting "unconscious hostility" or "phobic tendencies." In victory, these tendencies can be dismissed as eccentricities, explaining a colorful personality, perhaps, or a competitive impulse. In defeat, there must be a hidden failing to explain the reversal of fortunes, not a confluence of forces beyond any one person's control.

On the other hand, there is no reason a psychiatrist or psychologist should not contribute to an understanding of history as long as the facts are supportable even when the patient has not been "on the couch." Hofling's analysis squares in some respects with what others who knew Custer have said and written about him, but even that is open to interpretation. The Custer literature abounds with speculation about Custer's state of mind, especially during the last few days of his life. The true state of his psyche, however, must remain part of the mystery.

Philip Sheridan, no psychiatrist but a potential character witness who knew Custer well, summed him up rather more briefly in a letter to a friend after the battle: "Poor Custer, he was the embodiment of gallantry. . . . But I was always fearful that he would catch it if allowed a separate command. . . . He was too impetuous, without deliberation; he thought himself invincible and having a charmed life."[53]

CUSTER ON THE CHALKBOARD

Military assessment of Custer's actions at the Little Bighorn was underway even while the battle was in progress and hardly has slackened since. Just twenty years after the Little Bighorn, British army major C. E. Callwell used Custer as an example of the risks of divided commands in colonial wars. His book *Small Wars: Their Principles and Practice* became a widely read reference on irregular warfare against indigenous populations. By dividing his command, according to Callwell, the attacker risks poor coordination and confusion between the attacking wings. If properly executed by the attacker, however, this common tactic, which Custer used effectively in the Civil War and the Washita, can overwhelm an enemy.

Callwell, in general, did not think much of the fighting ability of "Red Indians" and other "uncivilized opponents and troops of inferior organization and morale." But even they, he claimed, could "see what is going on" when attacked by a divided force and defeat each wing in detail. Callwell gave them little credit for this, however, claiming that a military disaster such as the Little Bighorn "has usually been due not to the tactical skill of the adversary but to mistakes or mismanagement on the side of the assailants." Callwell acknowledged, "What occurred exactly is not known, for the force was annihilated and nothing but the bodies of men and horses served to tell the tale of the disaster." He credited Reno with finding a good position and entrenching, apparently after he was routed by overwhelming force.[54]

In 2006, researchers David C. Gompert and Richard L. Kugler applied an explanatory model of combat thinking developed at the National Defense University. The modern soldier, they explained, must rely on both intuition and information-based reasoning. Faced with a new situation at the Little Bighorn, Custer trusted the intuition he had developed based on his extensive Civil War experience and his more limited experience on the frontier. Custer was neither a compulsive risk taker nor a poor tactician, having won most of his Civil War battles decisively. His tactics at the Little Bighorn "were consistent with the Army doctrine of his time."[55]

His mistake was in relying on intuition, a mental model. Given Reno's retreat, Benteen's absence, and the size of the force he was facing, he could have extricated his beleaguered wing from its dangerous position. He had better options but stuck with his original plan for too long, even when presented with new information. Overconfidence, or "poor self-awareness," betrayed him, and at just the moment he was most vulnerable when facing capable adversaries, who employed "the leverage of rapid adaptation." The battle was lost when Custer remained in offensive posture while his divided command was spread out too far on the ridgeline in poor defensive position.[56]

By this logic, it might be argued (although Gompert and Kugler do not make the argument) that Reno and Benteen adapted better to new information than did Custer. If indeed they were not privy to Custer's plan, as they claimed, then they were free to improvise based on new information.

Writing in *Army History*, historian Dennis Showalter reviewed the decline in marksmanship and horsemanship that occurred in the cavalry in the years following the Civil War. Emergency tactics often involved "nothing more sophisticated than dismounting and improvising cover until relief arrived or the Indians drew off." In this kind of fighting, the horse "became a battle taxi." Showalter said there is reason to believe "Custer's immediate command was doomed when it dismounted because nobody except perhaps its commander knew any longer how to both move and fight mounted." This overstates the case. Custer had officers and veteran soldiers who could fight on horseback. The terrain was badly suited to that kind of warfare, however, and it was too late for much mobility with spent horses by the time Custer found himself surrounded and overwhelmed.[57]

Writing the foreword to a short biography of Custer in 2010, General Wesley K. Clark, the former Supreme Allied Commander Europe for NATO, thought Custer "overestimated his capabilities, underestimated the enemy, bulled through without a sound plan, and paid the supreme price." He credited Custer with giving the U.S. Army "the signal warning ingrained in the training, organization, and mindset of both our civilian and military leadership ever since. We don't reward impetuous, reckless behavior, especially not in our leaders. It's not about the glory—it's about the mission accomplished."[58]

How fortunate for the army, then, that Custer was defeated, thereby curbing future "impetuous, reckless behavior," circumscribing glory, and accomplishing missions. Such bloated chalkboard interpretations of the battle as object lesson seen through a modern lens have put Custer in the illustrious company of history's great military bunglers. Julian Spilsbury, who writes on military topics for the *Daily Telegraph* in the United Kingdom, included the Little Bighorn among twenty battles he reviewed in *Great Military Disasters*. It is in elite company, although hardly on the same scale as Moscow in 1812, Fredericksburg in 1862, Verdun and the Somme in 1916, or Stalingrad in 1942.[59]

And what if Custer had pulled it off and won? How close did he come to snatching victory from the jaws of defeat? Historian Paul Andrew Hutton contends that Custer remained on the offensive throughout almost the entire battle, a strategy that might have come close to working. In 1877, Sitting Bull supposedly told a correspondent for the *New York Herald* that early in the battle the Sioux "thought we were whipped," and there was "much doubt" as to the outcome. According to Utley, "Good arguments support a conclusion that he could have won." Utley acknowledged the element of chance but said Custer does not warrant the indictment of history. "Given what he knew at each decision point and what he had every reason to expect of his subordinates, one is hard pressed to say what he ought to have done differently. In truth, at the Little Bighorn 'Custer's Luck' simply ran out."[60]

Nathaniel Philbrick concluded Custer "came frighteningly close to winning the most spectacular victory of his career." Ambrose weighed in on Custer's behalf as well, while interpreting his premature demise as a kind of desperado's death straight out of the pages of a Western novel: "The attack had been a gamble, but so had all his attacks. It was a good plan. . . . Like all confirmed gamblers, however, he knew that someday he would have to lose. At least, when he lost, all the chips were on the table. It was a winner-take-all game, and Custer would have played it again if given the chance. He laughed. Then he died."[61]

Custer's wars were ended, Rebels and Indians were ended, and the now nearly 150-year war over his legacy had started. The great mystery of the Little Bighorn lived on, the story unfinished, the investigation inconclusive, the case unproved. The story Custer might have told died with him. The story Custer did tell was appearing in *Galaxy* even after his death. It was a story about the Civil War.

9

CUSTER AND THE PRESS

Mixed Verdict

Few persons have disregarded public opinion so much as I.

—George Armstrong Custer, 1863 [1]

Journalists, and Custer himself, were constructing what became his myth well before 1876. Journalists already had discovered Custer during the Civil War, more than a decade before his dramatic demise. He had found fame and acclaim in the Civil War press coverage of his battlefield feats. His natural flair was good copy, and his battlefield achievements merited coverage. The same would be true during the Indian Wars.

Journalists were not of one mind about him, just as Custer's military superiors were of mixed opinion about him, understanding that his boldness might bleed into brashness. In getting the Custer story, journalists have traversed factual deserts replete with mirages of "true" accounts. They have found witnesses, reported sometimes suspect recollections, and responded to audiences transfixed by the story and simply wanting more. So it is no surprise that the Custer whom America loves and loathes was invented in the popular press, where his image sparked the national imagination. Most Americans first learned of Custer in newspapers, whether in 1876 or during the Civil War. When newspapers began losing their primacy in the twentieth century to film, radio, and television, those new media largely adopted the tragic hero of legend created in the press.

Custer, the Sioux, and their allies bloodied the Little Bighorn battle-field when mass-mediated America was in its ascendency. That style of journalism was indiscriminate in its appeal, shamelessly seeking the low-est common denominator, going for the numbers, nuance be damned. It could be "yellow" and unsavory. It could be progressive and reformist. It became a style of journalism that eventually made its reputation on facts rather than opinion but at the same time could be exciting, righteous, even shrill.

Press coverage of Custer and the Little Bighorn has been approached a number of ways, most of them insightful. A number of historians have provided compendia of press accounts, including volumes by W. A. Gra-ham, Marc H. Abrams, Oliver Knight, and Thom Hatch, in particular. Beyond the Little Bighorn, Herbert Krause and Gary D. Olsen provided a good press collection in *Prelude to Glory: A Newspaper Accounting of Custer's 1874 Expedition to the Black Hills* (1974). All of the histories that address the role of the press—and many do so very well—have judged the press based on how well it gets the facts right. The standard is often an imaginary historical reality that is knowable and verifiable, which never will be the case for the Little Bighorn. Thus, the press coverage often has been judged on the basis of how well it measures up against contemporary norms and a set of unknown, and unknowable, facts.

Historians of the Little Bighorn have found the press both useful and frustrating. The press, then and now, is obliged to serve its audience through its public service function. This is the standard on which to condemn crude sensationalism. It was not sensationalism to report an important event that had an unexpected outcome and could have a sub-stantial impact on an important national issue—the Indian problem. That it was a good story in a traditional sense of containing heroes and villains, drama and tragedy, blood and gore is not a reason to fault the news coverage. The audience would have found it incredible that any news-paper could be so deaf to cultural values as to minimize or ignore the Little Bighorn story. Objectivity or balance was not an issue. So some correspondents' feelings about Indians were biased or one-sided. Those feelings were generally in concert with sentiments of the era in which they lived and worked. The Little Bighorn merited the coverage based on public policy, audience interest, and all the elements of great drama. Looking at how journalists wrote about Custer and the Little Bighorn is a way of understanding how the rest of America saw the event—not via military leaders and politicians but via a press to which virtually everyone had some degree of access.[2]

Unique aspects of the war with the Plains Indians also influenced the coverage. First, correspondents in 1876 had no desire to besmirch Custer because they and the military were not antagonists. That would have been impractical for both groups. During the Indian Wars, journalists generally were supportive of the soldiers and the cause. Journalists shared not only the discomfort of campaigning on the plains during the summer but the dangers of war, even joining in combat when fighting erupted. For example, correspondent Joe Wasson, of the *Idaho Avalanche* (Silver City), accompanied George Crook's 1867 Oregon-Idaho-California expedition. In November 1867, he joined troops in storming the high ground held by Indians, who threatened Fort Crook, in northeastern California. Military officers were attuned to the benefits of good press. Crook, for example, welcomed the correspondents, as he noted in his autobiography: "I regret to say that I learned too late that it was not what a person did, but it was what he got the credit for doing that gave him a reputation, and at the close of the [civil] war gave him position." Though Crook has not been lost to history, he is certainly less prominent than many of his contemporaries. One cannot help but wonder if he was thinking of Custer, who rose so quickly and won so many headlines in his brief career.[3]

Second, the conflict itself was unusual. The Indian Wars began before there was a United States, and so the post–Civil War conflict was a new phase in that enduring war, one focused on westward expansion. For twenty-five years, from 1866 to 1891, there was a continuous battle with different tribes without connections or geographic overlap. The experience of the journalists in the Indian Wars was unlike that of earlier war correspondents in that there was no front, no tactical or strategic plan to be kept from the public, no apparent castigation for criticism in the press. As compared to the Civil War and the Spanish-American War, there were relatively few correspondents covering the conflict. By Knight's count, only twenty accredited correspondents covered the Indian Wars, compared to three hundred for the Civil War and five hundred for the Spanish-American War. The disparity probably was as much a matter of economics as anything—the cost of fielding a correspondent being foremost. Only the *Chicago Times* and the *New York Herald* invested in firsthand coverage of the conflict on a consistent basis, and only the *Herald* did so for all the major campaigns from 1868 to 1881. There were other sources, such as officers who were paid to write dispatches and government reports. However, much of the coverage was a matter of taking news from other newspapers and using Associated Press reports that amalgamated various members' reports. Generally, according to Knight, the reporting held up pretty well in terms of accuracy, given the challenges of reporting on such a war.[4]

NEWS FLASH: HISTORIANS READ NEWSPAPERS

The dean of Custer historians, Robert M. Utley, certainly appreciated the role of the press in the history of the Little Bighorn. In *Custer and the Great Controversy: The Origin and Development of a Legend* (1962), Utley wrote that the "wildest rumors and grossest fabrications were printed and avidly read by a fascinated public. From the papers, they found their way into popular literature, into folklore, and into history. Almost every myth of the Little Bighorn that one finds today masquerading as history may be found also in the press accounts of July 1876." In the 1962 book, Utley was among the first to put the press at the foundation of the Custer legend. Correspondents interviewed people, and newspapers printed the accounts from other officers in the Montana Column. "Although historians have made little use of these accounts, they merit serious study, for they were recorded before angry partisanship had warped memories," he wrote. Utley understood the problems with interviewing sources who were often self-interested, such as officers in the Montana Column, let alone with collecting information from Indian sources and the oft-unreliable translators who were on hand: "Many of the interrogators were newspaper reporters for whom historical accuracy was an objective distinctly secondary to sensational copy, and many of the witnesses had a variety of motives for not telling the truth."[5]

In "The Enduring Custer Legend," published in the year and month of the Little Bighorn centennial, Utley added a few details to his analysis in *Custer and the Great Controversy*. His criticism of the press was a bit sharper. In print, he wrote, the battle became a political issue, and newspapers became a forum among army officers for sorting out blame for the disaster. The politics primarily concerned the Grant administration's Indian policy, or lack thereof, or a debate over whether the administration got Custer killed as an act of political vengeance. Utley concluded that in spite of the flood of sources over the course of the next century—reporters, army officers, Indians, popular writers, dramatists, poets, artists, television, cinema—"there is no consensus of what happened or why on the bleak Montana hilltop in the Centennial summer."[6]

Utley was not alone in viewing the press as legend maker. Karen Miller Russell, Janice Hume, and Karen Sichler focused very specifically on the Custer legend in "Libbie Custer's 'Last Stand': Image Restoration, the Press, and Public Memory" (2007). Using newspapers and magazines from 1876 to 1934, the authors looked at articles by Libbie Custer, news stories about her or her lectures, reviews and excerpts of her books, and, finally, her obituaries. She was nothing less than a "living publicity campaign" for her husband's image, the authors concluded. She understood how to create and preserve Custer's image. The press was the necessary juncture between her campaign and the public image. Like her husband, she artfully employed the press, and the press found a good story in her.[7]

In a volume dedicated solely to press coverage of the Little Bighorn, James E. Mueller provided extensive context for the battle's treatment in the press. He avoided a common problem in assessing the press in historical events—treating the events as though they occurred in a vacuum or as though everyone at the time knew this was a historical or legend-making moment. In *Shooting Arrows and Slinging Mud: Custer, the Press, and the Little Bighorn* (2013), Mueller focused in particular on the massacre in the context of the 1876 presidential campaign. He found, not surprisingly, that Democratic papers tended to blame the Grant administration and corruption for the tragedy. Republican newspapers were more likely to blame Custer. Mueller does not fault 1876 newspapers for lacking the details or perspectives of twentieth- and twenty-first-century media and historians. Forgoing modern sensibilities and political correctness, Mueller chronicles the puns and jokes—often tasteless—that went with the 1876 coverage. That chapter is titled "Custer's Death Was Sioux-icide."[8]

Like Mueller, Hugh J. Reilly found politics intruded heavily into coverage of the Little Bighorn. In *The Frontier Newspapers and the Coverage of the Plains Indian Wars* (2010), Reilly looked at various conflicts from the Great Sioux Uprising of 1862 to Wounded Knee on December 29, 1890, including the Little Bighorn. Republican and Southern newspapers, he wrote, were quick to castigate the Grant administration for the defeat. It also was an opportunity for some fairly outlandish speculation about the battle—for instance, that former Confederate officers had led the attack on Custer and that Sitting Bull had graduated from West Point. Generally, Reilly found the frontier newspapers did a fairly good job of covering the Indian Wars.[9]

Historian Brian Dippie went to the South, where he found newspapers used the tragedy as a political pawn, blaming corruption and ineptitude in the administration of their recent conqueror, U. S. Grant. The whole war with the Sioux, according to one Richmond paper, was the fault of the Indian Bureau, "which is directly controlled by Mr. Grant." That troops were sacrificed to Grant's partisan scheming was proven, in the eyes of many editors and publishers, by the fact that so many Federal troops still were loitering and loafing around the South. The involvement of Philip Sheridan and William Tecumseh Sherman only fueled Southern ire, neither general being a favorite in the region. But with praise for Custer and indignity about his death, the Southern press proved its patriotism and spirit of reunion.[10]

Marc H. Abrams, in *Sioux War Dispatches: Reports from the Field, 1876–1877* (2012), provided a compendium of the Sioux-war press coverage. Selected portions and full accounts are quoted at length and interspersed with informative narratives about the battles and soldiers as well as the correspondents and newspapers. Abrams's inclusion of coverage of the weeks before the battle throws light on how the press framed Custer and the defeat. Abrams showed Custer winning over the press well before the Little Bighorn. As in other histories, the *New York Herald* necessarily got the most attention as Abrams traced the story across the continent and the numerous sources, which were not just correspondents but also officers and Indians. The *Herald* offered what may have been the most extensive coverage of any newspaper of the battle, including stories that fueled the myth of Custer as fallen knight, giving him the epithet "Le Chevalier sans Peur et sans Reproche" and presenting him as a Christian knight. The coverage was extended to a reprinting of Sitting Bull's pictographic "autobiography," all of which supported the *Herald*'s exterminationist views as it elevated Custer's heroism and darkened the Indians as villains and savages.[11]

Similarly, Oliver Knight's *Following the Indian Wars: The Story of the Newspaper Correspondents among the Indian Campaigners* (1960) is dedicated to the press coverage of the Indian Wars. Knight devoted a chapter not only to the Little Bighorn but also to the Washita battle. He gave substantial attention to the background and movements of individual correspondents and sources of information, such as Mark Kellogg, leading up to the Little Bighorn and to the flow of information from the field, to various newspapers and telegraphic points, to publication. *Bismarck Tribune* correspondent Kellogg, the only newspaperman with the expedition, was providing articles for the *New York Herald*. He was killed at the Little Bighorn. Putting the individual correspondents' work in the context of the previous reporting, journalistic standards, and politics, Knight found their work accurate and reliable, largely a result of their personally observing the action on which they were reporting: "The stories were clear, they were understandable, they were often exciting. They were not, however, sensationalized." There were some exceptions, he noted, to the last point.[12]

W. A. Graham's book *The Custer Myth: A Source Book of Custeriana* (1953) is a classic among Custer titles. It was among the first generation of history books to view Custer more dispassionately, breaking from the template of adoration as history, ensconced for more than a half century in the mold of Frederick Whittaker's heroic 1876 biography, and then castigation as history, as shown in Frederic F. Van de Water's 1934 biography. Graham's source material included Native Americans, officers, and scouts and related chapters with the evidence against Marcus Reno, on whom Graham spent considerable time. Of interest in terms of media material are chapters titled "Why Helena Instead of Bozeman Scooped the News in 1876," "Five Tales with the Real Hollywood Touch," and "Dead Men Do Tell Tales," which is about Kellogg. An extensive annotated bibliography from Fred Dustin lists a number of press and media sources. Though dated, it is an important collection because Graham attempted to impose some order on the chaos of Custer material, though he admitted that he could only attend to a small part of it. Nevertheless, he managed to organize some of the most important sources up to the early 1950s, such as his Kellogg chapter, which reprinted correspondence to the *New York Herald* for July 11, 1876, and July 23, 1876.[13]

The most thorough treatment of Custer in popular culture, going well beyond the press, is Michael A. Elliott, *Custerology: The Enduring Legacy of the Indian Wars and George Armstrong Custer* (2007). It is expansive, including not just newspapers and magazines but also film, television, reenactors, national parks, and popular history. Elliott integrated the early press stories into the broader cultural response to Custer and so went well beyond just the original newspaper accounts of the battle, as he traced coverage even of reenactors in the 1960s. Elliott's research extended to the press and Sitting Bull, twentieth-century theatrics, and founders of the Little Big Horn Associates, which included a radio commentator and a newspaperman.[14]

Like Utley, Paul Andrew Hutton looked to the newspapers of the day for the genesis of the Custer myth. In *The Custer Reader* (1992), Hutton deferred to Utley and *Custer and the Great Controversy* for its attention to the press as the origin of the Custer myth. For example, Hutton acknowledged the significance of the press in Whittaker's biography, based largely on newspaper accounts of the Little Bighorn. Whittaker, "a hack writer," was "more drama than history," but Hutton conceded that Whittaker's heroic depiction prevailed for the next half century. Hutton's essay "From Little Bighorn to Little Big Man" (1992) put the press accounts in the stream of other popular sources of the Custer legend, including cinema, dime novels, Libbie Custer's three volumes, Buffalo Bill Cody's *Wild West* show, and even Otto Becker's barroom lithograph *The Last Stand*, which was commissioned by Anheuser-Busch and first published in 1896. The view of Custer changed in the popular media from positive (hero) to negative (symbol of American imperialism, exploitation of the West and native peoples). But dispassionate history was not the province of these popular media—which wrote for the day, not the ages—and the fascination with the story has endured.[15]

Custer was a minor celebrity before the Little Bighorn. *Prelude to Glory: A Newspaper Accounting of Custer's 1874 Expedition to the Black Hills* (1974) is a collection of press accounts from across the country, providing an excellent picture of the "popular" Custer before death made him myth. The compendium includes newspapers from St. Paul, New York, Chicago, and Bismarck. Herbert Krause and Gary D. Olsen offer an important resource for a picture of the public Custer before his end and the ensuing half-century campaign to lionize him.[16]

Robert G. Hays's *A Race at Bay: New York Times Editorials on "the Indian Problem," 1860–1900* (1997) is another collection from the popular press. However, it is much more than a catalog by virtue of his synopses and overviews of national Indian policy, public opinion, atrocities committed by each side, broken treaties, and corruption in the Indian agencies. These provide context for the editorial response to the Little

Bighorn. The book is limited in scope by collecting editorials from only one newspaper, which at the time did not have the preeminent position that it now holds in national reporting. [17]

Several popular and scholarly articles have made the press their primary object, but by definition any article must be narrow in scope. Bruce A. Rosenberg, in "How Custer's 'Last Stand' Got Its Name" (1972), traced the "last stand" designation to newspaper accounts of the battle. According to Rosenberg, newspapers tended to print one of two versions of the battle: that Custer and his men were drawn into a ravine or that they were surrounded and slaughtered in a last stand. "Overwhelmingly, the American people chose the latter account," Rosenberg decided, thanks to the news accounts and Whittaker's biography. His conclusion about the last stand myth is based only on reports from the *Chicago Tribune* and *New York Times*, both of which were reprinted by wire services. [18]

Rex C. Myers, in "Montana Editors and the Custer Battle" (1976), contrasted the coverage in Eastern and Western newspapers. In the East, the battle was a tragedy in a faraway place that had a bearing on policies concerning distant people. In the West, Indians killed people, so the problem was more concrete. The call for a militia was no mere posturing. Myers charged, "Scholars and buffs have almost universally ignored the reaction of Montana's Territorial residents to that engagement. By default, writers have assumed that word of Custer's defeat produced the same monumental reactions in Montana as it did in the eastern press." Noting the relevant work of Utley, Graham, Edgar Irving Stewart, and a few other chroniclers of the man and the battle, Myers said the concerns in Montana were simply more pragmatic and immediate, in contrast to those voiced in the press elsewhere in the country. The impact on audiences varied, especially from East to West—so the play and treatment in the newspapers of different regions reflected varied audience concerns. This put the military leadership in the uncomfortable position of fighting Indians in the West and humanitarians in the East. [19]

A very different perspective prevailed in Indian newspapers. John M. Coward found that the Little Bighorn directly affected two Native American newspapers' approach to promoting Indian progress. The *Cherokee Advocate* and the *Indian Journal* moved from advocating racial solidarity to emphasizing the differences between the eastern and western tribes of the northern plains. Coward said the newspapers were restrained in criticism of Custer and the U.S. government in order to promote assimilation into American society.[20]

Ulf Jonas Bjork offered what must be one of the more arcane studies in Custerology, but his research shows the vast interest in Custer, in this case in the Swedish American press. It is relevant because the Sioux and Swedish Americans intersected in Minnesota at one time, as the Sioux were pushed out and the Swedish Americans immigrated. From 1876 through the end of the century, the views of the Swedish American press evolved from hostility to the Indians to some ambivalence about their plight, much as the attitude in the general culture shifted.[21]

STOKING THE LEGEND

"The Boy General" headlines during the Civil War must have given Custer a hint of what good press could do for his career. By the time Custer became a frontier cavalryman, he already had been stoking the legend fires with his *Galaxy* articles, revealing a person enamored of his own accomplishments, many of them notable. The series titled "War Memoirs" was well written, even insightful, and a little presumptuous in assuming that such a young brevet general would be worthy of war memoirs. In his defense, though, he had won a substantial reputation by war's end. By comparison, Robert E. Lee's papers were assembled and published in 1887, Grant's in 1885 as he was dying, and Sherman's in 1875.

THE BLACK HILLS: CUSTER'S PR GOLD

Reading press accounts of the 1874 Black Hills expedition is akin to perusing a draft of a dime-novel Western—Indians lurking behind the buttes, grizzly bears and buffalo, punishing heat and cold, hardy men, and blooming, Eden-esque valleys. The reporters were along to chronicle the adventure. There were correspondents from the *New York Tribune*, the *Chicago Inter-Ocean*, the *St. Paul Press*, the *St. Paul Pioneer*, and the *Bismarck Tribune*. With the promise of that much coverage, a reporter needed to find something to stay ahead of the competition, whether it was the promise of gold, the adventure of hunting grizzlies, or the menace of wild Sioux who might burst out at any moment. On that last point, the correspondent for the *Bismarck Tribune* seemed a bit disappointed that the Indians were peaceful: "The dusky natives have been seen in small bands, but they have not interfered with us; we have not even had a good scare."[22]

The press helped justify the initial intrusions into the Black Hills and stoked the ensuing gold fever. The Fort Laramie Treaty of 1868 had given the Black Hills to the Lakota, but that was no deterrent to pioneers and gold hunters. A letter writer to the *New York Herald* in 1872 said the discovery of gold was of great national importance and stated that people of the Dakota Territory had been firm in their belief in the existence of Black Hills gold for the last five years. After disallowing several civilian forays into the area, he wrote, the government should "throw no further obstacles in the way" of an exploratory expedition. In some cases, press interest itself was feverish. In the spring and summer of 1872, the editor of the *Sioux City Times*, Charlie Collins, trumpeted his scheme to invade and colonize the Black Hills, with departure planned for September 1 of that year. Scores of pioneers and adventurers responded, but the army stepped in and ordered any expedition dispersed and its leaders arrested. That ended Collins's plans. Charles Windolph, who later survived the Little Bighorn, recounted his earlier service during the Black Hills expedition. He figured it to be a "big" newspaper story. "It'd help make them [the correspondents] famous, even if it would do a lot of harm."[23]

In June 1874, Sheridan named Custer to lead an expedition into the Black Hills. Long-running rumors of gold, as well as demands from railroads and lumbermen, trumped the legal detail of an existing treaty. Ten companies of the 7th Cavalry and two companies of infantry, as well as seventy-five Indian scouts, left Fort Abraham Lincoln on July 2. Also along for the adventure were several geologists and miners, three newspaper correspondents, and a photographer. During the sixty-day outing, soldiers and civilians hunted, fished, and watched for hostile Sioux. The gold was scant, but the imaginations were not. The geologists and miners studied the soil, panned the streams, and did find some flecks of gold. With the help of some exaggerations in the press about the gold prospects, those few specks were enough to set off a wave of gold speculation. When one of the geologists reported that he had seen no gold, Western newspapers excoriated him.[24]

The *Bismarck Tribune* was predictably promotional. The Black Hills were about two hundred miles from the town, and the publishers and town leaders believed Bismarck would be a natural gateway to the area. As the *Tribune* trumpeted the Black Hills' natural beauty and the potential for gold, it warned of an Indian menace, which served the *Tribune* in two ways: It made for exciting reading, and it helped justify the expedition. Custer was notable, as he had to be in his place as commander of the endeavor, and aggrandized for "much experience with the Indians" due to his having studied their history and customs. The expedition's economic potential for Bismarck overshadowed any soldier-celebrity sketches.[25]

The *St. Paul Pioneer* practically promised an Indian battle. "THERE WILL BE FIGHTING before this expedition returns. . . . The most noted of all Sioux chiefs, Tatanka Syotank, or Sitting Buffalo, is congregating his forces at Black Hills, and will oppose the advance" (emphasis in original). The *Pioneer* did not have a professional correspondent but employed the expedition's botanist to write dispatches, which the publisher claimed would be better than those of professional correspondents of other publications because his reporter was a professional scientist and therefore a "keen observer" and often more reliable than the competition. As for his powers of observation, the botanist did see things never seen before or since: "[Prairie] dogs, owls and rattlesnakes live together in the same holes. This latter statement is made upon sufficient evidence."[26]

If this had not convinced readers of the region's Edenic quality, the botanist-correspondent recounted in the final paragraph of his closing story upon the return of the expedition,

> Unused to the saddle and roughing it, my back failed the first day; and after that, for more than three weeks, existence was prolonged pain. Yet in pain I kept the saddle, climbed the buttes, "viewed the landscape o'er," and by lying flat upon my back, tablet overhead, wrote many letters to The Pioneer. My infirmity grew worse, till at the first crossing of the Belle Fourche, it seemed that my last day was near and that soon I should be left under the wayside turf. But we then entered the Black Hills, the water was no longer alkaline but sweet and pure, the air cool and delightful, my health improved daily and to the paradisciacal [*sic*] hygiene of the Hills I am indebted for complete recovery and return in perfect soundness to thank you for your attention, and bid you adieu.[27]

The *Pioneer* found Custer more interesting than had the *Bismarck Tribune*. The former seemed to have even more trepidation about Indians and devoted most of its coverage, like the *Tribune*, to descriptions of the country and details of Custer's hunting exploits. The *Pioneer* correspondent apparently was in good favor with Custer, who in a July 4 dispatch was featured for his rise through the military ranks and for the Washita campaign and praised for his knowledge as an Indian fighter: "It is safe to assert that there is little to know of Indian life and modes of warfare that Gen. Custer has not already learned." Custer was ready for a fight, but he negotiated from strength—as he assured the Sioux of his goodwill, according to the columns of the *Pioneer*.[28]

The crosstown rival to the *Pioneer* found Custer's adventure less compelling. That may have been a matter of the *St. Paul Press* being a Republican newspaper and its reservation about promoting the Dakota Territory over Minnesota. Still, it had a correspondent. He, too, reported that Custer was ready for an attack and was confident he could "handle all of the Indians in and around the Black Hills." However, the correspondent was less enamored of the country than had been the *Pioneer*'s botanist: "With regard to the country, it is only fit for Indians, buffalo, grasshoppers and mosquitoes." He downplayed the possibility of a fight with Indians, reporting that Custer was avoiding contact and trying "not to create any difficulty with the occupants of the Hills."[29]

Another Republican newspaper a little farther east, the *Chicago Inter-Ocean*, held nothing back in promoting the expedition and the possibility of a gold strike. This probably was a matter of the newspaper hoping for some economic rejuvenation in the wake of the 1873 panic, which had hit Chicago particularly hard on the heels of the city's fire of 1871. Chicago would be a natural thoroughfare for a gold rush, and a strike might spark the same sort of national economic energy as had the gold strike of 1849. The editor recognized the treaty issues but figured the federal government could take "speedy measures" to open the area up. Since the *Chicago Times* and the *Tribune* did not send correspondents, this left the *Inter-Ocean* to tout its local monopoly on the story.

Custer himself was newsworthy. He was a gentlemanly sort who did not smoke, drink, or swear. In fact, for vices, "he has none," unless hunting might be counted as one. The newspaper reported it as an adventure that included the "open question" as to whether there would be war with the Sioux. By the end of the month it was the "Custer Expedition."

By mid-August, the correspondent reported, the hopes for finding gold had dimmed. But that changed quickly when, a few weeks later, the *Inter-Ocean* headlined a dispatch "Gold." Particles in the soil, the correspondent speculated, meant possible riches. As the force turned homeward, the paper's tone was triumphant. "Already the expedition has done more than was even hoped of it, than even General Custer himself, who has never learned the use of the word failure, expected." Like the snakes, owls, and prairie dogs sharing their burrows, the return to Fort Lincoln must have been something to behold. The correspondent reported that the return was filled with jubilation, so much so that "the mules of the wagon trains lifted up their voices and wept for joy." Nearing the gate, Custer "leaped from his horse, and it took just two jumps of those Custerian legs to clear twenty feet of door yard." A story from Fargo, Dakota Territory, called the region nothing less than "The Gold Country." "The border newspapers, especially those on the line of the Northern Pacific Railway, are full of gold stories, gold hopes, and plans for golden realizations."[30]

The *New York Tribune*'s correspondent for the expedition, Samuel Barrows, was a personal friend of Custer's. Barrows had accompanied the Yellowstone expedition in 1873 as a *Tribune* correspondent. Unlike other newspapers, the *Tribune* published Black Hills reports that did not dwell on the drama of a possible fight with the Indians. It did report the possibility but said that anywhere from five to fifty Indians were seen almost daily, with soldiers' imaginations accounting for those numbers on the high end. Nine of ten accounts of Indian sightings were rejected upon examination, Barrows reported. Otherwise the coverage was conventional: descriptions of the land, the topography, the trials of the march, the soil, water, and flora. "The most exuberant flora this side of California."[31]

The *Tribune* reported gold in "promising quantities," even on the ground's surface. But admittedly, and somewhat in contradiction, the yields weren't all that great. There may have been a challenge in sustaining the narrative on such an expedition, given that one can only effuse for so long about the beauty of the landscape, the possibility of gold, and the wildlife. So on the return expedition, they encountered a band of Sioux, who told them a large number of Indians, about two thousand, were waiting for them and well armed. A fight was inevitable, they were told, but it never materialized. Barrows apparently never was severely afflicted with the gold fever, as he surmised in a closing dispatch that the value of the gold "can only be determined by future exploration." Two years later, Barrows was a natural choice for the *Tribune* to send to the West with missions to resolve the Indian problem. The *Tribune* publisher offered the assignment. Barrows was tempted, but his wife talked him out of it.[32]

The coverage of the Black Hills expedition is important to the Custer legend that quickly took form in 1876 newspapers and imprinted itself on the national imagination. The 1874 mission was an adventure story, replete with wild danger, the allure of the frontier, and the possibility of riches. The expedition's leader was of sufficient celebrity to be recognizable and known for his panache. He did not discover the gold, but he did deliver the story. By the time of the Little Bighorn disaster, the earlier news of Custer made unnecessary the creation of his myth from whole cloth. His "War Memoirs" in *Galaxy* gilded the image he had generated during the Civil War and the Black Hills expedition.

THE MASSACRE

Though the press was quick to the Little Bighorn story and proclamations of Custer's heroism, the initial coverage was conventional, listing casualties, speculating about events, recounting Marcus Reno's and Frederick Benteen's movements, and reprinting editorial responses from around the country. There were numerous mentions of the terrain—the hills and ravines of the Little Bighorn area—and even a "last stand." However, the last stand was not, at first, a consensus about the final moments for Custer and his troops. A number of newspapers figured the cavalrymen must have been trapped in one of the ravines, a much less glorious image than going down astride a hilltop with sabers flashing and pistols cracking. News stories variously depicted Custer as brave but brash, perhaps acting impetuously, maybe even disobeying orders. All agreed that it was a tragic massacre.

As with other Western newspapers, the *Bismarck Weekly Tribune* saw the Little Bighorn as local and immediate. It was not just a Washington policy debate. A headline on July 12 summed up the newspaper's perspective: "Now It's Business / No More Foolishness." The story noted a national wave of criticism leveled at Custer, Grant, and Alfred H. Terry. The latter two, by some accountings, were the authors of foolish policies. The *Weekly Tribune* started a fund for a Custer monument, as it reported "uneasiness" at the Standing Rock Agency, where the agent denied that Indians under his supervision were hostiles. A number of them even expressed sorrow over the event. This meant, according to a story a week later, that the government needed experienced troops to fight the Sioux, not raw recruits.[33]

Rumor and exaggeration erupted. The *Weekly Tribune* reported that Custer died at the head of the column and then, with rhetorical flourish, added, "Never, perhaps, in American history, did a family ever offer up so many lives for the flag in a single engagement. . . . Yes, they died as grandly as Homer's demigods." A rumor from the Cheyenne Agency held that Custer killed three Indians with his revolver. Another rumor claimed, "English voices were heard urging the Indians to attack." The newspaper seized the opportunity to brag about its own journalistic initiative:

> It will be remembered that the Bismarck Tribune sent a special corre-
> spondent with Gen. Terry, who was the only professional correspon-
> dent with the expedition. Kellogg's last words to the writer were: "We
> leave the Rosebud to-morrow, and by the time this reaches you we will
> have met and fought the red devils, with what result remains to be
> seen. I go with Custer and will be at the death." How true![34]

Both the *Helena Daily Herald* and the *Bismarck Weekly Tribune* saw a chance to raise awareness about the war. According to the latter:

> Perhaps the sacrifice of Custer were [*sic*] needed to wake the nation to
> the true nature of the war that was on hand. Some of those responsible
> for the conduct of this war may be aroused to the immediate demands
> for safety of many exposed frontiers. . . . Congress is still in session,
> and if they do not arouse themselves to provide adequately for the
> crisis, history will hold them criminally responsible for the ensuing
> exposure, suffering and slaughter.[35]

A few days later, the Helena newspaper reported that the "butchery of Custer is announced as the legitimate fruit of the present policy." The government was simply supplying the Indians with the arms to fight the soldiers, the paper charged, via the government storehouses at the agen-cies. The Custer massacre was proof of misguided policy:

> How much longer is this fatal and extravagant folly to be contin-
> ued? . . . Cannot Congress, among its other investigations, authorize

Figure 9.1. An imagined Custer bolted into American consciousness soon after the Little Bighorn, as evidenced by this Currier and Ives illustration, "Custer's Last Charge." Everything about this sketch is inaccurate, but it helped enshrine the already famous Custer. (Library of Congress)

one more to inquire and report whether there is any credible evidence of a single civilized or Christianized Indian ever produced as the result of its policy. . . .

The tidings from the Little Horn [*sic*] will convince Congress, we think, that the nation by some means has a war on its hands and no army to carry it on.[36]

Perhaps exaggerating the national sentiment, but probably not the regional, the *Daily Herald* proclaimed that war sentiment was widespread and the government should respond with "deadly aggression."[37]

No doubt, many saw the Little Bighorn as evidence for the necessity of a conflict that had been going on for decades, having shifted to the

West after the Civil War. War with Indians had preceded the Revolution, conflict with Mexico, the Civil War, and Reconstruction violence. With those conflicts more or less settled, a national policy of westward expansion justified civilizing the West and its inhabitants. Through somewhat circular logic, the Little Bighorn showed that the Indians needed to be subdued. By extension, the more resistant the Indians, the more needed the military response.

On the same day the *Daily Herald* issued its "wake-up" story, it reported on the inside pages, "Nothing is known of the operations of this detachment [Custer and five companies] only as they trace it by the dead." Yet "the Seventh fought like tigers." Here was the plot line that journalists, historians, and the general culture would embrace—lament the tragedy, admit that all the facts would never be known, and be certain of the heroism. According to Crow witnesses, in another story, "Custer and his command mowed the Sioux down like grass while he and his men lasted."[38] Here credibility is strained on several counts. First, the Crow versions of the battle were inconsistent and unreliable, as Utley and Graham have outlined. Second, it seems a bit incongruous, if Custer and his men were mowing the Sioux down, that the cavalrymen should be annihilated. A story datelined New York, July 13, and published in the *Herald* on July 18 reported that agency Indians, who heard accounts from hostiles, said Custer shot three Indians with his pistol, killed three with his saber, and was finally shot in the head by Rain-in-the-Face. It is great narrative detail and probably absolute fabrication, not only coming third-hand but also involving the improbably close accounting of one man's actions in the heat of battle.

A month after the battle, Terry wrote a letter to the *Helena Daily Herald* to clear up rumors of some soldiers having been captured and tortured by the Indians: "On the contrary, everything leads to the belief that every officer and man was killed while gallantly fighting." Subsequent coverage reiterated the unease among agency Indians, calls for action, and laying of blame, which often went to Custer for being impatient or not following orders. The latter point seemed intended to underline the fact that the Indians could not have beaten the U.S. Cavalry unless something or someone was in error.[39]

Two reports from Terry were the foundation of the earliest news stories about the battle. Terry gave one of his reports on the battle to John Gibbon's scout, Muggins Taylor, who was to take it to Fort Ellis, where it would be taken to Bozeman to be telegraphed east. The other report went to Bismarck via the *Far West* steamer. Taylor told his story the night of July 1, in Stillwater, to W. H. Norton, the *Helena Daily Herald* correspondent, who sent the story to Helena by courier. It was 180 miles, and the courier made it at about noon on July 4. A *Herald Extra* came out later that day. Later, the *Herald* editor wired the story to Salt Lake City. That version appeared in newspapers across the country two days later. This hasty action and the reprint from the *Herald Extra* of July 5 privileged a story littered with error and omission, extravagance and excitement. Though based largely on Taylor's report, the story assured readers that the men of the Seventh "fought like tigers, and were overcome by mere brute force." A brief report from Bozeman, dated July 3, continued the account, with more from Taylor. The twenty-five hundred to four thousand warriors, in this story, killed 315 soldiers. The Indians left with the approach of Reno and Gibbon. On July 12, the casualties were raised to 450. A day later, the number was 261 killed and 52 wounded.

On July 15, the *Herald* printed an account from the scout Curly and Lieutenant James H. Bradley, whom the newspaper claimed was a *Herald* reporter. From the battlefield, the morning of June 27, Bradley reported, "Custer fell upon the highest point of the field; and around him, within a space of five rods square, lay forty-two men and thirty-one horses. The dead soldiers all lay within a circle embracing only a few hundred yards square." Much of the story was informed speculation, but here was the "discovery," the verification, of the last stand. In a letter to the editor ten days later, Bradley criticized the press for sensational stories of mutilation, including one of an Indian removing Custer's heart and dancing around it. "Probably never did a hero who had fallen upon the field of battle appear so much to have died a natural death." Not only that, he wore the expression of a man who looked as though he had simply fallen asleep. "He had died as he lived—a hero."[40]

THE STORY GOES EAST

The *New York Herald* provided the most comprehensive coverage of the battle—East or West. It had the editor of the *Bismarck Tribune* in its employ, and it laid claim to the one correspondent to be killed at the Little Bighorn, as did the fledgling Associated Press. The *Herald* was first with the telegraphed verification of the massacre. After the *Far West* reached Bismarck, C. A. Lounsberry, owner of the *Bismarck Tribune*, and the telegraph operator spent the next twenty-four hours dictating and transmitting Kellogg's notes, interviews with officers, Crow scout Curly's version of the story, and a list of dead and wounded. In the end, they transmitted fifty thousand words, for which *Herald* publisher James Gordon Bennett gladly paid the $3,000 telegraph bill. Bennett and his son, James Gordon Bennett Jr., are notable figures in press history and in the history of press coverage of the Indian Wars. The elder Bennett had revolutionized the news business with the founding of the *Herald* in 1835 and his recognition of news as a commodity. One nineteenth-century journalist credited Bennett Sr. with revolutionizing the practice of gathering news and Bennett Jr. with the practice of winning news exclusives. A story such as the Custer massacre provided all the best news elements for the *Herald*—it was exclusive, exciting, and at the center of a bigger story on Indian affairs. The *Herald* had started regular coverage of the Indian Wars with the onset of hostilities in Kansas after the Civil War ended. The *Herald* usually was sympathetic to the military view in Indian affairs but was at the front of exposing the corruption of the Indian agencies and the Interior Department.[41]

During the 1868 conflicts in Kansas, when Sheridan could field only about eight hundred men at any one time in a 150,000-square-mile expanse, the *Herald*'s primary correspondent for Indian affairs had been Randolph Keim, who had covered the Civil War. He had the distinction of having been arrested as a spy by Sherman after the *Herald* printed a letter from Keim to Bennett reporting that the Confederate code had been broken. Keim was sent north with orders not to return. Covering the Indian Wars, Keim not only carried a correspondent's accouterments but also often lugged two pistols and a rifle. He had reported the Washita battle for the *Herald*, and he was part of the party, which included Sheridan, Custer, and several other officers, that went in search of Major Joel Elliott and eighteen of his men. Knight, in his history of newspaper correspondents in the Indian Wars, criticized Keim for simply being a "communiqué correspondent," one who stuck near headquarters and Sheridan. This also meant Keim did not get distracted by Custer, who was more newsworthy but was not the planner and tactician of the campaign.[42]

Though the *Herald*'s coverage of the Little Bighorn was extensive, it was rather conventional. The initial story was a rumor and quite wide of the mark in terms of fact: the "destruction of an entire village and a victory for United States troops not commanded by Crook." The source apparently was nonhostile Sioux at agencies. But when the facts appeared under the headline "A Bloody Battle," the initial details included a sketch of Custer that deemed him the "most reckless cavalry leader of the [Civil] war." As in early reports in other newspapers, there was no rush to create a hero. Instead, those reports either stated or implied that someone must have erred badly to be beaten so completely by savages. Custer failed to wait for reinforcements, the story charged, against an "enemy entrenched in a formidable position." The Indians were never entrenched. As though trying to explain the Indian victory over U.S. troops, the story noted that at West Point Custer did not display "any very marked brilliancy as a theoretical soldier." A day later, part of the blame shifted to Congress. An officer said the massacre was the fault of the Democratic House, "which invited Indian defeats by cutting down the army." An anonymous officer, probably Benteen, told the paper, "The truth about Custer is that he was a pet soldier who had risen not above his merit but higher than men of equal merit. He fought with Phil Sheridan and through the patronage of Sheridan he rose. But while Sheridan liked Custer's valor and dash, Sheridan never trusted his judgment. He was to Sheridan what Murat was to Napoleon." As if that were not enough, the *Herald* accused Custer of sacrificing his cavalry "to ambition and wounded vanity." The coverage vacillated between praise for gallantry and condemnation for brashness and poor judgment.[43]

On July 8, an inside page of coverage included a map of the region with details of the movements by Gibbon, Terry, Custer, Reno, and others. Even the last sighting of Kellogg, probably by *Herald* correspondent Keim, was noted: "The very last one I saw at the mouth of the Rosebud was Mr. Kellogg, the *Herald* correspondent, who was mounted on a mule and had a pair of canvas saddle bags in which were stored paper and pencil, sugar, coffee and bacon sufficient to last fifteen days. He sat on the right of General Gibbon."[44]

THE FALLEN HERO-SCRIBBLER

There were other reporters with Crook, but Kellogg gets special attention because, like Custer, he managed to get himself killed. Kellogg was the only professional correspondent to go with the expedition, and his doting dispatches about the commanding officers—including Gibbon, Terry, and Custer—make his reports appear to be payment, to some extent, for permission to accompany the troops. Kellogg was a former Civil War telegrapher who went to work for the *Bismarck Tribune* when it was established in 1873. *Bismarck Tribune* owner C. A. Lounsberry had been a friend of Custer's since the war and was to accompany the expedition, but his wife's illness changed his plans. He also had taken on the assignment as temporary correspondent for the *New York Tribune*. Lounsberry turned the job over to the forty-three-year-old Kellogg, who not only reported for the *Tribune* but also was to correspond with the *New York Herald*, the *Chicago Times*, and the *Chicago Tribune*. Lounsberry had been bragging to readers since March that they would get the first news of the campaign from his *Tribune*. In addition to his stringing for various newspapers, Kellogg's work as a telegrapher since the 1850s gave him numerous contacts and visibility, as he copied and sent messages throughout the Northwest. Sherman had warned Terry not to allow reporters along because they might "make mischief," but Terry did not take the advice. He must have known that Custer took Kellogg along, because Kellogg was with the forces when they left Fort Lincoln and when they started up Rosebud Creek in search of hostiles.

Kellogg left for Terry's camp of twelve hundred men on May 14. The march commenced three days later, and Kellogg sent regular dispatches, three of which appeared in the *Bismarck Tribune* under the name "Frontier," a moniker that also appeared in the *Chicago Times*. All of Kellogg's work went through Lounsberry, a town booster who wanted Bismarck to end up as a territorial capital. For the next several weeks, Kellogg wrote long, detailed letters on the progress of the columns and the nature of the countryside, all the while lauding Custer and the troops. In a column just before the departure of the expedition, Kellogg wrote,

> Gen. Geo. A. Custer, dressed in a dashing suit of buckskin, is prominent everywhere. Here, there, flitting to and fro, in his quick eager way, taking in everything connected with this command, as well as generally with the keen, incisive manner for which he is so well known. The General is full of perfect readiness for a fray with the hostile red devils, and woe to the body of scalp lifters that comes within reach of himself and brave companions in arms.[45]

Kellogg's accolades for the officers may have been genuine, or the words may have been a matter of practical politics. Whatever the motivation, though, he poured the praise on Custer—"brave," "dashing," "out in front," "fearless," "iron frame and constitution." Knight pegged Kellogg a "sycophant" who wrote with a "trained-seal quality." Kellogg's thinking about the Indians would have been in the mainstream of the region and period, though. "I have no romance in my nature as regards Indians. I look upon them as a whole, as a lying, thievish set; dirty, lazy and degraded, among the lowest of God's creatures, from whose treachery and evil work I have suffered, and with all my heart wish they could be safely 'corralled,' or colonized that they might never more be brought into contact or communion with the white races."[46] Kellogg appears to have taken up quarters on the *Far West* steamer several days before Terry arrived, and from there he sent his last dispatch to the *Herald*.

Exactly what happened to Kellogg, like much about the battle, is unknown. Gibbon found Kellogg's body on June 29, about three-quarters of a mile upstream from what is now Last Stand Hill. Kellogg's notes were recovered and were in that first dispatch wired to the *New York Herald* from Bismarck. Lounsberry may have been the first to receive Kellogg's letter/report of the battle, but it was not published because the *Bismarck Tribune*, a weekly, had already gone to press. Lounsberry did write in the July 5 edition that a full report on the Terry expedition would be published the next week. In an extra the next day, the *Tribune* printed Kellogg's statement from aboard the *Far West* on June 2, including the comment, "We leave the Rosebud tomorrow, and by the time this reaches you we will have met and fought the red devils, with what result remains to be seen. I go with Custer and will be at the death."[47]

Accounts are at odds as to precisely where Kellogg's body was found and when. Ultimately, his body was identified by the boots. Kellogg became a hero, lauded by *New York Evening Post* editor William Cullen Bryant: "If it is heroic to face danger and meet death calmly in the discharge of duty, then Mark Kellogg, the correspondent of the *New York Herald*, who died with Custer, was a hero. . . . The danger was as great to him as to any soldier in the column that he marched with, and he encountered it as coolly as they."[48] It was not clear how Bryan knew the details of Kellogg's temperament and behavior in his final minutes in a place so far away. As noted, newspapers made competing claims about having hired the fallen hero-scribbler. The *New York Herald*, the *Chicago Times*, and the Associated Press said he was theirs. Lounsberry said Kellogg was working for the *Bismarck Tribune*. Those other newspapers, he charged, were getting their material from officers. Lounsberry said he was the one who had passed on Kellogg's stories. After all, Lounsberry wrote, the *Tribune* was the paper that incurred the expense of outfitting Kellogg. [49]

"RED DEVILS" AND IMPRUDENCE

The *New York Times* initially reported a "slaughter-pen . . . in a narrow ravine" and many of the dead mutilated. The July 6 account came by way of Bozeman and Salt Lake City. The "Eastern attitude" was evident in reporting that was more critical of Custer and government policy and gave more credit to the Indians. "We have latterly fallen into the habit of regarding the Indians yet remaining in a wild or semi-subdued state as practically of little account." Although Sitting Bull and his warriors "invited war," Custer "attacked them impetuously" without waiting for support. He was "brave, dashing, but somewhat imprudent." [50]

The *Times* fell into the same exaggeration as other newspapers in explaining Custer's defeat: "No doubt, Custer dropped squarely into the midst of no less than ten thousand red devils and was literally torn to pieces. . . . [I]t was brought about to some extent by that pride which so often results in the defeat of men." Custer disobeyed orders, the story concluded, when he refused to wait for support. There was the speculative nonsense, too. Another account that came from the *Bismarck Tribune* said, "Custer was among the last who fell, but when his cheering voice was no longer heard, the Indians made easy work of the remainder." And thus were sowed the seeds of myth. In its sketch of Custer, the *Times* recounted his Civil War exploits and concluded with an officer's recollection of Custer in service with Sheridan:

> "At the head of the horsemen rode Custer of the golden locks, his broad sombrero turned up from his hard, bronzed face, the ends of his crimson cravat floating over his shoulder, gold galore spangling his jacket sleeves, a pistol in his boot, jangling spurs on his heels, and a ponderous claymore swinging at his side. A wild, dare-devil of a General and a prince of advance guards." . . . He was not a great General. He was a great fighter. [51]

For the *Times*, the bearing upon policy was important because the Little Bighorn brought new energy to the debate over war with the Indians: "Those who believe in the policy of the extermination of the Indians, and think the speedier the better it's accomplished, look upon the condition of war as inevitable, and are for pouring thousands of troops into the Indian country and giving them a terrible punishment." Such a policy was not popular, even in the army, according to the *Times*, and such action would be expensive and do nothing to advance the cause of civilization. True to *Times* tradition and its habit of being a bit more thoughtful and analytic and a bit less sensational than other New York newspapers, it identified the "immediate cause" of the disaster as Congress's failure to appropriate money for forts in the upper Yellowstone. The "remote cause" was the Black Hills expedition in violation of treaties.[52]

The *Tribune* also carried the lament about "Custer of the golden locks." Its obituary recounted his "brilliant achievements," the Washita campaign, and the "bold, dashing soldier" but added, "He does not seem to have been a soldier capable of real generalship." The page-one story, titled "Custer's Terrible Defeat," blamed Custer for failing to wait for support and being "full of impetuosity and ambition." Two different stories detailed the difficulties of the terrain, especially the job of finding the Indians in the vast expanse and among the endless ravines. Still, the *Tribune* surmised, Custer's actions were reckless, and he "died with a gallantry that must be called tragic rather than glorious." Like other newspapers, the *Tribune* thought the event signaled an opportune time to transfer Indian affairs to the War Department, a move that might reform "the most glaring abuses of our present system—or want of system."[53]

Though a number of Eastern newspapers saw the issue as an opportunity to address flawed policy, they recognized the immediate concerns of Westerners. Martin McGinnis, territorial delegate to Congress, charged in an interview published in the *Tribune*, "The cause of this war, or rather of these expeditions . . . may be summed up in the words, 'Sitting Bull and the outlaw Sioux.'" "Of course the Government has no alternative except to bring him to terms," the *Tribune* decided. Its account of the battle provided details of the terrain, especially the ravines, and the fact that people were surprised that Custer got caught in such a trap, especially in light of his alleged experience as an Indian fighter. The "last stand" had not yet materialized.[54]

THE FIRST CUSTERPHILE

Frederick Whittaker may be the most underappreciated of the Custer chroniclers, not for his objectivity but for his impact on history and myth. Whittaker, the hack writer of dime novels and bad history, also was, to some degree, an eyewitness to Custer in the Civil War. So he was no stranger to his subject. Whittaker was an opportunist who wrote fast and engagingly, drawing extensively on newspaper and magazine stories. A prolific Custerphile, Whittaker fleshed out those first news columns' sketches of the noble, dashing-knight Custer, an image that held a near-monopoly on the imaginations of the next two generations of Americans. Only Libbie Custer was a more ardent promoter of the mythic Custer, but she may not have had quite the impact of Whittaker because of his effusive writing and his rapid publication—only a few months after the Little Bighorn—of *A Complete Life of General George A. Custer*.

Whittaker was a Civil War veteran, having served in the 6th New York Cavalry before being wounded at the Wilderness in 1864. For a time, he and Custer served in the same division. He started his writing career after the war and produced more than eighty dime novels, along with songs, poems, and stories in a variety of publications. Whittaker had met Custer briefly in spring 1876, when Custer visited the publisher of his book, *My Life on the Plains*, and *Galaxy* magazine, noted earlier for its Custer articles. *Galaxy* published Whittaker's eulogy for Custer in September 1876. Within a month of the Little Bighorn, Sheldon and Company announced the coming biography. Whittaker contacted Libbie, who provided private papers and contacts with people in Monroe, Custer's adopted hometown. In addition, Whittaker tracked down a number of 7th Cavalry officers and finished the two-volume manuscript by mid-November. It gushed adulation. The public embraced "the last cavalier" portrayal. Whittaker also double-downed on the journalism by quoting at length from *My Life on the Plains* and from the Little Bighorn newspaper accounts, which were sometimes more speculative than factual. Though the book sold well enough to be reprinted, the reviews were mixed. Even the *Galaxy*, from which Whittaker borrowed liberally, found it overly partisan, though deeming it a good biography. [55]

Whittaker's primary culprits were Grant, Benteen, and Reno. The first two largely ignored the biography. Reno, though, was driven to request an investigation, which got underway in 1878. The Reno court of inquiry highlighted Whittaker's partisanship. One newspaper labeled Whittaker as Reno's "official accuser." At the hearing, Whittaker handed the recorder questions to ask of Reno. On the day the court began deliberations in the case, February 11, 1879, the *Chicago Times* ran a letter from Whittaker stating that the hearing would show Custer was "not defeated by the enemy, but abandoned by the treachery or timidity of his subordinates." The court ultimately found Reno innocent. In a letter to the *New York Sun* a few weeks later, Whittaker lambasted both Benteen and Reno, calling the court of inquiry a "whitewashing," a "mockery of justice" in spite of "enough facts . . . to sink Reno ten times over."[56]

Utley wrote that even though Whittaker wrote some dubious history, no serious student of Custer and the Little Bighorn can ignore him. Though a number of nineteenth-century critics scorned the work, it was almost the only comprehensive source for other writers, making Whittaker's legendary ideal and gallant last stand the prevailing picture of the era. The praise was so overblown as to leave one blushing for Whittaker, as in his conclusion to volume 2:

> Calumny and envy must be silent before the intrepid heroism of that immortal band as they rode into the "jaws of death," where perished not only the noble Custer and his adoring followers, but also the hope of a nation . . . cut off from aid; abandoned in the midst of incredible odds; waving aloft the sabre which had won him victory so often; the pride and glory of his comrades, the noble Custer fell; bequeathing to the nation his sword; to his comrades an example; to his friends a memory; and to his beloved one a Hero's name.[57]

Whittaker's *Life* read much like his dime-novel account of Custer, "The Dashing Dragoon," published in 1882 by Beadle and Adams in their *Boy's Library of Sport, Story and Adventure*. It concluded, "So ended the life of the flower of the American army, the brave, the gentle, the heroic, the people's idol, Cavalry Custer."[58]

A GREAT STORY

Daring, dashing, and suddenly dead. However much journalists and historians may dispute other facts of the man and the battle, those three things are irrefutable. This is the stuff not only of legend but also of news. The

newspapers of 1876 did exactly what their audiences expected of them—
they got the information fast, though often flawed, sorted it quickly, and
told a gripping story. Better yet, one of their own died in pursuit of the
story. Kellogg, too, was anointed a hero. Critics of the press have recognized its important place at the juncture of myth and history. It was a
source for both. However, the press of 1876 also was the genesis of the
antithesis, which blossomed fully in Van de Water. That antithesis was
the impulsive, brash, grandstanding colonel who failed to follow orders
and made bad decisions that caused his company to be wiped out. All of
those elements were present in the 1876 news, but the time and the
audience were not right for such an interpretation.

The verdicts on the press coverage of the Indian Wars, including the
Little Bighorn, are as mixed as the verdicts on Custer. The press did a
fairly good job of reporting on the 1876 massacre and other Indian conflicts, according to one historian. The coverage was one-sided bigotry
that provoked horrified outrage, according to another historian. Knight
found the reporting of the quarter century of Indian Wars "responsible
and accurate" for the most part. This was in light of the fact that newspapers had to depend largely on secondhand sources, which meant
sources as varied as letters from officers and soldiers, the Associated
Press, newspaper clippings, and announcements from Washington. To
their credit, frontier-war correspondents often actually witnessed the battles on which they reported. Knight said the stories were not examples of
brilliant writing, but they were "clear, they were understandable, they
were often exciting." James Welch, though, condemned coverage of the
Little Bighorn battle as biased, inflammatory, and dehumanizing of the
Indians, falsely portraying the soldiers as calm and heroic and ignoring
the injustice done to Indians (i.e., failing to explain their reasons for
mutilating the bodies of the fallen). Though Welch is correct about the
bias and the portrayal of the Indians, he imposes a 1990s sensibility and
ethic on the nineteenth-century press and an audience eager for news. A
journalist's first responsibility is to the day's citizens and readers, not to
the next generation's historians. As such, the facts of battle and stories of
lives are proffered for the moment, where the audience resides, not for the
future.[59]

Those to whom newspapers were primarily responsible, their audiences, varied so radically as to defy any single interpretation of the
known facts. The audiences differed not just geographically but also in

terms of education, income, and politics, particularly with regard to Indian policy. Those audiences, however, were more exposed than ever to one another due to the colliding realities and politics of urban and rural, educated and uneducated, rich and poor, native and immigrant. This was a result of expanding transportation and communication systems in nineteenth-century America. The former, especially railroads, connected disparate parts of a geographically large nation. What were once regional issues—such as the Indian problem—became national policy debates. The growing network of telegraph lines, cheap newspapers, and mass-market magazines meant more information and more ideas disseminated to more people than ever. The growth of press associations, such as the Associated Press, standardized the news and the norms. This standardization was a result of having to write for a wide range of publications with varying political sentiments and meant adhering to facts in the news, as opposed to expressing opinion or interpreting facts and events. Stories such as the Little Bighorn were filtered through the lens of mass consumption, making it comprehensible and palatable for the widest possible audience. In this respect, a familiar template of heroes and villains worked best.

In spite of the variability of the audiences and the press accounts, a cultural consensus came about fairly quickly after the Little Bighorn in favor of the tragic hero. In 1876, the press was "better" in terms of fact versus propaganda than its 1776 counterpart but not as good as its 1976 descendants. There were two versions of Custer in the 1876 press—the hero and the self-promoter. Both interpretations were based on evidence and interviews. Both versions survived. Both find their adherents in the twenty-first century.

10

THE FRONTIER, THE FITTEST, AND CUSTER

It is high time the sickly sentimentalism about humane treatment and conciliatory measures should be consigned to novel writers, and if the Indians continue their barbarities, wipe them out.

—*Montana Post*, January 26, 1867[1]

Americans historically have been ambivalent about both Custer and Indians and about what each represented. Well before the Little Bighorn, the larger culture romanticized and demonized Indians, who could be symbols of frontier strength or mere barbarians in the path of progress. The ambivalence is exemplified in such figures as James Fenimore Cooper's Hawkeye, of the *Leatherstocking Tales*. The character is a white man who knows Indians so well that he might pass for one. Hawkeye is part civilized and part savage, often working as the former to conquer the latter. But he draws his strength from the wilderness.

For almost a century and a half, Custer moved along a continuum from heroic Indian fighter to prima donna expansionist who got his comeuppance. The shifting legend, precariously positioned between extremes, has changed along with attitudes about Indians themselves. When Indians were viewed as mere savages who brutalized white settlers attempting to advance civilization, it was much easier to see Custer as a noble figure in the service of Manifest Destiny. Almost a century later, when many Americans were protesting their nation's imperialism and deaths in an undeclared war, Custer was more easily depicted as a vain fool. Ideas about Custer often have followed the cultural contours of ideas about race and progress, which were manifest not just in government policy but also in popular media.[2]

In the latter part of the nineteenth century, when Custer was still a hero, many believed in nothing less than extermination of the Indians. There were more liberal approaches that would have them civilized and Christianized. But even these more enlightened views presumed the inferiority of Indians and the need to improve them. Government policy was similarly divided but tilting toward elimination of native cultures, if not individuals, via the reservation system. Few proposed just letting them be, which may have been unrealistic anyway. For some, such as Custer's bosses in the campaign against the northern Plains Indians, Philip Sheridan and William Tecumseh Sherman, extermination was a viable option. In their eyes, not only did Indians behave barbarically, but their nomadic ways were doomed anyhow. By the twentieth century, with the rise of social Darwinism, which grew out of ideas developed by Herbert Spencer and others, what had earlier been jaundiced assumptions about other races had become a pseudoscientific rationale in which Indians were on the lower rungs of an evolutionary ladder of social progress.[3]

The national ambivalence about Indians began well before the westward migration in the postbellum years. In the *Leatherstocking Tales*, which defined "good" and "bad" Indians, Cooper created an enduring myth of white-Indian relations and frontier life. Good Indians knew how to operate in the wilderness and shared their knowledge with whites. Bad Indians also knew the wilderness but were dangerous to whites. As in any heroic tale, the villain was a measure of the hero. The greater the evil, the terror, and the menace, then the greater the individual who conquered them. In the years immediately after his death, Custer was elevated to a great warrior and frontiersmen. The Indians have a role similar in his legend to the one they play in the *Leatherstocking Tales*—they represent an untamed spirit, mystical, dangerous, and alluring. But in our historical imaginations and the popular media of the past, they also are uncivilized, un-Christian, and an impediment to progress. Custer's defeat and the Sioux-Cheyenne triumph at the Little Bighorn affirmed the power and menace of the frontier. The last stand speeded up the demise of the frontier and became an event that simply accentuated the fact that civilization and progress were unstoppable and inevitable.[4]

Paradoxically, eliminating the Indians meant weakening civilization, whose vitality depended on having a struggle. Lacking a contest, civilization would weaken. "Had there been no Indian," wrote historian Stanley Vestal, "there could have been no frontier, no wars, no pillage, no adventure, only a mob of lusterless clodhoppers moving into the empty wilds a little further each season." The solution to dealing with the American wild was, and remains, similarly ambivalent. Preserve the tradition, the wildness, by enclosing it on a reservation. The traditions are saved like pickled vegetables, the genetic pool preserved, the color retained.[5]

One aspect of the Custer myth that may most poignantly reflect the national and historical jumble of attitudes toward Indians is the story of his alleged Cheyenne mistress, Meotzi. She was among the captives of the Washita battle. The hard evidence for their liaison is thin, but the innuendo is thick. According to Custer, in *My Life on the Plains*, she was his interpreter. If Frederick Benteen is to be believed, she was Custer's tent mate. Scout Ben Clark tells a similar story. The story makes Custer more than a wilderness adventurer. With Meotzi, the conqueror consummated his intimacy with the savage, or perhaps it is simply a fable about whites ravishing the Indians. According to Cheyenne legend, Custer sired a child of mixed blood—savage and civilized. Since Custer and Libbie had no children, the fable of his fathering a child with Meotzi means his direct bloodline would survive, rather mysteriously, in the West. If one counts the children of his relatives, then his bloodline survives in both worlds.[6]

When news of Custer's death at the hands of Indians reached the East, the nation was celebrating itself at the 1876 Centennial International Exposition in Philadelphia, which drew nearly 10 million visitors from May to June. That event was an exhibition of American industrial power, which in the main building meant displays of everything from dental instruments to furniture to a one-hundred-ton steel gun. Innovations introduced at the centennial included typewriters, the telephone, a mechanical calculator, and agricultural machinery. Such technologic marvels were in contrast to a Smithsonian exhibit of Indian artifacts. This reframing of the Indians—museum Indians—as a primitive but valuable culture was a testament to American vitality and western expansion. During June, foreign leaders from around the world took part in the extravaganza. At this event, following an evening of drinks with foreign guests, when President Ulysses S. Grant and centennial officials were about to sit down to dinner, a messenger brought an urgent dispatch about the disaster just beyond the edge of civilization. It became known, in the midst of acclaim for modernity and industry, that the primitives had prevailed, this one time, over civilization. [7]

BRUTAL EXISTENCE

The image-stricken lieutenant colonel in a self-designed uniform, replete with braids and trim, is a sharp contrast to the buffalo-hunting frontiers-man in buckskins. Like his politics, Custer's image was fluid, adaptable to the circumstances. But the contrast is emblematic of Custer's embrace of both the frontier wilderness and civilized order. He is the organization man come to tame the West, the mountain man come to revel in wilderness. Each role—the mountain man and the military man—was exaggerated in Custer. The common strand between the two was the ever-constant menace of danger and a hard life. The Indian Wars realized and dramatized frontier brutality for many Americans, whether as personal witnesses or, more commonly, as readers of news and frontier tales. War with the Indians and stories of the war made it easier to type Indians as savages and barbarians and to set that type against the power and grace of civilization. Just as Custer fought the violators of national order in the Civil War, he would help bring to heel the Indians who resisted civilization.

Indian warfare was unconventional in a number of respects, particularly with regard to seeing Indians as "other," as from another place. Civil War veterans, of which there were many in the Plains Wars, had shared a military culture when they fought against one another in the Civil War. It was a culture based on orders, which came to correspond to an industrial culture that already supplied weapons, munitions, and such infrastructure as mail, telegraphs, railroads, and ships to aid in prosecuting war. The veterans even had fought classmates, as had Custer. That was not so in the Indian Wars. Unlike in the Civil War, there was no code of conduct. In the Civil War, there was some fraternization with the enemy, which was rare between soldiers and Indian foes. Language, too, was a barrier that had not existed in the Civil War. However, the whole mode of warfare was a change from the regimented actions and battle lines of the Union and Confederate forces. Both sides had experienced guerilla warfare, such as Custer's dealings with John Mosby and his rangers, who were reviled into the twentieth century for (allegedly) putting the wounded and captives to death and not being on a battlefield in the conventional sense. Many viewed the rangers as outlaws, robbers, and murderers. In dealing with Mosby, Custer, too, had been accused of not playing by the rules.[8]

Another sharp departure from the experience of Civil War veterans was simply the idea of war itself. For Indians and whites, war had different meanings, different purposes. For whites, there was a goal in war, such as taking land, establishing an independent nation, or restoring the Union. War would end when the goal was achieved. These goals paralleled those in Indian conflicts—protecting tribal lands and securing hunting grounds. But for Indians, war was important as a demonstration of courage and character. For white Americans and a considerable number of blacks on the Union side, war was a collective enterprise, a policy enacted by elected representatives and coordinated in a military hierarchy. For Indians, war was individualistic; they had little regard for tactics and coordination, and chiefs were spiritual and inspirational leaders, not strategists and regimental commanders.

In the minds of white Americans, Indian war was intentionally and peculiarly barbaric. Non–Native American accounts of Indian war often described scalping, torture, and mutilation, especially genital mutilation. Many deaths at the Little Bighorn were by clubbing or knifing, and bodies were mutilated afterward, scalped; some were dismembered. Readers of *Harper's Weekly* read of one instance outside Fort Wallace, Kansas, in which a warrior picked up a bugler "who had been pierced by three arrows, and stripped him as he rode along; after taking off all his clothing he mashed the head to a jelly with his tomahawk, and then threw the body under his horse's feet."[9]

Furthering the image of Indians as savages, closer to the animal end of the scale of existence, were tales of Indians gang-raping white female captives, who might be traded like slaves among the braves. Conventional wisdom held that men on the frontier were obligated to kill their wives if capture was imminent. Buffalo Bill Cody recounted being chased by Indians, reins in one hands, in the other a pistol held to his wife's head in case Indians caught up with them. He went on to make his name as a scout and hunter. She went back to St. Louis. Custer gave similar advice to his officers, telling them of a young woman who was raped, traded, and passed among her captors.

Later, Marcus Reno confirmed the brutality: "The harrowing sight of those mutilated and decomposing bodies crowning the heights on which poor Custer fell will linger in my memory till death." In this case, and in others, too, there were rumors of an arrow in the groin, which was a common practice among Indians, showing disrespect for the enemy. Tom Custer was so mutilated that he was identified only by a tattoo. [10]

The lot of recruits after the Civil War also may have exacerbated the harshness of Indian war. The soldiers were poorly paid, poorly trained, and poorly housed and fed. This was in contrast to the Indian warriors, who were products of a culture that glorified combat and the skills it required: courage, strength, cunning, horsemanship, and expertise with weapons. The *New York Sun* characterized the new regular army "as bummers, loafers and foreign paupers." Brutal living conditions on the plains and harsh military discipline also contributed to low morale among troops. Turnover was 25–40 percent, thanks to death, desertion, and discharge, which meant a constant, large number of fresh recruits in unfamiliar, harsh conditions. In addition to the usual afflictions of venereal disease and alcoholism, there were malaria, cholera, pneumonia, and dysentery. For the soldiers, contracting disease was five times more likely than sustaining a battle wound. It is small wonder that those who lived in and heard of such a world of danger and misery might adopt severe attitudes toward its native residents. What would a "civilized" soldier or consumer of dime novels conclude about those who thrived in animal-like conditions and reveled in bloody barbarism? [11]

CUSTER AND "THE RED MAN"

Custer's ideas about Indians were conventional, very much in the mainstream of mid-nineteenth-century thinking about Indians. Part of Custer was the romantic, which in the tradition of the *Leatherstocking Tales* cast the Indian as a child of nature, at one with the wilderness. The other part of Custer was the hard-edged realist who saw the Indians' doom in those same traits. Because they were children of nature, they would die in the path of progress. In 1858, twenty-one-year-old cadet Custer wrote an essay, "The Red Man," for his instructor in ethics in which Indians were all of these things. Though the prose was a bit florid, he summed up not just his thinking but also the view of many at the time:

> But now the home of his youth, the familiar forests . . . are swept away by the axe of the woodman; the hunting grounds have vanished from his sight and in every object he beholds the hand of desolation. We behold him now on the verge of extinction, standing on his last foothold, clutching his bloodstained rifle, resolved to die amidst the horrors of slaughter, and soon he will be talked of as a noble race who once existed but have now passed away.

The brief statement captured not just the ideas around him but also the romance-and-doom drama that would become integral to his complex myth. [12]

His orthodox views on race and Indians varied with audience and politics. In 1867, he wrote in *Turf, Field and Farm* and in correspondence to Libbie that recent trouble with the Cheyenne had been the result of a small group of young warriors, not all of the tribe. Their leaders had abandoned peace talks, Custer said, because they felt threatened by the military. Such a "liberal" view would have aligned him with some Easterners who blamed Grant and his policies for hostilities, not the Indians. However, Custer had to account for the views of Westerners, Sherman, and Sheridan. He wrote Libbie that if war resulted, "none would be more determined than I to make it a war of extermination. . . . [B]ut I consider we are not yet justified in declaring such a war." A few years later, Custer expressed some hope for Indians being assimilated into civilization. After the 1874 Black Hills expedition, he sent a group of scouts back with a letter commending their service and told of hearing "Rock of Ages" when he was in his tent one day. Coming out, he discovered not his cavalrymen singing but the "sons of those who had roamed over the prairies in barbarous wildness. . . . May the good work go on." [13]

In the campaign that would make Custer a legend, the mission and the orders to the military were open to some interpretation. Custer's take on those orders may shed light on his view of Indians. The 7th Cavalry was supposed to round up Indians and bring them to a reservation. However, he could use discretion against those he deemed hostile. So he could be an escort or a fighter? It is highly likely Custer would have taken into account that which would get more public attention, accelerate his career trajectory, and win more praise from his superiors. It is hard to imagine a telegram from Sheridan or Sherman lauding a job well done in walking the Indians to a reservation. That would be in contrast to bloodying and besting the ferocious Sioux warriors, perhaps even being the man to deliver the fatal blow to end their hostilities. His eagerness to do just that appears to be implied in John Gibbon's remark to Custer, as his column left for the Little Bighorn valley in June 1876, to save some Indians for the rest of the forces. James H. Bradley, who was Gibbon's chief of scouts, seemed of a similar mind about Custer. Bradley wrote, "We have little hope of being in at the death, as Custer will undoubtedly exert himself to the utmost to get there first and win all the laurels for himself and his regiment." For Custer, the issue of the Indians' place in the hierarchy of humanity was a nonissue. The presumption of their inferiority served his purposes. [14]

Perhaps more informative about Custer's ideas were those of his superiors, Sherman and Sheridan. As an ambitious career officer, Custer would not have the time nor inclination to ponder Indian policy, consider legal and ethical dimensions, and come to his own conclusions. Besides, it was the job of the military to carry out Washington's policies, not assert the position of field officers. As Custer surely would have seen it, such cogitations would have served no purpose. He would advance on the basis of his actions, not his thoughts.

PURPOSEFUL VIOLENCE

Sherman and Sheridan were among the foremost proponents of hard war against the Indians. During the Civil War, each had abandoned the idea of war as a gentlemanly slaughter and understood it to be a violent enterprise to subdue not only the opposing military but also to crush the warring spirit of enemy society. Both saw Indians as uncivilized savages who were impediments to progress. Both believed extermination of the Indians was a viable option. As a corporate man, Custer would have agreed. Not only are Sherman and Sheridan important in understanding Custer's attitude toward Indians, but they also are windows onto national sentiments. Those two generals had to deal with Washington and all the attendant politics and interests involved with the Indian issue, and so they could not be radically at odds with public sentiment. Sherman was general of the U.S. Army during the Plains Wars. Sheridan was Custer's immediate commander as head of the Missouri and Dakota territories.

Custer thrived on praise from his superiors. For example, when Sheridan heard the results of the Washita campaign, he sent a congratulatory note to Custer, who forwarded it to Libbie with the fawning statement, "Oh, is it not gratifying to be so thought of by one whose opinion is above all price?" Sherman also telegraphed commendations to Custer on the battle. A few years later, in 1871, when Sheridan returned from a tour of the Franco-Prussian War, Custer was there to greet him as he arrived in New York. Sheridan recounted to Custer stories of Prussian and French military incompetence and added that Custer and his old Civil War division would have been able to capture Kaiser Wilhelm a dozen times. [15]

Sherman began his postwar command in June 1865, when he was put in charge of the territory west of the Mississippi. His primary responsibility was to protect railroads and railroad construction from Indian attack. Sherman quickly found he was hindered by vast distances, too few troops, who were poorly trained and assigned to far-flung outposts, and the political reality of a multitude of opinions on how to deal with the Indians. In addition, conventional military tactics did not suit the new unconventional conflict with the Indians. Maintaining peace and herding the Indians onto reservations proved a challenge. The first order of business, as Sherman saw it, was to get management of the Indians under the control of the army and away from the Indian Bureau, which was under the Interior Department. Traders were providing Indians with ample amounts of arms and ammunition, far more, it seemed to Sherman, than they needed for hunting. As Sherman saw it, one part of the U.S. government was selling arms to the Indians, who used those rifles to fight another part of the government. In addition, the dual authority meant that when Indians were on reservations, they were under the authority of the Interior Department. When they left the reservation to hunt and raid, they were under army authority. Grant supported transferring authority to the army, and a bill was introduced in the Senate in January 1867 to do so. It was defeated in February. Sherman continued to chafe under the strictures of divided responsibility for the Indians. As long as the Interior Department was involved, the peace faction would be a formidable political presence, and a sentimental public in the East would be heard. [16]

The extermination option came up in the spring of 1867, when Sherman was planning for the coming summer. He figured it was time to get tough with the Indians, particularly the Sioux and Cheyenne, who were frequent offenders when it came to straying from the reservations to raid settlers and soldiers. However, white settlers increasingly encroached on the reservations and the hunting grounds. Sherman told his brother John, a U.S. senator, "The Sioux & Cheyenne are now so circumscribed that I suppose they must be exterminated, for they cannot & will not settle down, and our people will force us to it." One of Sherman's problems with Indian Bureau authority was that it hindered the army's ability to take, when appropriate, quick punitive action against the Indians. Under the control of the secretary of the interior, as Sherman saw it, the Indians were free to roam and raid, then show up at an agency to collect goods from the government. Sherman knew that extermination was easier said than done, either politically or militarily. His intent was to punish those who were guilty of atrocities against settlers, but he knew that innocent Indians might be killed in the process. For Sherman, it was civilization versus barbarism, and the result was inevitable. The Little Bighorn was a reminder that he was facing a tough opponent. Still, Sherman did not make extermination a policy. If the Indians behaved and stayed on the reservations, then they would be treated properly.[17]

Sherman became general of the army in March 1869 as his old boss, Grant, assumed the presidency. If Sherman were to carry out his get-tough policy, he needed a tough character to take charge of the Department of the Missouri, which encompassed more than 1 million square miles from the Mississippi River to the Rocky Mountains. He had that man in Sheridan, who has been immortalized in the history of the Plains Wars for remarking, "The only good Indian is a dead Indian." It sounds like something he would have said, but he did not. A Montanan attributed the remark to Sheridan in 1870 during the Piegan controversy.

Sheridan had ordered a group of cavalrymen to find the individual responsible for stealing horses and killing a trader in Montana. The military, mistaking a Piegan tribe for another believed to be harboring the guilty party, surrounded and killed 173 Piegans, many of them women and children. Only one soldier died, and that from falling off his horse. Public condemnation of the action erupted, particularly in the East, but it soon died out. A 10th Cavalry captain, though, put Sheridan at an 1869 peace conference at Fort Cobb. A Comanche leader supposedly approached Sheridan and declared, "Me, Toch-a-way; me good injun." Sheridan reportedly smiled and said, "The only good Indians I ever saw were dead." Sheridan denied ever making the statement. Still, it became synonymous with his Indian policy. He agreed with the peace policy that the goal was to assimilate Indians into an agrarian life, but he regarded them as savages who had lived too long with a "natural inclination" to war. Any transgressions had to be dealt with severely: "An attempt has been made to control the Indians, a wild and savage people, by moral suasion, while we all know that the most stringent laws have to be enacted for the government of civilized white people." Instead, his more common statement about Indians affairs, according to one historian, was "protection of the good, punishment for the bad." He said he had the interests of the Indians at heart in advocating severe punishment and confinement to reservations. The Indian Bureau, he believed, was a failure not just because of corruption but also because it was too humanitarian.[18]

Sheridan's experience as an Indian fighter predated the Civil War. His first Indian campaign was in 1855 in the Northwest. He was contemptuous of the uncivilized Indians, whom he believed should be controlled and disciplined. At that early date, well before his momentous Shenandoah Valley campaign of "total war" in 1864, he felt the only way to deal with Indians was to destroy their way of life. The idea carried over not only to the Civil War but also to the Indian Wars of the 1860s and 1870s. During both conflicts, General and later President Grant condoned the tactics. With Sherman as general of the army and Sheridan as territorial commander, it is small wonder that Custer burned the Washita village to the ground and planned to do the same at the Little Bighorn. It was a sanctioned way of conducting war at the time. It had been effective in Georgia and in the Shenandoah Valley in war against civilized people, so of course it would be employed against those who were deemed less than civilized.[19]

Sheridan was not the sort of man to philosophize about his mission, especially in the course of getting control of 1 million square miles populated by about 175,000 Sioux, Cheyenne, Arapaho, Kiowa, Apache, Comanche, Ute, Crow, Shoshone, Blackfoot, Pawnee, Pueblo, and Navajo. Like Sherman, Sheridan clearly saw the political dilemma for the military. He wrote in 1870, "If we allow the defenseless people on the frontier to be scalped and ravished, we are burnt in effigy and execrated as soulless monsters, insensible to the sufferings of humanity. If the Indian is punished to give security to these people, we are the same soulless monsters from the other side."[20]

Sheridan's Civil War experience gave him a sound appreciation of how effectively a band of raiders could tie up a force many times its own size, as Mosby's Rangers had done to Sheridan and Custer in Virginia. In that case, Sheridan warred against civilian opposition as well as the military. He thought to do the same thing on the plains. Sherman endorsed such action, having perfected the tactic in his March to the Sea. In October 1868, Sherman wrote, in approving Sheridan's plan for a winter campaign,

> If it results in the utter annihilation of these Indians, it is but the result of what they have been warned again and again. . . . I will say nothing and do nothing to restrain our troops from doing what they deem proper on the spot, and will allow no more vague general charges of cruelty and inhumanity to tie their hands, but will use all the powers confided in me to the end that these Indians, the enemies of our race and our civilization, shall not again be able to begin and carry out their barbarous warfare.[21]

Both Sherman and Sheridan thought Custer would be a good choice for command. Sheridan wired him at home in Michigan from Fort Hays, Kansas. Custer arrived three days later, in time for breakfast with Sheridan.

Sherman had a pretty good read on Custer and figured him the right sort of officer to take on the difficult job of chasing Indians around the plains. He called Custer "very brave even to rashness, a good trait for a cavalry officer," but "he has not too much sense." Before Custer headed to Fort Abraham Lincoln in 1876, Sherman and Sheridan expressed similar views of him. Sherman had written Sheridan in November 1875 that he thought a major battle with the Sioux was near and that he was eager to "finish this Sioux business, which is about the last of the Indians." After years of constraint, officers saw a chance to go to battle and even win promotions. Custer was among them, and he pleaded for a chance to join his command in the Dakota Territory. Grant was still put out with Custer for unfavorable testimony in the investigation of corruption in Indian affairs under Grant's secretary of war. When Custer headed to Chicago to personally plead his case with the general of the army, Sherman had Sheridan stop him and await further orders. Neither man was giving

Custer much sympathy. Sheridan recalled an incident eight years earlier when Custer left his regiment to visit his wife. If he were allowed to rejoin his command, Sheridan wrote, "I sincerely hope, if granted this time, it will have sufficient effect to prevent him from again attempting to throw discredit on his profession and his brother officers." Custer's luck was working, though, and in spite of the skepticism of his commanders, he was at Fort Abraham Lincoln in time for the summer campaign. [22]

The critics of hard-war tactics gained some momentum in 1869, shortly after Custer's Washita attack and the Piegan massacre in Montana. Both Sherman and Sheridan must have been surprised when, prior to Grant's inauguration, the Society of Friends, the Quakers, persuaded him to approach the Indian problem in a more Christian manner—from a policy of peace, in other words. Grant eventually named a Board of Indian Commissioners, and he appointed a number of agents from a list of names the Friends had given him. As with much else in the Grant administration, corruption and mismanagement eventually undermined the so-called Quaker policy. But men such as Sheridan and Sherman found themselves in a predicament because if they upheld the policy—followed orders—they would be denying frontier reality. Sheridan stated, "If a white man in this country commits a murder we hang him, if he steals a horse we put him in the penitentiary. If an Indian commits these crimes we give him better food & more blankets." Grant's peace policy ceased with the 1874 Red River campaign, which effectively ended Indian strength in the southern plains. This allowed the military to be less tolerant and more forceful in dealing with the Indians. [23]

Sherman, too, reflected not only a hard attitude toward the Indians but also some of the ambivalence of the times. He resented being accused of advocating extermination. Besides, he found it hypocritical of Easterners to criticize hard war in the West because those same critics were living on land that once was taken forcefully from its native inhabitants. He saw a general law of progress at work, and failing to recognize and respect such a historical force meant doom—not just for Indians but also for any society, including American society in general. Sherman chafed at criticism of war with the Indians because it seemed self-evident to him that opening up the West to settlement was progressive and moral, as opposed to siding with a people who were obsolete and doomed. [24]

Sherman summed up the collision of frontier reality and Eastern politics: "There are two classes of people, one demanded the utter extinction

of the Indians, and the other full of love for their conversion to civilization and Christianity. Unfortunately, the army stands between and gets
the cuffs from both sides." In short, ideas about policies with regard to the
Indians were a jumble of well-meaning principles, greed and self-interest,
old prejudices, untested assumptions, the impulse for revenge, and the
promise of the West. Sherman and Sheridan are best remembered for
their hard-war ideas and practices, not their ability to contend with the
confused policies, corrupt government agencies, inadequate military with
a large but vague mission, and web of intrigue and ambition that were
part of the job. They dealt with all that. They were popular figures in the
postwar period whose ideas and words mattered to the public and often
were simplified, such as in the comment about "the only good Indian."
By the time of the Little Bighorn, there was substantial sentiment for
wiping out the Indians. Racial prejudice, the Indians' brutal practices in
warfare, nationalism, and Manifest Destiny all fueled demonization of the
Indians. Fighting such barbarians in the quest for such noble goals neces-
sitated a place in the national imagination for heroes who would vanquish
and prevail.[25]

RACE AND INTELLECTUAL CURRENTS

The anti-Indian sentiments were not solely a matter of war and the rush to
claim the West and its natural wealth. A new defense of racism emerged
in the nineteenth century that claimed the inferiority of nonwhites was
grounded in science. Such ideas gained strong currency in the 1870s and
provided intellectual support for uncharitable or hostile actions toward
Native Americans. The ideas of Charles Darwin and Herbert Spencer
served as fashionable rationales for racism well into the twentieth century. However, considering that racism is as old as recorded human history,
social Darwinism was merely an intellectual garnish for an old idea. In
the nineteenth century, it just seemed self-evident to the mainstream
white culture that Indians, blacks, and other nonwhites or non-Europeans
were inferior. No explanation was needed. The issue was not their inferiority but how to deal with them—through the path of the social gospel,
which meant assimilation, or social Darwinism, which could mean extermination. In this context, the response to the Little Bighorn, which was
simply to speed up the end of tribal cultures by killing the Indians and/or

putting them on reservations, was logical for a large part of the public and for policymakers. That intellectual context also supported the image of Custer as hero, a tragic deviation in the historical course already determined by the laws of nature.

Long before the publication of *On the Origin of Species* (1860), Americans had employed racism and force as they defended slavery and moved west. Anglo-Saxonism, firmly established in American and English history during the nineteenth century without the benefit of Darwin, complemented nationalism and romanticism. The idea that a society was an "organic" entity that evolved was invoked before *Origin* was published. Even those who were not particularly Darwinian in perspective adopted a hierarchical view that at least implied placement of "more fit" and "less fit" people on a ladder in which societies moved up from savagery and barbarism toward civilization.[26]

The propellant for upward movement was a "progressive spirit." American Indians, some intellectuals believed, simply had no such spirit and so had no hope of becoming civilized. Geologist John Wesley Powell, director of the Bureau of Ethnology, denied the validity of the doctrine of the survival of the fittest but divided cultures into stages of savagery, barbarism, and civilization. Though individuals might regress to earlier stages, races and cultures generally progressed upward to civilization. When savage or barbaric cultures declined in the face of civilizing force, Powell believed, it was evidence of such a natural progression upward, not of inherent weakness or strength.[27]

Ethnologist Lewis Henry Morgan found the same hierarchy in his study of American Indians. The lower cultures would never catch up to the higher ones, and the direction of evolution also meant those lower realms of social evolution would die as more advanced cultures moved up more rapidly. Once those lower races had been in contact with higher cultures—such as the Aryan and Semitic races—the lower races' institutions and arts would decline, which meant they could not even progress within the confines of their own cultures.[28]

Drawing on Powell's stages, others offered an even more pessimistic outlook for Indians: they rarely ascended from their state of barbarism; those in existence were mere holdovers from prehistoric times as a result of putting all their energy into surviving in a harsh environment; when they came into contact with civilization, they would succumb. Not even education could help them, according to this bleak view, because trying to force Indians upward in stages of development had proved only nominally successful.[29]

This meant that those inclined to preserving Indians and their culture via humanitarian and Christian solutions were confronted with the harsh scientific "fact," according to some, that the mission was futile. Even if Indians could be elevated, they would forever remain inferior to the more rapidly evolving and progressing white civilization. By implication, they would be forever an impediment to civilization.[30]

Though some would never change their minds about the incapacity of Indians to be civilized, by the turn of the century a consensus was forming that Indians were not doomed to extinction. Even those who insisted that Indians were not disappearing conceded that their numbers might decline and be unstable in their transition to civilization. In 1887, the Dawes Act signaled shifting sentiments about the Indians. The law gave the president authority to allot part or all of any reservation to heads of households for agriculture or grazing. Indians could choose the allotments themselves, or if they failed to do so within four years of the president's order, agency officials could make the allotment. Eventually, the Indians would hold title to the land. Any land not allotted to Indians would be sold to "actual settlers," with the proceeds going into a trust for educating and civilizing Indians.

Historian Brian Dippie called the measure "a pure product of the reformer mind of the age—hostile to every vestige of tribalism, coercive, well-meaning, certain that the great Father knew what was best for his red children." The measure reflected two conclusions that Americans had reached. First, Indians were not disappearing as a result of natural law or innate necessity but would do so unless something was done to change their conditions. Second, while individuals might survive, even grow, cultural extinction was inevitable. The Dawes Act was the most substantial legislation concerning Indians until nearly four decades later, when they were granted full citizenship in 1924. The act was important, too, because it created a policy and a mechanism for assimilating Indians into the larger culture and a path out of what was seen as their backward ways. Such legislation naturally presumed the necessity of acting to elevate them as opposed to just leaving them alone, which might still imply inevitable doom.[31]

Still, as Americans increasingly embraced reform and progress, science and modernism, they were experiencing a sense of loss. The West of untainted wilderness and of people's imaginations was disappearing. Conquering the West may have been a measure of national character, but that same conquest meant losing a defining part of American exceptionalism and character. A frontier that was beyond the control of civilization was exciting and inspiring. If it was gone, inspiration and strength might atrophy. Much of the West remained undeveloped, but it was no longer out of the reach of development. Railroads, mining and timber interests, ranchers, and homesteaders had encroached. States, too, had taken their share—eventually amounting to about 73 million acres to pay for such developments as roads and schools. There remained a place and a need for a frontier and those who would tame it, even as it became more an idea and less a reality. In the nineteenth-century legend, Custer necessarily was a man of action, not one to ponder the fate of the vanishing American and the vanishing frontier. In the generation of the new century, though, the nation had a man who was a frontiersman, warrior, and intellectual. He did ride and hunt the remnants of wilderness, and he would ponder the meaning of a vanishing people and the vanishing West. That man was Theodore Roosevelt.[32]

TR: FRONTIERSMAN AND CIVILIZER

The East-West divide in sentiments about the Indians grew more pronounced after the Civil War. The hard-war proponents of the West endorsed severe action and had the sympathy of Sherman and Sheridan. Peace policy advocates in the East, which included the Friends as well as numerous other denominations and newspapers, found President Grant amenable to their exhortations. Political and philosophical tensions, as well geographic differences, came together in Theodore Roosevelt, a gentleman cowboy who came from the Eastern establishment to revel in the Wild West. He simultaneously embraced frontier and progress. He was no typical American in any respect, but he was emblematic of late-nineteenth- and early-twentieth-century ideas in a number of ways, including his mixture of admiration and contempt for Indians. Unlike that of Sherman, Sheridan, and Custer, Roosevelt's generation was seeing the end of the frontier and witnessing that conclusion with some sense of loss, not just of geographic wildness but also of something especially American that had defined the national character. Roosevelt lived in the Dakota

Territory in the early 1880s, about five years after the Little Bighorn. He formulated most of his ideas about Indians when he returned East from the territory. Thoughts about the West became more nuanced around the turn of the century, as did his ideas about the Indians and their place in the American story. Any generational turn invites reassessment, as happened with the frontier and the Indians for the leaders coming into the new century. Custer remained a hero, but the Indians became something more than simple villains, though they continued to serve that purpose, especially in fiction and film. Indians were coming into their own as an important part of the American idea. The rise of ethnographic studies, of new visual media, of new ideas about the rights of individuals—laborers and women, among others—all suggested that more intellectual energy was being expended on understanding and improving society in the progressive spirit of the day. That would be good for recognizing the importance of native culture.[33]

Unlike Custer, Roosevelt was an intellectual frontiersman. His ideas about the Indians were couched in terms of intellectual trends about ethnicity, race, and social hierarchies. In the evolutionary hierarchy to which Roosevelt subscribed, people proceeded from savage (disorganized chaos), to barbarism (military virtues developed), to a blend of military virtues with love of order and race fecundity (this was "social efficiency"). In such a scheme, savages and barbarians might invigorate civilization with energy and martial spirit. In the fourth stage, the individual strength and fighting vigor declined and were replaced with love of ease and too much emphasis on the contemplative life and material possessions. Roosevelt called this final stage "race suicide," which was a decadent, dying social order. In order to avoid that final stage, civilization needed some barbarian energy to remain vigorous and dynamic. He agreed that Indians were in a savage state of human development, which was the lowest state. He cited the Algonquin of the Northwest as savages, not as far along as tribes of the South; the nomadic Plains Indians were even more savage, even further removed from civilization. In this racial scheme, Indians were doomed to extinction by white migration westward, and so genocide was justified. Roosevelt had reached the same conclusion as historian Francis Parkman, whom he admired and after whom he modeled his own work, *The Winning of the West*. In it, Roosevelt said contact with a superior race meant the demise of the Indians: "The conquest and settlement by the whites of the Indian lands was necessary to the greatness of the race and to the well-being of civilized mankind."[34]

But Roosevelt was not an exterminationist. He admired Indians as warriors. When he organized the Rough Riders before the outbreak of the Spanish-American War, he included a number of Indian descendants because he recognized their fighting ability. Even if he thought Indian culture would perish, he believed those who survived their encounters with whites should be brought into American society. It was the assimilation philosophy. In his First Annual Message to Congress (1901), Roosevelt said Indians should be treated like whites and should receive an education, which should be elementary and industrial, not college or university level. The main issue was how to absorb Indians into the larger culture. Though Roosevelt objected to interracial marriage between whites and blacks and between whites and Orientals, he advocated white-Indian intermarriage, which he believed accelerated Indian progress toward civilization. He wanted fair treatment of Indians, and during his presidency he tried to clean up corruption in the Indian Bureau.[35]

A reformer at heart, President Roosevelt had softened his tone from his earlier years, probably in keeping with a growing sense of social justice. His increased regard for Indian culture is shown, too, in his encouragement of studies of Indian society and recognition of some of its unique aspects. Like Sheridan, Roosevelt encouraged ethnologic studies to identify and understand some the admirable strengths of Indian culture. It was a parallel to preserving, geographically, the vast tracts of the American frontier that Roosevelt would later induct into a national park system. If the ideas on race, hierarchy, savagery, and civilization seem a bit tortuous, it may be because they are. There was a growing awareness in the period of different ideas about race, the increasing use of scientific rationales for racism, and an attempt not just to fit blacks and foreigners into a "proper" place in the hierarchy but also to discover the place of Indians in American society and history. A new generation of historians and chroniclers of the West came into their own in this period of worry and intellectual mayhem about race and science. They would begin to present Custer in different lights.[36]

Presumptions of racial inferiority and superiority began to come under more critical scrutiny in the late nineteenth and early twentieth centuries. Roosevelt was a neo-Lamarckian, meaning he believed that characteristics acquired during life could be passed on to subsequent generations and that this principle could be applied to races and societies, not just individual organisms. For Roosevelt and other neo-Lamarckians, race was not necessarily a defining factor in social evolution. Racial heredity could explain some social phenomena, which were largely a matter of social and environmental forces. Though *survival of the fittest* was a popular catchall term, and still is, Roosevelt found it an unsatisfactory explanation of progress. In fact, he disagreed with Herbert Spencer's idea that *evolution* and *progress* were synonymous. Roosevelt's fourth stage of social hierarchy—"race suicide"—meant he had come to a very different conclusion about evolution's necessarily progressive direction. He was skeptical of natural selection's application to society. Here is where Roosevelt represented a departure from ideas of simple social Darwinism—that Indians were doomed to extinction because they were inherently less fit, a "weaker" race. He agreed they were doomed, but not simply on the basis of biology, let alone biologic theory applied to sociology.[37]

In *The Winning of the West*, Roosevelt disdained "sentimental historians" who failed to understand the savage frontier. Conflict between whites and Indians was inevitable, he wrote, as was the triumph of the white race. Besides, Indians had no title to the land and "at the most were in possession merely by having butchered the previous inhabitants." While Roosevelt rejected sentimentality and embraced progressivism, society lurched toward some idea of social justice, even if it did not mean what later generations would recognize as equality. But it definitely was a move away from the extermination philosophy, rationalized post hoc by a simplistic notion of social Darwinism—that is, that the weaker would be vanquished by the stronger. Roosevelt's inconsistency on the subject reflected social and political inconsistencies in attitudes about race and Indians. His approach illustrated a way to embrace evolution and the scientific-technologic progress that it implied and, at the same time, to provide a scientific rationale for preserving Native Americans and the wildness that they represented. They were reservoirs of frontier energy for civilization and would help keep it from degenerating into race suicide.[38]

In the early twentieth century, those committed to the idea that Indians were inferior no longer needed the romantic tradition, such as Cooper's "bad Indian" or the savages and barbarians who killed heroic cavalrymen. The romantic ideals of the West still existed, but they just were not as necessary before. Modernism and science could provide the logic for conquering the Indians. Romantic-tradition icons, which Custer had become by now, were no longer as central to the national rationale for the treatment of the Indians. Custer and his ilk were less important, and so the possibility opened up of a critical history of Custer, the Little Bighorn, and the West. Concurrently, the assimilationist ideal reached its peak in 1924 with the Indian Citizenship Act, which granted full citizenship to all American Indians. Up to that point, many Indians had acquired citizenship via marriage, land allotments, or treaties. But not all Indians were citizens. World War I had speeded up this high point of the assimilation ideal because Indians had fought alongside white troops, not in segregated units, as had blacks. Many interpreted this as showing their ability to assimilate. At the same time, the Indian symbolized the lost frontier, which was already a treasured national memory. Museums packed in the Indian artifacts as the vanishing American was revived in the American imagination.[39]

GLORY HUNTER?

The Custer of the popular imagination was almost wholly heroic before the 1920s, when biographical writing became more critical, not just of Custer but also of other historical figures. The changing sentiments about Indians correlated with changing attitudes about Custer and the Little Bighorn. These more critical assessments of the man and the battle found him neither necessarily heroic nor just a deviation in American history because inferior savages had defeated the white man. Historical memory became more critical and complex. When the nation commemorated the fiftieth anniversary of the Little Bighorn, the *New York Times* lamented the fallen hero. Films, novels, and barroom art celebrated Custer's gallantry. It was more than Libbie Custer's death in 1933 that opened the way for the first critical biography of and novel about Custer in 1934. By then, the frontier, more than a generation removed from the battle itself, was undoubtedly subdued. The nation could be more magnanimous to the losers and more discerning in assessing the victory. Frederic F. Van de Water's *Glory-Hunter* corrected Frederick Whittaker's hagiography by simply taking the perfectly opposite tack. The tragedy of the fearless soldier became the tale of an egoist who rose in rank due to luck and was solely responsible for the massacre of himself and his men. Shortly after

Van de Water's biography, the novel *Montana Road*, by Harry Sinclair, had Custer bumbling into a trap after ignoring his scouts as he subverted the efforts of an Indian agent to avoid war. In both Van de Water's and Sinclair's tellings, the dashing cavalier had become the handsome dolt who used up his good luck and blundered into death.[40]

Film remained faithful to a heroic Custer with several low-budget cinematic portrayals. Those included, among others, *The Last Frontier* (1932) and *Custer's Last Stand* (1936). The apex of Custer love must have been, at least for cinema, the 1941 *They Died with Their Boots On*. Errol Flynn's Custer moves from being a reckless, naive cadet to becoming an officer who saves the day several times in the Civil War, attracting the notice of his superiors. He goes on to lament the plight of the Indians and eventually sacrifices himself and his soldiers for the greater tactical good. Reviewers noted the historical malfeasance of the film. The public loved it.

POST WORLD WAR II: ANTI-CUSTER

Racism as policy became more disreputable after World War II. The United States and its Allies had defeated rabidly racist regimes in Germany and Japan, both of which embraced exterminationist philosophies toward others. In the wake of that triumph, it was hypocritical for the United States to maintain its own course of segregation and discrimination, as minorities began to challenge the laws and institutions of those policies. Though most of the historical attention has been on the plight of black Americans, Native Americans were part of the fight against racism and marginalization. The American Indian Movement came into its own nearly a decade later than the major civil rights groups for blacks. The new awareness and appreciation of Indian culture in the 1960s correlated with a decidedly downward turn in the heroic Custer legend.

One of the first anti-Custer films, *Fort Apache*, appeared in 1948. Henry Fonda plays Colonel Owen Thursday, the Custer character. Thursday is an ambitious officer who mistreats his men, holds his foes in contempt, and finally attacks a large force of Indians that wipes him out. By depicting Thursday as uncommon, director John Ford avoided a negative image of the military, which would have been a poor draw so soon after World War II. John Wayne plays the second in command, Captain

York, based on Benteen. York hates Thursday but refuses to criticize him before reporters. Several other films continued the anti-Custer trend, including a few that told the story of the Little Bighorn from the Indian perspective, even though historical accuracy was not an issue. Those films included *Sitting Bull* (1954) and *Chief Crazy Horse* (1955), which seized upon the trend of more sympathy for the Indians.[41]

Fiction, too, discovered the dark side of Custer. Will Henry's *No Survivors* (1950) picks up Van de Water's theme of glory hunting but allows Custer to die bravely. The anti-Custer sentiments gained momentum with Mari Sandoz's *Cheyenne Autumn* (1954), which resurrects the Meotzi story and has Custer bedding an Indian woman after the Washita massacre. By the mid-1950s, Custer the villain had become a common motif in fiction and film, and the legend came full circle in *Convenient Coward* (1961), in which author Ken Shiflet elevates Reno by having him contend with an unbalanced Custer. Reno is similarly redeemed in the biography *Faint the Trumpet Sounds* (1966). One of the authors, the American Legion, and a Reno descendant petitioned the army for a review of Reno's dismissal. They succeeded, and Reno was given an honorable discharge in May 1967. *The Winter War* (1961), by William Wister Haine, finds Custer's vanity to be the cause of the Little Bighorn slaughter. *Little Big Man* (1964), by Thomas Berger, while more nuanced, is nevertheless in that vein of writing that finds Custer anything but a hero. The 1970 film version of Berger's novel simplifies and demonizes Custer and idealizes the Indians. Its Custer also is an attack on the American military and Vietnam. Three other films of the decade were similarly anti-Custer or at least portrayed a nonheroic Custer: *The Great Sioux Massacre* (1965), *Custer of the West* (1968), and *The Glory Guns* (1965). By the end of the decade, Custer had degenerated into an egomaniacal bumbler with a homicidal streak.[42]

In contrast, the Indians were elevated not only as part of the new consciousness of race and injustice but also in conjunction with a rising environmental movement that sometimes portrayed Indians as especially ecologically conscientious. This idealization fit well with Dee Brown's *Bury My Heart at Wounded Knee* (1970), which tells the history of Native Americans from the Indian point of view. This completed a cycle of history in which Indians had evolved from savage primitives in the way of enlightenment to themselves being the enlightened ones, the good and the noble. Custer's legend, conversely, is at best mixed. He still has admirers, but history, new information, and changing politics complicate his legacy.[43]

11

THE CUSTER STORY
IN HISTORY

History is like the sky at midnight.

—Frederick Whittaker[1]

Libbie Custer recalled a peculiar image as her husband and the cavalry column left Fort Lincoln that May morning in 1876. They seemed a mirage "equally plain to the sight on the earth and in the sky." For nearly 150 years, Custer has been suspended between fact and ephemera for everyone from historians to dime novelists to cinematographers.[2]

The Custer story first arrived via journalists, who in a few cases became biographers or historians of the Little Bighorn. Custer has come to us from scholars, popular writers, dime novelists, literary figures, screenwriters, other soldiers, his widow and a great grandnephew, and his Indian foes. Sometimes the story is from "none of the above" but from someone who simply is fascinated with Custer, such as the podiatrist who added a pair of Custer boots to his collection and came down with a case of Custerphilia. Custer historiography would be a volume unto itself, were it even possible to assemble in its entirety because of the sheer volume of material. A half-century-old count ran to nearly 650 items. In 2010, Larry Sklenar estimated that the total number of published Custer books exceeded sixteen hundred—just the books, not such miscellany as articles, comics, television, and film. Even if it were possible to review comprehensively the Custer–Little Bighorn histories, such an undertaking probably would not be useful because much of the material simply is redundant or poorly done. The challenge is not to compile an exhaustive catalog but instead to assess works that best represent a perspective or are the most useful or influential. For example, Frederick Whittaker's biography of Custer is not the best, but it ranks among the most influential by virtue of being first and in concert with Libbie Custer's successful image campaign of the next half century. Even the categories offered here are selective because of the number of books, some of which we have discussed elsewhere. This ever-expanding trove of material is part of the Custer legend, which exists amid the inconstant winds of history and vacillating moods of culture.[3]

Gregory J. W. Urwin summed up well the imbalance of the Custer literature, which obsesses with "an insignificant Indian battle" and short-changes or even omits his Civil War accomplishments. Urwin documented Custer's skill as a field commander and showed how his Civil War record was not at all congruent with his performance in the Plains Wars. He documented Custer's buildup in the press and showed how his fighting reputation affected his relationships with other commanders as well as his own men. Urwin was understandably annoyed with the hole in the historical literature when he published *Custer Victorious* in 1983. Though Urwin took Custer research and writing into a neglected but not unknown area, he fit an earlier tradition of exuberant interpretation of Custer's actions. The Civil War was for Custer the defining event of his life. His death at the Little Bighorn defined Custer for posterity.[4]

Several other Civil War works have since provided the sort of context that Urwin advocated: Jay W. Simson's *Custer and the Front Royal Executions of 1864* (2009) and David Coffey's *Sheridan's Lieutenants: Phil Sheridan, His Generals, and the Final Year of the Civil War* (2005). In September 1864, Union soldiers executed at least five of John Mosby's Rangers. Mosby hanged three Union prisoners in reprisal. Mosby blamed Custer. Such a charge later rang true for many Custer critics who wanted to put the Washita battle in the context of a previous atrocity. Simson, though, found Custer not guilty, pointing out that he ordered no executions, probably was not at the executions, and did not have the command authority Mosby attributed to him. In fact, according to Simson, Custer was a very good brigade and divisional commander. Coffey, too, found admirable qualities in the Civil War Custer—a young officer who was flamboyant but willing to fight. Philip Sheridan cultivated a number of very bright and brave young officers, including Custer. It was not Custer's luck that won him promotions and recognition but the fact that he and others earned their postwar positions with substantial contributions to Sheridan's success.[5]

In *The Real Custer: From Boy General to Tragic Hero* (2014), James S. Robbins showed Custer to have been a brave, sometimes reckless, and skillful commander in the Civil War. In documenting the facts of Custer's ability, Robbins balanced the rise to fame against "Custer's luck"—his just being in the right place at the right time and having the right connections. For example, the shortcomings of Judson Kilpatrick as a cavalry commander were ultimately to Custer's advantage, but the latter had the talent to fill the vacuum of Kilpatrick's ineptitude. It was not a hollow promotion. Undeniably, Custer was charismatic and good press material. Still, according to Robbins, Custer had the skill and panache to take full advantage of such opportunities. Robbins's argument is well documented, particularly with regard to the public Custer, who became a newspaper staple during the war, to the chagrin of a few other officers. Robbins defended Custer's postwar record, including the years in Texas and the Plains Wars, in the context of Custer's Civil War years, particularly vis-à-vis Mosby in northern Virginia. The plains were a far larger theater of operations, Robbins noted, and Custer had far fewer men, fighting enemies who were not only mobile but also moved their whole communities, meaning Shenandoah Valley–style scorched-earth tactics were of no use.[6]

Thom Hatch, in *Glorious War: The Civil War Adventures of George Armstrong Custer* (2013), saw Custer first and foremost as a Civil War soldier who served his country and usually won. But his record was eclipsed by the Little Bighorn:

> With this book as a testament, George Armstrong Custer's entire military career should be reassessed by fair-minded historians under a more favorable light and found to have been commendable. Few officers before or after have served with such honor and distinction. In the end he should receive praise rather than vilification for his patriotic service to America and be awarded his rightful place in history books alongside the greatest of cavalry commanders.

Like Urwin's *Custer Victorious*, *Glorious War* is in the tradition of the heroic Custer and demonstrates especially good command of secondary sources and narrative force.[7]

The heroic Custer theme had its genesis in publications well before the Little Bighorn. Custer himself developed it, first in his *Galaxy* series and then in *My Life on the Plains: or, Personal Experiences with Indians*. Whittaker and Libbie Custer effectively promoted the legend, which was for the most part accepted uncritically among historians and popularizers until the 1930s.[8]

CUSTERPHILES AND CUSTERPHOBES

Consideration of almost any historical figure or event needs to give some deference to the first rendering, not necessarily for its historiographic qualities but because being first often means creating a template for others or being the one to which subsequent historians respond. Libbie Custer and journalist-Custerphile Whittaker are not among the must-reads if one is looking to become better acquainted with the man and the battle. However, they are must-reads if one is to appreciate the Custer myth, its nineteenth-century origins, and the people who helped create the legend. Whittaker's *A Complete Life of General George A. Custer* (1876) is the biography that people of the era wanted. *A Complete Life* finished the portrait Custer started in *My Life on the Plains*. *My Life* was autobiographical. More critically, it was lavish self-promotion. With eloquent acidity, Frederick Benteen dubbed it "My Lie on the Plains." Whittaker produced the only substantial Custer biography in the nineteenth century, and the earliest biographies in the twentieth century remained in Whittaker's hagiographic tradition. He and Libbie helped spawn nearly two generations of Custerphiles, such as Frazier Hunt, who oozed adoration for someone they believed embodied the noble qualities of American myth and heroism, of the bold and fearless leader, the dashing frontiersman taking on the wilderness, both real and symbolic. For Custerphiles, he was all of the above or some combination thereof. *Boots and Saddles; or, Life in Dakota with General Custer* (1885) was the first of three books Libbie Custer wrote about her deceased husband. It is illustrative of her influence on the Custer myth and subsequent Custer histories. Two subsequent volumes were *Tenting on the Plains; or, General Custer in Kansas and Texas* (1887) and *Following the Guidon* (1890).[9]

Sentiments began to change in the 1920s, with the rising tide of modernism and a more critical look at American traditions and icons, including heroic and romantic history. Among the array of antihero books and articles about Custer, many were hypercritical, to the point that later historians deemed some of the authors "Custerphobes." Frederic F. Van de Water's critical biography of Custer began the Custer-as-villain phase of Little Bighorn history. *Glory-Hunter: A Life of General Custer* (1934) remains influential because the character flaws Van de Water found still pervade the Custer literature—the main faults being vanity and egoism. Van de Water presented Custer as an incompetent egoist who squandered his men's lives for self-aggrandizement. The historians in this new, Custerphobic vein were just as unbalanced as the Custerphiles, except the primary theme was contempt for Custer, who now embodied the dark side of American culture—imperialism, vanity, violation of Christian principles, violence. Van de Water and other Custerphobes puzzled Robert M. Utley, who wondered how people without connection to the event or the person, other than historical interest, could develop such a passionate hatred of Custer:

> Unlike the participants in the Little Bighorn campaign and their friends, the writers of the 20th century have no perceptible reason to become emotionally involved in the events of 1876. Yet partisanship in this century has been even more bitter than in the last. Loudest were the Custerphobes of the 1920s and 1930s, led by Frederic F. Van de Water, E. A. Brininstool, C. E. DeLand, and Fred Dustin. Although they quarreled incessantly among themselves over details and interpretations, they shared a passionate, almost unhealthy, hatred of Custer. [10]

It took a few more decades to find the center. In the 1950s, several notable volumes were much more objective, fitting neither the Whittaker–Libbie Custer tradition nor the Van de Water antithesis. Those historians included Jay Monaghan, who wrote *Custer: The Life of General George Armstrong Custer* (1959); William A. Graham, whose body of work included *The Custer Myth: A Source Book of Custeriana* (1953); and Edgar Irving Stewart, who wrote *Custer's Luck* (1955). Graham's *Myth* was not a narrative biography but a collection of historical essays and primary materials about Custer and the Little Bighorn. Nevertheless, his approach was dispassionate, and in this and other publications he looked to understand the man and the battle. Stewart, too, sought more than a battle epic with heroes and scoundrels in his much more objective military history of the Little Bighorn. [11]

In *Custer: The Life of General George Armstrong Custer*, Monaghan stuck with the knowable facts from a wide range of sources, even in those places where others seemed unable to avoid judgment, such as the Meotzi legend. Noting the gossip and the baby's birth date and checking the citations from Mari Sandoz, who assumed Custer had fathered the child, Monaghan concluded in a footnote, "Until the various documents are found, then, and show more than has been reported from the Sandoz notes, the Custer-baby stories must be considered Indian gossip. It should be remembered, too, that the Indian Bureau would not have been averse to circulating tales against the army."[12]

Monaghan was an accomplished historian of the West, though not an academic historian. His strong narrative style and colorful language drew critical praise, especially from Stephen Ambrose, who called his book "a model biography—scholarly, detailed, and lively. It cannot be surpassed."[13] Ambrose praised Monaghan's detailed account of Custer's Civil War experiences. A pioneer in oral history, he launched a project in 1935 in which he interviewed Indians for the Colorado Historical Society and owners of sheep and cattle ranches in Wyoming and Utah in 1920s and 1930s. His treatment of Marcus Reno and Benteen exemplifies the balance that Monaghan brought to the story. He found flaws and virtues in both men, especially Benteen. At the Little Bighorn, Reno

> displayed a distressing weakness of character . . . wanting in resolution. Benteen, on the other hand, took over heroically. Although second in rank, this gossipy and garrulous fellow, like the Duke of Austria and Shakespeare's "King John," found that "courage mounteth with occasion." He ordered foxholes dug, rearranged duffel for defense in case the Indians renewed the attack tomorrow.

While Reno thought the only way to save the command was to slip away in the night, leaving the wounded, Benteen would not consider such a thing, leaving the men to be tortured to death. Monaghan called Benteen "Custer's enemy and a chronic whiner" and charged both Benteen and Reno with being "dark with hatred of the commander." Though Monaghan disliked Reno, he did not accept the accusation of Reno's critics in 1876 that, had he continued the charge at the river, he would have scattered the disorganized warriors. As for Reno's chief accusers, Libbie Custer and Whittaker were looking for someone to blame, and Reno was the best target. Was Reno at fault for not continuing the charge? "Who can say?" Monaghan asked. [14]

Custer himself received similarly dispassionate treatment. Monaghan noted, for example, that Custer may have been eager to get the glory for himself in the 1876 expedition, but all of the officers wanted first crack at and credit for whipping the Indians. Custer's leadership and preparation for the 1876 expedition were "Custer at his best." At the Washita, Monaghan pointed out, Custer acted bravely and effectively. The transgression of abandoning Elliott and his men meant that "his enemies would say that he either became frightened or so elated over victory that he wanted to get back regardless of Elliott's fate. Who can analyze motives?" [15]

Jeffry D. Wert's *Custer: The Controversial Life of George Armstrong Custer* (1996) was a particularly good account of Custer's early years, recounting his pandering to the press during the Civil War, his brashness and ambition, and his image fetish as demonstrated in the attention he gave details of his uniform. Like other historians, Wert found that Custer coveted fame and glory. Wert stated that historians should be unsparing in seeking the truth but admitted they probably never will be satisfied, for at the core of the battle story "lies a mystery." [16]

THE LITTLE BIGHORN

Among historians who have provided the most comprehensive, balanced accounts of Custer and the Little Bighorn, Utley merits first mention. It is not so much because of a single premier volume but because of his body of work, which began in 1962 with *Custer and the Great Controversy*. Unlike many of his predecessors, Utley is neither Custerphile nor Custerphobe. *Cavalier in Buckskin* (1998) put the story in its proper time and place, viewing Custer through the perspective of America's westward movement, and Utley is among the senior fellows of that genre of national history that facilitated placing Custer and the Little Bighorn in proper context. Militarily, he faulted Custer when the evidence led him there and commended the Indians when appropriate. Utley also acknowledged the role of publicity in shaping Custer's persona and his legend. He concluded that history has been a little too tough on Custer.

Like Utley, Louise Barnett cited Custer's lack of information about the size of the Indian encampment and the unfamiliar terrain. As a result, he launched his attack before the rest of his command showed up. In *Touched by Fire: The Life, Death and Mythic Afterlife of George Armstrong Custer* (1996), Barnett, more than the other historians in this group, used the battle to contemplate the role of women in the nineteenth century, as well as the fate of women and children captured by Indians. It was a good addition that helps the reader understand frontier brutality, Indian culture, and the military response. Custer, she showed, was not peculiarly brutal but was of his time and place. She did not condone the violence but explained it. Barnett also gave ample—some might say excessive—attention to Libbie Custer and her experiences with army life, the frontier, and widowhood. Barnett did have an affinity for premonitions and "what-if" history that some might find off-putting. For example, she noted Libbie's dream of her husband being shot from his horse. Libbie's widowhood provoked some speculation about what would have happened to Custer had it been Libbie who died first. "Given his strong will and natural buoyancy, it seems unlikely that he would have been destroyed." It is historically irrelevant but makes for great reading and reinforces the point that Custer is a gateway into any number of issues with innumerable perspectives. [17]

Two comprehensive Custer biographies of the last decade were James Donovan's *A Terrible Glory: Custer and the Little Bighorn—the Last Great Battle of the American West* (2008) and Nathaniel Philbrick's *The Last Stand: Custer, Sitting Bull, and the Battle of the Little Bighorn* (2010). Donovan, too, found that Custer's confidence devolved to arrogance and proved his undoing. Donovan credited Crazy Horse and Sitting Bull for their leadership, both spiritual and tactical, but was not an apologist for either side. Just as the soldiers were inept horsemen and incompetent with their guns, the Indians were chaotic and disorganized in their fighting. Donovan drew on the archeological evidence unearthed at the battle site in the 1980s and 1990s, which challenged the idea that a "last stand" place or moment ever existed. There were failures in command, such as Reno's drunkenness and Benteen's sullen dithering. Donovan gave more weight to the Reno hearing than most other historians. The public did not blame Custer, Donovan concluded, until Reno was found not guilty.

Philbrick hewed closely to Custer and the Little Bighorn, with only brief forays into related topics, such as Indian life and women. Philbrick did not take an omniscient view of events and instead imparted great appreciation for what the three columns—Custer, Reno, and Benteen—did not know about one another's positions, the strength of the Indians, and the terrain. In short, none of the three knew what the other two were doing. Philbrick followed the aftermath of the Little Bighorn and how it defined the lives of a number of individuals, including Libbie Custer, Crazy Horse, Benteen, and Reno. This extension of the narrative was especially good because it offered the chance to appreciate the impact of Custer's defeat and provided some context for the emerging mythology of Custer and the Little Bighorn.

Several good volumes were limited to military history, which became very minute at times with regard to movements, logistics, chain-of-command issues, tactics, and strategy. Most of the above biographies ably covered the battle. However, a few narratives stand apart because biography was not so much their concern as the raw military history. Stewart's *Custer's Luck* traced troop movements so closely that it threatened to be incomprehensible to all but the most ardent devotees of the battle itself. Stewart explained what it took to move a large force that included supplies and ammunition over the rough terrain and across swollen streams with poor communications and the language problems with the Crow scouts. Stewart's convincing assessment of the difficulties drew on a wide range of primary and secondary sources, including numerous contemporaneous accounts from newspapers and magazines. When Stewart looked at a variety of the tales and legends of the battle—such as soldiers being drunk, images of drawn sabers, of Custer being killed in the river rather than at Last Stand Hill—he deftly separated fact, legend, and the unknowable. The admission that so much is just not knowable and the declaration that it may be pointless to squabble ceaselessly about Custer and the battle would make Stewart a killjoy for many. [18]

In *To Hell with Honor: Custer and the Little Bighorn* (2000), Sklenar was similarly attentive to military minutiae, which included biographies of lower-ranking officers, the demography of the enlisted men, details of what each man carried, problems with mule pack trains, and even the kind of knot used to tie packs on the mules. Sklenar put a lot of the burden on the mules, so to speak, and the difficulties of packing and handling them. Sklenar found both Reno and Benteen lacking, the former for drunkenness, dishonesty, and cowardice, the latter for pettiness, obstinacy, and dishonesty. Sklenar called his book an analysis of "conflicting evidence relative to the Battle of the Little Bighorn." He succeeded, as his speculation was informed and probabilistic. [19]

Others literally dug into the battle, beginning with archeological studies in the 1980s and 1990s that uncovered thousands of pieces of ammunition remnants. Douglas D. Scott and Richard Allan Fox Jr., in separate studies, applied archeology to the Custer puzzle. With the help of metal detectors, several research teams scanned the main battlefield as well as the Reno-Benteen defense sites, land around Weir Point, and other areas. Perhaps most significantly, the research showed the Indians to have been much better armed than previously believed. Scott's forensics identified forty-seven different guns used by the warriors, as well as bows and arrows, knives, lances, tomahawks, and war clubs. Conservatively assuming 1,500 warriors, about 200 had repeating rifles, and another 375 were equipped with muzzle loaders and single-shot rifles. The same evidence was used to test witnesses' accounts, validating some and refuting others. The archeology added another difference of opinion concerning the Little Bighorn when the archeologists concluded that Custer accompanied the left wing down Medicine Tail Coulee to the ford rather than going with the right wing on the Nye-Cartwright Ridge. [20]

A number of Custer–Little Bighorn histories have been produced primarily for popular consumption and offer well-written, entertaining accounts of the general's life and campaigns. No contemporary Custer book fits this genre so well as Evan S. Connell's *Son of the Morning Star* (1984), the popularity of which was greatly expanded by a successful 1991 television film of the same name. *Son of the Morning Star* is narrative history with literary flair. Western novelist and historian Larry McMurtry called it "a masterpiece that is unlikely to be bettered: a literary mosaic on the one hand and a feat of literary archaeology on the other, with Connell working patiently in the inexhaustible dig of the Little Bighorn, where he frequently unearths shards of commentary that no one else has found." [21]

Connell, a respected novelist and short story writer, leveraged an essay about Custer into what became a significant nonfiction best seller. Custer is an actor playing a small, sometimes absurd role in the great sweep of Western history, buffeted by vanity, military politics, and clashing cultures. The wandering narrative gallops across a vast terrain of facts toward a tragic denouement at the Little Bighorn. Although Connell does not cite his sources through notes, the documents from which they are drawn are cited in a voluminous bibliography. This technique compromises the historical value of the work for some readers, even as it facilitates the narrative. It is an ambitious, modernist approach, not quite the masterpiece McMurtry says it is, but a memorable contribution to Custer studies and, for better or worse, the source of a great many public impressions as to what actually happened.

Like Connell, McMurtry is sensitive to the way historical narratives shape a useable past. As a Western writer with a Pulitzer Prize and a large following, McMurtry could hardly avoid entering the Custer literary wars, although he admits he is not "a battlefield buff, and I am not even sure I should call myself a historian." Asked to write a short biography, *Crazy Horse*, for a series of historical essays by noted writers, McMurtry began an inquiry that he continued in *Custer* (2012), another short work he intended as a clarifying commentary and reassessment of the Custer literature. He found it challenging as he wound his way along myriad, twisting paths of Little Bighorn history, strewn with legend and fact. Like many others before him, however, McMurtry raised as many questions about the Little Bighorn as he answered, speculating that "the immense dust cloud so obscured the scene, or limited his focus, that [Custer] never really knew the extent of his own misjudgment. It may be that he even thought he was winning, until he was suddenly dead."[22]

McMurtry gets to the heart of the difficulties that come with this sort of popular approach to Custer when he references Stephen E. Ambrose's *Crazy Horse and Custer: The Parallel Lives of Two American Warriors* (1975). As usual, Ambrose, a prolific and best-selling historian, appeals to audiences with a good story of the two men up through the Little Bighorn and their separate, violent deaths. But his research is suspect because he was accused of plagiarizing passages from Monaghan's *Custer*, the biography he so admired. Ambrose subsequently was accused of plagiarism and errors in other books he wrote. He brushed aside many of these charges by claiming the problems were not substantive and that he was interested primarily in telling a good story. In the Custer book, however, he conceded that "much of the fun of studying this battle is the free rein it gives to the imagination." McMurtry warned, "Once pointed toward this battle, historical imaginations tend to bolt" like a runaway horse.[23]

Duane Schultz, a psychology professor who also writes military history, provided a somewhat different approach and purpose in the popular genre. His *Custer: Lessons in Leadership* (2010) is part of a series of books about famous American generals. In this short, crisply written biography, Schultz concluded that while Custer was the "ideal cavalry general" in the Civil War, he came up short as a leader in what was a new kind of warfare, "an insurgency, a guerrilla war in which the enemy typically attacked civilians rather than military units, and quickly disappeared, melting into the countryside." This is hardly the case, however, as small unit action was the norm for American soldiers until the massed battles of the Mexican War and Civil War, and even then such partisan rangers as Mosby and such brigands as William Quantrill were active combatants. As a psychological case study of leadership, the book appeared to offer lessons for budding generals and CEOs who must adapt tactics and strategies to face unexpected situations. [24]

THE CUSTER MYTH

Custer and the Little Bighorn seem both inevitable and aberrant in the course of American history. Custer himself is much of what makes the Little Bighorn a compelling story. Without such a dashing figure, the story of the battle would not be nearly so interesting or controversial. He is mythologized in American history and culture because he fits any number of roles, from tragic hero to inept villain. He has been the face of Manifest Destiny, of middle-class accomplishment, of the mediocre student rising above expectations, of bravery and daring under fire, of reckless youth and the allure of the West. His is a story of the menace of the frontier and of civilization's triumph over savagery. He symbolizes the sins of the whites against Indians. Recent decades have seen numerous biographies that are commendable in detail, readability, reliance on sound sources, and balance. In spite of little new evidence or insight, the Custer industry runs unabated.

Utley is among the most prominent of Custer and Little Bighorn historians in part due to the fact that too often other histories were distilled in presentism and garnished with politics. In addition to his productivity and quality of work, Utley came first to Western history, then to Custer. This is in contrast to some who found in Custer an icon or demon for their causes. Utley evaluated Custer in his historical context and relied on primary sources. He did the same with Custer's adversaries, particularly

Sitting Bull. Utley spent his career with the National Park Service, retiring in 1980. During his time with the service and in his retirement, he wrote Western history, which included biographies of Custer, Sitting Bull, and Geronimo and histories of the Indian Wars, Texas lawmen, frontier violence, the mountain men, and the National Park Service, as well as guides to the Little Bighorn battlefield. The scope of Utley's work gave him a unique ability to understand Custer and the Little Bighorn as part of a larger story and not treat him as a wildly deviant moment in history.

Western histories can't avoid Custer, but, as part of the American epic, he is a bit more problematic, in no small part because of the controversy, as Utley pointed out in *Custer and the Great Controversy*. The epic, though, is more than a battle story or a tragedy. Such history discovered Custer's place in the larger stories of the American West and in American culture. Richard Slotkin fitted Custer to that larger history, which was one of expansion, growth, and violence, along with the inevitable doom of the Indians and their way of life. In *The Fatal Environment: The Myth of the Frontier in the Age of Industrialization, 1800–1890* (1985), Slotkin showed that violence and the exterminationist philosophy were characteristic of American frontier life and mentality:

> The violent spirit of the warrior hero, and the violent means by which he has gained his wisdom, are inseparable from the regenerative process he initiates. Thus this hero can only function as a social benefactor when he operates on the edge of society, where it confronts the unsocial wilderness. The spectacular violence underscoring his achievement is morally acceptable only when it occurs beyond the borders and when its objects are those primitive and alien races whose existence is antithetical to the triumph of the Metropolis.[25]

Though Custer needed to be extraordinary to be legend and myth, this view made him common, perhaps extraordinary only in that he was an exaggeration of typical ideas and attitudes. Thus, Custer was not an aberration in American history but an expectation.

Any credible Custer–Little Bighorn history acknowledges the myth and ponders it to some extent. This important subset of Custer–Little Bighorn history focuses on and attempts to understand the American culture's fascination, even obsession, with the man and the battle. Like the battlefield, the intellectual terrain can be hard to decipher. One of the greatest challenges for any historian venturing into this territory is simply defining the terms *legend* and *myth*, which authors have treated in varied fashion. For Lawrence Frost, legends were untruths. Utley's myth ranged from an unsettled question to controversial historical issues. Graham, too, seemed to view myth as unanswered questions, which he did not presume to answer, instead offering a grounding in sources for one to approach the problems. Michael Elliott and Brian Dippie approached myth as a complex representation of a larger truth and cultural values.

In 1962, with *Custer and the Great Controversy*, Utley was the first to give book-length consideration to the Custer myth. Utley sorted through the myriad, sometimes conflicting stories that followed the Little Bighorn. He stated that almost every myth of the Little Bighorn could be found in the press accounts of 1876. He used the press extensively in tracing the development of the controversy, a term he appeared to prefer over the word *myth*. He was highly skeptical of the veracity of the news stories but found them useful as an entry into the myth. In a 1976 article, published between the first and later editions of *Custer and the Great Controversy*, Utley credited newspapers with sensationally exploiting the battle and inspiring a number of pulp and popular writers, including Whittaker, but faulted reporters for not being historians. In discussing the problem of recording Indian testimony about the Little Bighorn, Utley noted that it was extremely difficult to interpret from one language to another, let alone when "the average Sioux or Cheyenne interpreter was scarcely proficient in the science. Beyond this, many of the interrogators were newspaper reporters for whom historical accuracy was an objective distinctly secondary to sensational copy, and many of the witnesses had a variety of motives for not telling the truth." Such criticism did not stop Utley from using the press as the foundation for his study of the controversy, however. He placed individual reporters in the history of the legend, including Mark Kellogg and Whittaker, who first met Custer in the New York offices of *Galaxy* and immediately became an admirer. In addition to writing his *Life of Custer*, Whittaker was provocateur in chief for the creation of the Reno court of inquiry.[26]

Though offering a slightly jaundiced view of the press, Utley put newspapers among four aspects of the story that are necessary to understanding the Custer controversy: the press, the military "great debate" over Reno's role, Indian contributions, and the blossoming of legend and myth. Utley had a somewhat simplistic view of the press. He did not appreciate the fact that "objectivity" is a modern press value; in the nineteenth century, the mass press and modern media values were just emerging. Second, it was not the job of the press to provide historical narrative. It was the job of the press to provide information for the masses, and to this extent press accounts necessarily pandered—as they still do—to the prejudices and perspectives of the moment and to audience tastes.

Slotkin's *The Fatal Environment* is not a Custer history, but it merits mention among studies of the Custer myth because of Slotkin's profound insights about Custer's place in American myth and history. Slotkin devoted several chapters to Custer, whom he placed at the "narrative core of the Last Stand myth." Any interpretation of the myth, therefore, depended on the reading of Custer's character and motives. Slotkin called the last stand myth a variant of the frontier myth, one that might be applied to any number of social and political conflicts, such as race or labor. Custer was not unique in military accomplishments, nor in westward wandering or even defeat. "But none did all of these things in sequence and at a time when western affairs were accorded center stage." Unlike the pattern set out in literary conventions to that point, Custer moved from West to East in search of opportunity. When he did go West, it was with an eye toward succeeding in the hierarchical structures of the military and New York society. "He is an early type of organization man, hiding in the costumes of the cavalier trooper and the Frontier buckskin."[27]

Graham's *The Custer Myth: A Source Book of Custeriana* is prominent among Custer histories but is not a study of Custer as myth. The subhead better reflects the content. Though the title is misleading, it is a necessary volume for anyone interested in Custer and is an excellent window onto the problem of doing Custer history. The collection of battle stories incorporates numerous Indian accounts, the versions of a wide variety of military officers, including Benteen and Reno, some writings, and an extensive bibliography by Custerphobe Fred Dustin, who wrote a scathing indictment of Custer in the *Michigan History Journal* in 1946. Graham's reprint of important primary sources includes Benteen's narrative, Kellogg's letters, scout George Herendeen's story, and details of the Reno hearings.[28]

In *Custer Legends* (1981), Frost meant *legend* as controversy or speculation about the man and the battle, not in the sense of a mythic person or event that reflects larger truths about the culture. Frost's legends included the number of soldiers who died in the battle, who actually killed

Custer, whether Benteen disobeyed orders, rumors of Custer having a woman at the battle, and stories of a sole survivor. Generally, he was even-handed. For example, he concluded that Custer did not have a son by Meotzi and that the nature of the relationship between her and Custer was simply unknowable.

Frost argued that a lot more than luck was at work in Custer's Civil War leadership and ascension through the ranks. He was a good commander. Frost recounted Custer's alleged hanging of several of Mosby's Rangers, who some claimed were war criminals. Frost found Custer not guilty. Via a number of passages with a "charge-countercharge" structure, Frost argued the evidence in lawyerly fashion. In the chapter titled "Hero or Fool," Frost favored the heroic and declared that much of the command, Benteen in particular, had failed to come to Custer when he summoned them. Benteen, Frost charged, abandoned Custer. This is not surprising, given that Frost was a certified Custerphile. He wrote a dozen books on Custer, which included volumes on Custer's horses, his photographers, and his wife, Libbie. His collection of Custer lore included thousands of telegrams, military orders, and even a photo album that had belonged to the couple. Frost was central to the 1967 founding of the Little Big Horn Associates and assisted Urwin with the important research that led to publication of *Custer Victorious*.[29]

Michael A. Elliott, in *Custerology: The Enduring Legacy of the Indian Wars and George Armstrong Custer* (2007), pondered the Custer myth, its celebrations in contemporary culture, and how the myth seeped into far and near corners of American culture. Custer's place in the national imagination is a contradictory one, according to Elliott, an English professor. He called Custer's death at the Little Bighorn a "national mythic spectacle," more significant as spectacle than military loss. Elliott's focus was not the man and the battle but the ongoing production of knowledge and material about Custer and the Indian Wars. Elliott declared himself a "thorough presentist—someone whose interest in history is focused on how that history, including prior acts of historical commemoration, is experienced in our current age." He traced the historical and collective fascination through the history of the Little Bighorn Battlefield National Monument, consideration of violence in American history (for which he gives ample credit to Slotkin), the interests of members of the Little Big Horn Associates, the impact of Indian testimony, and reenactments. Elliott noted it is a bit curious that Custer actually became a point of conciliation when Indians and whites cooperated to produce an annual reenactment. His range of source material included newspapers, magazines, national organizations devoted to the subject, television, and cinema.[30]

Brian W. Dippie's *Custer's Last Stand: The Anatomy of an American Myth* (1976) was perhaps the best study of Custer myth creators, which included cinema, fiction, poetry, and paintings. Dippie was a professor of history at the University of Victoria in Canada. His study of the cultural response to the man and the battle reflected an appreciation for how the competing myths arose in various media and how the myths shifted with the cultural mood. His chronological bibliography of Custer biography and related history is helpful in navigating the Great Plains of Custer studies. He, too, admitted the impossibility of a genuinely exhaustive bibliography on the subject of Custer.[31]

HISTORY FOR THE MASSES

Utley's designated Custerphobes of the 1920s and 1930s—Van de Water, Brininstool, DeLand, and Dustin—were not academic historians but instead seemed to fall somewhere between hobbyists and obsessives. Like Utley, Elliott listed Brininstool as among the most influential early-twentieth-century figures in Custer studies. Elliott added Walter Camp, John S. Gray, and Frost. This coterie of Custer fanatics was composed of a journalist, a professor of physiology, a railroad construction superintendent, and a podiatrist. None came to Custer professionally, but all dealt with the subject passionately.

Brininstool collected numerous stories of alleged survivors of the battle and eventually turned to the defense of Benteen and Reno. Brininstool began his journalism career in Los Angeles in 1895 and soon turned to freelancing, writing extensively about Western life for magazines. His publications included *A Trooper with Custer and Other Historic Incidents of the Battle of the Little Big Horn* (1925) and *The Custer Fight: Capt. Benteen's Story of the Battle of the Little Big Horn, June 25–26, 1876* (1933). Like Van de Water, Brininstool deemed Custer's arrogance a major factor in his undoing at the Little Bighorn. Brininstool was among those at whom Utley marveled for being able to harbor such a "passionate, almost unhealthy, hatred of Custer." Graham likewise commented on Brininstool's "long, continued effort 'to cut Custer down to size' and make a hero of Reno."[32]

Dustin published a 641-item Custer bibliography between 1939 and 1952. Like Brininstool and Van de Water, Dustin defended Reno. Graham, who reprinted the bibliography in *The Custer Myth*, called Dustin a master of research and commended the bibliography to any student of Custer and the Little Bighorn. Graham granted masterpiece status to Dustin's *The Custer Tragedy* (1939), in spite of its slant. DeLand, an attorney in South Dakota, also collected interviews of alleged survivors and did his own studies of the battlefield. *The Sioux Wars* (1930, 1934) was a two-volume history that followed the Sioux from Minnesota through the Little Bighorn and Wounded Knee. Thus, it provided historical context for the battle.[33]

Gray approached Custer and the Little Bighorn more empirically than the others. The professor of physiology at Northwestern University used his more systemic approach to calculate the fighting strength of the Indians and to assess the 7th Cavalry's movements via a "time-motion" study. He even devoted a chapter in *Custer's Last Campaign: Mitch Boyer and the Little Bighorn Reconstructed* (1991) to mapping scout Curly's escape route. Similarly meticulous, *Centennial Campaign: The Sioux War of 1876* (1976) is a highly detailed history of the Battle of the Little Bighorn and provided a history of the fighting that led up to the battle. Whatever one may think of his approach or the assumptions behind his models, he in some respects anticipated a different approach to history. A few decades later, archeologists used their science to get a better picture of the "last stand," or lack thereof. Such close, factual attention to details of troop movement may appeal only to a more limited audience, but Little Bighorn diehards regard that detail highly.[34]

Walter Camp became central to the Custer literature with his extensive collection of interviews of Indian Wars survivors, both white and Indian. He was especially interested in the Little Bighorn. His job as construction superintendent with the Englewood and Chicago Railway meant he had free passes to travel the West. He began visiting battlefields and by 1917 wrote that he had interviewed more than 60 survivors of Reno's command and more than 150 Indian survivors. He died in 1925 without completing his planned volume, but since 1976 four books based solely on his notes have been released, including *Camp on Custer: Transcribing the Custer Myth* (1995) and *Custer in '76: Walter Camp's Notes on the Custer Fight* (1990).[35]

Frost began his acquaintance with the Custer legend in 1929, when he moved to Monroe, Michigan, to start his podiatry practice. Brice Custer, great grandnephew of General Custer and defender of the family's honor, gave Frost a pair of the general's boots that had a bullet hole from one of the general's Civil War wounds. For Frost, the game was afoot, as the boots appear to have left a deep imprint among his collection of unusual footwear. It was the start of a case of Custerphilia, as Frost collected thousands of Custer books, articles, original telegrams, orders, letters, and photos. He was among the founders of the Little Big Horn Associates. He wrote twelve books on Custer, which include a few arcane titles: *General Custer's Thoroughbreds* (1989) and *General Custer's Photographers* (1986). In a more conventional vein, he also produced *The Custer Album* (1964) and *General Custer's Libbie* (1976).[36]

INDIAN HISTORY VIA CUSTER

As though Custer–Little Bighorn history is not sufficiently cumbersome in its own right, it is a significant part of another genre of American history. That is Indian history. According to Elliott, there are more than 250 Indian accounts of the Little Bighorn. Several historiographic assessments of those stories, including those by Elliott and Utley, leave only more doubts about the elusive details of the Little Bighorn and Custer's final moments. In Utley's estimation, the Indian accounts only deepen the mystery and confusion. "Most of the Indian testimony is so confused, contradictory, and weirdly divorced from known reality that one is tempted to ignore all such evidence," he wrote. Obstacles came from translation, cultural traditions, and chronological narrative versus non-chronological impressions. Even the purpose of a narrative—whether to clarify historical facts or fit a tradition of entertaining braggadocio—was at issue. Still, Utley noted, it is valuable material that must be understood in its proper context and should not be dismissed out of hand. Elliott agreed. "Native testimony is simply too alluring to ignore altogether," even when it claimed Custer believed a Little Bighorn victory would make him a viable presidential candidate or that some soldiers committed suicide during the battle. A major weakness is that the testimony was given individually and excluded any larger, coherent narrative of the battle. "Paradox, contradiction, and inscrutability are the ideal grist for a mill that desires to keep grinding interminably," according to Elliott. So, ironically, the Indians have helped Custer live.[37]

PERSONAL HISTORIES

Utley's memoir, *Custer and Me* (2004), is a readable but peculiar book. It's not a history story but a historian's story, a sort of early tell-all memoir. Utley even got into some of the details of an affair that led to the breakup of his first marriage. He considered the changing nature of Custer history; the politics surrounding Park Service decisions, such as renaming of the Custer Battlefield to Little Bighorn Park; and the writing of history. His insights are valuable, especially for those interested in the intersection of history, culture, and media. He suggests, for example, that entertainment and historical interpretation are necessarily at odds. While that may be true in general, the relationship is sometimes symbiotic— witness such phenomena as Ken Burns's *The Civil War* series. In *Custer and Me*, Utley was freed from the constraints of historical sources and impartiality and so provided learned lessons and engaging observations. Among the former, he observed that, as a symbol, the Custer name is akin to the Confederate flag: "Neither Custer nor the Confederate flag should be expurgated from the national memory, but their uses should be sharply examined to limit or remove offense to the offended groups."[38]

Brice Custer wrote a very personal history of the Little Bighorn, *The Sacrificial Lion: George Armstrong Custer, from American Hero to Media Villain* (1999). The World War II veteran appears to have been motivated by his perception of injustice done to his relative. It was a competent synopsis of the general's military career and the Little Bighorn battle. A visit to the Black Kettle Museum in Oklahoma and apparent misinformation about the Washita battle inspired Brice Custer to set the record straight as he saw it. He presented evidence of Custer's competence and reasons for the Little Bighorn loss. But *Sacrificial Lion* seems written primarily as an attack on any negative assessment of the general. In the course of defending his great granduncle, the author assailed the political correctness that absolves Indians of any wrongdoing in the Plains Wars. He denounced the "national guilt movement," movies and television, and "bigots," including Russell Means of the American Indian Movement. Throughout, Brice Custer refers to his relative as "Autie," making his ire even more personal. Among the historians at whom Brice Custer directs his historical-political arrows are Mari Sandoz and Edgar Stewart.[39]

Brice Custer also targeted Vine DeLoria Jr.'s *Custer Died for Your Sins: An Indian Manifesto* (1969), which he cited for its crude manipulation of 1876 facts in order to appease 1960s sentiments and fashions. DeLoria used Custer as a convenient foil for a cause. Utley likewise criticized DeLoria for pandering to the intellectual fashions of the moment instead of writing history. The book was not, Utley wrote, written for historical understanding or clarity. In essence, its main title and subtitle are reversed. It's a manifesto with a patina of history.[40]

Historians have been glassing the ghosts from afar for nearly a century and a half through the lenses of military history, biography, documentary and oral history, ethnography, archeology, Native American studies, and cultural history. The view is of the same lonely battlefield, but the lens remains fogged.

12

VISITORS

In 1975, less than ten months before the centennial of the Battle of the Little Bighorn, CBS newsman Charles Kuralt arrived at the site with a television crew. Then at the height of his fame as the host of *On the Road*, a series of popular and typically cheerful documentary vignettes about extraordinary people in ordinary places, Kuralt was uncharacteristically somber. "This is about a place where the wind blows, the grass grows, and a river flows below a hill," he intoned, embalming the scene in lyrical prose rich with the pathetic fallacy. "There is nothing here but the wind and the grass and the river. But of all the places in America, this is the saddest place I know. . . . Come here sometime, and you'll see. There is melancholy in the wind and sorrow in the grass, and the river weeps."[1]

Kuralt had begun his *On the Road* reports in 1967 as part of the *CBS Evening News*, capturing some of the reportorial authority of that storied half-hour newscast. From the beginning the segments were seen as "a two-minute cease-fire" from the mayhem of the Vietnam War and national domestic turmoil, reaffirming homespun values as Kuralt played the part of a surrogate national tourist traveling the back roads, a gadabout with a purpose, whimsical and dedicated in his treks to find America. Kuralt visited historical sites, especially in the run-up to the bicentennial in 1976, usually offering a Whiggish spin on the national past.[2]

At the Little Bighorn, Kuralt painted a picture of a barren landscape, notable, perhaps, because he anticipated something different. The jocular style of most of his road pieces is absent; here his tone is more suggestive of disappointment and regret. Interviewed about the story for a broadcast-

ing textbook, Kuralt said the challenge he faced was the absence of people to interview. After looking over the battlefield, he returned to the CBS
bus and wrote the elegiac script in a few minutes. He was pleased with
the result when it aired, the austere script matched to the work of his
camera crew and the arid landscape, "beautiful . . . all mood." Kuralt
boasted elsewhere of his travels in search of the authentic America, yet
this was the "saddest place" on his itinerary.[3]

THE SADDEST PLACE

Millions saw Kuralt's vignette and could vicariously share the same be-
wilderment that began when Frederick Benteen asked Alfred H. Terry
where Custer had gone and was told that Custer and his battalion were all
dead on the field. Benteen didn't believe him. He was sure Custer had
abandoned his command, just as Benteen thought he had at the Washita,
and was somewhere on the Bighorn. "I think you are mistaken," Terry
said with some ire, "and you will take your company and go down where
the dead are lying and investigate for yourself." When Benteen's party
reached the battlefield abattoir, they found Custer, naked and reposing
against the recumbent bodies of two soldiers. Some thought his countenance bore the rictus of a smile. "By God, that is him," said Benteen, who
became one of the first visitors to the saddest place.[4]

Of course, there may have been other visitors before Benteen, before
Terry, before even Lieutenant James H. Bradley, who "found the body."
Calamity Jane, the legendary Western adventuress called "the heroine of
the plains," whose real name was Martha Canary, claimed she was along
on the Yellowstone expedition in 1876 and saw the mutilated corpses. "I
went to the battlefield after Custer's battle and I never want to see such a
sight again," Calamity allegedly wrote her daughter in 1879. Other clai-
mants also came forward, including Buffalo Bill, although his visit seems
to have originated in a dime novel before it made its way into his *Wild
West* shows.[5]

The visitors kept coming, and each saw something different because
the battle site marked, in the storied frontier, a dual loss—the defeat of
the 7th Cavalry and the beginning of the end for the victors. Over time,
the site began to take on new meanings.

Descended from Native Americans, novelist and poet James Welch was born on the Blackfeet Indian Reservation in Montana in 1940. "Like any kid in America," he recalled,

> I had grown up with the legend of Custer's Last Stand. . . . I can't think of a hero who has taught kids more about dying in mock battles than General George Armstrong Custer. I had even been Custer myself once, standing on a small sandy hill in the backyard when I was six or seven, suddenly clutching my chest when one of the "Indians" shot me, falling and tumbling down the hill to lie motionless while the battle raged on about me.[6]

Welch's first visit in 1974 made little impression on him other than his encounter with a National Park Service employee who told him not to eat on the battlefield. But he recalled the 1970s and 1980s as a time when he and many Native Americans experienced "consciousness raising" about the past. Welch returned to the battlefield as the scriptwriter for a 1992 documentary film expanding the Indian perspective, a project he later described in his book *Killing Custer*. He recalled sneaking onto the battlefield in 1990 on Halloween night and giving his movie-inspired imagination free rein. He was not far away from the "small sandy hill" in his backyard. But is it possible to see anything at the Little Bighorn without the glistening moonlight of the imagination?[7]

> It is difficult, if not impossible, to truly imagine the battle if you are a daytime visitor. There are too many man-made assaults on the senses. . . .
> But at night you are alone with your imagination. Especially if the moon has lit up the battlefield for you. You can see the soldiers racing their horses up Calhoun Ridge from the ford at Medicine Tail Coulee. . . . You can see the waves of horsemen charging from the south, led by Gall, and from the north, led by Crazy Horse. You can see the soldiers, in a blind, terrified panic, running from Calhoun Hill toward Custer Hill, seeking safety in numbers.[8]

A REALITY MORE ABSTRACT

University of Chicago English professor Norman Maclean, who grew up in Missoula, Montana, worked on a book about Custer and the Little

Bighorn primarily between 1959 and 1963. He corresponded with his friend Robert Utley while developing the Custer project, visiting the battlefield often and reflecting on its meaning. "Since what we see in the Battle is largely something in us, it is natural that behavior on the Battlefield is varied, though patterned. Many make a point of touching the white grave markers as they walk by, others just as clearly avoid doing so, and I have seen several standing in tears and probably not for anyone buried here."[9]

Like Welch, Maclean found special resonance in visiting the battlefield at night, when the battle becomes something spectral, a universal tragedy.

> After the traffic of the day is gone and the gates are shut, the Hill takes on another appearance that again alters dimensions, proportions, and reality. In the moonlight, the Hill is very small, the sky enormous, and in a universe of white diffusion it is hard to tell where the Hill ends and the sky begins and there is no reason to. . . .
>
> This, then is the Custer Battlefield, a slight and distant elevation on which men died in bloody socks and since have been transformed into a universe of other meanings by their own ashy soil, by identities established however irrelevantly with our own lives, and by a power that for a better word is here called spectral.[10]

The project remained unfinished as Maclean turned to the book that made him famous—*A River Runs through It and Other Stories*, published in 1976. Maclean devoted his final years to a book focusing on the 1949 Mann Gulch wildfire in Montana, during which a dozen young smokejumpers were killed. *Young Men and Fire*, published posthumously in 1992, explored the tragic parallels between the cavalrymen and the smokejumpers:

> The hill on which they died is a lot like Custer Hill. In the dry grass on both hills are white scattered markers where the bodies were found, a special cluster of them just short of the top, where red terror closed in from behind and above and from the sides. The bodies were of those who were young and thought to be invincible by others and themselves. They were the fastest the nation had in getting to where there was danger, they got there by moving in the magic realm between heaven and earth, and when they got there they almost made a game of

it. None were surer they couldn't lose than the Seventh Cavalry and
the Smokejumpers. [11]

Mann Gulch, for Maclean, reprised the Little Bighorn in the boldness
and confidence of young men jumping or riding into the midst of danger
on a Montana hillside, only to be surrounded by "red terror." Arrogance
was their undoing as much as flame, bullets, and arrows.

POIGNANT, AMBIGUOUS, PROLEPTIC

In 1988, British American journalist and travel writer Bill Bryson, meandering around the United States in search of amusing material for his
book *The Lost Continent*, stopped at the Little Bighorn. In his writing
about it, his irreverent style is initially on full display:

> There's not much to it, but then there wasn't much to the battle. . . .
> Custer was an idiot and a brute and deserved his fate. . . .
>   All that is known for sure is that Custer screwed up in a mighty big
> way and got himself and 260 other men killed.
>   Scattered as they are around such a desolate and windy bluff, the
> marker stones are surprisingly, almost disturbingly, poignant. It's im-
> possible to look at them and not imagine what a strange and scary
> death it must have been for the soldiers who dropped there, and it left
> me yet again in a reflective frame of mind as I walked down the hill to
> the car and returned to the endless American highway. [12]

Bryson, affecting the insouciance of a bemused, angry, Everyman
narrator at war with kitsch, tourists, and commercialism on his "lost
continent," played the scene for laughs. As a rule, he said, he did not care
for battlefields. "I fail to see the appeal in them once they have carted off
the bodies and swept up." Like Kuralt, he found the site desolate, even
insignificant. This was no Antietam, no Gettysburg. Just a skirmish on the
plains. Why mince words? Custer was a brute, an idiot, a butcher. He
screwed up. He had it coming. Bryson's readers expected prejudices and
gags, history without complexity, and he delivered. The mood changed
abruptly, however, when he was compelled to look at the scattered head-
stones, suggestive of a thousand Boot Hills in Western films. The historical tableau, no longer so funny, turned "almost disturbingly poignant,"

unleashing the visitor's imagination, perhaps a cinematic memory of the "strange and scary" killings that occurred on this grassy heath. Like many visitors to the Little Bighorn, the chastened, wisecracking comedian walked down the hill to his own steed, abandoned the battle site and history, to ride toward a never-quite-setting sun on the endless road, a parody of innumerable horse opera endings. [13]

Larry McMurtry was among those visitors for whom the Little Bighorn failed to evoke much imaginative interest or emotion. "I walked the Custer battlefield twice, without, I confess, being very moved by what can now be seen. I was more interested in what the Crow guides were telling the tourists," he wrote in *Custer*. He found himself "wondering why my fellow tourists were there. Few of them looked like history buffs. The battlefield was a major listing in the tour guides: it was just something you did if you were in that part of Montana." McMurtry thought of little more than dust kicked up by "two thousand milling, charging horses," leaving the field "a hell of dust, smoke, shooting, hacking." All that dust obscured the battle then, just as the Indian side of the story remains "permanently ambiguous, potent rather than conclusive." [14]

Tim Dee brought the sensibilities of an ornithologist, naturalist, cultural critic, and BBC radio producer to the Little Bighorn in his 2013 book *Four Fields*. In his studied view, the fight was about grass. As white settlement spread into the West, the Native Americans, especially the Sioux, lost the free range. Enclosed spaces ended their way of life. This forcible estrangement meant that the Native Americans "were basically caged," cut off from the fields that sustained them. Dee viewed the battle literally from the ground up and saw abundant lushness where others have seen only desolation. "Grass still covers the battlefield at the Little Bighorn and stretches as far as you can see. . . . There seems more than enough grass to go round. Yet that is what the battle was about. Grass and its fencing. The conjuring of proleptic fields." This fecundity, however, belies a sinister history, an ironic truth: [15]

> Today, despite the green and despite what the plains grow, the world here is curtailed and depleted, and in many places speaks only of the end of things. Standing in the battlefield makes you look into the distance and eventually something arrives through the heat shimmer and grass gloss of July. Nowhere else that I know has the enclosing of wild grass seemed so humanly germane . . . yet so precisely terminal

(to know anything of this place's past is to know how much death lies just below its surface).[16]

The battlefield has never been plowed; nor has grazing been permitted since 1891. "One of the ironies that the straw-headed Custer bequeathed to the world is that the best surviving shortgrass prairie in southern Montana is at the Little Bighorn battlefield," a thriving ecosystem, according to Dee. With further irony, he noted that a stone marking where Custer allegedly fell lies within a fenced square of grass, "a field of comrades who are sown around him in death like so many bags of flour." This, too, he noted, is a fiction, Custer probably having died elsewhere on the field and his partial remains later being interred at West Point.[17]

Not all visitations to the saddest place have involved personal engagements with the battlefield or séances with history. From the beginning, public awareness and understanding of Custer have been shaped by fiction, beginning with dime novels, mostly adventure tales written for young boys. According to Kent L. Steckmesser, Custer is made to seem boyish and heroic. In the interest of telling a good story, fiction writers have ignored the facts when it suited them. By connecting stories to historical events, "they helped to confuse fact and fancy and to disseminate legends about Custer and his last battle," Steckmesser wrote in 1964. Early adult-oriented fiction about Custer tended to be "disputatious" and moralistic, with long editorial passages taking sides in the Custer controversies or transforming Custer "into a sober and prudent figure who resembles George Washington." Novels that emphasized Custer's maturity tended to exonerate him for the Little Bighorn disaster and shift responsibility. As historical interpretation about Custer and Native Americans began to shift after 1934, literary interpretation changed, too, as polemical novelists turned to debunking Custer or psychoanalyzing him.[18]

Also important to Custer lore are paintings and illustrations, songs, films, television shows, and other popular culture productions. This area of Custer studies has been explored exhaustively and entertainingly by an impressive troop of writers, including Robert Utley, Bruce Rosenberg, Michael Elliott, and Brian Dippie. Some interesting and important material largely has been overlooked, however, and new material warrants attention.

HEMINGWAY AND CUSTER

Both of Ernest Hemingway's grandfathers served in Union Army regiments during the Civil War. His maternal grandfather, Ernest Hall, was mustered into the 1st Iowa Volunteer Cavalry in 1861. He was promoted to corporal in April 1862 but was then discharged for wounds in August under mysterious circumstances. Rumors circulated that he had been a deserter. Ernest's mother, Grace Hall Hemingway, adored her father and told her son, his namesake, about his grandfather's alleged gallantry and impeccable character so often that Ernest came to resent her expectations of him. Ernest's paternal grandfather, Anson Hemingway, served as a private in the 72nd Illinois Infantry, most notably during the Vicksburg Campaign, and later as a first lieutenant in the 70th U.S. Colored Infantry. Although Ernest Hall, especially, was said to have been reticent about discussing his Civil War experiences, young Hemingway was able to cobble together enough information about his grandfathers to create fictional characters with imagined battle-hardened ancestry.[19]

Hemingway had a lifelong fascination with Custer, who appears in some form in six of his novels and is mentioned in several of his letters. Robert Jordan, the University of Montana Spanish instructor who goes to Spain in 1937 to fight in its civil war in *For Whom the Bell Tolls*, has a grandfather who fought in the cavalry during the American Civil War and the Plains Indian Wars. Jordan comes from Red Lodge, Montana, about 120 miles west of the Little Bighorn battlefield. As he waits to blow up a bridge behind the fascist lines, Jordan wishes his grandfather, "a hell of a good soldier," were there to help him fight with his partisan band. "They said if he had been with Custer that day he never would have let him be sucked in that way," Jordan muses. "How could he ever not have seen the smoke nor the dust of all those lodges down there in the draw along the Little Big Horn unless there must have been a heavy morning mist? But there wasn't any mist." He recalls that his fictional grandfather, who knew Custer, had told him, "Custer was not an intelligent leader of cavalry, Robert. . . . He was not even an intelligent man. . . . He just had great ability to get himself in and out of trouble . . . and on the Little Big Horn he got into it but he couldn't get out."[20]

Jordan resented his grandfather's assessment of Custer because it was at odds with the famous *Custer's Last Fight*, painted by Cassilly Adams in 1886, then repainted and lithographed in 1895 by Otto Becker. After

Anheuser-Busch distributed the lithograph to promote beer, the iconic image of a saber-wielding Custer in buckskin became a ubiquitous ornament on American barroom walls. Jordan saw it often on the wall of a Red Lodge poolroom. His discomfort, Dippie noted, reflects "the annoyance that history should dare intrude upon a good story, however false." Moreover, the greatest cavalry leader of all time, according to Jordan's grandfather, was John Mosby. But Jordan has a letter Philip Sheridan wrote to Judson Kilpatrick claiming that Jordan's grandfather was an even better leader of irregular cavalry than Mosby. His grandfather's authority, then, must be acknowledged, even if the comparison with Custer is spurious. Custer was not leading guerrillas. [21]

Literary scholar David M. McClellan noticed a resemblance between Custer and a fascist officer, Captain Mora, who leads a failed attack on Loyalist partisans in *For Whom the Bell Tolls*. El Sordo, the leader of another guerrilla band cooperating with Jordan's group, is surrounded by 150 men on a hilltop that seems inspired by Custer's Last Stand, five men "spread out like the points of a five-pointed star" behind their own dead horses. By feigning suicide, El Sordo's men induce the fascists to charge the hill led by the overconfident Mora, who ignores the warnings of his subordinates. The captain, a Custer doppelgänger, has a "red face and a blond, British-looking moustache and there was something wrong about his eyes. They were a light blue and the lashes were light, too. As you looked at them they seemed to focus slowly." El Sordo shoots him just before fascist aircraft bomb and strafe the hill. When the attackers reach the crest of the hill, they decapitate all the corpses. [22]

McClellan sees Mora's countenance as inspired by familiar photographs of Custer, while the "wrongly-focusing eyes of both the captain and the general match fatal flaws in intellectual perception." Additionally, photographs of Sitting Bull "are visual equivalents of Hemingway's description of El Sordo." Mora (Custer) walks into a trap while attacking the hill defended by El Sordo (Sitting Bull). The decapitations reverse the mutilations that occurred after the Little Bighorn. Literary scholar Dean Rehberger points out that in "Hemingway's retelling of the Custer myth . . . savagery is displaced to the side of military order and technological superiority." [23]

Hemingway's novel *Across the River and into the Trees* similarly is infused with the last stand myth. Like Marcus Reno, Richard Cantwell was ordered to lead an ill-advised attack. In Cantwell's case, the attack was directed against a fortified German town in the Hürtgen Forest campaign in World War II. Like Reno's battalion, Cantwell's regiment sustained heavy casualties and had a desperate fight on a rocky hillside. Cantwell, recently promoted to brigadier general before the battle, had fought bravely but apparently was made a scapegoat by his incompetent superiors. Unlike Reno, he was demoted. Cantwell had served with the Montana National Guard and has little respect for Custer, who seems to represent the glory-seeking generals who needlessly get their men killed. He tells his lover, Renata, in Venice that they will drive someday to the hill "where they killed that fool George Armstrong Custer, and you can see the markers where everybody died and I'll explain the fight to you." Elsewhere he thinks of Custer as that "beautiful horse-cavalryman. I guess it is fun to be that way and have a loving wife and use sawdust for brains. But it must have seemed like the wrong career to him when they finished up on that hill above the Little Big Horn."[24]

Islands in the Stream also shows just how much Hemingway absorbed the imagery of Custer's Last Stand. Thomas Hudson, a death-obsessed painter, pursues the crew of a sunken German U-boat through the Jardines del Rey archipelago along the northern coast of Cuba during World War II. Hudson and his companions are aboard a yacht disguised as a research vessel but equipped by U.S. authorities with machine guns, grenades, bombs, and communications equipment. Navigating treacherous channels, they find bodies in a fishing village burned by the Germans, who have stolen boats and fled up the coast. Near the bodies is a dead German who had "very long hair, blond and sun-streaked, and he was face down in the sand." Further along the coast they find a dying German sailor in a lean-to. His blond hair is "long and uncombed and in the late afternoon light, with the sun almost down, he looked like a saint."[25]

The pursuit continues as Hudson contemplates the mission with increasing dread: "It is my duty and I want to get them and I will. But I have a sort of fellow death-house feeling about them." They sail into a trap but manage to kill all the Germans, who are "fighting Custer's Last Stand in the mangroves." Hudson is mortally wounded during the battle. According to McClellan, "Hudson follows to his doom the outlines of the pattern Custer fatally pursued. . . . Like Custer, Hudson meets his end in an ambush along a river after patiently tracking his human prey, who left signs of their passing presence for days."[26]

Invert the pattern, however, and Hudson becomes an Indian chieftain pursuing Custer, whose demise is foreshadowed by the discovery of the blond sailors and realized during the fight in the mangroves. This reading would explain Hudson's revulsion after discovering the massacre of the islanders by the submariners, perhaps reprising the Washita. McClellan notes that in his later fiction, Hemingway increasingly identified with the Indians in the battle. And about the time he was writing *Islands in the Stream*, Hemingway wrote a friend about the tall tales he was telling during an African safari: "At night I tell them how we killed George Armstrong Custer and the 7th Cavalry and they think we are wasting our time here and should get the hell to America."[27] Hemingway knew how to take a good story, change it around as it suited him, and work it into his novels in any number of ways. He was writing fiction, drawing on history and his own journalism. The mythic Custer was lively source material, even for songwriters.

"MR. CUSTER"

In 1960, Custer's Last Stand inspired a tune that, for a week in October, was the most popular song played on radio stations in the United States. Titled "Mr. Custer," it capitalized on the public's growing enthusiasm for novelty songs played by Top 40 radio stations during the genre's golden age, roughly from 1956 to 1969. A novelty song typically responded to a news item, a season, a cartoon, a fad, or a broader cultural trend in a humorous way, with universal appeal. The humor might take the form of parody or edgy social commentary exploiting an understated anxiety. If the songwriting formula worked, the song might extend its influence by becoming a comical annoyance, like singing chipmunks at Christmas, indefinitely recycled and imitated. The novelty would only work if the listener recognized the hook, or reference.[28]

"Mr. Custer" was a response to television's obsession with Westerns. Between 1957 and 1959, about one-third of the evening network programs were Westerns. Custer had made occasional appearances in early television Westerns but had left a larger boot print in the cinema and other forms of popular culture. Custer and the West were practically synonymous. His heroic reputation already was in decline and would slide further during the coming decade.

The timing was right, in 1960, for songwriters Al DeLong, Fred Darian, and Joseph Van Winkle to pitch a song narrated by a cowardly soldier who repeatedly pleads that he does not want to go on the expedition, while backed by a chorus of crooning troopers on their way to the Little Bighorn. The source of his anxiety is a dream in which he has an arrow in his back. The song is full of stereotypical images of Indians drawn from such television Westerns as *The Lone Ranger*. The writers recruited Larry Verne, who worked near their office in a photography studio, to drawl the mostly spoken lyrics. The public liked the gimmick and bought the record, which outsold all other novelty records in a year of abundance for that genre. Its popularity coincided with the closing month of the presidential campaign of 1960. Perhaps the public had tired of high-minded Cold War rhetoric about American power and welcomed some comic relief at Custer's expense. A cover version of the song by Charlie Drake also sold well in the United Kingdom.[29]

Just how resilient the Custer image was to the winds of social change in the 1960s was tested by the ABC network television series *Custer*, which lasted through seventeen episodes during the fall 1967 season. *Custer*, only loosely grounded in history, was canceled after awful reviews and forceful protests by Native American groups that took exception to Indians being typecast as savages.[30]

ALTERNATIVE HISTORY CUSTERS

"Custer's Last Jump," a story of alternative history written by Steven Utley and Howard Waldrop in 1972, introduces fixed-wing aircraft and dirigibles into the Civil War. The plot involves Mosby leading an expedition into Kansas to divert Union troops to the western theater. Mosby's Raiders, equipped with sixteen aircraft, form the 1st Western Interdiction Wing of the Confederate States Army Air Corps, which rules the skies from Missouri to Illinois in early 1864. They are challenged by the Union Army's 5th Cavalry attached to the 12th Air Destroyer Squadron and 2nd Airship Command.

Crazy Horse and a hunting party believe the Confederate aircraft to be mythical Thunderbirds. Crazy Horse visits Mosby, who earlier had tried to persuade the Confederate government to recruit Indians for aircraft operations. In exchange for permission to open an airbase in Sioux territory, the Confederates agree to train Crazy Horse and ten warriors as pilots and gunners, and they go on to distinguish themselves in dogfights and bombing raids. At the end of the war, which continues until 1867, the Indians escape by flying their aircraft to the Black Hills and hiding them in mountain caves.

In 1869, Custer, who had trained as a parachute infantryman during the Civil War and was the army's only jump-qualified general officer, is appointed commander of the 7th Cavalry, which also includes the 505th Balloon Infantry and 12th Airship Squadron. The unit attacks Black Kettle at the Washita River, with Custer among the jumpers who slaughter more than three hundred Indians. Crazy Horse vows revenge.

He gets it in 1876, when Custer moves against Sitting Bull's forces camped along the Little Bighorn with a flotilla of four airships. The War Department, amazingly, remains ignorant that the Confederates have equipped tribes with combat aircraft. As Custer's dirigibles approach the Little Bighorn, they are attacked by Indian pilots and shot down. Custer and his balloon infantrymen jump from the flaming dirigibles, and the general apparently is hit by shrapnel and killed before he hits the ground. Sheridan, who later becomes president, covers up the fiasco, which has cost the lives of 430 men. Exactly what happened in the battle remains, in the story, uncertain and becomes a legend of the West. The future looks back on the jaunty air cavalrymen flying off to the tune of "Chutes and Saddles," celebrated in the film *They Died with Their Chutes On*. Custer's Last Stand, of course, is remembered as "Custer's Last Jump."

Racism is implicit in the notion that technologically backward Indians are not supposed to be capable of flying aircraft, much less destroying a regiment of paratroopers in an air battle. Custer, who arrogantly sets out to avenge his brother and win political power by exterminating a troublesome tribe of primitives, is himself exterminated along with his command. Later generations would question the ability of minorities to master technologies and engage in combat. The story, however, really calls attention to the disparities in technologies that made the Indians' situation hopeless in the long run. Availability of twentieth-century technologies would not have changed the balance of power.

One element that does succeed is the seamless extension of the Civil War into the Indian Wars and twentieth- and twenty-first-century wars to come. An expansionist power, in this case a Confederacy seeking to defend its borders by enlarging its territory, arms tribesmen as a matter of expediency. As one war ends, another begins, or resumes, with unpredictable consequences. [31]

Harry Turtledove's *The Great War* alternative history series varies the theme by projecting not only the Civil War and technology into the future but Custer as well. The Confederacy and Canada are waging war against the United States, while the European conflict rages in the early twentieth century. Turtledove's Custer is vain, egotistical, and lustful, but apparently a pretty good commander. Now, at seventy-seven, Custer is smoking cigars and tipping the flask, all to Libbie Custer's disapproval. His few peroxided strands of long hair coil from under a hat he always wears to hide his baldness. His mustache has been dyed, and as he sits in his study with an aide, Custer ogles the housemaid.

Custer is a glory hound who criticizes others for being glory hounds: "Custer was a firm believer in a variation of the Ptolemaic theory: he was convinced the world revolved around him. Anything good that happened anywhere near him had to redound to his credit and no one else's; nothing bad was ever his fault. In that as in few other things, Libbie aided and abetted him." [32]

By now, though, Custer's cavalry fights with tanks, which he employs against Confederate lines in Tennessee. He develops a tactic for massing his tanks and breaks through the lines near Nashville, which becomes headquarters for the 1st U.S. Army. A few months later, Custer heads toward Murfreesboro, and the Confederates request an armistice. President Theodore Roosevelt agrees to it, infuriating Custer because he has to stop his attack. Custer's success brings a change in thinking across the army as to how to use tanks—bunching them up instead of spreading them out, anticipating the German blitzkrieg. In two earlier volumes in the trilogy, Turtledove has Custer invade and conquer Kentucky, returning it to the Union, being similarly bold and innovative in his tactics. [33]

GHOST STORIES

From the moment of its departure from Fort Lincoln, the 7th Cavalry has inspired supernatural speculation. Libbie Custer observed that the disappearing line of cavalry appeared to march away into the sky, and "already there seemed a premonition in the supernatural translation as their forms were reflected from the opaque mist of the early dawn." Frederick Whittaker, her collaborator in preserving Custer's memory, practiced spiritualism "with a fervor approaching insanity." Along with Native American rituals, such as Sitting Bull's visions prior to the battle and the subsequent Ghost Dance religion, the Custer myth has its share of survivor tales, zombies, and old-fashioned ghost stories.[34]

Not surprisingly, an episode of the supernatural thriller series *The Twilight Zone* brought the Little Bighorn into the 1960s and television, the medium that defined the decade and the Vietnam War. Written by series creator and host Rod Serling, "The 7th Is Made Up of Phantoms" was first broadcast on December 6, 1963. The story begins when a scout and two troopers on patrol from the 7th Cavalry find a tepee and a warm fire near the junction of the Bighorn and the Little Bighorn. The scout instructs the troopers to tell Custer that if he's looking for the Sioux, "he's gonna have his britches full of 'em before sundown." The scout gets an arrow in the back, and the scene shifts to three Montana National Guardsmen standing in front of a tank during training exercises on June 24, 1964. They have disobeyed orders and are near the Little Bighorn. They hear shots nearby and find a tepee and a 7th Cavalry canteen.

"You know there must be a lot of ghosts running around a place like this," says Master Sergeant William Connors, who knows the history of the battle and admits to a youthful obsession with it. His wisecracking corporal, Richard Langsford, knows little history but is skeptical of the supernatural. The youngest of the three, Private Michael McCluskey, looks like a young Custer and is rash and audacious as the story unfolds. The wind picks up, and some ominous Indian war whoops are heard in the distance. Serling, as narrator, explains, "Past and present are about to collide head-on, as they are wont to do in a very special bivouac area known as the Twilight Zone."

When the three return late to the command post, Connors tells his hard-nosed commanding officer, Captain Dennet, what they have seen and is chewed out. The captain suspects Connors has been drinking or is imagining things. He orders Connors to take the tank up Rosebud Creek early the next morning. Connors knows he will be following Custer's route and is worried. The next day they see smoke signals and hear drums and war cries. McCluskey fires several rounds in the direction of a large dust cloud, and a riderless horse gallops by. Langsford starts walking when he realizes Connors intends to either stop the massacre or join it, then finds a half dozen tepees. McCluskey investigates and returns with an arrow in his back. Langsford says, "It's like chasing history and trying to change it." Another patrol goes out and finds the tank with the message "Crossing Rosebud Creek. Trying to Reach 7th Cavalry. Have to." The three guardsmen, meanwhile, have climbed a ridge and joined Custer, guns blazing.

In the final scene, the captain, a lieutenant, and the rest of the unit reach the Little Bighorn Battlefield National Monument and find the names of the three missing men on the monument. "Too bad they couldn't have brought the tank up. It would have helped," says the captain. Serling intones, "Look for this one under 'P' for phantom in a historical ledger located in a reading room known as the Twilight Zone."

The Indians are never seen, suggesting the possibility of a rational explanation. Custer did not see the Indians either, until he was doomed. But if the guardsmen have fallen victim to an illusion or madness, why are their names on the battlefield monument, unless the other guardsmen have been drawn into the fantasy as well? Their bodies are not found, just as some of Custer's men were never found. If they did step into the past, why, the captain asks, did they abandon the tank? Presumably because the tank would have changed history, and the Indians' battlefield ghosts would have lost their mythic roles and ethereal existence. The time-travel element—a rip in the fabric of time, for example—is not explained but is metaphoric. The sergeant is a surrogate for those under the spell of the Custer myth, the large audience that first encountered the last stand as an adventure story in their youth and then revisited the battlefield in their imaginations later in life.

"Chasing history and trying to change it" doesn't work, however, because either the outcome is the same or it isn't history. The abandoned tank symbolizes the twilight zone between the past and the present. The narrative temptation is to have the guardsmen drive the tank over the ridge right into the Sioux village, but Serling isn't interested in that kind of alternative history. The 7th Cavalry is made up of ghosts we can chase through history, myth, and popular culture. We can get close to the Little Bighorn, and we may even take an arrow in the back—the danger of obsession—but we can never really get there, and if we did, we could not come back.

Mark Sumner's *Devil's Tower*, a fantasy novel published in 1996, features a megalomaniacal Custer cast as a Western sorcerer seeking magical powers released by the carnage of the Civil War. Those who have the powers strive to control a degraded Western landscape after the war. Custer defeats Sitting Bull and other medicine men at the Valley of the Greasy Grass with stronger magic and firepower. A final showdown with another conjurer ends Custer's quest for unlimited power and reveals he has been taken over by a rogue demon. The story is a variation on the Faust theme. The demon of ambition gets the better of Custer in this fantasy world and brings him down. The real-life Custer's bravado made him a likely choice for such a spectral parable.[35]

Custer himself narrates his life story in Michael Blake's 1996 novel *Marching to Valhalla*. Blake's previous novel was adapted for the popular film *Dances with Wolves*. Presented in the form of a private journal that Custer is writing as he advances toward the Little Bighorn, *Marching to Valhalla* begins as little more than a standard biography written in first person. Midway through the story, Custer begins to muse that he lives only in the moment, controlling almost nothing and "caring little about answers" to questions about destiny that have vexed him throughout his life. But as he approaches the fateful river, his mood darkens with regret.[36]

"Sometimes it seems that I am the bad boy, called forth only when exploitation of my abilities might suit the aims of others," he writes. He suspects his career has been suppressed because he is too well known and the army "does not want fighters to assume such power. Perhaps they fear that the tigers they create today will turn and devour them tomorrow." Custer knows he will not survive the battle, nor will he resolve his inner tensions. "There are trails of smoke about my head that hold the answers, yet each time I reach for one, my hand passes straight through. It seems that I am dying, yet I feel nothing. . . . I am watching myself from outside in complete calm." The manuscript ends on the morning of the battle, with Custer anticipating his arrival in Valhalla, "to be carried up from the earth by ravishing women warriors; to be transported to a heavenly kingdom where food and drink and joy are limitless; to wander such a place for eternity in perfect satisfaction."[37]

Custer holds in view later visitors trying to find answers in the smoke rings that twirl around the Custer myth. As he observes himself from outside, his self-reflexive detachment is ghostly, already a shade in conflict with history, just as the story he is telling has begun to overwhelm events. He rides to his doom, ready to collect his ticket to Valhalla, lamenting that he has "knowledge defying definition . . . that resides beyond mortal boundaries. It is a maddening knowledge, elusive as it is distinct."[38]

Also troubled by a maddening knowledge is Lieutenant Michael Crofton, the protagonist of Keith Coplin's 2004 novel *Crofton's Fire*. Crofton, part of a squadron of twenty-two pathfinders attached to Custer's wagon train, observes the last stand alone from a ridge. The men "all disliked Custer, a braggart, a malefactor, a hound for glory," says Crofton, whose commanding officer, a major, declines to rush to Custer's aid. Crofton sees Custer "in the middle, standing, arrogant to the end, aiming and firing his long-barreled pistol deliberately. And then he was hit. In the back. Then hit again. And I saw it was his own men shooting him," the coup de grâce delivered by a rifle shot to the back of the head after Custer falls to his knees.[39]

Crofton escapes and keeps quiet during subsequent investigations to protect Custer's reputation. "Sitting in room after room, with intense men seeking answers, I lied. I said I saw nothing, that hostile savages barred my way to the battlefield and that I barely escaped with my life. I told no one of the end of Custer that I had witnessed, his ready killing by his own men. Custer was the fair-haired boy, and I was willing to leave it like that."[40] So here, as fiction, we see a commentary on Custer's conflicted legacy as real knowledge, historical fact, is subsumed by lies, half-truths, and a narrative that serves ulterior motives. Crofton is wise to let it be so because he knows it would be folly to think he could change it.

Soon Custer is the army's "prince of fools. . . . His reputation was, as far as we could tell, far greater than the man. . . . [H]is grasp of tactics was nonexistent and his concern for the safety of his troopers equally remote." Nevertheless, the major has second thoughts about not trying to save Custer and shoots himself. "He might have put the gun to his head," says Crofton, "but it was Custer's ghost who pulled the trigger."[41]

Crofton tells his sweetheart Lucinda that the major's death "is another sin that Custer will have to take into the beyond. What I cannot understand is how the rash and destructive actions of one man can have such devastating consequences." She sees Custer as "a great man and a great hero," who, unlike the major, "gave his all in sacrifice to duty and honor and country." Crofton understands that the Custer myth already has overtaken reality.[42]

The scene he witnesses over the ridge is nothing less than the Anheuser-Busch lithograph, *Custer's Last Fight*, viewed with the novelist's twentieth-century sensibilities, a Vietnam-era dispatching of an unpopular officer. The major's suicide, caused by a guilty conscience, shifts blame from Custer by implicitly discrediting all the officers who did not try to rescue him, with Lucinda taking the part Libbie Custer would play in preserving the Custer myth. Crofton's official silence supports the myth that prevailed until Libbie's death and Frederic F. Van de Water's biography, after which a new Custer emerged, a foolish and vainglorious narcissist who rashly disobeyed orders and led his command into a charnel house. Crofton, meanwhile, struggles with the morality of war, racism, and empire as William Tecumseh Sherman sends him on a secret mission to Cuba and then to Africa to observe the Anglo-Zulu War in 1879, another colonial misadventure.

The cigar-smoking ghost in G. G. Boyer's *Custer, Terry, and Me*, published in 2005, chats up narrator Tom Ballard, also a surviving eyewitness to the last stand, as Ballard writes his memoirs in 1945. His late-night visitor is the once teetotaling general himself, evidently off the wagon in the spirit world and imbibing Ballard's cognac as he comments on the manuscript. Ballard, a teenage waif adopted by Terry, knows the truth the history books missed. Custer realized as soon as he saw the village that he had to concentrate his command. He expected Terry to arrive by way of Tullock's Creek and tried to protect him by bringing up Benteen and the wagons and rescuing Reno. After sending Myles Keogh to the ridge to wait for the rest of the command, Custer led three companies down Medicine Tail Coulee to take hostages and was shot at the ford. Ballard had ridden off with a message. After witnessing the slaughter of Custer's battalion, Ballard escaped with the Crow scouts. [43]

Then the cover-up began. Terry changed Custer's orders after the fact to disguise his own mistakes. Benteen and Reno shifted the blame to Custer. "When those people who were covering up learned that I was alive and realized that the truth I carried around in my head could ruin them, my life was in danger every moment," Ballard explains. Ballard tells the truth to Terry, who sends him to Sheridan before the Reno court of inquiry. Sheridan believes Ballard but tells him everyone from Ulysses S. Grant on down, especially Terry, will be ruined if Ballard testifies. When Ballard arrives in Chicago, Benteen hires two thugs to murder him. Ballard kills them first and leaves the city without testifying, saving Grant, Sherman, Sheridan, Terry, and the army itself while sacrificing Custer, who seems content to live in the limbo of Ballard's memories.

"It's nice to have visitors when you're old and lonely," Ballard confesses. "Especially when they are the ultimate authority that can confirm your own tricky convictions."[44]

Ballard, therefore, is not so different from modern Little Bighorn visitors, who commune with Custer's ghost but are more commonly inspired by the conflicted legacy than burdened by history and "tricky convictions."

In Dan Simmons's 2010 novel *Black Hills*, Custer's ghost haunts a Sioux boy, Paha Sapa, who touches Custer at the Little Bighorn just as he expires. Paha Sapa, whose name roughly translates as Black Hills, is a mystic who sees into the future as well as the past and has to deal with channeling Crazy Horse as well as Custer. The Custer who inhabits Paha Sapa's brain as a "memory tumor" for sixty years is a garrulous, lusty time traveler cuckolded by history. Custer rants about Indian hypocrisy ("You Sioux were a ruthless, relentless invasion machine"), recounts his intimate life with Libbie in heavy-breathing detail, and eventually reveals the real reason he lost at the Little Bighorn: too many Indians!

A few days before Libbie dies, Paha Sapa gains an audience at her Park Avenue apartment. Libbie seems to sense Custer's presence in this séance as he chides her for remaining a widow. "Instead, you 'lived' to serve a ghost. And there are no ghosts, my dear." He is not a shade haunting Paha Sapa's mind, he says, "but only a node in his unique empathic consciousness, a sort of simulation of a self-aware memory." This "node" might be another way of explaining the Custer myth lodged in the national consciousness, if that is what Simmons, a well-regarded and much reviewed writer, had in mind in this bizarre historical science fiction tale.[45]

GHOSTS ABROAD

Mystery sets the Little Bighorn battlefield apart. No major highway takes one to the Little Bighorn Park. It's not on the way to anything in particular, and even at that, it's surrounded by the Crow Indian Reservation, not national or private land. But the road to the battlefield seems to be a side road that isn't really a side road in the American story. It's a detour that some must take to find some elusive piece of the American character or American place. Amble across it in the evening, a park ranger noted, and

Figure 12.1. David T. Wright portrays Custer in educational films, such as *Destiny at Dawn: Loss and Victory on the Washita*, reenactments, and "living history" productions. He is one of many Custer reenactors who create a costumed character easily recognized by the public. (Courtesy of David T. Wright)

with a little imagination, "you'll see a place where ghosts walk in broad daylight." After twenty-five summers at the battlefield and forty-two years of studying the battle, author and ranger Michael Donahue knows those wraiths as well as the popular misconceptions about them and the foibles of history and historians.

But Donahue is no mere romanticizer of history. One hot July afternoon, as he graciously suffered questions about the park, visitors, and his experience, Donahue noted, "The good news is that Custer was killed near the interstate. Otherwise we wouldn't have much visitation today." The park is located about halfway between Mount Rushmore and Yellowstone National Park, just off Interstate 90 in south-central Montana. But, more seriously, Donahue said, easy access for the Little Bighorn Battlefield National Monument is a factor. The Washita battle site in Oklahoma is not close to an interstate or any main road and so does not have nearly as many visitors.

Custer himself undeniably is a factor. "There is a monument that is very similar to this, the exact same distance off the interstate. And it's just hours south. But you may have only six people a day stop there. . . . What I'm talking about is the [William J.] Fetterman Fight in 1866 . . . more than 80 men killed by a huge number of warriors." The difference between a half dozen a day and thousands? Custer, a "media star" of his day, and Sitting Bull and Crazy Horse. People have heard of them. Even though most people know little of Indian history, they have heard of Sitting Bull and Crazy Horse. The interstate sign alerts them to something they know about.

But the Little Bighorn is mysterious. The Fetterman Fight in present-day Wyoming is not. "And we as human beings all have a little Sherlock Holmes in us. You know, we want to know what happened on a grassy knoll in Dallas, Texas. We want to know what sunk the *Titanic*, how big the rip was, was it faulty rivets . . . ? We want to know what happened at the Alamo."

The mystery is enhanced by the battlefield itself, unlike any other in the world, Donahue points out, in that it has individual markers for combatants on both sides. One can see those places where people died in combat:

> So when you walk across that beautiful landscape, and some people see it barren and some people see it as a beautiful spot, you see those beautiful white marble markers sticking out of the grass. When that sunlight catches those markers and you have a little imagination, you can see maybe a man dying right here. . . . It adds to the mystery, but it also adds to an atmosphere. This battle has an atmosphere that I don't get at the Alamo, I don't get at Gettysburg. I've been to those places, Vicksburg. I don't get that same feeling, because there is quietness here. There's a pristine quality to the battlefield.[46]

Even Custer's bones are a mystery. In September 1991 the Associated Press reported some confusion about who was buried in Custer's tomb at West Point. An anthropologist who examined bones at the Little Bighorn in 1985 had some doubts that the troops who exhumed Custer's remains had got the right man. Bodies at the battlefield were often poorly identified and buried hastily in shallow graves. Custer was so interred for a year, exposed to the elements and animals, before he was dug up and sent east. Later, remains at the battlefield also were exposed to souvenir seekers. The Custer family has denied permission to exhume the remains. Whether it is Custer or not, West Point visitors still leave flowers at the popular monument.[47]

Custer and the battlefield are at the center of another, more important highway—our historical imaginations, which embrace conquest and wilderness, a romanticized West and heroic moments. The national story is about conflict, clashing armies and ideas. So is Custer's story, from the

Figure 12.2. What were believed to be Custer's remains were interred at West Point with great pomp and pageantry in 1877. Just who is buried in Custer's tomb remains a mystery, however. The engraving is from *Harper's Weekly*, October 1877. (Library of Congress)

Civil War to his contested legacy. Custer and the Little Bighorn are worth a footnote in American history, but his story is worth a library. There is a public consensus that a "last stand" occurred, but its history is evasive, and some historians demur. At the Little Bighorn, the National Park Service has brought order to an elusive moment in history.

Rangers, such as Donahue, maintain and explain, provide maps, and answer questions about the tragedy. The site and story are managed with markers, monuments, paths, regulations, schedules, bookstores, and gates. The last stand monument affirms the debatable idea that a last stand actually occurred. The park itself is surrounded by a model of control, the Crow reservation, which has corralled the people of the tribe, but not necessarily to their benefit, as they cling to the idea of nomadic and noble traditions. Meanwhile, they live within the confines of treaty land and at the hand of government. More than three hundred thousand people a year come to the park's 765-acres of wind-blown grass, where rangers ably account for events, leaving most visitors enlightened while some remain gawkers at the dead with only the illusion of understanding, as they sit comfortably in the shade, out of the glare of Montana's summer sun and historical reality.[48]

It is an alluring landscape. There is the appearance of solitude, but the windy quiet of the high-plains grasslands vanishes quickly before the daily columns of cars and buses charging the park, many visitors aiming and firing their cameras as indiscriminately as panicked, doomed cavalrymen would have fired their carbines. The cavalrymen at least knew what they intended to hit. Visitors must drive a long way from somewhere to get to the Little Bighorn. But it is at the center of the collective, cultural imagination.

LIONIZING CUSTER

Still, the Custer myth and the public interest in him seem excessive with respect to his historical significance. His legend began with his own hand, in his articles for *Galaxy*, and with the good press he received—properly so—for his Civil War service. It looked as though Custer was creating a character for himself. That character was the one who designed his own flashy costumes in the Civil War, the one inordinately bold in his cavalry charges, a man who appeared in a great many photographs. The Little

Bighorn simply took the story out of his hands and amplified the gallant individualist, the bold frontiersman, the man who would help civilize the untamed West. Then, his last stand grabbed hundreds of headlines and sold thousands of newspapers, books, and magazines. The Custer legend factory began production.

Custer's career was largely commendable, from Manassas to the Plains Wars, except for that one day and perhaps the Washita. The Civil War never really ended for Custer, as he and many other veterans kept fighting to quell unrest in the South and bring the West into the Union. In some respects, the lessons of Manassas and Gettysburg were his undoing in the unconventional warfare with the Indians. The story has remained largely a simple narrative, however.

A PBS documentary, *Custer's Last Stand*, which premiered in January 2012, did little with the last stand, perhaps because so little is known of the actual battle or perhaps because everyone in audience already knows what happened. Instead, it is a documentary about a man who not only looked like a soldier and frontiersman but also acted the part. Autie and Libbie Custer put forth the image of a cavalier and his lady. Custer, in the documentary, is an outsize personality of great theatrical sensibility, and he knows how to generate publicity. It is the Custer first seen in Civil War headlines.

Similarly, in the 2002 Vietnam War movie *We Were Soldiers*, Mel Gibson plays Lieutenant Colonel Hal Moore. When informed he will command the 1st Battalion, 7th Cavalry, Moore recalls that was Custer's unit, something the scriptwriter could only get away with if the audience knew, or thought it knew, the earlier story. A few scenes later, at home, he signs his last will and testament, with books about and pictures of Custer next to him. Audiences all across the nation knew things were going to get bad for the colonel. He and his four hundred soldiers go into the Ia Drang Valley, where they are outnumbered about ten to one. After several days of intense combat, Moore evacuates his command. Unlike Custer, though, Moore survives. As at the Little Bighorn, the "savages" inflict substantial casualties and eventually take the ground. It is another affirmation of the Custer narrative, which the popular culture owns in cinema, fiction, and television. The story is not so different from the one in the 1876 headlines.

Custer's story remains vital in the twenty-first century because it is part of an American creation myth via the frontier, and it is a simple frame, no matter which side is cast as the good guys or the bad guys. The battle was warfare on a human scale, compared to, say, the Peninsula Campaign of the Civil War, the Tet Offensive in Vietnam, or Anzio or Tarawa in World War II. The Little Bighorn seems almost comprehensible, as opposed to cyberwar or the irrationality of terrorism conducted merely for the sake of killing. It is a fathomable anomaly—the primitives beat the modern army. It is tragedy because the brave, young husband was slain in the course of fulfilling the nation's destiny.

The Civil War Custer was a man with flaws and virtues. After he brushed up against glory and fame, his celebrity outran both rank and accomplishment, thanks to the press and his own writing. The last stand became an iconic defeat, a burden that had to mean something. It became both heroic and a metaphor for imperial overreach and military stupidity—the dark side of the American character—arrogance, overconfidence, brutality, genocide, racism, the survival of the fittest.

Custer resides in our historical, national imagination in the same way he is in his tomb at West Point. Some of him is there; at least we think those few bones are his. Some of him must still be at the battlefield. And some of him was claimed by the elements, becoming eternally of the landscape, where our monuments pretend certainty about history and its meaning.

Like the cavaliers of the Old South whom he helped defeat and then adopted in affectation, he is gone. But like the Lost Cause myth, Custer's story endures and appeals, recalling national sin while celebrating the warrior spirit—and leaving some visitors unsure why they stopped at this spot along the highway but glad they had their cameras along.

Visitors to the Little Bighorn, both the terrain of battle and fields of fantasy, will continue to quarry new riches to fire the imagination. "Come here sometime, and you'll see," Kuralt advised. That terrain remains contested ground, a field of blood, the saddest place.

NOTES

INTRODUCTION

1. John M. Carroll, ed., *Custer in the Civil War: His Unfinished Memoirs* (San Rafael, CA: Presidio Press, 1977). This book includes Custer's eleven official action reports [hereafter Custer, *War Reports*] and Custer's unfinished war memoirs [hereafter Custer, *War Memoirs*] published in *Galaxy* in 1876; Custer, *War Memoirs*, 146–47.

2. Custer, *War Memoirs*, 68, 146.

3. John V. Quarstein and J. Michael Moore, *Yorktown's Civil War Siege: Drums along the Warwick* (Charleston, SC: History Press, 2012), 119–20; Frederick Stansbury Haydon, *Aeronautics in the Union and Confederate Armies, with a Survey of Military Aeronautics Prior to 1861* (Baltimore: Johns Hopkins Press, 1941), 306; Custer, *War Memoirs*, 145–47.

4. Custer, *War Memoirs*, 148.

5. Jay Monaghan, *Custer: The Life of General George Armstrong Custer* (1959; Lincoln: University of Nebraska Press, 1971), 29. Custer began writing for *Galaxy* while he commanded a 7th Cavalry company at Elizabethtown, Kentucky, from September 1871 until April 1873. *Galaxy* published twenty of his articles from January 1872 to October 1874 and subsequently issued them in book form. See George Armstrong Custer, *My Life on the Plains*, ed. Milo Milton Quaife (1874; Lincoln: University of Nebraska Press, 1966), 21.

6. Custer, *War Memoirs*, 148–50; Monaghan, *Custer*, 78–80.

7. Edward Caudill and Paul Ashdown, *Sherman's March in Myth and Memory* (Lanham, MD: Rowman & Littlefield, 2008), 111, 116–18; Paul Ashdown and Edward Caudill, *The Myth of Nathan Bedford Forrest* (Lanham, MD: Rowman & Littlefield, 2005), 160–65; Paul Ashdown and Edward Caudill, *The Mos-*

by Myth: A Confederate Hero in Life and Legend (Wilmington, DE: Scholarly Resources, 2002), 146, 152–53, 155, 165.

8. Heather Cox Richardson, *West from Appomattox: The Reconstruction of America after the Civil War* (New Haven, CT: Yale University Press, 2007), 4, 74–75; see also Brenda Wineapple, *Ecstatic Nation: Confidence, Crisis, and Compromise, 1848–1877* (New York: Harper, 2013); Douglas R. Egerton, *The Wars of Reconstruction: The Brief, Violent History of America's Most Progressive Era* (New York: Bloomsbury, 2014); Kevin Phillips, *The Cousins' Wars: Religion, Politics, and the Triumph of Anglo-America* (New York: Basic Books, 1999), 486–506; Elliott West, "The Civil War and Reconstruction in the American West," Gilder Lehrman Institute of American History, 2014, www.gilderlehrman.org/history-by-era/reconstruction/essays/civil-war-and-reconstruction-american-west (accessed May 14, 2014).

9. Robert Kagan, *Dangerous Nation* (New York: Knopf, 2006), 66.

10. Claudio Saunt, *West of the Revolution: An Uncommon History of 1776* (New York: W. W. Norton, 2014), 150, 152, 156–57.

11. Thomas Powers, *The Killing of Crazy Horse* (New York: Knopf, 2010), 36.

12. Ray C. Colton, *The Civil War in the Western Territories* (Norman: University of Oklahoma Press, 1959), 121–22, 144–45, 164–65; Ned Blackhawk, "Remember the Sand Creek Massacre," *New York Times*, November 28, 2014; see also Ned Blackhawk, *Violence over the Land: Indians and Empires in the Early American West* (Cambridge, MA: Harvard University Press, 2006).

13. Tony Horwitz, "Massacre at Sand Creek," *Smithsonian* 45, no. 8 (December 2014): 50–57; see also Ari Kelman, *A Misplaced Massacre: Struggling over the Memory of Sand Creek* (Cambridge, MA: Harvard University Press, 2013).

14. William T. Sherman to Ellen Sherman, August 10, 1862, Sherman Papers, University of Notre Dame, South Bend, IN; Charles H. Devens Jr. and William T. Sherman, *Addresses to the Graduating Class of the U.S. Military Academy, West Point, N.Y., June 14th, 1876* (New York, 1876), 36–37; John F. Marszalek, *Sherman: A Soldier's Passion for Order* (New York: Free Press, 1993), 380; Michael Fellman, *Citizen Sherman: A Life of William Tecumseh Sherman* (New York: Random House, 1995), 263–65.

15. Rita Parks, *The Western Hero in Film and Television* (Ann Arbor, MI: UMI Research Press, 1982), 42.

I. THE DREAM

1. The spelling of Emanuel or Emmanuel Custer's name is inconsistent throughout the Custer literature. Jeffry D. Wert, *Custer: The Controversial Life of George Armstrong Custer* (New York: Simon & Schuster, 1996), 15–17.

2. Wert, *Custer*, 17–19.

3. Frederick Whittaker, *A Complete Life of General George A. Custer* (1876; Lincoln: University of Nebraska Press, 1993), 2:5–6; Frazier Hunt, *Custer: The Last of the Cavaliers* (New York: Cosmopolitan Book Corporation, 1928), 4, 8, 55. Hunt's obituary in the *New York Times* on December 28, 1967, describes him as a "swashbuckling 240-pound Midwesterner who stood 6 feet 3 inches tall and whose habitual attire was a trenchcoat and a fedora. . . . [Hunt] enjoyed a reputation for gusto and a hearty, self-confident roughness." Hunt may have found a kindred romantic spirit in the subject of his biography. His Custer is a "swashbuckling boy general," albeit without a fedora, "the darling of the gods . . . the last of the cavaliers." Wert, *Custer*, 15. Evan S. Connell, *Son of the Morning Star* (San Francisco, CA: North Point Press, 1984), 352; Marguerite Merington, ed., *The Custer Story: The Life and Intimate Letters of General George A. Custer and His Wife Elizabeth* (New York: Devin-Adair, 1950), 3, 291–92. Local resident John Giles told a turn-of-the-century visitor that the Custer family came from Hesse-Cassel and fought with the Hessians in the Revolutionary War. See Henry Howe, *Historical Collections of Ohio: An Encyclopedia of the State* (Cincinnati: State of Ohio, 1907), 1:899–900.

4. Whittaker, *A Complete Life*, 6. A later biographer said the suit "resembled nothing military." It was on display at the Custer Battlefield National Monument. See Jay Monaghan, *Custer: The Life of General George Armstrong Custer* (1959; Lincoln: University of Nebraska Press, 1971), 178; Frederic F. Van de Water, *Glory-Hunter: A Life of General Custer* (1934; Lincoln: University of Nebraska Press, 1988), 22; Wert, *Custer*, 5.

5. Quentin Reynolds, *Custer's Last Stand* (New York: Random House, 1951), 6–12; Hunt, *Custer*, 10.

6. Wert, *Custer*, 19–20; Monaghan, *Custer*, 6.

7. Wert, *Custer*, 20–21.

8. Wert, *Custer*, 20–22; Stephen E. Ambrose, *Crazy Horse and Custer: The Parallel Lives of Two American Warriors* (Garden City, NY: Doubleday, 1975), 91.

9. Monaghan, *Custer*, 7; Wert, *Custer*, 20–22.

10. Wert, *Custer*, 22–23.

11. Reynolds, *Custer's Last Stand*, 23–26.

12. Monaghan, *Custer*, 10; Wert, *Custer*, 23–25; Ambrose, *Crazy Horse and Custer*, 94.

13. Monaghan, *Custer*, 11; Jim Donovan, *Custer and the Little Bighorn: The Man, the Mystery, the Myth* (2001; New York: Crestline, 2011), 23; Lawrence A. Frost, *Custer Legends* (Bowling Green, OH: Bowling Green University Popular Press, 1981), 138.

14. Wert, *Custer*, 26–38.

15. Wert, *Custer*, 38–40; James S. Robbins, *Last in Their Class: Custer, Pickett and the Goats of West Point* (New York: Encounter Books, 2006), 188–89.

16. Whittaker, *A Complete Life*, 16–17.

17. Reynolds, *Custer's Last Stand*, 61, 70, 78–83.

18. Custer, *War Memoirs*, 86; Van de Water, *Glory-Hunter*, 30; James Donovan, *A Terrible Glory: Custer and the Little Bighorn—the Last Great Battle of the American West* (New York: Little, Brown & Co., 2008), 41.

19. Robbins, *Last in Their Class*, xii; Nathaniel Philbrick, *The Last Stand: Custer, Sitting Bull, and the Battle of the Little Bighorn* (New York: Viking, 2010), 47; Robert M. Utley, *Cavalier in Buckskin: George Armstrong Custer and the Western Military Frontier* (Norman: University of Oklahoma Press, 1988), 15.

20. Ambrose, *Crazy Horse and Custer*, 100–101.

21. Robbins, *Last in Their Class*, 194.

22. Custer, *War Memoirs*, 83.

23. Morris Schaff, *The Spirit of Old West Point, 1858–1862* (Boston: Houghton, Mifflin, 1907), 194.

2. THE SUN OF GLORY

1. Samuel Lover, "The Girl I Left behind Me," in *The Poetical Works of Samuel Lover* (New York: D. and J. Sadlier, 1872), 175.

2. Gregory J. W. Urwin, *Custer Victorious: The Civil War Battles of General George Armstrong Custer* (East Brunswick, NJ: Associated University Presses, 1983), 13, 17.

3. Urwin, *Custer Victorious*, 31, 33, 37–38. A few earlier books covered the Civil War period. See, for example, D. A. Kinsley, *Favor the Bold* (1967; New York: Promontory Press, 1968). Kinsley favored narrative over documentation, inventing conversations ("carefully constructed from paraphrases") and scenes and flavoring his story with speculation.

4. Urwin, *Custer Victorious*, 12; Thom Hatch, *Glorious War: The Civil War Adventures of George Armstrong Custer* (New York: St. Martin's Press, 2013); James S. Robbins, *The Real Custer: From Boy General to Tragic Hero* (Washington, DC: Regnery, 2014).

5. Don Russell, "Custer's First Charge," *By Valor & Arms: The Journal of American Military History* 1, no. 1 (October 1974): 20, quoted in Urwin, *Custer Victorious*, 31.

6. Jay Monaghan, *Custer: The Life of General George Armstrong Custer* (1959; Lincoln: University of Nebraska Press, 1971), 372; Custer, *War Memoirs*, 71.

7. Custer, *War Memoirs*, 71–73.

8. Custer, *War Memoirs*, 75. Union brigadier general John Beatty, an Ohio congressman after the war, agreed with Custer. He wrote that many battle reports were "base exaggerations—romances, founded upon the smallest conceivable amount of fact. They are simply elaborate essays, which seek to show that the author was a little braver, a little more skillful in the management of his men, and a little worthier, than anybody else." Stephen Z. Starr, *The Union Cavalry in the Civil War* (Baton Rouge: Louisiana State University Press, 1981), 2:265.

9. Monaghan, *Custer*, 43.

10. Custer, *War Memoirs*, 89.

11. Custer, *War Memoirs*, 90.

12. Custer, *War Memoirs*, 90; Ronald S. Coddington, "Custer and His Roommate Part Ways," *New York Times*, February 15, 2012.

13. Custer, *War Memoirs*, 91–92.

14. Custer, *War Memoirs*, 91–92.

15. Custer, *War Memoirs*, 92; Monaghan, *Custer*, 38.

16. Quentin Reynolds, *Custer's Last Stand* (New York: Random House, 1951), 90–91.

17. Custer, *War Memoirs*, 102; Frederic F. Van de Water, *Glory-Hunter: A Life of General Custer* (1934; Lincoln: University of Nebraska Press, 1988), 36.

18. Charles Aldrich, ed., "Captain Thomas Drummond," *The Annals of Iowa* 6, no. 3 (Des Moines: Historical Department of Iowa, 1903–1905), 150, available at iagenweb.org/benton/bios/thomas_drummond.htm (accessed April 24, 2014).

19. Reynolds, *Custer's Last Stand*, 94; Ethan S. Rafuse, *A Single Grand Victory: The First Campaign and Battle of Manassas* (Wilmington, DE: Scholarly Resources, 2002), xiii; David J. Eicher, *The Longest Night: A Military History of the Civil War* (New York: Touchstone, 2001), 99. The battle had its share of depredations as well. Both sides claimed the other was guilty of atrocities, and this impression was fanned by the press. Among the Union casualties was Major Sullivan Ballou, made famous in 1990 when the poignant letter he wrote to his wife a week before the battle was read during PBS's first episode of Ken Burns's *The Civil War* series, seen by some 14 million people. Some months after the battle, William B. Sprague, the governor of Rhode Island who had been on the flanking expedition through the woods with Custer and in the fighting on Chinn Ridge, led a delegation to the Manassas battlefield to rebury the remains of

Ballou and other officers from the 2nd Rhode Island Regiment. Informants revealed that Ballou's body had been exhumed by some Georgians, then decapitated and burned. Apparently this was done in error, as they were looking for the corpse of Colonel John Slocum, commander of the 2nd Rhode Island, which had inflicted most of the two hundred casualties on the 8th Georgia. See Robert Brent Toplin, ed., *Ken Burns's The Civil War: Historians Respond* (New York: Oxford University Press, 1996), xv, 26; Virgil Carrington Jones, *Gray Ghosts and Rebel Raiders* (1956; New York: Promontory Press, 1995), 66–73, 380–81; Evan C. Jones, "The Macabre Fate of a Civil War Major," Historynet.com, June 12, 2006, www.historynet.com/sullivan-ballou-the-macabre-fate-of-a-american-civil-war-major.htm (accessed April 26, 2014); orig. pub. in *America's Civil War* (November 2004).

20. JoAnna M. McDonald, *"We Shall Meet Again": The First Battle of Manassas (Bull Run)* (New York: Oxford University Press, 1999), 19; Rafuse, *A Single Grand Victory*, 97–99; William C. Davis, *Battle at Bull Run: A History of the First Major Campaign of the Civil War* (Baton Rouge: Louisiana State University Press, 1977), 143.

21. Davis, *Battle at Bull Run*, 143–48; Rafuse, *A Single Grand Victory*, 140–41.

22. Rafuse, *A Single Grand Victory*, 120–21.

23. Custer, *War Memoirs*, 102.

24. Custer, *War Memoirs*, 102; McDonald, *"We Shall Meet Again,"* 49–53; Davis, *Battle at Bull Run*, 171–72.

25. Monaghan, *Custer*, 48–53.

26. Custer, *War Memoirs*, 104; Brian Steel Wills, *A Battle from the Start: The Life of Nathan Bedford Forrest* (New York: HarperCollins, 1992), 137; Eicher, *The Longest Night*, 99.

27. Rafuse, *A Single Grand Victory*, 157–60; McDonald, *"We Shall Meet Again,"* 96–97.

28. Report of Major Innis N. Palmer, U.S. War Department, *The War of the Rebellion: Official Records of the Union and Confederate Armies*, 128 vols. (Washington, DC: Government Printing Office, 1881–1901), vol. 2, pt. 1, 393 (hereafter cited as *OR*; except as otherwise noted, all references are to series 1).

29. Custer, *War Memoirs*, 100; McDonald, *"We Shall Meet Again,"* 152–54; Rafuse, *A Single Grand Victory*, 181–89; Davis, *Battle at Bull Run*, 233.

30. *OR*, vol. 2, pt. 1, 393; Monaghan, *Custer*, 54–55; Davis, *Battle at Bull Run*, 242; Custer, *War Memoirs*, 110.

31. Reynolds, *Custer's Last Stand*, 100; Marguerite Merington, ed., *The Custer Story: The Life and Intimate Letters of General George A. Custer and His Wife Elizabeth* (New York: Devin-Adair, 1950), 12–13.

32. Custer, *War Memoirs*, 100, 106–8.

33. Custer, *War Memoirs*, 114; Monaghan, *Custer*, 57.

34. Custer, *War Memoirs*, 115–18; David B. Sabine, "Philip Kearny," in *Historical Times Illustrated Encyclopedia of the Civil War*, ed. Patricia L. Faust (New York: HarperCollins, 1991), 408–9.

35. Jeffry D. Wert, *Custer: The Controversial Life of George Armstrong Custer* (New York: Simon & Schuster, 1996), 46; Merington, *The Custer Story*, 26.

36. Custer, *War Memoirs*, 118.

37. Custer, *War Memoirs*, 129–30; Monaghan, *Custer*, 64–66; "The Reconnaissance toward Warrenton," *New York Tribune*, March 21, 1862; Tom Carhart, *Lost Triumph: Lee's Real Plan at Gettysburg and Why It Failed* (New York: G. P. Putnam's Sons, 2005), 70–72; Merington, *The Custer Story*, 27–28.

38. Merington, *The Custer Story*, 27–28; Custer, *War Memoirs*, 134.

39. Custer, *War Memoirs*, 137, 143.

40. Eicher, *The Longest Night*, 216.

41. Custer, *War Memoirs*, 142; Merington, *The Custer Story*, 28–29.

42. Custer, *War Memoirs*, 144–45.

43. John V. Quarstein and J. Michael Moore, *Yorktown's Civil War Siege: Drums along the Warwick* (Charleston, SC: History Press, 2012), 119–20; Frederick Stansbury Haydon, *Aeronautics in the Union and Confederate Armies, with a Survey of Military Aeronautics Prior to 1861* (Baltimore: Johns Hopkins Press, 1941), 306; Custer, *War Memoirs*, 145–46.

44. Eicher, *The Longest Night*, 270; Monaghan, *Custer*, 72.

45. Custer, *War Memoirs*, 151–56; Wert, *Custer*, 51–52.

46. Custer, *War Memoirs*, 68, 156.

47. David M. Jordan, *Winfield Scott Hancock: A Soldier's Life* (Bloomington: Indiana University Press, 1996), 44; Urwin, *Custer Victorious*, 46–47; Monaghan, *Custer*, 74; Merington, *The Custer Story*, 30. Jeff Shaara devoted a chapter to Custer and Hancock at Williamsburg in his 1996 novel *Gods and Generals*. In the novel, Sumner assigns Custer to Hancock as his personal observer when it was Custer who had asked Smith for the assignment. Hancock does not know Custer and sees only a foppish young lieutenant, "blond hair falling in loose curls, a red scarf tied loosely around the man's neck, a long feather sprouting from the band in the man's hat." This description is imaginative, conforming to the romantic Custer myth. Custer did wear a red scarf after he became a general. At the time of the Williamsburg battle, Custer, according to Whittaker, was "a queer figure" who looked more like a disheveled newspaperman than a soldier. He wore a slouch hat and an open cavalry jacket. His hair was beginning to lengthen because he had vowed he would not have it cut until he reached Richmond, but it wasn't yet the foot-long flowing locks noted by a friend after Gettysburg. The plume was favored by some cavalrymen, such as Mosby, but was not part of Custer's attire at the time he was a staff officer. "It was not for

more than a year after, that he came out as a dandy," according to Whittaker. Shaara was writing fiction. Such details illustrate how readily Custer's image trumped realism in popular culture. Jeff Shaara, *Gods and Generals* (New York: Ballantine Books, 1996), 176–90; Frederick Whittaker, *A Complete Life of General George A. Custer* (1876; Lincoln: University of Nebraska Press, 1993), 2:106; Wert, *Custer*, 105; Kevin Dougherty, *The Peninsula Campaign of 1862: A Military Analysis* (Jackson: University Press of Mississippi, 2005), 88–89.

48. Monaghan, *Custer*, 76–78; Eicher, *The Longest Night*, 273; Urwin, *Custer Victorious*, 41; Wert, *Custer*, 52; *New York Times*, April 3, 1863.

49. Wert, *Custer*, 52–53; Monaghan, *Custer*, 78–83; Whittaker, *A Complete Life*, 2:108–18; George B. McClellan, *McClellan's Own Story: The War for the Union, the Soldiers Who Fought It, the Civilians Who Directed It, and His Relations to It and to Them*, ed. William C. Prime (New York: Charles L. Webster, 1887), 365; Urwin, *Custer Victorious*, 48.

3. THE GENERAL

1. Robert Louis Stevenson, "A Gossip on Romance," *Longman's Magazine* 1, no. 1 (November 1882): 69–79; see also *Essays of Robert Louis Stevenson* (New York: Scribner, 1909), 103.

2. Bruce Catton, *Terrible Swift Sword* (Garden City, NY: Doubleday, 1963), 295–305.

3. Catton, *Terrible Swift Sword*, 311–12.

4. Catton, *Terrible Swift Sword*, 312–14; David J. Eicher, *The Longest Night: A Military History of the Civil War* (New York: Touchstone, 2001), 278–81; George B. McClellan, *The Civil War Papers of George B. McClellan: Selected Correspondence, 1860–1865*, ed. Stephen W. Sears (New York: Ticknor & Fields, 1989), 287–88.

5. Clifford Dowdey, *The Seven Days: The Emergence of Robert E. Lee* (1964; New York: Fairfax Press, 1978), 136.

6. Custer, *War Memoirs*, 143.

7. Thomas B. Buell, *The Warrior Generals: Combat Leadership in the Civil War* (New York: Three Rivers Press, 1997), 70–71.

8. Buell, *The Warrior Generals*, 76–77, 220.

9. Custer, *War Memoirs*, 143; Frederick Whittaker, *A Complete Life of General George A. Custer* (1876; Lincoln: University of Nebraska Press, 1993), 2:102.

10. Dowdey, *The Seven Days*, 152, 189; Eicher, *The Longest Night*, 284–85.

11. Jeffry D. Wert, *Custer: The Controversial Life of George Armstrong Custer* (New York: Simon & Schuster, 1996), 56; Buell, *The Warrior Generals*, 77–78; Catton, *Terrible Swift Sword*, 329.

12. Buell, *The Warrior Generals*, 79–81; Jay Monaghan, *Custer: The Life of General George Armstrong Custer* (1959; Lincoln: University of Nebraska Press, 1971), 84–86.

13. Eicher, *The Longest Night*, 285–88; Dowdey, *The Seven Days*, 241–42; Marguerite Merington, ed., *The Custer Story: The Life and Intimate Letters of General George A. Custer and His Wife Elizabeth* (New York: Devin-Adair, 1950), 32; Stephen W. Sears, *To the Gates of Richmond: The Peninsula Campaign* (New York: Ticknor & Fields, 1992), 256; Wert, *Custer*, 56; Kevin Dougherty, *The Peninsula Campaign of 1862: A Military Analysis* (Jackson: University Press of Mississippi, 2003), 110–22.

14. Eicher, *The Longest Night*, 288; Catton, *Terrible Swift Sword*, 333; Dowdey, *The Seven Days*, 258.

15. Eicher, *The Longest Night*, 288–97; Dowdey, *The Seven Days*, 283–315.

16. Eicher, *The Longest Night*, 293–97; D. H. Hill, "McClellan's Change of Base and Malvern Hill," in *Battles and Leaders of the Civil War*, ed. Robert Underwood Johnson and Clarence Clough Buel (New York: Century, 1887–1888), 2:394.

17. Whittaker, *A Complete Life*, 121.

18. Catton, *Terrible Swift Sword*, 325; Merington, *The Custer Story*, 52; Sears, *To the Gates*, 345–46; Wert, *Custer*, 56.

19. Wert, *Custer*, 56–57.

20. Sears, *To the Gates*, 337, 353; Whittaker, *A Complete Life*, 122–24; Wert, *Custer*, 57.

21. Whittaker, *A Complete Life*, 122–24. An abridged version of the letter is quoted in Merington, *The Custer Story*, 32.

22. Monaghan, *Custer*, 89.

23. Whittaker, *A Complete Life*, 126; Monaghan, *Custer*, 89–90; Daniel Davis, "Brothers at Bassett Hall," *Emerging Civil War*, October 25, 2011, http://emergingcivilwar.com/2011/10/25/brothers-at-bassett-hall (accessed April 17, 2014).

24. Whittaker, *A Complete Life*, 126–29; Monaghan, *Custer*, 90–93; Wert, *Custer*, 57; Duane Schultz, *Custer: Lessons in Leadership* (New York: Palgrave Macmillan, 2010), 22–23; Merington, *The Custer Story*, 34–35.

25. Wert, *Custer*, 57–58; James M. McPherson, *Crossroads of Freedom: Antietam* (New York: Oxford University Press, 2002), 79, 88.

26. McPherson, *Crossroads of Freedom*, 97–100, 106.

27. McPherson, *Crossroads of Freedom*, 104–5; Monaghan, *Custer*, 95.

28. McPherson, *Crossroads of Freedom*, 106–7, 111.

29. Monaghan, *Custer*, 96–98; Eicher, *The Longest Night*, 342–44; Stephen W. Sears, *Landscape Turned Red* (New Haven, CT: Ticknor & Fields, 1983), 157.

30. McPherson, *Crossroads of Freedom*, 112–15; Sears, *Landscape Turned Red*, 158–61.

31. Monaghan, *Custer*, 102–3; Buell, *The Warrior Generals*, 121; McPherson, *Crossroads of Freedom*, 116–31; Catton, *Terrible Swift Sword*, 452.

32. Custer, in a letter to his sister, written in Sharpsburg on September 21, quoted in Whittaker, *A Complete Life*, 129; Merington, *The Custer Story*, 35; Monaghan, *Custer*, 103–5; Stephen E. Ambrose, *Crazy Horse and Custer: The Parallel Lives of Two American Warriors* (Garden City, NY: Doubleday, 1975), 170–71; Ethan S. Rafuse, *McClellan's War: The Failure of Moderation in the Struggle for the Union* (Bloomington: Indiana University Press, 2005), 335, 338; Wert, *Custer*, 58, 132–33.

33. Wert, *Custer*, 59; Catton, *Terrible Swift Sword*, 476–77.

34. Custer, *War Memoirs*, 113–14.

35. George B. McClellan, *McClellan's Own Story: The War for the Union, the Soldiers Who Fought It, the Civilians Who Directed It, and His Relations to It and to Them*, ed. William C. Prime (New York: Charles L. Webster, 1887), 652; Whittaker, *A Complete Life*, 132–33; James Harrison Wilson, *Under the Old Flag: Recollections of Military Operations in the War for the Union, the Spanish War, the Boxer Rebellion, etc.* (New York: D. Appleton, 1912), 126; Frederic F. Van de Water, *Glory-Hunter: A Life of General Custer* (1934; Lincoln: University of Nebraska Press, 1988), 45; Monaghan, *Custer*, 106.

36. Ambrose, *Crazy Horse and Custer*, 169; Robert M. Utley, *Cavalier in Buckskin: George Armstrong Custer and the Western Military Frontier* (Norman: University of Oklahoma Press, 1988), 19. Such talk may have been circulating among McClellan's officers before Antietam. See Sears, *Landscape Turned Red*, 111.

37. Thomas J. Rowland, *George B. McClellan and Civil War History: In the Shadow of Grant and Sherman* (Kent, OH: Kent State University Press, 1998), 43; McClellan, *McClellan's Own Story*, 365; McPherson, *Crossroads of Freedom*, 14.

38. Mark Thompson, "Guns of the Revolution: Henry Knox, George Washington, and the War of American Independence," in *Sons of the Father: George Washington and His Protégés*, ed. Robert M. S. McDonald (Charlottesville: University of Virginia Press, 2013), 121–48.

39. Dowdey, *The Seven Days*, 25; Rafuse, *McClellan's War*, 30–40, 382, 393; Dennis Showalter, "The U.S. Cavalry: Soldiers of a Nation, Policeman of an Empire," *Army History* 8 (Fall 2001): 13–14.

40. Whittaker, *A Complete Life*, 132.

41. Monaghan, *Custer*, 108–10; Wert, *Custer*, 66–67.

42. Wert, *Custer*, 66–67; Gregory J. W. Urwin, *Custer Victorious: The Civil War Battles of General George Armstrong Custer* (East Brunswick, NJ: Associated University Presses, 1983), 51.

43. Urwin, *Custer Victorious*, 53; Wert, *Custer*, 76–77; Samuel Harris, *Personal Reminiscences of Samuel Harris* (Chicago: Rogerson Press, 1897), 17, 23–24.

44. Monaghan, *Custer*, 113–15; Wert, *Custer*, 70–72; Whittaker, *A Complete Life*, 147.

45. Whittaker, *A Complete Life*, 145; Showalter, "The U.S. Cavalry," 7–23.

46. Whittaker, *A Complete Life*, 144.

47. Gregory J. W. Urwin, "Custer: The Civil War Years," in *The Custer Reader*, ed. Paul Andrew Hutton (1992; Norman: University of Oklahoma Press, 2004), 13; Charles Francis Adams Jr., *A Cycle of Adams Letters, 1861–1865*, vol. 2, edited by Worthington Chauncey Ford (Boston: Houghton Mifflin, 1920), 8 (May 12, 1863); Stephen Z. Starr, *The Union Cavalry in the Civil War* (Baton Rouge: Louisiana State University Press, 1981), 1:314n75, 315; Wert, *Custer*, 74–75; Ambrose, *Crazy Horse and Custer*, 177.

48. Wert, *Custer*, 72–74.

49. Monaghan, *Custer*, 117–20; Whittaker, *A Complete Life*, 149.

50. Monaghan, *Custer*, 120–22; Whittaker, *A Complete Life*, 149–50; John W. Hardy, "Tales from a Civil War Prison," *Archeology*, August 30, 1999, archive.archaeology.org/online/features/civil/words/hardy.html (accessed April 17, 2014).

51. *OR*, vol. 25, pt. 1, 1116; Merington, *The Custer Story*, 53–54, 69.

52. Steven E. Woodworth, *Beneath a Northern Sky: A Short History of the Gettysburg Campaign* (Wilmington, DE: Scholarly Resources, 2003), 11.

53. Tom Carhart, *Lost Triumph: Lee's Real Plan at Gettysburg and Why It Failed* (New York: G. P. Putnam's Sons, 2005), 110; Eicher, *The Longest Night*, 491–92.

54. Carhart, *Lost Triumph*, 109; Woodworth, *Beneath a Northern Sky*, 12; Burke Davis, *Jeb Stuart: The Last Cavalier* (1957; New York: Wings Books, Random House 1994), 303–4.

55. Buell, *The Warrior Generals*, 230; Richard M. McMurry, *John Bell Hood and the War for Southern Independence* (Lexington: University Press of Kentucky, 1982), 73; Emory M. Thomas, *Bold Dragoon: The Life of J. E. B. Stuart* (New York: Harper & Row, 1986), 217–20, 281–82; Davis, *Jeb Stuart*, 304–5. Stuart had a flair for pageantry. On January 8, 1864, he attended a charades party in Richmond. Participants acted out scenes suggested by various words, one of which was *pilgrimage*. A flower-strewn cross was brought out on a stage. As a band played "See! The Conquering Hero Comes," Stuart emerged, an actor

recalled, "in full uniform, his stainless sword unsheathed, his noble face luminous with inward fire. Ignoring the audience and its welcome, he advanced, his eyes fixed on the shrine until he laid the blade, so famous, upon it." Actors dressed as monks and nuns then followed, chanting the "Miserere." Thomas Cooper DeLeon, *Belles, Beaux and Brains of the 60's* (New York: G. W. Dillingham, 1909), 222, quoted in Davis, *Jeb Stuart*, 370.

56. Jeffry D. Wert, "Battle of Brandy Station, Va.," in *Historical Times Illustrated Encyclopedia of the Civil War*, ed. Patricia L. Faust (New York: HarperCollins, 1991), 76; Monaghan, *Custer*, 125–26; Davis, *Jeb Stuart*, 306; Woodworth, *Beneath a Northern Sky*, 12–13; Eicher, *The Longest Night*, 492.

57. Carhart, *Lost Triumph*, 110–11; Merington, *The Custer Story*, 58–59; Thomas, *Bold Dragoon*, 221–22; Eric J. Wittenberg, *The Battle of Brandy Station: North America's Largest Cavalry Battle* (Charleston, SC: History Press, 2011), 78–82.

58. Thomas C. Devin's Report, Joseph Hooker Papers, Huntington Library, cited in Wert, *Custer*, 78; Monaghan, *Custer*, 127; Urwin, *Custer Victorious*, 53; Ambrose, *Crazy Horse and Custer*, 186.

59. Eicher, *The Longest Night*, 493.

60. Thomas, *Bold Dragoon*, 225–31; Davis, *Jeb Stuart*, 310–13; Eicher, *The Longest Night*, 492–93.

61. Woodworth, *Beneath a Northern Sky*, 7–8; Stephen W. Sears, *Gettysburg* (Boston: Houghton Mifflin, 2003), 15–16; Thomas, *Bold Dragoon*, 225.

62. Woodworth, *Beneath a Northern Sky*, 11, 16–17; Thomas, *Bold Dragoon*, 234; Wert, *Custer*, 79–80; Eicher, *The Longest Night*, 494; Samuel J. Martin, *Kill-Cavalry: The Life of Union General Hugh Judson Kilpatrick* (1996; Mechanicsburg, PA: Stackpole Books, 2000), 92–96; E. A. Paul, "The Cavalry Fight at Aldie," *New York Times*, June 20, 1863; Sears, *Gettysburg*, 97–98.

63. Merington, *The Custer Story*, 54–55; Whittaker, *A Complete Life*, 155–60; Van de Water, *Glory-Hunter*, 49–50. The Rebels apparently did not notice his blue uniform.

64. Davis, *Jeb Stuart*, 316–20; Thomas, *Bold Dragoon*, 237–43; Woodworth, *Beneath a Northern Sky*, 18; Monaghan, *Custer*, 131–32.

65. Wert, *Custer*, 80–81, 84; Carhart, *Lost Triumph*, 118.

66. Ambrose, *Crazy Horse and Custer*, 188; Arnold Gates, "Galusha Pennypacker," *Historical Times Illustrated Encyclopedia of the Civil War*, 574; William E. Marvel, "Who Was the Youngest Civil War General?" Historynet.com, June. 13, 2011, www.historynet.com/who-was-the-youngest-civil-war-general.htm (accessed April 19, 2014); "General Charles C. Dodge," *New York Tribune*, November 5, 1910; Jeffry D. Wert, "Edmund Kirby" and "William Paul Roberts," in *Historical Times Illustrated Encyclopedia of the Civil War*, 419, 636–37.

67. Custer, *War Memoirs*, 112.

68. Whittaker, *A Complete Life*, 162–63; Monaghan, *Custer*, 132–33; Ambrose, *Crazy Horse and Custer*, 187–88; Quentin Reynolds, *Custer's Last Stand* (New York: Random House, 1951), 103–4; Van de Water, *Glory-Hunter*, 50–53.

69. Wert, *Custer*, 83–84; Merington, *The Custer Story*, 60; J. H. Kidd, *Riding with Custer: Recollections of a Cavalryman in the Civil War* (1908; Lincoln: University of Nebraska Press, 1997), 129.

70. D. A. Kinsley, *Favor the Bold* (1967; New York: Promontory Press, 1968), 135.

71. Kidd, *Riding with Custer*, 164–65.

72. Kidd, *Riding with Custer*, 165; Monaghan, *Custer*, 15; Martin *Kill-Cavalry*, 59–61, 134–35.

73. Kidd, *Riding with Custer*, 124–25; Wert, *Custer*, 83–85.

74. Wert, *Custer*, 86–87; *OR*, vol. 27, pt. 1, 992, 999, 1000; Kidd, *Riding with Custer*, 126–27.

75. Kidd, *Riding with Custer*, 128; Wert, *Custer*, 85–86; Monaghan, *Custer*, 138; Woodworth, *Beneath a Northern Sky*, 45.

4. GETTYSBURG

1. George R. Agassiz, ed., *Meade's Headquarters, 1863–1865: Letters of Colonel Theodore Lyman from the Wilderness to Appomattox* (Boston: Atlantic Monthly Press, 1922), 17.

2. Gregory J. W. Urwin, *Custer Victorious: The Civil War Battles of General George Armstrong Custer* (East Brunswick, NJ: Associated University Presses, 1983), 66–68; Tom Carhart, *Lost Triumph: Lee's Real Plan at Gettysburg and Why It Failed* (New York: G. P. Putnam's Sons, 2005), 203.

3. Jay Monaghan, *Custer: The Life of General George Armstrong Custer* (1959; Lincoln: University of Nebraska Press, 1971), 138; Emory M. Thomas, *Bold Dragoon: The Life of J. E. B. Stuart* (New York: Harper and Row, 1986), 245; David J. Eicher, *The Longest Night: A Military History of the Civil War* (New York: Touchstone, 2001), 516–21; Steven E. Woodworth, *Beneath a Northern Sky: A Short History of the Gettysburg Campaign* (Wilmington, DE: Scholarly Resources, 2003), 100–101; Stephen W. Sears, *Gettysburg* (Boston: Houghton Mifflin, 2003), 224.

4. Penrose G. Mark, *Red, White, and Blue Badge, Pennsylvania Veteran Volunteers: A History of the 93rd Regiment, Known as the "Lebanon Infantry" and "One of the 300 Fighting Regiments" from September 12th, 1861, to June 27th, 1865* (1911; Baltimore: Butternut and Blue, 1993), quoted in Eicher, *The*

Longest Night, 520–21; Carl Schurz, *The Reminiscences of Carl Schurz* (New York: McClure, 1907–1908), 3:19–20, quoted in Sears, *Gettysburg*, 225.

5. Monaghan, *Custer*, 139–40; Sears, *Gettysburg*, 246; J. H. Kidd, *Riding with Custer: Recollections of a Cavalryman in the Civil War* (1908; Lincoln: University of Nebraska Press, 1997), 134; Jeffry D. Wert, *Custer: The Controversial Life of George Armstrong Custer* (New York: Simon & Schuster, 1996), 88.

6. Thomas, *Bold Dragoon*, 246–47; Sears, *Gettysburg*, 257; Burke Davis, *Jeb Stuart: The Last Cavalier* (1957; New York: Wings Books, Random House, 1994), 332–33; Carhart, *Lost Triumph*, 142; Wert, *Custer*, 88; Eric J. Wittenberg, *Protecting the Flank at Gettysburg: The Battles for Brinkerhoff's Ridge and East Cavalry Field, July 2–3, 1863* (El Dorado Hills, CA: Savas Beatie, 2013), 34.

7. Custer, *War Memoirs*, 82.

8. Edward G. Longacre, *The Cavalry at Gettysburg: A Tactical Study of Mounted Operations during the Civil War's Pivotal Campaign, 9 June–14 July 1863* (London: Associated University Presses, 1986), 198–99.

9. Longacre, *The Cavalry at Gettysburg*, 199–201; Wert, *Custer*, 89; Urwin, *Custer Victorious*, 70–72; *New York Times*, July 21, 1863.

10. Urwin, *Custer Victorious*, 72.

11. Longacre, *The Cavalry at Gettysburg*, 201, 222–23; Stephen Z. Starr, *The Union Cavalry in the Civil War* (Baton Rouge: Louisiana State University Press, 1979), 1:430–31.

12. Carhart, *Lost Triumph*, 127–34.

13. Monaghan, *Custer*, 141–42; Carhart, *Lost Triumph*, 187; Wittenberg, *Protecting the Flank*, 29.

14. Longacre, *The Cavalry at Gettysburg*, 221–23; Wittenberg, *Protecting the Flank*, 40; Carhart, *Lost Triumph*, 188; Urwin, *Custer Victorious*, 72; Kidd, *Riding with Custer*, 136.

15. Urwin, *Custer Victorious*, 73; Longacre, *The Cavalry at Gettysburg*, 221; Carhart, *Lost Triumph*, 188; Kidd, *Riding with Custer*, 136; Sears, *Gettysburg*, 392, 463–64.

16. Carhart, *Lost Triumph*, 202–3, 210; Wittenberg, *Protecting the Flank*, 44–45; Longacre, *The Cavalry at Gettysburg*, 223–25; John W. Busey and David G. Martin, *Regimental Strengths and Losses at Gettysburg* (Hightstown, NJ: Longstreet House, 1994), quoted in Carhart, *Lost Triumph*, 210, 279n24. The numbers vary widely depending on the source. Sears, for example, estimated the Federals had about 3,250 men on the field, the Confederates about 3,500. See Sears, *Gettysburg*, 459–60.

17. Davis, *Jeb Stuart*, 337; Thomas, *Bold Dragoon*, 247–48; Carhart, *Lost Triumph*, 205, 211.

18. H. B. McClellan, *I Rode with Jeb Stuart* (Bloomington: Indiana University Press, 1958), 338; Wittenberg, *Protecting the Flank*, 56, 162.

19. Thom Hatch, *Glorious War: The Civil War Adventures of George Armstrong Custer* (New York: St. Martin's Press, 2013), 141; Wittenberg, *Protecting the Flank*, 44–49; Longacre, *The Cavalry at Gettysburg*, 223–29; Kidd, *Riding with Custer*, 139.

20. Longacre, *The Cavalry at Gettysburg*, 229; Urwin, *Custer Victorious*, 74.

21. Kidd, *Riding with Custer*, 144–45.

22. Mathematics professor Michael Jacobs of Pennsylvania College, later Gettysburg College, recorded the time. Michael Jacobs, *Notes on the Rebel Invasion of Maryland and Pennsylvania and the Battle of Gettysburg* (Philadelphia: Lippincott, 1864), 41; Woodworth, *Beneath a Northern Sky*, 176, 192; Monaghan, *Custer*, 143; Eicher, *The Longest Night*, 544; Sears, *Gettysburg*, 406–7, 415; Kathy Georg Harrison and John W. Busey, *Nothing but Glory: Pickett's Division at Gettysburg* (Gettysburg, PA: Thomas Publications, 1993), 39.

23. Longacre, *The Cavalry at Gettysburg*, 229–31; Carhart, *Lost Triumph*, 216–21; Wert, *Custer*, 93; Kidd, *Riding with Custer*, 149–52.

24. Longacre, *The Cavalry at Gettysburg*, 231, 237; Monaghan, *Custer*, 146; Kidd, *Riding with Custer*, 153.

25. Thomas, *Bold Dragoon*, 247; Carhart, *Lost Triumph*, 41–54, 142–48, 155–59, 173–85, 269. Carhart speculated that Lee, a keen student of military history, formulated his plan by drawing on the battles of Cannae in 216 BCE, Leuthen in 1757, Castiglione in 1796, and Austerlitz in 1805. Wittenberg, *Protecting the Flank*, 124–25, 138–57.

26. Wittenberg, *Protecting the Flank*, 124–25, 138–57; Carhart, *Lost Triumph*, 240, 251, 253, 269.

27. Longacre, *The Cavalry at Gettysburg*, 237; *OR*, vol. 27, pt. 2, 698, 724–25; Carhart, *Lost Triumph*, 222–29.

28. Carhart, *Lost Triumph*, 229–32; Hatch, *Glorious War*, 146–47.

29. Carhart, *Lost Triumph*, 232–33; Urwin, *Custer Victorious*, 80; William E. Miller, "The Cavalry Battle Near Gettysburg," in *Battles and Leaders of the Civil War*, ed. Robert Underwood Johnson and Clarence Clough Buell (New York: Century, 1887–1888), 3:401, 404–5; Longacre, *The Cavalry at Gettysburg*, 238–39.

30. *OR*, vol. 27, pt. 1, 958; Wert, *Custer*, 95; Wittenberg, *Protecting the Flank*, 118; Frederick Whittaker, *A Complete Life of General George A. Custer* (1876; Lincoln: University of Nebraska Press, 1993), 2, 178; Hatch, *Glorious War*, 149.

31. See Carhart, *Lost Triumph*, 266–69.

32. Woodworth, *Beneath a Northern Sky*, 212; Sears, *Gettysburg*, 471, 478–79; Urwin, *Custer Victorious*, 86–89.

33. Wert, *Custer*, 96–98; Kidd, *Riding with Custer*, 165–71; *New York Times*, July 21, 1863.

34. Sears, *Gettysburg*, 479–87.

35. Wert, *Custer*, 99–101; Busey and Martin, *Regimental Strengths*, 239; Sears, *Gettysburg*, 491–92, 498; *OR*, vol. 27, pt. 1, 193.

36. Monaghan, *Custer*, 155; Wert, *Custer*, 103–4; Edward G. Longacre, *Custer and His Wolverines: The Michigan Cavalry Brigade, 1861–1865* (Cambridge, MA: Da Capo Press, 1997), 177–78.

37. Whittaker, *A Complete Life*, 181.

38. E. A. Paul, "The Cavalry Service: Details of the Operations of Our Cavalry during the Campaign against Lee," *New York Times*, July 21, 1863.

39. James A. Ramage, *Gray Ghost: The Life of Col. John Singleton Mosby* (Lexington: University Press of Kentucky, 1999), 46, 103.

40. Ramage, *Gray Ghost*, 106–15; Monaghan, *Custer*, 157; Virgil Carrington Jones, *Gray Ghosts and Rebel Raiders*; Kevin H. Siepel, *Rebel: The Life and Times of John Singleton Mosby* (1983; New York: Da Capo Press, 1997), 97–99.

41. *OR*, vol. 29, pt. 1, 78; Wert, *Custer*, 108.

42. Samuel J. Martin, *Kill-Cavalry: The Life of Union General Hugh Judson Kilpatrick* (1996; Mechanicsburg, PA: Stackpole Books, 2000), 132; *New York Times*, September 17, 1863.

43. Wert, *Custer*, 108–10; *New York Times*, September 28, 1863.

44. Martin, *Kill-Cavalry*, 132–34; Urwin, *Custer Victorious*, 95–99, Davis, *Jeb Stuart*, 358; *OR*, vol. 29, pt. 1, 111–12, 118–19.

45. Monaghan, *Custer*, 159–62; Agassiz, *Meade's Headquarters*, 17; Hatch, *Glorious War*, 188–90; *New York Times*, September 17, September 28, 1863; Martin, *Kill-Cavalry*, 117, 134–35; *Harper's Weekly*, October 3, 1863.

46. Martin, *Kill-Cavalry*, 113–18, 134, 140–41.

47. Wert, *Custer*, 113.

48. Wert, *Custer*, 115–17; Martin, *Kill-Cavalry*, 136–38.

49. Louis N. Boudrye, *Historic Records of the 5th New York Cavalry in the Civil War* (Albany, NY: J. Munsell, 1868), 79–80, quoted in Vincent L. Burns, *The Fifth New York Cavalry in the Civil War* (Jefferson, NC: McFarland, 2014), 140.

50. Wert, *Custer*, 118; Martin, *Kill-Cavalry*, 139; Custer, *War Reports*, No. 2, October 24, 1863, 12.

51. Martin, *Kill-Cavalry*, 139–41; *OR*, vol. 29, pt. 1, 382, 391, 451–53.

52. Martin, *Kill-Cavalry*, 142–43; Kidd, *Riding with Custer*, 213–26; Brian D. Kowell, "Pell-Mell Cavalry Chase," *America's Civil War* 5, no. 2 (July 1992): 40–45, 72–74.

53. William W. Blackford, *War Years with Jeb Stuart* (New York: Charles Scribner's Sons, 1946), 242.

54. Martin, *Kill-Cavalry*, 139–43; Kidd, *Riding with Custer*, 214–26.

55. Custer, *War Reports*, No. 2, October 24, 1863, 12; Whittaker, *A Complete Life*, 214.

56. Wert, *Custer*, 127–28.

57. Quentin Reynolds, *Custer's Last Stand* (New York: Random House, 1951), 107.

58. Wert, *Custer*, 125–40; Marguerite Merington, ed., *The Custer Story: The Life and Intimate Letters of General George A. Custer and His Wife Elizabeth* (New York: Devin-Adair, 1950), 84.

5. SHINING STAR

1. *Omaha Daily Bee*, July 11, 1876.

2. For more on the origins of the raid, see Virgil Carrington Jones, *Eight Hours before Richmond* (New York: Holt, 1957); Duane Schultz, *The Dahlgren Affair: Terror and Conspiracy in the Civil War* (New York: W. W. Norton, 1998); Eric J. Wittenberg, *Like a Meteor Blazing Brightly: The Short but Controversial Life of Colonel Ulrich Dahlgren* (Roseville, MN: Edinborough Press, 2009); Samuel J. Martin, *Kill-Cavalry: The Life of Union General Hugh Judson Kilpatrick* (1996; Mechanicsburg, PA: Stackpole Books, 2000), 144–50.

3. Martin, *Kill-Cavalry*, 150–51.

4. Gregory J. W. Urwin, *Custer Victorious: The Civil War Battles of General George Armstrong Custer* (East Brunswick, NJ: Associated University Presses, 1983), 117; Martin, *Kill-Cavalry*, 152–53; Jeffry D. Wert, *Custer: The Controversial Life of George Armstrong Custer* (New York: Simon & Schuster, 1996), 140.

5. Wert, *Custer*, 140–41; Urwin, *Custer Victorious*, 118–20.

6. Custer, *War Reports*, No. 5, March 1 and 3, 1864, 18–20; Robert Moore, "Custer and the Shadow Soldiers," *Civil War Times* 39, no. 1 (March 2000): 29–34, 58.

7. Wert, *Custer*, 141–42; Custer, *War Reports*, No. 5, March 1 and 3, 1864, 18–20; Urwin, *Custer Victorious*, 123; *New York Times*, March 3, 1864; *Harper's Weekly*, March 19 and 26, 1864.

8. Martin, *Kill-Cavalry*, 154–71; George R. Agassiz, ed., *Meade's Headquarters, 1863–1865: Letters of Colonel Theodore Lyman from the Wilderness to Appomattox* (Boston: Atlantic Monthly Press, 1922), 79; Thom Hatch, *Glorious War: The Civil War Adventures of George Armstrong Custer* (New York: St. Martin's Press, 2013), 229.

9. J. H. Kidd, *Riding with Custer: Recollections of a Cavalryman in the Civil War* (1908; Lincoln: University of Nebraska Press, 1997), 235–36.

10. Kidd, *Riding with Custer*, 235–36, 241–42. Kidd began writing his memoirs in the 1880s. Articles appeared in the *Ionia* (Michigan) *Sentinel*, which he edited, and other publications. These articles subsequently appeared as chapters in his book. See Gregory Urwin's introduction to the 1997 edition of Kidd's book, xvi–xvii; Custer, *War Reports*, No. 5, March 1 and 3, 1864, 18–19.

11. Wert, *Custer*, 142–45.

12. Marguerite Merington, ed., *The Custer Story: The Life and Intimate Letters of General George A. Custer and His Wife Elizabeth* (New York: Devin-Adair, 1950), 87–88; Wert, *Custer*, 150.

13. Jay Monaghan, *Custer: The Life of General George Armstrong Custer* (1959; Lincoln: University of Nebraska Press, 1971), 187–88; Merington, *The Custer Story*, 89.

14. Roy Morris Jr., *Sheridan: The Life and Wars of General Phil Sheridan* (New York: Crown, 1992), 111, 147.

15. Morris, *Sheridan*, 157–59.

16. David J. Eicher, *The Longest Night: A Military History of the Civil War* (New York: Touchstone, 2001), 659–63.

17. Michael P. Gray, "The Wilderness during the Civil War," *Encyclopedia Virginia*, Virginia Foundation for the Humanities, April 15, 2011, www.encyclopediavirginia.org/Wilderness_During_the_Civil_War_The (accessed May 8, 2014).

18. E. M. Law, "From the Wilderness to Cold Harbor," *Century* (June 1887): 277–300; Eicher, *The Longest Night*, 662–63.

19. Kidd, *Riding with Custer*, 264–66; Gordon C. Rhea, *The Battle of the Wilderness, May 5–6, 1864* (Baton Rouge: Louisiana State University Press, 1994), 341, 344–45; Urwin, *Custer Victorious*, 131–32; Eicher, *The Longest Night*, 669; Custer, *War Reports*, No. 6, July 4, 1864, 21; Monaghan, *Custer*, 189–90; Burke Davis, *Jeb Stuart: The Last Cavalier* (1957; New York: Wings Books, Random House, 1994), 379.

20. Rhea, *The Battle of the Wilderness*, 345.

21. Kidd, *Riding with Custer*, 267–75; Wert, *Custer*, 152–53; Thomas B. Buell, *The Warrior Generals: Combat Leadership in the Civil War* (New York: Three Rivers Press, 1997), 303; George M. Neese, *Three Years in the Confederate Horse Artillery* (New York: Neale, 1911), 261–62; Rhea, *The Battle of the Wilderness*, 349–50.

22. Custer, *War Reports*, No. 6, July 4, 1864, 22.

23. Eicher, *The Longest Night*, 662–66; Thomas W. Hyde, *Following the Greek Cross; or, Memories of the Sixth Army Corps* (Boston: Houghton Mifflin, 1894), 184–85; Bruce Catton, *A Stillness at Appomattox* (Garden City, NY: Doubleday, 1953), 80–81.

24. Eicher, *The Longest Night*, 666–72; Kidd, *Riding with Custer*, 274–75. Confederate casualties have been estimated at higher levels, as high as 11,400.

25. David Coffey, *Sheridan's Lieutenants: Phil Sheridan, His Generals, and the Final Year of the Civil War* (Lanham, MD: Rowman & Littlefield, 2005), 20; Wert, *Custer*, 154–55; Kidd, *Riding with Custer*, 288–89.

26. Urwin, *Custer Victorious*, 136.

27. Custer, *War Reports*, No. 6, July 4, 1864, 22–23; Morris, *Sheridan*, 166–67; Emory M. Thomas, *Bold Dragoon: The Life of J. E. B. Stuart* (New York: Harper and Row, 1986), 289–90.

28. Thomas, *Bold Dragoon*, 291–92.

29. Urwin, *Custer Victorious*, 138–40; Custer, *War Reports*, No. 6, July 4, 1864, 23–24; Kidd, *Riding with Custer*, 296–97; Gordon C. Rhea, *The Battles for Spotsylvania Court House and the Road to Yellow Tavern, May 7–12* (Baton Rouge: Louisiana State University Press, 1997), 201–6.

30. Rhea, *The Battles for Spotsylvania Court House*, 206–7.

31. Clint Johnson, *In the Footsteps of J. E. B. Stuart* (Winston-Salem, NC: John F. Blair, 2003), 65; Rhea, *The Battles for Spotsylvania Court House*, 207–9. A sharpshooter, Private John A. Huff of the 5th Michigan, is usually identified as the man who shot Stuart, but eyewitnesses made other claims. See Urwin, *Custer Victorious*, 144; Thomas, *Bold Dragoon*, 292–95.

32. Rhea, *The Battles for Spotsylvania Court House*, 212; *New York Herald*, May 17, 1864; *Daily Alta California* (San Francisco), June 15, 1864; James Harrison Wilson, *Under the Old Flag: Recollections of Military Operations in the War for the Union, the Spanish War, the Boxer Rebellion, etc.* (New York: D. Appleton, 1912), 1:407–8; Merington, *The Custer Story*, 97.

33. Coffey, *Sheridan's Lieutenants*, 24; Kidd, *Riding with Custer*, 308; Morris, *Sheridan*, 169–70.

34. Urwin, *Custer Victorious*, 145–51; Kidd, *Riding with Custer*, 307–14; Gordon C. Rhea, *To the North Anna River: Grant and Lee, May 13–25, 1864* (Baton Rouge: Louisiana State University Press, 2000), 62; Rhea, *The Battles for Spotsylvania Court House*, 212. In a letter written to her parents on May 22, 1864, Libbie said Custer's men were sorry Stuart was dead, "for they consider Wade Hampton who will succeed him a superior officer." Presumably this was her husband's opinion. Hampton and Fitz Lee were capable successors to Stuart after Yellow Tavern. As Urwin put it, the Confederate cavalry "had been badly mauled and humiliated at Yellow Tavern, but it had not been destroyed, and Sheridan's 10,000 had many miles to go before they would be safe again." Merington, *The Custer Story*, 98; Urwin, *Custer Victorious*, 145.

35. Eicher, *The Longest Night*, 679, Urwin, *Custer Victorious*, 151–52; Custer, *War Reports*, No. 6, July 4, 1864, 26; Morris, *Sheridan*, 172–73.

36. Eicher, *The Longest Night*, 686; Morris, *Sheridan*, 174; Custer, *War Reports*, No. 6, July 4, 1864, 28–29.

37. Custer, *War Reports*, No. 6, July 4, 1864, 29.

38. Coffey, *Sheridan's Lieutenants*, 29–30; Wert, *Custer*, 162.

39. Custer, *War Reports*, No. 6, July 4, 1864, 29–30; Coffey, *Sheridan's Lieutenants*, 31.

40. Kidd, *Riding with Custer*, 344–57.

41. Kidd, *Riding with Custer*, 357–61; Custer, *War Reports*, No. 6, July 4, 1864, 29–30; Urwin, *Custer Victorious*, 154–64; Wert, *Custer*, 165; Merington, *The Custer Story*, 104–5.

42. Coffey, *Sheridan's Lieutenants*, 31.

43. Coffey, *Sheridan's Lieutenants*, 33–35; Eicher, *The Longest Night*, 694; Custer, *War Reports*, No. 6, July 4, 1864, 31.

44. Morris, *Sheridan*, 179–81.

45. Morris, *Sheridan*, 182–83; Coffey, *Sheridan's Lieutenants*, 42–43; Wert, *Custer*, 170.

46. Morris, *Sheridan*, 182–84; Coffey, *Sheridan's Lieutenants*, 42–43; Henry C. Lockwood, "General Philip Henry Sheridan," *Frank Leslie's Popular Monthly* 26, no. 5 (November 1888): 520.

47. Wert, *Custer*, 170–71; James E. Taylor, *The James E. Taylor Sketchbook: With Sheridan up the Shenandoah Valley in 1864. Leaves from a Special Artist's Sketch Book and Diary* (Dayton, OH: Morningside House, 1989), 1, 35, 534.

48. Eicher, *The Longest Night*, 743; Wert, 171–72.

49. Wert, *Custer*, 172–73; Scott C. Patchan, "The Battle of Crooked Run: George Custer's Opening Act in the Shenandoah Valley," *North and South* 11, no. 2 (December 2008): 76–82.

50. Urwin, *Custer Victorious*, 171–74.

51. Urwin, *Custer Victorious*, 174.

52. Kidd, *Riding with Custer*, 375–77.

53. *New York Times*, August 25, 1864.

54. Philip H. Sheridan, *Personal Memoirs of P. H. Sheridan* (New York: Charles L. Webster, 1888), 1:500.

55. James A. Ramage, *Gray Ghost: The Life of Col. John Singleton Mosby* (Lexington: University Press of Kentucky, 1999), 194–95; *New York Times*, August 25, 1864. According to Morris, in the years after the Civil War on the western plains, Sheridan thought "the Indians were uncomfortably reminiscent of John Singleton Mosby's Confederate rangers in the Shenandoah Valley, the sole exception being that Mosby's men had not scalped their victims after killing them." Morris, *Sheridan*, 307.

56. Urwin, *Custer Victorious*, 175; Jones, *Eight Hours*, 280–83; Kevin H. Siepel, *Rebel: The Life and Times of John Singleton Mosby* (1983; New York: Da Capo Press, 1997), 118.

57. Urwin, *Custer Victorious*, 175–77; Kidd, *Riding with Custer*, 378–82; Wert, *Custer*, 176.

58. Ramage, *Gray Ghost*, 302, 306.

59. Ulysses S. Grant, *Personal Memoirs of U. S. Grant* (New York: Charles L. Webster, 1885), 2:329; Sheridan, *Personal Memoirs*, 2:9; Eicher, *The Longest Night*, 743.

60. Morris, *Sheridan*, 196–97.

61. Urwin, *Custer Victorious*, 176; Morris, *Sheridan*, 198; Coffey, *Sheridan's Lieutenants*, 52, 56; Wert, *Custer*, 180–82; Custer, *War Reports*, No. 7, September 28, 1864, 35.

62. Coffey, *Sheridan's Lieutenants*, 55–57

63. Coffey, *Sheridan's Lieutenants*, 57–60 (Merritt quoted on page 58); Urwin, *Custer Victorious*, 184–87. Colonel Rutherford B. Hayes, commanding one of Crook's brigades, was also on the field. Hayes would become the Republican presidential nominee shortly before the Little Bighorn. Colonel George S. Patton, fighting with the 2nd Virginia Infantry, was killed in Winchester. He was the grandfather of the World War II general.

64. Coffey, *Sheridan's Lieutenants*, 58; J. Cutler Andrews, *The South Reports the Civil War* (Princeton, NJ: Princeton University Press, 1970), 420, quoted in Brayton Harris, *Blue & Gray in Black & White: Newspapers in the Civil War* (Washington, DC: Batsford Brassey, 1999), 293. "Early so distrusted his cavalry that he relied almost solely on his veteran infantry and artillery. . . . Confederate cavalry units from the Shenandoah Valley were so undisciplined and poorly led . . . that it made scant sense to depend on them for serious work." See Gary W. Gallagher, "Two Generals and a Valley: Philip H. Sheridan and Jubal A. Early in the Shenandoah," in *The Shenandoah Valley Campaign of 1864*, ed. Gary W. Gallagher (Chapel Hill: University of North Carolina Press, 2006), 20.

65. Custer, *War Reports*, No. 7, September 28, 1864, 38.

66. Eicher, *The Longest Night*, 746.

67. Coffey, *Sheridan's Lieutenants*, 61–65; Jay W. Simson, *Custer and the Front Royal Executions of 1864* (Jefferson, NC: McFarland, 2009), 34–36.

68. Simson, *Custer and the Front Royal Executions*, 46–47; Kidd, *Riding with Custer*, 395–96.

69. Simson, *Custer and the Front Royal Executions*, 11–16.

70. Simson, *Custer and the Front Royal Executions*, 16–17, 58–59; Siepel, *Rebel*, 121, 128; Ramage, *Gray Ghost*, 198; Morris, *Sheridan*, 207, 226.

71. John S. Mosby, "Retaliation: The Execution of Seven Prisoners by Col. John S. Mosby—A Self-Protective Necessity," *Southern Historical Society*

Papers 27 (1899): 314–22. John S. Mosby, *The Memoirs of John S. Mosby*, ed. Charles Wells Russell (1917; Nashville: J. S. Sanders, 1995), 300–302; Jones, *Gray Ghosts and Rebel Raiders*, 294–94, 407n26–27.

72. Joseph J. Mathews, *Reporting the Wars* (Minneapolis: University of Minnesota Press, 1957), 92–94; Simson, *Custer and the Front Royal Executions*, 57.

73. "Mosby and His Men," *Confederate Veteran* 7, no. 9 (September 1899): 388; Thomas L. Rosser to A. E. Richards, November 23, 1899, in Richards's "Major Richards Cites Authorities for His Conclusion," *Southern Historical Society Papers* 27 (1899): 23; Simson, *Custer and the Front Royal Executions*, 133; Adolphus E. Richards, "Address for Monument Dedication," September 23, 1899, *Southern Historical Society Papers* 27 (1899): 254, 282–83; John S. Mosby, "Retaliation: The Execution of Seven Prisoners by Col. John S. Mosby—A Self-Protective Necessity," *Southern Historical Society Papers* 27 (1899): 314–22.

74. *Richmond Times*, September 24 and November 12, 1899; Simson, *Custer and the Front Royal Executions*, 133–50.

75. Simson, *Custer and the Front Royal Executions*, 143; *Richmond Times*, November 12, 1899.

76. *Richmond Times*, December 8 and 24, 1899; Mosby to Robert L. "Bob" Walker, December 12, 1899, in Adele H. Mitchell, ed., *The Letters of John S. Mosby*, 2nd ed. (N.p.: Stuart-Mosby Historical Society, 1986), 96–97.

77. Frederic F. Van de Water, *Glory-Hunter: A Life of General Custer* (1934; Lincoln: University of Nebraska Press, 1988), 81.

78. Monaghan, *Custer*, 221–22.

79. D. A. Kinsley, *Favor the Bold* (1967, 1968; New York: Promontory Press, 1968), 260.

80. Lawrence A. Frost, *Custer Legends* (Bowling Green, OH: Bowling Green University Popular Press, 1981), 56.

81. Wert, *Custer*, 185.

82. Hatch, *Glorious War*, 279.

83. Coffey, *Sheridan's Lieutenants*, 69.

84. Jones, *Eight Hours*, 294.

85. Ramage, *Gray Ghost*, 199–200.

86. Eicher, *The Longest Night*, 752.

87. Siepel, *Rebel*, 120–21.

88. Joseph Wheelan, *Terrible Swift Sword: The Life of General Philip H. Sheridan* (Cambridge, MA: Da Capo Press, 2012), 133.

89. Longacre, *Custer and His Wolverines*, 261.

90. Simson, *Custer and the Front Royal Executions*, 82.

6. CHECKMATE

1. Quoted in Frederick Whittaker, *A Complete Life of General George A. Custer* (1876; Lincoln: University of Nebraska Press, 1993), 2:612.

2. Jeffry D. Wert, *Custer: The Controversial Life of George Armstrong Custer* (New York: Simon & Schuster, 1996), 186–89, 198; Marguerite Merington, ed., *The Custer Story: The Life and Intimate Letters of General George A. Custer and His Wife Elizabeth* (New York: Devin-Adair, 1950), 120.

3. Roy Morris Jr., *Sheridan: The Life and Wars of General Phil Sheridan* (New York: Crown, 1992), 186–87, 207–9; Philip H. Sheridan, *Personal Memoirs of P. H. Sheridan* (New York: Charles L. Webster, 1888), 1:413–17; *Harper's Weekly*, October 11, 1864.

4. Morris, *Sheridan*, 205–6, 209.

5. Charles Moore, "The Days of Fife and Drum," in *Collections and Researches Made by the Michigan Pioneer and Historical Society* (Lansing: Michigan Pioneer and Historical Society, 1900), 28:450; Wert, *Custer*, 190–91; *OR*, vol. 43, pt. 1, 521.

6. Custer, *War Reports*, No. 8, October 13, 1864, 41.

7. David Coffey, *Sheridan's Lieutenants: Phil Sheridan, His Generals, and the Final Year of the Civil War* (Lanham, MD: Rowman & Littlefield, 2005), 74–76; John Brown Gordon, *Reminiscences of the Civil War* (New York: Charles Scribner's Sons, 1904), 333–36; David J. Eicher, *The Longest Night: A Military History of the Civil War* (New York: Touchstone, 2001), 749.

8. J. H. Kidd, *Riding with Custer: Recollections of a Cavalryman in the Civil War* (1908; Lincoln: University of Nebraska Press, 1997), 409–12; Wert, *Custer*, 194–95; Gregory J. W. Urwin, *Custer Victorious: The Civil War Battles of General George Armstrong Custer* (East Brunswick, NJ: Associated University Presses, 1983), 206–7; Custer, *War Reports*, No. 8, October 22, 1864, 42–43.

9. Kidd, *Riding with Custer*, 413–14.

10. Jonathan A. Noyalas, *The Battle of Cedar Creek: Victory from the Jaws of Defeat* (Charleston, SC: History Press, 2011), 44–45; Coffey, *Sheridan's Lieutenants*, 78–81.

11. Coffey, *Sheridan's Lieutenants*, 81–82; Noyalas, *The Battle of Cedar Creek*, 53.

12. Brayton Harris, *Blue & Gray in Black & White: Newspapers in the Civil War* (Washington, DC: Batsford Brassey, 1999), 287–98. The poem first appeared in the November 8 edition of the *New York Tribune*.

13. Harris, *Blue & Gray*, 298, 301–2.

14. Morris, *Sheridan*, 215–17; Urwin, *Custer Victorious*, 210–11; *OR*, vol. 43, pt. 1, 434, 450; Jay Monaghan, *Custer: The Life of General George Armstrong Custer* (1959; Lincoln: University of Nebraska Press, 1971), 216.

15. Custer, *War Reports*, No. 8, October 22, 1864, 45; Gordon, *Reminiscences*, 348.

16. Wert, *Custer*, 195; Morris, *Sheridan*, 218; *OR*, vol. 43, pt. 1, 525–26; Urwin, *Custer Victorious*, 212–14; *New York Times*, October 27, 1864; Eicher, *The Longest Night*, 752.

17. Urwin, *Custer Victorious*, 215; Morris, *Sheridan*, 218–19; *Harper's Weekly*, November 5, 1864; Coffey, *Sheridan's Lieutenants*, 94.

18. Jay W. Simson, *Custer and the Front Royal Executions of 1864* (Jefferson, NC: McFarland, 2009), 87–92; James A. Ramage, *Gray Ghost: The Life of Col. John Singleton Mosby* (Lexington: University Press of Kentucky, 1999), 214–15; *New York Times*, November 10 and 12, 1864; Morris, *Sheridan*, 226–27.

19. Wert, *Custer*, 199–201; Merington, *The Custer Story*, 95, 132. Sheridan also attended Christ Episcopal Church. Custer was raised Methodist but described himself in a May 1, 1864, letter to Libbie as "a non-professing (tho not an unbeliever) Christian." Libbie was raised Presbyterian, and the Custers were married at the First Presbyterian Church in Monroe.

20. Wert, *Custer*, 202–3; *OR*, vol. 43, pt. 1, 675–76; Urwin, *Custer Victorious*, 221–24.

21. Custer, *War Reports*, No. 9, December 23, 1864, 52–55; *OR*, vol. 43, pt. 1, 677–79; Sheridan, *Memoirs*, 2:102.

22. Wert, *Custer*, 203–4.

23. Wert, *Custer*, 204–5; Urwin, *Custer Victorious*, 224–25; Coffey, *Sheridan's Lieutenants*, 98–99.

24. Morris, *Sheridan*, 236–37.

25. Wert, *Custer*, 205–6; Custer, *War Reports*, No. 10, March 20, 1865, 56; Urwin, *Custer Victorious*, 225.

26. Wert, *Custer*, 206–8; *New York Times*, March 21, 1865; Custer, *War Reports*, No. 10, March 20, 1865, 56–58; Urwin, *Custer Victorious*, 226–28; Morris, *Sheridan*, 238; Eicher, *The Longest Night*, 804. Custer wrote in his report that he had taken eighteen hundred prisoners. One of Merritt's staff members heard Custer say he had two thousand prisoners, but he may have been referring to the total number of prisoners taken by all units. On March 11 he told Libbie the division had captured three thousand prisoners, one thousand more men than Early had in his command, unless he was including prisoners taken after the battle. In the same letter he boasted that neither Merritt nor Sheridan was closer than ten miles from wherever these prisoners were captured. See George B. Sanford, *Fighting Rebels and Redskins: Experiences in Army Life of Colonel George B. Sanford, 1861–1892*, ed. E. R. Hagemann (Norman: University of Oklahoma Press, 1969), 316, quoted in Urwin, *Custer Victorious*, 230; Merington, *The Custer Story*, 141–42.

27. Merington, *The Custer Story*, 141, 143.

28. Morris, *Sheridan*, 239; Custer, *War Reports*, No. 10, March 20, 1865, 58. Mosby's friend and mentor, Professor William Holmes McGuffey (1800–1873), may have been among the faculty trying to save the university. McGuffey was the author of the *McGuffey Readers* textbooks. With a price on his head, Mosby briefly visited McGuffey in Charlottesville in May 1865 and left just before Federal cavalry arrived to arrest him. Mosby grew up at Tudor Grove, a 398-acre farm four miles south of Charlottesville and within sight of Monticello. He studied Greek at the University of Virginia until he was expelled in 1853 for shooting another student. He was convicted of a misdemeanor, incarcerated, and then pardoned later that year. He took advantage of the sentence to study law. See Ramage, *Gray Ghost*, 17–27, 267.

29. Custer, *War Reports*, No. 10, March 20, 1865, 58–59.

30. Merington, *The Custer Story*, 141.

31. Merington, *The Custer Story*, 144.

32. *New York Times*, March 20 and 22, 1865; Monaghan, *Custer*, 229–30; Merington, *The Custer Story*, 137.

33. Morris, *Sheridan*, 242–43.

34. Morris, *Sheridan*, 243; Coffey, *Sheridan's Lieutenants*, 107–8, 155n7; *OR*, vol. 46, pt. 3, 266.

35. Morris, *Sheridan*, 244–46; *OR*, vol. 46, pt. 1, 1130.

36. Wert, *Custer*, 216–17; Urwin, *Custer Victorious*, 236–38.

37. Morris, *Sheridan*, 247–51; Eicher, *The Longest Night*, 808; Urwin, *Custer Victorious*, 242. A court of inquiry vindicated Warren in 1882, three months after his death.

38. Edward G. Longacre, *The Cavalry at Appomattox: A Tactical Study of Mounted Operations during the Civil War's Climactic Campaign, March 27–April 9, 1865* (Mechanicsburg, PA: Stackpole Books, 2003), 115–18. Roberts was the youngest Confederate general. Barringer was captured soon after by some Federal scouts disguised as Confederates. He had breakfast with Sheridan the next morning and later met Lincoln at City Point. Lincoln served with the general's brother, Daniel Barringer, in Congress and was a personal friend.

39. Longacre, *The Cavalry at Appomattox*, 120–21; Custer, *War Reports*, No. 11, April 15, 1865, 62; Bruce Catton, *A Stillness at Appomattox* (Garden City, NY: Doubleday, 1953), 365–66.

40. Morris, *Sheridan*, 253–54.

41. Longacre, *The Cavalry at Appomattox*, 128–29, 148–56; Urwin, *Custer Victorious*, 244–46; Coffey, *Sheridan's Lieutenants*, 123; *OR*, vol. 46, pt. 1, 1108, 1120.

42. Eicher, *The Longest Night*, 816; Longacre, *The Cavalry at Appomattox*, 156; Henry Edwin Tremain, *The Last Hours of Sheridan's Cavalry* (New York: Bonnell, Silver and Bowers, 1904), 133, 149–52; Monaghan, *Custer*, 238–39;

Custer, *War Reports*, No. 11, April 15, 1865, 63. Custer claimed his division captured Ewell. Monaghan said Ewell personally surrendered to Custer. He also said Brigadier General Paul Semmes, mortally wounded at Gettysburg, was among those captured during the battle. Ewell's biographer, Donald Pfanz, reported that the 5th Wisconsin asserted that it captured Ewell, but he judged Custer's claim the stronger. See Donald Pfanz, *Richard S. Ewell: A Soldier's Life* (Chapel Hill: University of North Carolina Press, 1998), 525. The battle is known variously as Sayler's Creek, Saylor's Creek, and Little Sailor's Creek.

43. Longacre, *The Cavalry at Appomattox*, 163–65; Coffey, *Sheridan's Lieutenants*, 124.

44. Longacre, *The Cavalry at Appomattox*, 166–70; Coffey, *Sheridan's Lieutenants*, 124.

45. Longacre, *The Cavalry at Appomattox*, 171–74; W. F. Robinson, "Last Battle before Surrender," *Confederate Veteran* 32, no. 11 (November 1924): 471, quoted in Longacre, *The Cavalry at Appomattox*, 174; William E. Marvel, *Lee's Last Retreat: The Flight to Appomattox* (Chapel Hill: University of North Carolina Press, 2006), 147–49.

46. Longacre, *The Cavalry at Appomattox*, 174–77; Tremain, *The Last Hours*, 229–31.

47. Custer, *War Reports*, No. 11, April 15, 1865, 63; Tremain, *The Last Hours*, 231.

48. Longacre, *The Cavalry at Appomattox*, 180–85.

49. Longacre, *The Cavalry at Appomattox*, 192–94.

50. Longacre, *The Cavalry at Appomattox*, 194; Wert, *Custer*, 402; Coffey, *Sheridan's Lieutenants*, 129–31.

51. Coffey, *Sheridan's Lieutenants*, 131. There are several versions of what happened during the negotiations. By one account, Captain (or Major—sources differ) Robert Moorman Sims, one of Longstreet's staff officers, approached Custer and asked him to suspend hostilities by request of Lee. Custer said he had no authority to do so and sent Lieutenant Colonel Edward Whitaker, his chief of staff, to accompany Sims back to the Confederate lines and tell Lee that, without an unconditional surrender, he could not suspend hostilities. Sheridan recalled that Custer had told him Lee had surrendered. Meanwhile, rumors that Lee had capitulated spread through Custer's lines, prompting cheers and provoking Gary's South Carolinians to open fire. Urwin, *Custer Victorious*, 254–56; Wert, *Custer*, 224–25; Sheridan, *Memoirs*, 2:193–94; James Longstreet, *From Manassas to Appomattox: Memoirs of the Civil War in America* (1896; Bloomington: Indiana University Press, 1960), 627; Benjamin Albert Botkin, *A Civil War Treasury of Tales, Legends, and Folklore* (New York: Random House, 1960), 484–86; Duane Schultz, *The Dahlgren Affair: Terror and Conspiracy in the Civil War* (New York: W. W. Norton, 1998), 39. Monaghan, *Custer*, 243–44, has the

fullest treatment of the conflicting accounts, assessing the evidence and errors. But he has his own error, confusing Sims (1837–1898) with William Gilmore Simms (1806–1870), an author whose novel *Eutaw* Custer once checked out of the West Point library. Utley, *Cavalier in Buckskin*, 33, has the unnamed Sims riding up to Custer bearing a white towel tied to a pole and telling him Lee wanted to meet with Grant. "Fittingly," wrote Utley, "this emblem of war's end came to the young general who, by age twenty-five, had written a record of military exploits that few soldiers exhibit in a lifetime." Custer likely was among the first Federal officers to learn of a pending surrender, but stating it this way enlarges his role. In his own report, Custer wrote that he did agree to a truce after he had taken precautions to align his troops either to attack or repel an attack. Custer, *War Reports*, No. 11, April 15, 1865, 64. Sheridan already knew of negotiations between Grant and Lee but expected Lee to continue to fight and was at least momentarily disappointed when he learned of the white flag. Gordon had yet another account, describing the arrival of

> an officer of strikingly picturesque appearance. This Union officer was slender and graceful, and a superb rider. He wore his hair very long, falling almost to his shoulders. Guided by my staff officer, he saluted me with his sabre and said: "I am General Custer, and bear a message to you from General Sheridan. The general desires me to present to you his compliments, and to demand the immediate and unconditional surrender of all the troops under your command." I replied: You will please, general, return my compliments to General Sheridan, and say to him that I shall not surrender my command. "He directs me to say to you, general, if there is any hesitation about your surrender, that he has you surrounded and can annihilate your command in an hour." To this I answered that I was probably as well aware of my situation as was General Sheridan; that I had nothing to add to my message informing him of the contents of the note from General Lee; that if General Sheridan decided to continue the fighting in the face of the flag of truce, the responsibility for the blood shed would be his and not mine.

Gordon, *Reminiscences*, 439. Libbie Custer tried to suppress some versions of the surrender story. Merington, *The Custer Story*, 156–57.

52. Morris, *Sheridan*, 257–58; Merington, *The Custer Story*, 160; Eicher, *The Longest Night*, 819.

53. *Detroit Advertiser*, May 1, 1865; *New York Times*, May 7, 1865; Wert, *Custer*, 227.

54. Merington, *The Custer Story*, 164.

55. Wert, *Custer*, 228.

56. Wert, *Custer*, 228; Coffey, *Sheridan's Lieutenants*, 134–35; *New York Times*, May 24, 1865; *Daily National Intelligencer*, May 24, 1865. Sheridan had been given command of Federal forces in the West on May 17 and was on a steamboat heading down the Mississippi for New Orleans at the time of the parade. Van de Water predictably made the most of the incident. "The whole man with his flaws and flairs is epitomized in that dash," he wrote. "He has been, he will ever be, prone to spectacular outbursts against ordered regularity; insurgent in his hunt for Glory. That runaway is at once his biography and his epitaph." Frederic F. Van de Water, *Glory-Hunter: A Life of General Custer* (1934; Lincoln: University of Nebraska Press, 1988), 126.

57. Merington, *The Custer Story*, 160–61.

58. Charles Capehart to Captain Charles King, August 16, 1890, E. B. Custer Collection, Little Bighorn National Battlefield, quoted in Urwin, *Custer Victorious*, 35. Urwin attributes the letter to Capehart's brother, Henry, even though he cites Charles Capehart as the writer of the letter. Both brothers served in the 1st West Virginia Cavalry, both served under Custer, and both won the Congressional Medal of Honor.

59. Merington, *The Custer Story*, 142.

60. Urwin, *Custer Victorious*, 268; H. A. Sommers, "The History of Elizabethtown," *Elizabethtown News*, May 27, 1921.

7. FROM CIVIL WAR TO
INDIAN WARS

1. Jeffry D. Wert, *Custer: The Controversial Life of George Armstrong Custer* (New York: Simon & Schuster, 1996), 231–36; Jeff Barnes, *The Great Plains Guide to Custer: 85 Forts, Fights & Other Sites* (Mechanicsburg, PA: Stackpole Books, 2012), 2, 4, 10–11.

2. Wert, *Custer*, 240–42; Barnes, *The Great Plains Guide*, 17–20. The word *Indian* is used here as a general term, as it was used in the nineteenth and earlier twentieth centuries, and there was awareness of tribes and tribal differences. The term *Native Americans* is a later designation.

3. Paul Andrew Hutton, ed., *The Custer Reader* (Norman: University of Oklahoma Press, 1992), 93–94; Oliver Knight, *Following the Indian Wars: The Story of the Newspaper Correspondents among the Indian Campaigners* (Norman: University of Oklahoma Press, 1960), 6–17, 21.

4. Thom Hatch, *The Custer Companion: A Comprehensive Guide to the Life of George Armstrong Custer and the Plains Indian Wars* (Mechanicsburg, PA: Stackpole Books, 2002), 35–36; Wert, *Custer*, 245–48. Stanley was a freelancer whose clients included the *Missouri Democrat* and the *New York Tribune*. He

said Custer was the right man for fighting the Indians: "A certain impetuosity and undoubted courage are his principal characteristics."

5. Barnes, *The Great Plains Guide*, 41–43; Wert, *Custer*, 256. See Charles K. Hofling, "General Custer and the Battle of the Little Big Horn," *Psychoanalytic Review* 54 (Summer 1967): 303–28.

6. Barnes, *The Great Plains Guide*, 45–46, 50–51; Wert, *Custer*, 258.

7. Wert, *Custer*, 261; Barnes, *The Great Plains Guide*, 56–57, 61.

8. Stan Hoig, *The Battle of the Washita: The Sheridan-Custer Indian Campaign of 1867–69* (Lincoln: University of Nebraska Press, 1976), 20; Wert, *Custer*, 262–64; Hatch, *The Custer Companion*, 63–64, 72–73.

9. Hatch, *The Custer Companion*, 69–72.

10. Hatch, *The Custer Companion*, 69–72; Brian Dippie, ed., introduction to *Nomad: George A. Custer in Turf, Field and Farm* (Austin: University of Texas Press, 1980), xiv–xvi. Dippie reprints the *Turf, Field and Farm* articles.

11. Wert, *Custer*, 265–68; Hatch, *The Custer Companion*, 75, 83–84.

12. Hoig, *The Battle of the Washita*, 52–53.

13. Wert, *Custer*, 270–74; John F. Marszalek, *Sherman: A Soldier's Passion for Order* (New York: Free Press, 1993), 378–79.

14. Hatch, *The Custer Companion*, 76–79, 92; Wert, *Custer*, 270–74; Hoig, *The Battle of the Washita*, 128–31. Ranger Joel Shockley of the National Park Service at the Washita Battlefield National Historic Site provided information on the battle, including the number of men with Custer at the time of the fight, which Shockley put at 689, and the number of Indians who pinned Custer's troops down for about three hours. More recent scholarship has added both detail and nuance to the history of the battle. Among these notable histories are Duane Schultz, *Coming through Fire: George Armstrong Custer and Chief Black Kettle* (Yardley, PA: Westholme, 2012); Richard G. Hardorff, ed., *Washita Memories: Eyewitness Views of Custer's Attack on Black Kettle's Village* (Norman: University of Oklahoma Press, 2006); Jerome A. Greene, *Washita: The U.S. Army and the Southern Cheyennes, 1867–1869* (Norman: University of Oklahoma Press, 2004).

15. Hatch, *The Custer Companion*, 76–79, 92; Wert, *Custer*, 270–74. According to Shockley, the Cheyenne nation said only sixty were killed: six children, twelve women, and forty-two men. Schultz, *Coming through Fire*, 249.

16. Quoted in Hoig, *The Battle of the Washita*, 141.

17. Hoig, *The Battle of the Washita*, 141, 154–56. Joel Shockley points out that Myers reported traveling two miles and not seeing Elliott. But Elliott was killed only one mile east of Custer's knoll along the east bank of Sergeant Major Creek. If Myers went two miles, then he would have been killed by the same Indians who were attacking Elliott. Myers, Shockley believes, lied to Custer.

Personal correspondence, October 19, 2014. Hardorff, *Washita Memories*, 27–28; Greene, *Washita*, 125.

18. Hoig, *The Battle of the Washita*, 149, 160–62.

19. Wert, *Custer*, 279.

20. Hutton, *The Custer Reader*, 95–96; Hoig, *The Battle of the Washita*, xiv.

21. Hatch, *The Custer Companion*, 87–89; Barnes, *The Great Plains Guide*, 112; Wert, *Custer*, 284–85. Joel Shockley, personal correspondence, October 19, 2014.

22. Barnes, *The Great Plains Guide*, 96–97.

23. Robert M. Utley, *Cavalier in Buckskin: George Armstrong Custer and the Western Military Frontier* (Norman: University of Oklahoma Press, 1988), 107; see Hatch, *The Custer Companion*, 94, for citations explicating the rumor. John Stands in Timber and Margot Liberty, *Cheyenne Memories* (New Haven, CT: Yale University Press, 1967), use the same oral tradition to dismiss the story; Hatch, *The Custer Companion*, 92–94. Meotzi is one of several names used for the Indian woman who supposedly gave birth to Custer's child. She also is cited as Monahsetiah. According to Shockley, she gave birth to a healthy Indian boy in February 1869 at Fort Sill. And any fair-haired child she may have given birth to in late 1869 would have been Tom Custer's because George Custer, Shockley states, was sterile. Personal correspondence, October 19, 2014.

24. Hatch, *The Custer Companion*, 132–34; Barnes, *The Great Plains Guide*, 117–19; Wert, *Custer*, 290.

25. Wert, *Custer*, 291–92.

26. Wert, *Custer*, 291–96.

27. Barnes, *The Great Plains Guide*, 125–26, 136–39, 142–43, 147; Hatch, *The Custer Companion*, 107.

28. Hutton, *The Custer Reader*, 108; Barnes, *The Great Plains Guide*, 149–52, 161–62.

29. Wert, *Custer*, 303; Hatch, *The Custer Companion*, 128–29; Barnes, *The Great Plains Guide*, 165–73.

30. Jay Monaghan, *Custer: The Life of General George Armstrong Custer* (1959; Lincoln: University of Nebraska Press, 1971), 342–43, 350–51; Hutton, *The Custer Reader*, 108–10.

31. Utley, *Cavalier in Buckskin*, 117–19; Wert, *Custer* 304–5.

32. Hatch, *The Custer Companion*, 128–29; Utley, *Cavalier in Buckskin*, 120–23.

33. Hutton, *The Custer Reader*, 109–10; Barnes, *The Great Plains Guide*, 168–73, 179.

34. Hatch, *The Custer Companion*, 138–39; Hutton, *The Custer Reader*, 97, 108–10; Barnes, *The Great Plains Guide*, 179.

35. Barnes, *The Great Plains Guide*, 177; Hatch, *The Custer Companion*, 138–39; James E. Mueller, *Shooting Arrows and Slinging Mud: Custer, the Press, and the Little Bighorn* (Norman: University of Oklahoma Press, 2013), 17.

36. Wert, *Custer*, 312–34; Barnes, *The Great Plains Guide*, 185–89.

37. Monaghan, *Custer*, 352–56. On press coverage and exaggeration of the trip, see Herbert Krause and Gary D. Olsen, *Prelude to Glory: A Newspaper Accounting of Custer's 1874 Expedition to the Black Hills* (Sioux Falls, SD: Brevet Press, 1974).

38. Wert, *Custer*, 321–25.

39. Barnes, *The Great Plains Guide*, 203–13.

8. CROSSING THE RIVER

1. *The Holy Bible*, Revised Standard Version (New York: Thomas Nelson, 1952), 582.

2. James Donovan, *A Terrible Glory: Custer and the Little Bighorn—the Last Great Battle of the American West* (New York: Little, Brown, 2008), 304; John F. McBlain, "With Gibbon on the Sioux Campaign of 1876," *Journal of the U.S. Cavalry Association* 9, no. 33 (1896), quoted in Evan S. Connell, *Son of the Morning Star* (San Francisco: North Point Press, 1984), 2–3.

3. Donovan, *A Terrible Glory*, 303; Nathaniel Philbrick, *The Last Stand: Custer, Sitting Bull, and the Battle of the Little Bighorn* (New York: Viking, 2010), 253–55; Charles F. Roe, *Custer's Last Battle* (New York: Bruce, 1927), cited in Philbrick, *The Last Stand*, 254, and Donovan, *A Terrible Glory*, 304; McBlain, cited in Connell, *Son of the Morning Star*, 2–3.

4. Donovan, *A Terrible Glory*, 305; Connell, *Son of the Morning Star*, 3; Philbrick, *The Last Stand*, 255.

5. Robert M. Utley, *Cavalier in Buckskin: George Armstrong Custer and the Western Military Frontier* (Norman: University of Oklahoma Press, 1988), 187.

6. Quentin Reynolds, *Custer's Last Stand* (New York: Random House, 1951), 185.

7. Donovan, *A Terrible Glory*, 310–11; see also Drew Gilpin Faust, *The Republic of Suffering: Death and the American Civil War* (New York: Knopf, 2008). In 1876, the nation was not far removed from the Civil War, during which bodies often were buried hastily where they fell or never recovered.

8. Utley, *Cavalier in Buckskin*, 194–95; Robert M. Utley, foreword to John S. Gray, *Custer's Last Campaign: Mitch Boyer and the Little Bighorn Reconstructed* (Lincoln: University of Nebraska Press, 1991), x. Reynolds did make up dialogue for Crazy Horse and Sitting Bull. Example: "'We have won a battle,'

Sitting Bull said gravely, 'but we have lost a war. Yellow Hair has beaten us. Oh yes, we killed him, but he and his men killed hundreds of our greatest warriors.'" Reynolds, *Custer's Last Stand*, 182. About one hundred Indians were killed, according to estimates. Larry Sklenar, *To Hell with Honor: Custer and the Little Bighorn* (Norman: University of Oklahoma Press, 2000), 19–25, 327–28; Philbrick, *The Last Stand*, 207–12.

9. David Hardin, *After the War: The Lives and Images of Major Civil War Figures after the Shooting Stopped* (Chicago: Ivan R. Dee, 2010), 277; Sklenar, *To Hell with Honor*, xiii, 276.

10. Sklenar, *To Hell with Honor*, 103–4; Philbrick, *The Last Stand*, 139; Jeffry D. Wert, *Custer: The Controversial Life of George Armstrong Custer* (New York: Simon & Schuster, 1996), 339.

11. Utley, *Cavalier in Buckskin*, 175–80; Donovan, *A Terrible Glory*, 183, 205–8; Sklenar, *To Hell with Honor*, 105–11.

12. Sklenar, *To Hell with Honor*, 111–12; Philbrick, *The Last Stand*, 146–49; Donovan, *A Terrible Glory*, 208–9; Utley, *Cavalier in Buckskin*, 181–82.

13. Philbrick, *The Last Stand*, 152. The spellings *Sundance* and *Sun Dance* are inconsistent. The creek was also known as Ash Creek before the name was changed to Reno Creek.

14. Philbrick, *The Last Stand*, 313–16; Donovan, *A Terrible Glory*, 212, 216, 218; Wert, *Custer*, 342; Sklenar, *To Hell with Honor*, 119. There is some variation in the estimates.

15. Philbrick, *The Last Stand*, 153–58; Sklenar, *To Hell with Honor*, 127–35.

16. Donovan, *A Terrible Glory*, 214.

17. Donovan, *A Terrible Glory*, 215; Philbrick, *The Last Stand*, 344; Utley, *Cavalier in Buckskin*, 183; Sklenar, *To Hell with Honor*, 146–53, 168.

18. Sklenar, *To Hell with Honor*, 157–58; Donovan, *A Terrible Glory*, 217, 438n61.

19. W. A. Graham, *The Custer Myth: A Source Book of Custeriana* (New York: Bonanza Books, 1953), 289–90.

20. Sklenar, *To Hell with Honor*, 162–63.

21. Quoted in Sklenar, *To Hell with Honor*, 163.

22. Utley, *Cavalier in Buckskin*, 176; Philbrick, *The Last Stand*, 10.

23. Sklenar, *To Hell with Honor*, 168–76; Donovan, *A Terrible Glory*, 228–29; John Koster, "Slaper's Side of he Story," *Wild West* 27, no. 1 (June 2004): 40.

24. Philbrick, *The Last Stand*, 174–84; Robert M. Utley, ed., *The Reno Court of Inquiry: The Chicago Sun Times Account* (Fort Collins, CO: Old Army Press, 1983), 154, 214, quoted in Philbrick, *The Last Stand*, 177; Donovan, *A Terrible Glory*, 237–40.

25. Sklenar, *To Hell with Honor*, 257–58; Donovan, *A Terrible Glory*, 240; Mari Sandoz, *The Battle of the Little Bighorn* (1966; Lincoln: University of Nebraska Press, 1978), 80.

26. Donovan, *A Terrible Glory*, 240–44; Sandoz, *The Battle of the Little Bighorn*, 84; Philbrick, *The Last Stand*, 193–94.

27. Donovan, *A Terrible Glory*, 245–48; Sandoz, *The Battle of the Little Bighorn*, 85–86; Philbrick, *The Last Stand*, 194–200.

28. Philbrick, *The Last Stand*, 201–3; Donovan, *A Terrible Glory*, 254–56.

29. Utley, *Cavalier in Buckskin*, 186; Donovan, *A Terrible Glory*, 250–51, 256–58; Philbrick, *The Last Stand*, 203. Novelist-historian Larry McMurtry found Custer's "We've got them" shout highly dubious. "By the time he would have delivered this famous cry he must have known that something close to the reverse was true: they had him." Larry McMurtry, *Custer* (New York: Simon & Schuster, 2012), 16.

30. Philbrick, *The Last Stand*, 203–5. Cooke's hastily written note is difficult to read. He clearly intended to write, "P.S. bring packs," but it appears to be "P. bring pacs." The letter *S* may be superimposed over the letter *P*. Most sources interpret this as "P.S.," but Utley prefers the single "P.," and that is how it appears in Utley's *Little Bighorn Battlefield: A History and Guide to the Battle of the Little Bighorn* (1988; Washington, DC: U.S. Department of the Interior, 1994), 61, 63. Just what Martin told Benteen is, along with just about everything else that happened, in dispute. Barnett, for example, questioned the likelihood that Martin, an Italian immigrant whose name, before it was Anglicized, was Giovanni Martini, would have used a neologism like *skedaddling*, a word more in keeping with Benteen's argot. Yet Benteen insisted while testifying before the court of inquiry that Martin, who had a poor command of English at the time, had used the word. In an interview years later, Martin said he did not use the word, nor did he say anything about Indians leaving the village. He had, in fact, left before Custer mounted any kind of attack. Louise Barnett, *Touched by Fire: The Life, Death and Mythic Afterlife of George Armstrong Custer* (New York: Henry Holt, 1996), 292–93.

31. Donovan, *A Terrible Glory*, 258–59.

32. Donovan, *A Terrible Glory*, 259–60; Barnett, *Touched by Fire*, 293–94; Sklenar, *To Hell with Honor*, 298–302; Philbrick, *The Last Stand*, 220–22.

33. Sklenar, *To Hell with Honor*, 302–3; Philbrick, *The Last Stand*, 222–23; Donovan, *A Terrible Glory*, 264–65, 280.

34. Philbrick, *The Last Stand*, 224–26. Connell, *Son of the Morning Star*, 282, described Reno's column as "a mob of frightened, angry, irresolute, bewildered men held together spasmodically by a recollection of what they were, or were supposed to be, and by a realization that if they dispersed they would be chopped up like raw liver." Sklenar, *To Hell with Honor*, 306–11.

35. Philbrick, *The Last Stand*, 228–33, 238, 394; Donovan, *A Terrible Glory*, 283–88, 292; Sklenar, *To Hell with Honor*, 314–15; Connell, *Son of the Morning Star*, 282.

36. Donovan, *A Terrible Glory*, 291–92; Charles Windolph, *I Fought with Custer: The Story of Sergeant Windolph, Last Survivor of the Battle of the Little Big Horn as Told to Frazier and Robert Hunt* (1947; Lincoln: University of Nebraska Press, 1987), 102.

37. Donovan, *A Terrible Glory*, 292–96; Philbrick, *The Last Stand*, 237–44.

38. Donovan, *A Terrible Glory*, 296–98; Windolph, *I Fought with Custer*, 106.

39. Donovan, *A Terrible Glory*, 306. Less than a week earlier, Custer had met with his officers to explain the mission. Wallace had been uneasy. Something in Custer's manner had seemed unnatural to him. Returning to his bivouac with Godfrey and McIntosh, his company commander, Wallace had said he thought Custer was going to be killed. After McIntosh was killed during Reno's charge, Wallace had taken command of G Company, which almost had been wiped out. When he reached Terry, Wallace learned his prediction about Custer had come true. Donovan, *A Terrible Glory*, 194.

40. Sklenar, *To Hell with Honor*, 257, 268–90.

41. Donovan, *A Terrible Glory*, 252; Philbrick, *The Last Stand*, 216; Utley, *Cavalier in Buckskin*, 187; Wert, *Custer*, 350; Richard Allan Fox Jr., *Archaeology, History, and Custer's Last Battle: The Little Big Horn Reexamined* (Norman: University of Oklahoma Press, 1993), 319; Gray, *Custer's Last Campaign*, 360–61; Sklenar, *To Hell with Honor*, 264–75; Michael N. Donahue, *Drawing Battle Lines: The Map Testimony of Custer's Last Fight* (El Segundo, CA: Upton and Sons, 2008), 17–19; see also Douglas D. Scott, "Archeologists: Detectives on the Battlefield," in Herman J. Viola, *Little Bighorn Remembered: The Untold Indian Story of Custer's Last Stand* (New York: Times Books, 1999). Custer had met Yates in Monroe in January 1863 after Yates had been wounded at Fredericksburg. The two later served together on Pleasonton's staff. Custer had recommended his appointment, and Yates served as Custer's aide-de-camp on the Charlottesville raid. Their friendship continued in the 7th Cavalry after the war. As commander of Company F, called the Bandbox Troop for its spit and polish, Yates was considered a model officer. The left wing's other unit, Company E, was called the Gray Horse Troop after its imposing light-gray mounts.

42. Sklenar, *To Hell with Honor*, 59, 272–74; Paul Andrew Hutton, "Could Custer Have Won?" *Quarterly Journal of Military History* 25, no. 2 (Winter 2013): 35; Donovan, *A Terrible Glory*, 266; Utley, *Cavalier in Buckskin*, 188–89; Philbrick, *The Last Stand*, 257. Donovan suggests that if Custer learned Sturgis had been killed at the river, the subsequent course of the battle was a foregone conclusion. He could not face pulling out and returning to Fort Lincoln

without a success that would have mitigated the loss of his colonel's son. As it turned out, Colonel Sturgis blamed Custer for his son's death.

43. Hutton, "Could Custer Have Won?" 36–37; Philbrick, *The Last Stand*, 257–58, 262; Donovan, *A Terrible Glory*, 266–67.

44. Sklenar, *To Hell with Honor*, 278–80; Philbrick, *The Last Stand*, 264–66.

45. Hutton, "Could Custer Have Won?" 39; Donovan, *A Terrible Glory*, 268–71, 273–75. Donovan does an admirable job of sorting out a wide variety of evidence. It is well to keep in mind his own caveat, however. "Every reconstruction of the final actions of Custer's battalion—the events on and around Last Stand Hill toward the end of the battle—is fraught with difficulty, and none that I have seen is completely satisfactory. There is not enough evidence, historical or archaeological, to come up with a description that satisfactorily incorporates all the Indian accounts and archaeological finds." Donovan, *A Terrible Glory*, 457n40.

46. D. A. Kinsley, *Favor the Bold* (1967; New York: Promontory Press, 1968), 533; Reynolds, *Custer's Last Stand*, 180.

47. Custer has been put on trial in fiction. See Douglas C. Jones, *The Court-Martial of George Armstrong Custer: A Novel* (New York: Charles Scribner's Sons, 1976). The novel was filmed for television in 1977.

48. Richard White, "Frederick Jackson Turner and Buffalo Bill," in *The Frontier in American Culture*, ed. James R. Grossman (Berkeley: University of California Press, 1994), 29.

49. Merrill D. Peterson, *Lincoln in American Memory* (New York: Oxford University Press, 1994), 271, 285–86; John F. Marszalek, *Sherman: A Soldier's Passion for Order* (New York: Free Press, 1993), 163–64; Stephen E. Ambrose, "William T. Sherman: A Personality Profile," *American History Illustrated* 1 (January 1967): 54–57; Nassir Ghaemi, "Sherman's Demons," *Atlanta* (November 2006): 76–82; *Cincinnati Commercial*, December 11, 1861.

50. Paul Andrew Hutton, introduction to *Glory-Hunter: A Life of General Custer* by Frederic F. Van de Water (1934; Lincoln: University of Nebraska Press, 1988), 12–13; Charles K. Hofling, "General Custer and the Battle of the Little Big Horn," *Psychoanalytic Review* 54 (Summer 1967): 303–28; Charles K. Hofling, *Custer and the Little Big Horn: A Psychobiographical Inquiry* (Detroit: Wayne State University Press, 1981), 98.

51. Charles K. Hofling, "George Armstrong Custer: A Psychoanalytic Approach," *Montana: The Magazine of Western History* 21, no. 2 (1971): 32–43.

52. Hofling was a professor in the Department of Psychiatry at St. Louis University. See also Edgar Irving Stewart, "A Psychoanalytic Approach to Custer: Some Reflections," *Montana: The Magazine of Western History* 21, no. 3 (1971): 74–77. Stewart, a historian, attempted to refute some of Dr. Hofling's conclusions.

53. Henry Greiner, *General Phil Sheridan as I Knew Him, Playmate-Comrade-Friend* (Chicago: J. S. Hyland, 1908), 357, quoted in Joseph Wheelan, *Terrible Swift Sword: The Life of General Philip H. Sheridan* (Cambridge, MA: Da Capo Press, 2012), 281; Bess Lovejoy, "Raising the Dead," *International Herald Tribune*, November 27, 2012.

54. C. E. Callwell, *Small Wars: Their Principles and Practice*, 3rd ed. (1896; 3rd ed., 1906; Lincoln: University of Nebraska Press, 1996), 178–80.

55. David C. Gompert and Richard L. Kugler, "Custer and Cognition," *Joint Force Quarterly* 41, no. 2 (2006): 87–93.

56. Gompert and Kugler, "Custer and Cognition."

57. Dennis Showalter, "The U.S. Cavalry: Soldiers of a Nation, Policeman of an Empire," *Army History* 8 (Fall 2001): 16.

58. Wesley K. Clark, foreword to Duane Schultz, *Custer: Lessons in Leadership* (New York: Palgrave Macmillan, 2010), x.

59. Julian Spilsbury, *Great Military Disasters: A History of Incompetence* (New York: Metro Books, 2010). The British edition, published in London by Quercus, has a different subtitle: *From Cannae to Stalingrad*.

60. Hutton, "Could Custer Have Won?" 39. The publisher of Hutton's article, *Quarterly Journal of Military History*, made the thesis more explicit on the cover: "New Analysis / Custer / His Surprising Strategy Nearly Won the Day at Little Bighorn"; *New York Herald,* November 16, 1877; Utley, *Cavalier in Buckskin*, 200, 202.

61. Philbrick, *The Last Stand*, 260; Ambrose, "William T. Sherman," 444.

9. CUSTER AND THE PRESS

1. Letter, October 9, 1863, cited in Frederick Whittaker, *A Complete Life of General George A. Custer* (1876; Lincoln: University of Nebraska Press, 1993), 2:212.

2. Oliver Knight, *Following the Indian Wars: The Story of the Newspaper Correspondents among the Indian Campaigners* (Norman: University of Oklahoma Press, 1960), xiii. He cites the *Chicago Times* correspondent who wrote that he detested Indians. That correspondent was covering Crook's actions during the 1876 Sioux War.

3. Knight, *Following the Indian Wars*, xii, 43–44, 55–56.

4. On the Indian war correspondents, see Knight, *Following the Indian Wars*, 4, 316–17, 325–27.

5. Robert M. Utley, *Custer and the Great Controversy: The Origin and Development of a Legend* (Lincoln: University of Nebraska Press, 1962), 39, 148, 86–87.

6. Robert M. Utley, "The Enduring Custer Legend," *American History Illustrated* 11, no. 3 (June 1976): 4–9, 42–49.

7. Karen Miller Russell, Janice Hume, and Karen Sichler, "Libbie Custer's 'Last Stand': Image Restoration, the Press, and Public Memory," *Journalism and Mass Communication Quarterly* 84, no. 3 (September 2007): 582–99.

8. James E. Mueller, *Shooting Arrows and Slinging Mud: Custer, the Press, and the Little Bighorn* (Norman: University of Oklahoma Press, 2013).

9. Hugh J. Reilly, *The Frontier Newspapers and the Coverage of the Plains Indian Wars* (Santa Barbara, CA: Praeger, 2010). The speculations about the Confederate officers and Sitting Bull are at 41–42.

10. Brian Dippie, "The Southern Response to Custer's Last Stand," *Montana: The Magazine of Western History* 21, no. 2 (April 1971): 18–31.

11. Marc H. Abrams, *Sioux War Dispatches: Reports from the Field, 1876–1877* (Yardley, PA: Westholme, 2012); chapter 6 is "The Battle of the Little Big Horn." Richard Slotkin, *The Fatal Environment: The Myth of the Frontier in the Age of Industrialization, 1800–1890* (New York: Harper Perennial, 1994), 458–59.

12. Knight, *Following the Indian Wars*, 326–29; Abrams, *Sioux War Dispatches*, 125–26.

13. W. A. Graham, *The Custer Myth: A Source Book of Custeriana* (New York: Bonanza Books, 1953).

14. Michael A. Elliott, *Custerology: The Enduring Legacy of the Indian Wars and George Armstrong Custer* (Chicago: University of Chicago Press, 2007), 149, 201–10.

15. Paul Andrew Hutton, "From Little Bighorn to Little Big Man," in *The Custer Reader*, ed. Paul Andrew Hutton (Norman: University of Oklahoma Press, 1992), 574, 395–423.

16. Herbert Krause and Gary D. Olsen, *Prelude to Glory: A Newspaper Accounting of Custer's 1874 Expedition to the Black Hills* (Sioux Falls, SD: Brevet Press, 1974).

17. Robert G. Hays, *A Race at Bay: New York Times Editorials on "the Indian Problem," 1860–1900* (Carbondale: Southern Illinois University Press, 1997).

18. Bruce A. Rosenberg, "How Custer's 'Last Stand' Got Its Name," *Georgia Review* 26, no. 3 (Fall 1972): 279–96.

19. Rex C. Myers, "Montana Editors and the Custer Battle," *Montana: The Magazine of Western History* 26, no. 2 (Spring 1976): 18–31; Knight, *Following the Indian Wars*, 21–22.

20. John M. Coward, "Explaining the Little Bighorn: Race and Progress in the Native Press," *Journalism and Mass Communication Quarterly* 71, no. 3 (Autumn 1994): 540–49.

21. Ulf Jonas Bjork, "The Swedish-American Press and the Sioux," *Swedish-American Historical Quarterly* 60, no. 2 (April 2009): 72–90.

22. Krause and Olsen, *Prelude to Glory*, 15, 24, reported in the *Bismarck Tribune*, August 19, 1874.

23. Neil Mangun, foreword to *I Fought with Custer: The Story of Sergeant Windolph, Last Survivor of the Battle of the Little Big Horn as Told to Frazier and Robert Hunt* (1954; Lincoln: University of Nebraska Press, 1987), 33–35, cited from Windolph's narrative in Mangun, foreword, 42.

24. Jeffry D. Wert, *Custer: The Controversial Life of George Armstrong Custer* (New York: Simon & Schuster, 1996), 312–17.

25. Krause and Olsen, *Prelude to Glory*, 13.

26. Krause and Olsen, *Prelude to Glory*, 43, 52, 39; *St. Paul Pioneer*, July 3 and 11, 1874.

27. Krause and Olsen, *Prelude to Glory*, 77; *St. Paul Pioneer*, August 30, 1874.

28. Krause and Olsen, *Prelude to Glory*, 45, 59–63; *St. Paul Pioneer*, July 8, 1874.

29. Krause and Olsen, *Prelude to Glory*, 79, 82, 89–90; *St. Paul Press*, July 28 and August 16, 1874.

30. Krause and Olsen, *Prelude to Glory*, 97–98, 102, 107, 126, 136, 139, 140; *Chicago Inter-Ocean*, July 9, 29, and 30; August 17 and 27; September 2, 5, and 8, 1874.

31. *New York Tribune*, June 26, August 17, and August 20, 1874.

32. Krause and Olsen, *Prelude to Glory*, 224–228, 187–188; *Chicago Inter-Ocean*, August 10 and September 14, 1874.

33. *Bismarck Weekly Tribune*, July 12 and 19, 1876.

34. *Bismarck Weekly Tribune*, July 12, 1876.

35. *Bismarck Weekly Tribune*, July 5, 1876.

36. *Helena Daily Herald*, July 10, 1876.

37. *Helena Daily Herald*, July 13, 1876.

38. *Helena Daily Herald*, July 5, 1876.

39. *Helena Daily Herald*, July 5 and 18, 1876; Abrams, *Sioux War Dispatches*, 188.

40. See Graham, *The Custer Myth*, 349–51, on the details about who was first with the Bighorn story and his explanation for why Helena and Bozeman beat Bismarck. See also Knight, *Following the Indian Wars*, 213–14; "The Custer Massacre," *Helena Daily Herald*, July 5, 1876; "A Terrible Fight," *Helena Daily Herald*, July 5, 1876; "The Valley of Death," *Helena Daily Herald*, July 15, 1876; "Custer's Death," *Helena Daily Herald*, July 25, 1876.

41. Utley, *Custer and the Great Controversy*, 37; Knight, *Following the Indian Wars*, 68–70.

42. Knight, *Following the Indian Wars*, 70–72, 94–101, 196–97.

43. "The War with the Sioux," *New York Herald*, July 3, 1876; "A Bloody Battle," *New York Herald*, July 6, 1876; "The Massacre," *New York Herald*, July 7, 1876. Joachim-Napoleon Murat was a brother-in-law to Napoleon Bonaparte and had a reputation as a daring cavalryman, having served with distinction in several campaigns, including the Austrian campaign, when he was commander of cavalry. He also was noted for his flashy, distinctive attire. As commander of cavalry, he served Napoleon ably, making possible the lightning strikes that enabled Napoleon to defeat superior forces on several occasions.

44. "Custer's Death," *New York Herald*, July 8, 1876.

45. Clement A. Lounsberry, *Early History of North Dakota: Essential Outlines of American History* (Washington, DC: Liberty Press, 1919), 316; Knight, *Following the Indian Wars*, 196–206; Sandy Barnard, *I Go with Custer: The Life and Death of Reporter Mark Kellogg* (Bismarck, ND: Bismarck Tribune, 1996), 3–8, 13, 25, 110.

46. Knight, *Following the Indian Wars*, 202–6.

47. Knight, *Following the Indian Wars*, 195–206; Lounsberry, *Early History*, 315; Edgar Irving Stewart, *Custer's Luck* (Norman: University of Oklahoma Press, 1955), 138; Utley, *Custer and the Great Controversy*, 36; Barnard, *I Go with Custer*, 94–96, 130–33; James Donovan, *A Terrible Glory: Custer and the Little Bighorn—The Last Great Battle of the American West* (New York: Little, Brown, 2008), 312.

48. Quoted in Knight, *Following the Indian Wars*, 216–17.

49. Knight, *Following the Indian Wars*, 211–12, 216–17.

50. "Another Account," *New York Times*, July 6, 1874; "An Indian Victory," *New York Times*, July 7, 1876.

51. "Confirmation of the Disaster," "Details of the Battle," and "Sketch of Custer," *New York Times*, July 7, 1876.

52. "The Causes and Consequences," *New York Times*, July 7, 1876; for *Times* editorial views on Indians, see Hays, *A Race at Bay*.

53. "Obituary," *New York Tribune*, July 7, 1876; "Custer's Terrible Defeat," *New York Tribune*, July 7, 1876; "The Montana Slaughter," *New York Tribune*, July 7, 1876.

54. "Custer's Terrible Defeat."

55. Donovan, *A Terrible Glory*, 344–53.

56. Donovan, *A Terrible Glory*, 344–53, 366, 371, 377–78; Graham, *The Custer Myth*, 326–29.

57. Robert M. Utley, introduction to Whittaker, *A Complete Life*, 2: xi–xii, 642–43.

58. Bruce A. Rosenberg, "How Custer's 'Last Stand' Got Its Name," *Georgia Review* 26, no. 3 (Fall 1972): 288–92; Frederick Whittaker, "The Dashing Dra-

goon; or, the Story of Gen. George A. Custer," *Beadle's Boy's Library of Sport, Story and Adventure* 1, no. 98 (April 26, 1882): 15.

59. Knight, *Following the Indian Wars*, 327–29; James Welch with Paul Stekler, *Killing Custer: The Battle of the Little Bighorn and the Fate of the Plains Indians* (1994; New York: W. W. Norton, 1995), 192.

10. THE FRONTIER, THE FITTEST, AND CUSTER

1. *Montana Post*, January 26, 1867, cited in Robert G. Athearn *William Tecumseh Sherman and the Settlement of the West* (Norman: University of Oklahoma Press, 1995), 101.

2. Richard Slotkin, *Gunfighter Nation: The Myth of the Frontier in Twentieth-Century America* (New York: Harper Perennial, 1993), 16.

3. A classic of social Darwinian thought in American history is Richard Hofstadter, *Social Darwinism in American Thought* (Boston: Beacon Press, 1955). See also Richard Bannister, *Social Darwinism: Science and Myth in Anglo-American Social Thought* (Philadelphia: Temple University Press, 1979).

4. Michael Kammen, *Mystic Chords of Memory: The Transformation of Tradition in American Culture* (New York: Vintage Books, 1993), 27.

5. Stanley Vestal, *Short Grass Country* (New York: Duell, Sloan & Pearce, 1941), 173.

6. Louise Barnett, *Touched by Fire: The Life, Death and Mythic Afterlife of George Armstrong Custer* (New York: Henry Holt, 1996), 194–97; Philbrick, *The Last Stand: Custer, Sitting Bull, and the Battle of the Little Bighorn* (New York: Viking, 2010), 59, 138–139.

7. Paul van Develder, *Savages and Scoundrels: The Untold Story of America's Road to Empire through Indian Territory* (New Haven, CT: Yale University Press, 2009), 224.

8. Barnett, *Touched by Fire*, 117–20. On the reaction to Mosby and his tactics, see Paul Ashdown and Edward Caudill, *The Mosby Myth: A Confederate Hero in Life and Legend* (Wilmington, DE: Scholarly Resources, 2001).

9. *Harper's Weekly* is quoted in Barnett, *Touched by Fire*, 122.

10. Barnett, *Touched by Fire*, 299–300; she recounts the stories of outrages, 168–71.

11. Barnett, *Touched by Fire*, 301; *New York Sun* quoted in Roy Morris Jr., *Sheridan: The Life and Wars of General Phil Sheridan* (New York: Crown, 1992), 301.

12. George Armstrong Custer, "The Red Man," May 5, 1858, is reprinted in *The Harrisonian* (Journal of the Harrison County, Ohio, Historical Society), no. 2 (1989).

13. Richard Slotkin, *The Fatal Environment: The Myth of the Frontier in the Age of Industrialization, 1800–1890* (New York: Harper Perennial, 1994), 393–94; Barnett, *Touched by Fire*, 102.

14. Barnett, *Touched by Fire*, 286.

15. Paul Andrew Hutton, *Phil Sheridan and His Army* (Lincoln: University of Nebraska Press, 1985), 69; Morris, *Sheridan*, 332.

16. Athearn, *William Tecumseh Sherman and the Settlement of the West*, 110, 232.

17. Athearn, *William Tecumseh Sherman*, 100–101, 113, 160; Charles Royster, *The Destructive War: William Tecumseh Sherman, Stonewall Jackson, and the Americans* (New York: Knopf, 1991), 393–402.

18. Hutton, *Phil Sheridan*, 180–81.

19. Hutton, *Phil Sheridan*, 8, 10–11, 17.

20. Morris, *Sheridan*, 324–25; Hutton, *Phil Sheridan*, 185.

21. Morris, *Sheridan*, 307–10.

22. Athearn, *William Tecumseh Sherman*, 132, 309.

23. Morris, *Sheridan*, 324–25, 342, 346–47.

24. Royster, *The Destructive War*, 396–97, 401–2.

25. Brian Dippie, *The Vanishing American: White Attitudes and U.S. Indian Policy* (Middletown, CT: Wesleyan University Press, 1982), 148.

26. Hofstadter, *Social Darwinism*, 171–72.

27. John S. Haller, *Outcasts from Evolution: Scientific Attitudes of Racial Inferiority, 1859–1900* (Urbana: University of Illinois Press, 1971), 100.

28. Haller, *Outcasts from Evolution*, 107–8, 111–12, 140, 142.

29. Haller, *Outcasts from Evolution*, 107–8, 111–12, 140, 142.

30. Not all science of the period was bad news for Indians. At an 1877 meeting in Nashville of the American Society for the Advancement of Science, an ethnologist challenged the assumptions that Indians were dying out and their demise was inevitable. Garrick Mallery, with the U.S. Geological Survey, presented data to upend what historian Brian Dippie called the "vanishing American" thesis. In fact, Mallery argued, Indian populations were increasing. He said that the vanishing American idea was based on faulty data and logic. First, estimates of past Indian populations were inaccurate and inflated. Second, in cases where Indian populations had declined, it was a result of murder, not because they died in the face of civilization. He cited tribes of Oregon and California as examples of killing versus "natural" deaths. And finally, it was fallacious to argue that population decline in the face of civilization was a result of innate racial inferiority. He did not deny the principle of evolution but instead

applied it to his own thesis: "It is silly to expect a sudden improvement among any people by the *presto change!* of political conjuration, when their old modes of life are forbidden and none furnished instead" (emphasis in original). The withering away of the race was "absolutely false," and the transition from savagery to civilization and a growing population would continue "unless repressed by causes not attributable to civilization, but to criminal misgovernment." Mallery had his allies, such as the *New York Times*, which wrote in 1878 that those who believed Indians were declining in numbers were themselves diminishing in number faster than the Indians. However, popular opinion still held strong to the idea of the vanishing American. See Dippie, *The Vanishing American*, 127–30.

31. Dippie, *The Vanishing American*, 137–38, 174–75, 177, 199.

32. Robert G. Athearn, *The Mythic West in Twentieth-Century America* (Lawrence: University Press of Kansas, 1986), 190–91.

33. Thomas Dyer, *Theodore Roosevelt and the Idea of Race* (Baton Rouge: Louisiana State University Press, 1980), 81.

34. Quoted in Dyer, *Theodore Roosevelt*, 42, 70, 74–75, 78, 82.

35. Dyer, *Theodore Roosevelt*, 82–84, 87.

36. On Roosevelt's reform ideas about the Indians, see Dyer, *Theodore Roosevelt*, 86–87.

37. Dyer, *Theodore Roosevelt*, 31–33, 37–38.

38. Dyer, *Theodore Roosevelt*, 80; Theodore Roosevelt, *The Winning of the West* (New York: G. P. Putnam's Sons, 1903), 1:90–94, 257–64.

39. Dippie, *The Vanishing American*, 199.

40. Paul Andrew Hutton, ed., *The Custer Reader* (Norman: University of Oklahoma Press, 1992), 409.

41. Hutton, *The Custer Reader*, 411–12.

42. Hutton, *The Custer Reader*, 112–13, 413–16.

43. On the myth of Indians as environmentalists and conservationists, see Shepard Krech III, *The Ecological Indian: Myth and History* (New York: W. W. Norton, 1999).

11. THE CUSTER STORY IN HISTORY

1. Frederick Whittaker, "General George A. Custer," *Galaxy* (September 1876): 362. There is some irony achieved by taking the quote out of context. Whittaker was not providing insight into historiography or pondering complexity or the mystery of things past. He went on to say, "The regal stars are few, the planets fewer. Every now and then comes a bright meteor flashing from the multitude, and vanishes as swiftly as it came, leaving behind only a legend of

light." So it was quite the opposite—that history was only helping us see, in that midnight sky, the brightness of the Custer meteor. As in his biography of Custer, his comment on history contained a grain of truth, even if unintended.

2. Larry Sklenar, *To Hell with Honor: Custer and the Little Bighorn* (Norman: University of Oklahoma Press, 2000), 63.

3. Duane Schultz, *Custer: Lessons in Leadership* (New York: Palgrave Macmillan, 2010), 180.

4. Gregory J. W. Urwin, *Custer Victorious: The Civil War Battles of General George Armstrong Custer* (East Brunswick, NJ: Associated University Presses, 1983), 37–38, 12.

5. Jay W. Simson, *Custer and the Front Royal Executions of 1864* (Jefferson, NC: McFarland, 2009), 3–10, 149–151; "Appendix III. Custer's Second Atrocity: The Washita" explains how Custer's critics used the Front Royal atrocity to justify labeling the Washita as a massacre. David Coffey, *Sheridan's Lieutenants: Phil Sheridan, His Generals, and the Final Year of the Civil War* (Lanham, MD: Rowman & Littlefield, 2005), xvi–xvii, 147.

6. James S. Robbins, *The Real Custer: From Boy General to Tragic Hero* (Washington, DC: Regnery, 2014), 262.

7. Thom Hatch, *Glorious War: The Civil War Adventures of George Armstrong Custer* (New York: St. Martin's Press, 2013), 308.

8. The "War Memoirs" series ran in *Galaxy* in March 1876, 319–24; April 1876, 448–60; May 1876, 624–32; June 1876, 809–16; October 1876, 447–55; November 1876, 684–94. "Battling with the Sioux on the Yellowstone" ran on July 1876, 91–102.

9. Paul Andrew Hutton, ed., *The Custer Reader* (Norman: University of Oklahoma Press, 1992), 561; Elizabeth Custer, *Boots and Saddles; or, Life in Dakota with General Custer* (New York: Harper & Brothers, 1885); Elizabeth Custer, *Tenting on the Plains; or, General Custer in Kansas and Texas* (New York: Charles L. Webster, 1887); Elizabeth Custer, *Following the Guidon* (New York: Harper & Brothers, 1890).

10. Robert M. Utley, *Custer and the Great Controversy: The Origin and Development of a Legend* (1962; Lincoln: University of Nebraska Press, 1998), 30, 162–66.

11. Jay Monaghan, *Custer: The Life of General George Armstrong Custer* (1959; Lincoln: University of Nebraska Press, 1971); W. A. Graham, *The Custer Myth: A Source Book of Custeriana* (New York: Bonanza Books, 1953); Edgar Irving Stewart, *Custer's Luck* (Norman: University of Oklahoma Press, 1955).

12. Monaghan, *Custer*, 328.

13. Stephen E. Ambrose, *Crazy Horse and Custer: The Parallel Lives of Two American Warriors* (Garden City, NY: Doubleday, 1975), 168.

14. Monaghan, *Custer*, 328, 388–99, 322, 370.

15. Monaghan, *Custer*, 319–23, 375–76.

16. Jeffry D. Wert, *Custer: The Controversial Life of George Armstrong Custer* (New York: Simon & Schuster, 1996), 353–58.

17. Louise Barnett, *Touched by Fire: The Life, Death and Mythic Afterlife of George Armstrong Custer* (New York: Henry Holt, 1996), 300, 352.

18. Stewart's remarks about the veracity of stories about the Little Bighorn are on 431–32; on the blame for the tragedy, see 493–95.

19. Sklenar, *To Hell with Honor*, 336.

20. Douglas D. Scott, "Archeologists: Detectives on the Battlefield," in Herman J. Viola, *Little Bighorn Remembered: The Untold Indian Story of Custer's Last Stand* (New York: Times Books, 1999), 165, 167, 169, 177; Richard Allan Fox Jr., *Archaeology, History, and Custer's Last Battle: The Little Big Horn Reexamined* (Norman: University of Oklahoma Press, 1993), 17.

21. Larry McMurtry, *Custer* (New York: Simon & Schuster, 2012), 8.

22. McMurtry, *Custer*, 105, 172.

23. McMurtry, *Custer*, 8; Ambrose, *Crazy Horse*, 445, 91.

24. Schultz, *Custer*, x, 181.

25. Richard Slotkin, *The Fatal Environment: The Myth of the Frontier in the Age of Industrialization, 1800–1890* (New York: Harper Perennial, 1985), 374–75.

26. Utley, *Custer and the Great Controversy*, 39, 30–31, 51–53, 86–87; Robert M. Utley, "The Enduring Custer Legend," *American History Illustrated* 11, no. 3 (June 1976): 7–8.

27. Slotkin, *The Fatal Environment*, 373–478.

28. Fred Dustin, "George Armstrong Custer," *Michigan History Journal* 30 (April–June 1946), 226–54.

29. Lawrence A. Frost, *Custer Legends* (Bowling Green, OH: Green University Popular Press, 1981), 66.

30. Michael A. Elliott, *Custerology: The Enduring Legacy of the Indian Wars and George Armstrong Custer* (Chicago: University of Chicago Press, 2007), 9, 26, 90, 224–28. Elliott called his work "public history," 13.

31. Brian W. Dippie, *Custer's Last Stand: The Anatomy of an American Myth*, rev. ed. (1976; Lincoln: University of Nebraska Press, 1994).

32. Utley, *Custer and the Great Controversy*, 77–78, 163–64; Graham, *The Custer Myth*, 301.

33. Graham, *The Custer Myth*, 380–405; Fred Dustin, *The Custer Tragedy* (1939; El Segundo, CA: Upton and Sons, 1987); Charles Edmund DeLand, *The Sioux Wars* (Pierre: South Dakota Historical Collections, 1930, 1934).

34. John S. Gray, *Centennial Campaign: The Sioux War of 1876* (1976; Norman: University of Oklahoma Press, 1988).

35. Kenneth Hammer, ed., *Custer in '76: Walter Camp's Notes on the Custer Fight* (Norman: University of Oklahoma Press, 1990); Richard G. Hardorff, ed., *On the Little Bighorn with Walter Camp: A Collection of Walter Mason Camp's Letters, Notes and Opinions on Custer's Last Fight* (El Segundo, CA: Upton and Sons, 2002); Elliott, *Custerology*, 211, 215–17, 196–97.

36. Lawrence Frost, "The Beginnings of the LBHA," *Little Bighorn Associates Newsletter* 20, no. 1 (1987): 3–4.

37. Elliott, *Custerology*, 194–95; Utley, *Custer and the Great Controversy*, 86–90.

38. Robert M. Utley, *Custer and Me* (Norman: University of Oklahoma Press, 2004), 133–34, 212, 59–60.

39. Brice Custer, *The Sacrificial Lion: George Armstrong Custer, from American Hero to Media Villain* (El Segundo, CA: Upton and Sons, 1999), 5–21.

40. Utley, *Custer and Me*, 117–18; Vine DeLoria Jr., *Custer Died for Your Sins: An Indian Manifesto* (New York: Macmillan, 1969).

12. VISITORS

1. Charles Kuralt, "Place of Sorrows," *On the Road with Charles Kuralt* (New York: Putnam, 1985), 281–82. The episode was broadcast on September 4, 1975.

2. "Travels with Charley," *Time*, January 19, 1968, 44; Matthew C. Ehrlich, "Myth in Charles Kuralt's 'On the Road,'" *Journalism and Mass Communication Quarterly* 79, no. 2 (Summer 2002): 327–38.

3. Ted White, *Broadcast News Writing, Reporting and Producing*, 4th ed. (Burlington, MA: Focal Press, 2005), 46–49.

4. James Donovan, *A Terrible Glory: Custer and the Little Bighorn—The Last Great Battle of the American West* (New York: Little, Brown, 2008), 308; Nathaniel Philbrick, *The Last Stand: Custer, Sitting Bull, and the Battle of the Little Bighorn* (New York: Viking, 2010), xxii, 256. Custer's body had been abused but not scalped or severely mutilated, especially compared to the condition of his brother Tom's body. Evan S. Connell, *Son of the Morning Star* (San Francisco: North Point Press, 1984), 409–10; Jeffry D. Wert, *Custer: The Controversial Life of George Armstrong Custer* (New York: Simon & Schuster, 1996), 355.

5. Brian W. Dippie, *Custer's Last Stand: The Anatomy of an American Myth*, rev. ed. (1976; Lincoln: University of Nebraska Press, 1994), 79–80; see also Richard W. Etulain, *The Life and Legends of Calamity Jane* (Norman: University of Oklahoma Press, 2014).

6. James Welch with Paul Stekler, *Killing Custer: The Battle of the Little Bighorn and the Fate of the Plains Indians* (1994; New York: Penguin Books, 1995), 96.

7. Welch, *Killing Custer*, 96–98.

8. Welch, *Killing Custer*, 109, 212. Welch also recommends crossing the river to shift the perspective. "In fact, you might even forget that you're here because a battle occurred on those hills beyond the river. . . . Imagine that it's an immense campground filled with eight thousand people."

9. Norman Maclean, *The Norman Maclean Reader*, ed. O. Alan Weltzien (Chicago: University of Chicago Press, 2008), 24.

10. Maclean, *The Norman Maclean Reader*, 25.

11. Maclean, *The Norman Maclean Reader*, 152.

12. Bill Bryson, *The Lost Continent: Travels in Small-Town America* (New York: Harper & Row, 1989), 280–81.

13. Bryson, *The Lost Continent*, 279. Earlier in his travels, Bryson passed through Monroe, Michigan, and saw a sign: "Welcome to Monroe—Home of General Custer." "A mile or so later there was another sign, even larger, saying, *Monroe, Michigan—Home of La-Z-Boy Furniture*. Goodness, I thought, will the excitement never stop?" He anticipated the visit to the Little Bighorn when, in Dodge City, Kansas, he considered a detour to Holcomb, the site of the Clutter murders in 1959 made famous by Truman Capote in his book *In Cold Blood*. "All that a trip to Holcomb would achieve would be to provide me with the morbid thrill of gawping at a house in which a family had long before been senselessly slaughtered." But he went to Holcomb anyway, assuming it would be more interesting than Dodge City's historic district. Bryson, *The Lost Continent*, 179, 216.

14. Larry McMurtry, *Custer* (New York: Simon & Schuster, 2012), 105–6, 171; Larry McMurtry, *Crazy Horse* (New York: Viking, 1999), 101, 104.

15. Tim Dee, *Four Fields* (New York: Random House, 2013), 120.

16. Dee, *Four Fields*, 120.

17. Dee, *Four Fields*, 123, 127, 130.

18. Kent L. Steckmesser, "Custer in Fiction: George Custer, Hero or Villain?" *American West* 1, no. 4 (Fall 1964): 47–52, 63–64.

19. Kenneth Lynn, *Hemingway* (New York: Simon & Schuster, 1987), 20, 30; Peter Griffin, *Along with Youth: Hemingway, the Early Years* (New York: Oxford University Press, 1985), 4–5.

20. Carl P. Eby, *Hemingway's Fetishism: Psychoanalysis and the Mirror of Manhood* (Albany: State University of New York Press, 1999), 216, 220–21; Ernest Hemingway, *Ernest Hemingway: Selected Letters, 1917–1961*, ed. Carlos Baker (New York: Charles Scribner's Sons, 1981), 694, 811, 827; Ernest Hem-

ingway, *For Whom the Bell Tolls* (New York: Charles Scribner's Sons, 1940), 337–39.

21. Hemingway, *For Whom the Bell Tolls*, 339; Dippie, *Custer's Last Stand*, 51, 54. Hemingway also mentions the painting in the novels *To Have and Have Not* and *Islands in the Stream*. Hemingway informally led a small group of partisans during the liberation of Paris in 1944. In a letter written October 15, 1944, he told a friend, "After some very interesting times, straight out of Mosby, we entered Paris with very first troops." Hemingway, *Ernest Hemingway: Selected Letters*, 574; Carlos Baker, *Ernest Hemingway: A Life Story* (New York: Charles Scribner's Sons, 1969), 409–10.

22. Hemingway, *For Whom the Bell Tolls*, 308, 316–22; David M. McClellan, "Is Custer a Model for the Fascist Captain in *For Whom the Bell Tolls*?" in *Fitzgerald/Hemingway Annual 1974*, ed. Matthew J. Bruccoli and C. E. Frazer Clark Jr. (Englewood, CO: Information Handling Services, 1975), 239–40.

23. McClellan, "Is Custer a Model," 239–40; Dean Rehberger, "'I Don't Know Buffalo Bill'; or, Hemingway and the Rhetoric of the Western," *Blowing the Bridge: Essays on Hemingway and* For Whom the Bell Tolls, ed. Rena Sanderson (New York: Greenwood, 1992), 177, quoted in Eby, *Hemingway's Fetishism*, 236.

24. David McClellan, "The Battle of the Little Big Horn in Hemingway's Later Fiction," in *Fitzgerald/Hemingway Annual 1976*, ed. Matthew J. Bruccoli (Englewood, CO: Information Handling Services, 1978), 245–48; Ernest Hemingway, *Across the River and into the Trees* (New York: Charles Scribner's Sons, 1950), 169, 265.

25. Ernest Hemingway, *Islands in the Stream* (New York: Charles Scribner's Sons, 1970), 338, 362.

26. Hemingway, *Islands in the Stream*, 376, 459; McClellan, "The Battle of the Little Big Horn," 246; Ernest Hemingway to Harvey Breit, January 3, 1954, *Ernest Hemingway: Selected Letters*, 827.

27. Ernest Hemingway to Harvey Breit, January 3, 1954, in *Ernest Hemingway: Selected Letters*, 827.

28. Steven Otfinoski, *The Golden Age of Novelty Songs* (New York: Billboard Books, 2000), 3, 6.

29. Rita Parks, *The Western Hero in Film and Television* (Ann Arbor, MI: UMI Research Press, 1982), 130; Dippie, *Custer's Last Stand*, 96–119; Roberta E. Pearson, "White Network/Red Power: ABC's *Custer* Series," in *The Revolution Wasn't Televised: Sixties Television and Social Conflict*, ed. Lynn Spigel and Michael Curtin (New York: Routledge, 1997), 327–31; Otfinoski, *The Golden Age*, 97–98, 109.

30. Pearson, "White Network/Red Power," 327–46.

31. Steven Utley and Howard Waldrop, "Custer's Last Jump!" in *Custer's Last Jump and Other Collaborations*, by Howard Waldrop et al. (Urbana, IL: Golden Gryphon Press, 2003), 45–75.

32. Harry Turtledove, *The Great War: Breakthroughs* (New York: Random House, 2001), 40.

33. Turtledove, *The Great War: Breakthroughs*; Harry Turtledove, *The Great War: Walk in Hell* (New York: Random House, 2000); Harry Turtledove, *The Great War: American Front* (New York: Random House, 1999).

34. Elizabeth Custer, *Boots and Saddles; or, Life in Dakota with General Custer* (Norman: University of Oklahoma Press, 1980), 218; Robert M. Utley, *Custer and the Great Controversy: The Origin and Development of a Legend* (1962; Lincoln: University of Nebraska Press, 1998), 64; Philbrick, *The Last Stand*, 31–36, 293; Michael A. Elliott, *Custerology: The Enduring Legacy of the Indian Wars and George Armstrong Custer* (Chicago: University of Chicago Press, 2007), 19–20.

35. Mark Sumner, *Devil's Tower* (New York: Ballantine Books, 1996).

36. Michael Blake, *Marching to Valhalla* (New York: Random House, 1996), 183.

37. Blake, *Marching to Valhalla*, 278, 280, 282–83.

38. Blake, *Marching to Valhalla*, 282–83.

39. Keith Coplin, *Crofton's Fire* (New York: G. P. Putnam's Sons, 2004), 4, 7.

40. Coplin, *Crofton's Fire*, 10.

41. Coplin, *Crofton's Fire*, 13, 15.

42. Coplin, *Crofton's Fire*, 15–16.

43. G. G. Boyer, *Custer, Terry, and Me* (New York: Dorchester, 2005).

44. Boyer, *Custer, Terry, and Me*, 183, 187.

45. Dan Simmons, *Black Hills* (2010; New York: Back Bay Books, 2011), 319, 392, 429.

46. The comments from Michael Donahue are from a July 2013 interview at the park, where he has been a seasonal ranger for more than twenty-five years. Donahue's upcoming book is *Where the Rivers Ran Red: The Indian Fights of George A. Custer*, which he said would put the Little Bighorn in perspective vis-à-vis Custer's other Indian-fighting experience, in addition to providing new information about the battle.

47. David Germain, Associated Press, September 15, 1991. The sources cited in the story were forensic anthropologist Clyde Snow, who examined newly found bones at the Little Bighorn in 1985, and Doug McChristian, chief historian at Custer Battlefield National Monument in Montana. Snow looked into the records of Custer's burial and his exhumation. "I have a suspicion they got the wrong body," said Snow, of Norman, Oklahoma. "The only way to put those

suspicions to bed would be to look at the bones interred at West Point and see how they gibe with information we have on Gen. Custer."

48. Personal visits to the park occurred in July 2012 and July 2013. Interviews with rangers were from July 2013.

BIBLIOGRAPHY

BOOKS

Abrams, Marc H. *Sioux War Dispatches: Reports from the Field, 1876–1877*. Yardley, PA: Westholme, 2012.

Adams, Charles Francis, Jr. *A Cycle of Adams Letters, 1861–1865*. Vol. 2. Edited by Worthington Chauncey Ford. Boston: Houghton Mifflin, 1920.

Agassiz, George R., ed. *Meade's Headquarters, 1863–1865: Letters of Colonel Theodore Lyman from the Wilderness to Appomattox*. Boston: Atlantic Monthly Press, 1922.

Aldrich, Charles, ed. "Captain Thomas Drummond." *The Annals of Iowa* 6, no. 3. Des Moines: Historical Department of Iowa, 1903–1905.

Ambrose, Stephen E. *Crazy Horse and Custer: The Parallel Lives of Two American Warriors*. Garden City, NY: Doubleday, 1975.

Andrews, J. Cutler. *The South Reports the Civil War*. Princeton, NJ: Princeton University Press, 1970.

Ashdown, Paul, and Edward Caudill. *The Mosby Myth: A Confederate Hero in Life and Legend*. Wilmington, DE: Scholarly Resources, 2001.

———. *The Myth of Nathan Bedford Forrest: Life and Legend*. Wilmington, DE: Scholarly Resources, 2005.

Athearn, Robert G. *The Mythic West in Twentieth-Century America*. Lawrence: University Press of Kansas, 1986.

———. *William Tecumseh Sherman and the Settlement of the West*. Norman: University of Oklahoma Press, 1995.

Baker, Carlos. *Ernest Hemingway: A Life Story*. New York: Charles Scribner's Sons, 1969.

Bannister, Richard. *Social Darwinism: Science and Myth in Anglo-American Social Thought*. Philadelphia: Temple University Press, 1979.

Barnard, Sandy. *I Go with Custer: The Life and Death of Reporter Mark Kellogg*. Bismarck, ND: Bismarck Tribune, 1996.

Barnes, Jeff. *The Great Plains Guide to Custer: 85 Forts, Fights & Other Sites*. Mechanicsburg, PA: Stackpole Books, 2012.

Barnett, Louise. *Touched by Fire: The Life, Death and Mythic Afterlife of George Armstrong Custer*. New York: Henry Holt, 1996.

Blackford, William W. *War Years with Jeb Stuart*. New York: Charles Scribner's Sons, 1946.

Blake, Michael. *Marching to Valhalla*. New York: Random House, 1996.

Botkin, Benjamin Albert. *A Civil War Treasury of Tales, Legends, and Folklore*. New York: Random House, 1960.

Boudrye, Louis N. *Historic Records of the 5th New York Cavalry in the Civil War.* Albany, NY: J. Munsell, 1868.

Boyer, G. G. *Custer, Terry and Me.* New York: Dorchester, 2005.

Bryson, Bill. *The Lost Continent: Travels in Small-Town America.* New York: Harper & Row, 1989.

Buell, Thomas B. *The Warrior Generals: Combat Leadership in the Civil War.* New York: Three Rivers Press, 1997.

Burns, Vincent L. *The Fifth New York Cavalry in the Civil War.* Jefferson, NC: McFarland, 2014.

Busey, John W., and Kathy G. Harrison. *Nothing but Glory: Pickett's Division at Gettysburg.* Gettysburg, PA: Thomas, 1993.

Busey, John W., and David G. Martin. *Regimental Strengths and Losses at Gettysburg.* Hightstown, NJ: Longstreet House, 1994.

Callwell, C. E. *Small Wars: Their Principles and Practice.* 3rd ed. Lincoln: University of Nebraska Press, 1996; orig. pub. 1896; 3rd ed. orig. pub. 1906.

Carhart, Tom. *Lost Triumph: Lee's Real Plan at Gettysburg and Why It Failed.* New York: G. P. Putnam's Sons, 2005.

Carroll, John M., ed. *Custer in the Civil War: His Unfinished Memoirs.* San Rafael, CA: Presidio Press, 1977.

Catton, Bruce. *A Stillness at Appomattox.* Garden City, NY: Doubleday, 1953.

———. *Terrible Swift Sword.* Garden City, NY: Doubleday, 1963.

Caudill, Edward, and Paul Ashdown. *Sherman's March in Myth and Memory.* Lanham, MD: Rowman & Littlefield, 2008.

Coffey, David. *Sheridan's Lieutenants: Phil Sheridan, His Generals, and the Final Year of the Civil War.* Lanham, MD: Rowman & Littlefield, 2005.

Connell, Evan S. *Son of the Morning Star.* San Francisco: North Point Press, 1984.

Coplin, Keith. *Crofton's Fire.* New York: G. P. Putnam's Sons, 2004.

Curtin, Michael, and Lynn Spigel, eds. *The Revolution Wasn't Televised: Sixties Television and Social Conflict.* New York: Routledge, 1997.

Custer, Brice. *The Sacrificial Lion: George Armstrong Custer, from American Hero to Media Villain.* El Segundo, CA: Upton and Sons, 1999.

Custer, Elizabeth. *Boots and Saddles; or, Life in Dakota with General Custer.* Norman: University of Oklahoma Press, 1980; orig. pub. 1885.

Custer, George Armstrong. *My Life on the Plains.* Edited by Milo Milton Quaife. Norman: University of Oklahoma Press, 1962; orig. pub. 1874.

Davis, Burke. *Jeb Stuart: The Last Cavalier.* New York: Wings Books, Random House, 1994; orig. pub. 1957.

Davis, William C. *Battle at Bull Run: A History of the First Major Campaign of the Civil War.* Baton Rouge: Louisiana State University Press, 1977.

Dee, Tim. *Four Fields.* New York: Random House, 2013.

DeLand, Charles Edmund. *The Sioux Wars.* Pierre: South Dakota Historical Collections, 1934.

DeLeon, Thomas Cooper. *Belles, Beaux and Brains of the 60's.* New York: G. W. Dillingham, 1909.

DeLoria, Vine, Jr. *Custer Died for Your Sins: An Indian Manifesto.* New York: Macmillan, 1969.

Derby, W. R., and W. C. King. *Camp-Fire Sketches and Battlefield Echoes of the Rebellion.* Cleveland, OH: N. G. Hamilton, 1887.

Develder, Paul van. *Savages and Scoundrels: The Untold Story of America's Road to Empire through Indian Territory.* New Haven, CT: Yale University Press, 2009.

Dippie, Brian W. *Custer's Last Stand: The Anatomy of an American Myth.* Rev. ed. Lincoln: University of Nebraska Press, 1994.

———, ed. *Nomad: George A. Custer in Turf, Field and Farm.* Austin: University of Texas Press, 1980.

———. *The Vanishing American: White Attitudes and U.S. Indian Policy.* Middletown, CT: Wesleyan University Press, 1982.

Donahue, Michael N. *Drawing Battle Lines: The Map Testimony of Custer's Last Fight.* El Segundo, CA: Upton and Sons, 2008.

Donovan, James. *A Terrible Glory: Custer and the Little Bighorn—The Last Great Battle of the American West.* New York: Little, Brown, 2008.

Donovan, Jim. *Custer and the Little Bighorn: The Man, the Mystery, the Myth.* New York: Crestline, 2011; orig. pub. 2001.

Dougherty, Kevin. *The Peninsula Campaign of 1862: A Military Analysis.* Jackson: University Press of Mississippi, 2005.

Dowdey, Clifford. *The Seven Days: The Emergence of Robert E. Lee.* New York: Fairfax Press, 1978; orig. pub. 1964.

Dustin, Fred. *The Custer Tragedy.* El Segundo, CA: Upton and Sons, 1987.

Dyer, Thomas. *Theodore Roosevelt and the Idea of Race.* Baton Rouge: Louisiana State University Press, 1980.

Eby, Carl P. *Hemingway's Fetishism: Psychoanalysis and the Mirror of Manhood.* Albany: State University of New York Press, 1999.

Egerton, Douglas R. *The Wars of Reconstruction: The Brief, Violent History of America's Most Progressive Era.* New York: Bloomsbury, 2014.

Eicher, David J. *The Longest Night: A Military History of the Civil War.* New York: Touchstone, 2001.

Elliott, Michael A. *Custerology: The Enduring Legacy of the Indian Wars and George Armstrong Custer.* Chicago: University of Chicago Press, 2007.

Etulain, Richard W. *The Life and Legends of Calamity Jane.* Norman: University of Oklahoma Press, 2014.

Faust, Drew Gilpin. *The Republic of Suffering: Death and the American Civil War.* New York: Knopf, 2008.

Fellman, Michael. *Citizen Sherman: A Life of William Tecumseh Sherman.* New York: Random House, 1995.

Fishel, Edwin C. *The Secret War for the Union: The Untold Story of Military Intelligence in the Civil War.* Boston: Houghton Mifflin, 1996.

Fox, Richard Allan, Jr. *Archaeology, History, and Custer's Last Battle: The Little Big Horn Reexamined.* Norman: University of Oklahoma Press, 1993.

Frost, Lawrence A. *Custer Legends.* Bowling Green, OH: Bowling Green University Popular Press, 1981.

Gordon, John Brown. *Reminiscences of the Civil War.* New York: Charles Scribner's Sons, 1904.

Graham, W. A. *The Custer Myth: A Source Book of Custeriana.* New York: Bonanza Books, 1953.

Grant, Ulysses S. *Personal Memoirs of U. S. Grant.* Vol. 2. New York: Charles L. Webster, 1885.

Gray, John S. *Centennial Campaign: The Sioux War of 1876.* Norman: University of Oklahoma Press, 1988; repr. of 1976.

———. *Custer's Last Campaign: Mitch Boyer and the Little Bighorn Reconstructed.* Lincoln: University of Nebraska Press, 1991.

Greene, Jerome A. *Stricken Field: The Little Bighorn since 1876.* Norman: University of Oklahoma Press, 2008.

———. *Washita: The U.S. Army and the Southern Cheyennes, 1867–1869.* Norman: University of Oklahoma Press, 2004.

Greiner, Henry. *General Phil Sheridan as I Knew Him, Playmate-Comrade-Friend.* Chicago: J. S. Hyland, 1908.

Griffin, Peter. *Along with Youth: Hemingway, the Early Years.* New York: Oxford University Press, 1985.

Grossman, James R., ed. *The Frontier in American Culture.* Berkeley: University of California Press, 1994.

Haller, John S. *Outcasts from Evolution: Scientific Attitudes of Racial Inferiority, 1859–1900.* Urbana: University of Illinois Press, 1971.

Hammer, Kenneth, ed. *Custer in '76: Walter Camp's Notes on the Custer Fight*. Norman: University of Oklahoma Press, 1990.

Hardin, David. *After the War: The Lives and Images of Major Civil War Figures after the Shooting Stopped*. Chicago: Ivan R. Dee, 2010.

Hardorff, Richard G., ed. *On the Little Bighorn with Walter Camp: A Collection of Walter Mason Camp's Letters, Notes and Opinions on Custer's Last Fight*. El Segundo, CA: Upton and Sons, 2002.

———, ed. *Washita Memories: Eyewitness Views of Custer's Attack on Black Kettle's Village*. Norman: University of Oklahoma Press, 2006.

Harris, Brayton. *Blue & Gray in Black & White: Newspapers in the Civil War*. Washington, DC: Batsford Brassey, 1999.

Harris, Samuel. *Personal Reminiscences of Samuel Harris*. Chicago: Rogerson Press, 1897.

Harrison, Kathy Georg, and John W. Busey. *Nothing but Glory: Pickett's Division at Gettysburg*. Gettysburg, PA: Thomas Publications, 1993.

Hatch, Thom. *Black Kettle: The Cheyenne Chief Who Sought Peace but Found War*. Hoboken, NJ: John Wiley & Sons, 2004.

———. *The Custer Companion: A Comprehensive Guide to the Life of George Armstrong Custer and the Plains Indian Wars*. Mechanicsburg, PA: Stackpole Books, 2002.

———. *Glorious War: The Civil War Adventures of George Armstrong Custer*. New York: St. Martin's Press, 2013.

Haydon, Frederick Stansbury. *Aeronautics in the Union and Confederate Armies, with a Survey of Military Aeronautics Prior to 1861*. Baltimore: Johns Hopkins Press, 1941.

Hays, Robert G. *A Race at Bay: New York Times Editorials on "the Indian Problem," 1860–1900*. Carbondale: Southern Illinois University Press, 1997.

Hemingway, Ernest. *Across the River and into the Trees*. New York: Charles Scribner's Sons, 1950.

———. *Ernest Hemingway: Selected Letters, 1917–1961*. Edited by Carlos Baker. New York: Charles Scribner's Sons, 1981.

———. *For Whom the Bell Tolls*. New York: Charles Scribner's Sons, 1940.

———. *Islands in the Stream*. New York: Charles Scribner's Sons, 1970.

Hofling, Charles K. *Custer and the Little Big Horn*. Detroit: Wayne State University Press, 1981.

Hofstadter, Richard. *Social Darwinism in American Thought*. Boston: Beacon Press, 1955.

Hoig, Stan. *The Battle of the Washita: The Sheridan-Custer Indian Campaign of 1867–69*. Lincoln: University of Nebraska Press, 1976.

Howe, Henry. *Historical Collections of Ohio: An Encyclopedia of the State*. Vol. 1. Cincinnati: State of Ohio, 1907.

Hunt, Frazier. *Custer: The Last of the Cavaliers*. New York: Cosmopolitan Book Corporation, 1928.

Hutton, Paul Andrew, ed. *The Custer Reader*. Norman: University of Oklahoma Press, 1992.

———. *Phil Sheridan and His Army*. Lincoln: University of Nebraska Press, 1985.

Hyde, Thomas W. *Following the Greek Cross; or, Memories of the Sixth Army Corps*. Boston: Houghton Mifflin, 1894.

Jacobs, Michael. *Notes on the Rebel Invasion of Maryland and Pennsylvania and the Battle of Gettysburg*. Philadelphia: Lippincott, 1864.

Johnson, Clint. *In the Footsteps of J. E. B. Stuart*. Winston-Salem, NC: John F. Blair, 2003.

Johnson, Robert U., and Clarence C. Buel, eds. *Battles and Leaders of the Civil War*. New York: Century, 1887–1888.

Jones, Douglas C. *The Court-Martial of George Armstrong Custer: A Novel*. New York: Charles Scribner's Sons, 1976.

Jones, Virgil Carrington. *Eight Hours before Richmond*. New York: Holt, 1957.

———. *Gray Ghosts and Rebel Raiders*. New York: Promontory Press, 1995; orig. pub. 1956.

Jordan, David M. *Winfield Scott Hancock: A Soldier's Life*. Bloomington: Indiana University Press, 1996.

Kagan, Robert. *Dangerous Nation*. New York: Knopf, 2006.

Kammen, Michael. *Mystic Chords of Memory: The Transformation of Tradition in American Culture.* New York: Vintage Books, 1993.

Kidd, J. H. *Riding with Custer: Recollections of a Cavalryman in the Civil War.* Lincoln: University of Nebraska Press, 1997; orig. pub. 1908.

Kinsley, D. A. *Favor the Bold.* New York: Promontory Press, 1968; orig. pub. 1967, 1968 as two volumes: *"Favor the Bold" in Custer: Civil War Years.* Vol. 1. New York: Holt, Rinehart and Winston, 1967.

Knight, Oliver. *Following the Indian Wars: The Story of the Newspaper Correspondents among the Indian Campaigners.* Norman: University of Oklahoma Press, 1960.

Krause, Herbert, and Gary D. Olsen. *Prelude to Glory: A Newspaper Accounting of Custer's 1874 Expedition to the Black Hills.* Sioux Falls, SD: Brevet Press, 1974.

Krech, Shepard, III. *The Ecological Indian: Myth and History.* New York: W. W. Norton, 1999.

Kuralt, Charles. *On the Road with Charles Kuralt.* New York: Putnam, 1985.

Longacre, Edward G. *The Cavalry at Appomattox: A Tactical Study of Mounted Operations during the Civil War's Climactic Campaign, March 27–April 9, 1865.* Mechanicsburg, PA: Stackpole Books, 2003.

———. *The Cavalry at Gettysburg: A Tactical Study of Mounted Operations during the Civil War's Pivotal Campaign, 9 June–14 July 1863.* London: Associated University Presses, 1986.

———. *Custer and His Wolverines: The Michigan Cavalry Brigade, 1861–1865.* Cambridge, MA: Da Capo Press, 1997.

Longstreet, James. *From Manassas to Appomattox: Memoirs of the Civil War in America.* Bloomington: Indiana University Press, 1960; orig. pub. 1896.

Lounsberry, Clement A. *Early History of North Dakota: Essential Outlines of American History.* Washington, DC: Liberty Press, 1919.

Lynn, Kenneth. *Hemingway.* New York: Simon & Schuster, 1987.

Maclean, Norman. *The Norman Maclean Reader.* Edited by O. Alan Weltzien. Chicago: University of Chicago Press, 2008.

Mark, Penrose G. *Red, White, and Blue Badge, Pennsylvania Veteran Volunteers: A History of the 93rd Regiment, Known as the "Lebanon Infantry" and "One of the 300 Fighting Regiments" from September 12th, 1861, to June 27th, 1865.* Baltimore: Butternut and Blue, 1993; orig. pub. 1911.

Marszalek, John F. *Sherman: A Soldier's Passion for Order.* New York: Free Press, 1993.

Martin, Samuel J. *Kill-Cavalry: The Life of Union General Hugh Judson Kilpatrick.* Mechanicsburg, PA: Stackpole Books, 2000; orig. pub. 1996.

Marvel, William. *Lee's Last Retreat: The Flight to Appomattox.* Chapel Hill: University of North Carolina Press, 2006.

Mathews, Joseph J. *Reporting the Wars.* Minneapolis: University of Minnesota Press, 1957.

McClellan, George B. *The Civil War Papers of George B. McClellan: Selected Correspondence, 1860–1865.* Edited by Stephen W. Sears. New York: Ticknor & Fields, 1989.

———. *McClellan's Own Story: The War for the Union, the Soldiers Who Fought It, the Civilians Who Directed It, and His Relations to It and to Them.* Edited by William C. Prime. New York: Charles L. Webster, 1887.

McClellan, H. B. *I Rode with Jeb Stuart.* Bloomington: Indiana University Press, 1958.

McDonald, JoAnna M. *"We Shall Meet Again": The First Battle of Manassas (Bull Run).* New York: Oxford University Press, 1999.

McMurry, Richard M. *John Bell Hood and the War for Southern Independence.* Lexington: University Press of Kentucky, 1982.

McMurtry, Larry. *Crazy Horse.* New York: Viking, 1999.

———. *Custer.* New York: Simon & Schuster, 2012.

McPherson, James M. *Crossroads of Freedom: Antietam.* New York: Oxford University Press, 2002.

Merington, Marguerite, ed. *The Custer Story: The Life and Intimate Letters of General George A. Custer and His Wife Elizabeth.* New York: Devin-Adair, 1950.

Mitchell, Adele H., ed. *The Letters of John S. Mosby*. 2nd ed. N.p., Stuart-Mosby Historical Society, 1986.

Monaghan, Jay. *Custer: The Life of General George Armstrong Custer*. Lincoln: University of Nebraska Press, 1971; orig. pub. 1959.

Morris, Roy, Jr. *Sheridan: The Life and Wars of General Phil Sheridan*. New York: Crown, 1992.

Mosby, John S. *The Memoirs of John S. Mosby*. Edited by Charles Wells Russell. Nashville, TN: J. S. Sanders, 1995; orig. pub. 1917.

Mueller, James E. *Shooting Arrows and Slinging Mud: Custer, the Press, and the Little Bighorn*. Norman: University of Oklahoma Press, 2013.

Neese, Gordon M. *Three Years in the Confederate Horse Artillery*. New York: Neale, 1911.

Noyalas, Jonathan A. *The Battle of Cedar Creek: Victory from the Jaws of Defeat*. Charleston, SC: History Press, 2011.

Oftinoski, Steven. *The Golden Age of Novelty Songs*. New York: Billboard Books, 2000.

Olson, Gary D. *Prelude to Glory: A Newspaper Accounting of Custer's 1874 Expedition to the Black Hills*. Sioux Falls, SD: Brevet Press, 1974.

Parks, Rita. *The Western Hero in Film and Television*. Ann Arbor, MI: UMI Research Press, 1982.

Peterson, Merrill D. *Lincoln in American Memory*. New York: Oxford University Press, 1994.

Pfanz, Donald. *Richard S. Ewell: A Soldier's Life*. Chapel Hill: University of North Carolina Press, 1998.

Philbrick, Nathaniel. *The Last Stand: Custer, Sitting Bull, and the Battle of the Little Bighorn*. New York: Viking, 2010.

Phillips, Kevin. *The Cousins' Wars: Religion, Politics, and the Triumph of Anglo-America*. New York: Basic Books, 1999.

Powers, Thomas. *The Killing of Crazy Horse*. New York: Knopf, 2010.

Quarstein, John V., and J. Michael Moore. *Yorktown's Civil War Siege: Drums along the Warwick*. Charleston, SC: History Press, 2012.

Rafuse, Ethan S. *McClellan's War: The Failure of Moderation in the Struggle for the Union*. Bloomington: Indiana University Press, 2005.

———. *A Single Grand Victory: The First Campaign and Battle of Manassas*. Wilmington, DE: Scholarly Resources, 2002.

Ramage, James A. *Gray Ghost: The Life of Col. John Singleton Mosby*. Lexington: University Press of Kentucky, 1999.

Reilly, Hugh J. *The Frontier Newspapers and the Coverage of the Plains Indian Wars*. Santa Barbara, CA: Praeger, 2010.

Reynolds, Quentin. *Custer's Last Stand*. New York: Random House, 1951.

Rhea, Gordon C. *The Battle of the Wilderness, May 5–6, 1865*. Baton Rouge: Louisiana State University Press, 1994.

———. *The Battles for Spotsylvania Court House and the Road to Yellow Tavern, May 7–12*. Baton Rouge: Louisiana State University Press, 1997.

———. *To the North Anna River: Grant and Lee, May 13–25, 1864*. Baton Rouge: Louisiana State University Press, 2000.

Richardson, Heather Cox. *West from Appomattox: The Reconstruction of America after the Civil War*. New Haven, CT: Yale University Press, 2007.

Robbins, James S. *Last in Their Class: Custer, Pickett and the Goats of West Point*. New York: Encounter Books, 2006.

———. *The Real Custer: From Boy General to Tragic Hero*. Washington, DC: Regnery, 2014.

Roe, Charles F. *Custer's Last Battle*. New York: Bruce, 1927.

Roosevelt, Theodore. *The Winning of the West*. Vol. 1. New York: G. P. Putnam's Sons, 1903.

Rowland, Thomas J. *George B. McClellan and Civil War History: In the Shadow of Grant and Sherman*. Kent, OH: Kent State University Press, 1998.

Royster, Charles. *The Destructive War: William Tecumseh Sherman, Stonewall Jackson, and the Americans*. New York: Knopf, 1991.

Sanderson, Rena, ed. *Blowing the Bridge: Essays on Hemingway and* For Whom the Bell Tolls. New York: Greenwood, 1992.

Sandford, George B. *Fighting Rebels and Redskins: Experiences in Army Life of Colonel George B. Sanford, 1861–1892.* Edited by E. R. Hagemann. Norman: University of Oklahoma Press, 1969.

Sandoz, Mari. *The Battle of the Little Bighorn.* Lincoln: University of Nebraska Press, 1978; orig. pub. 1966.

Saunt, Claudio. *West of the Revolution: An Uncommon History of 1776.* New York: W. W. Norton, 2014.

Schaff, Morris. *The Spirit of Old West Point, 1858–1862.* Boston: Houghton, Mifflin, 1907.

Schultz, Duane. *Coming through Fire: George Armstrong Custer and Chief Black Kettle.* Yardley, PA: Westholme, 2012.

———. *Custer: Lessons in Leadership.* New York: Palgrave Macmillan, 2010.

———. *The Dahlgren Affair: Terror and Conspiracy in the Civil War.* New York: W. W. Norton, 1998.

Schurz, Carl. *The Reminiscences of Carl Schurz.* Vol. 3. New York: McClure, 1907–1908.

Sears, Stephen W. *Gettysburg.* Boston: Houghton Mifflin, 2003.

———. *Landscape Turned Red.* New Haven, CT: Ticknor & Fields, 1983.

———. *To the Gates of Richmond: The Peninsula Campaign.* New York: Ticknor & Fields, 1992.

Shaara, Jeff. *Gods and Generals.* New York: Ballantine Books, 1996.

Sheridan, Philip H. *Personal Memoirs of P. H. Sheridan.* Vol. 1. New York: Charles L. Webster, 1888.

Sherman, W. T. *Sherman Papers.* South Bend, IN: University of Notre Dame, 1862.

Siepel, Kevin H. *Rebel: The Life and Times of John Singleton Mosby.* New York: Da Capo Press, 1997; orig. pub. 1983.

Simmons, Dan. *Black Hills.* New York: Back Bay Books, 2011; orig. pub. 2010.

Simson, Jay W. *Custer and the Front Royal Executions of 1864.* Jefferson, NC: McFarland, 2009.

Sklenar, Larry. *To Hell with Honor: Custer and the Little Bighorn.* Norman: University of Oklahoma Press, 2000.

Slotkin, Richard. *The Fatal Environment: The Myth of the Frontier in the Age of Industrialization, 1800–1890.* New York: Harper Perennial, 1994.

———. *Gunfighter Nation: The Myth of the Frontier in Twentieth-Century America.* New York: Harper Perennial, 1993.

Spigel, Lynn, and Michael Curtin, eds. *The Revolution Wasn't Televised: Sixties Television and Social Conflict.* New York: Routledge, 1997.

Spilsbury, Julian. *Great Military Disasters: A History of Incompetence.* New York: Metro Books, 2010.

Stands in Timber, John, and Margot Liberty. *Cheyenne Memories.* New Haven, CT: Yale University Press, 1967.

Starr, Stephen Z. *The Union Cavalry in the Civil War.* 2 vols. Baton Rouge: Louisiana State University Press, 1979 and 1981.

Stewart, Edgar Irving. *Custer's Luck.* Norman: University of Oklahoma Press, 1955.

Sumner, Mark. *Devil's Tower.* New York: Ballantine Books, 1996.

Taylor, James E. *The James E. Taylor Sketchbook: With Sheridan up the Shenandoah Valley in 1864. Leaves from a Special Artist's Sketch Book and Diary.* Dayton, OH: Morningside House, 1989.

Thomas, Emory M. *Bold Dragoon: The Life of J. E. B. Stuart.* New York: Harper & Row, 1986.

Tidball, Eugene C. *"No Disgrace to My Country": The Life of John C. Tidball.* Kent, OH: Kent State University Press, 2002.

Toplin, Robert Brent, ed. *Ken Burns's The Civil War: Historians Respond.* New York: Oxford University Press, 1996.

Tremain, Henry Edwin. *The Last Hours of Sheridan's Cavalry.* New York: Bonnell, Silver and Bowers, 1904.

Turner, Frederick J. *History, Frontier, and Section: Three Essays.* Albuquerque: University of New Mexico Press, 1993.

Turtledove, Harry. *The Great War: American Front*. New York: Random House, 1999.
———. *The Great War: Breakthroughs*. New York: Random House, 2001.
———. *The Great War: Walk in Hell*. New York: Random House, 2000.
Urwin, Gregory J. W. *Custer Victorious: The Civil War Battles of General George Armstrong Custer*. East Brunswick, NJ: Associated University Presses, 1983.
Utley, Robert M. *Cavalier in Buckskin: George Armstrong Custer and the Western Military Frontier*. Norman: University of Oklahoma Press, 1988.
———. *Custer and Me*. Norman: University of Oklahoma Press, 2004.
———. *Custer and the Great Controversy: The Origin and Development of a Legend*. Lincoln: University of Nebraska Press, 1962.
———. *Little Bighorn Battlefield: A History and Guide to the Battle of the Little Bighorn*. Washington, DC: U.S. Department of the Interior, 1994; orig. pub. 1988.
———, ed. *The Reno Court of Inquiry: The Chicago Sun Times Account*. Fort Collins, CO: Old Army Press, 1983.
Van de Water, Frederic F. *Glory-Hunter: A Life of General Custer*. Lincoln: University of Nebraska Press, 1988; orig. pub. 1934.
Vestal, Stanley. *Short Grass Country*. New York: Duell, Sloan & Pierce, 1941.
Viola, Herman J. *Little Bighorn Remembered: The Untold Indian Story of Custer's Last Stand*. New York: Times Books, 1999.
Waldrop, Howard, et al. *Custer's Last Jump and Other Collaborations*. Urbana, IL: Golden Gryphon Press, 2003.
Welch, James, with Paul Stekler. *Killing Custer: The Battle of the Little Bighorn and the Fate of the Plains Indians*. New York: W. W. Norton, 1994.
Wert, Jeffry D. *Custer: The Controversial Life of George Armstrong Custer*. New York: Simon & Schuster, 1996.
Wheelan, Joseph. *Terrible Swift Sword: The Life of General Philip H. Sheridan*. Cambridge, MA: Da Capo Press, 2012.
Wheeler, Richard, ed. *Lee's Terrible Swift Sword: From Antietam to Chancellorsville, an Eyewitness History*. New York: HarperCollins, 1992.
Whittaker, Frederick. *A Complete Life of General George A. Custer*. 2 vols. Lincoln: University of Nebraska Press, 1993; repr. of 1876.
Williams, Roger L. *Military Register of Custer's Last Command*. Norman, OK: Arthur C. Clark, 2009.
Wills, Brian Steel. *A Battle from the Start: The Life of Nathan Bedford Forrest*. New York: HarperCollins, 1992.
Wilson, James Harrison. *Under the Old Flag: Recollections of Military Operations in the War for the Union, the Spanish War, the Boxer Rebellion, etc.* New York: D. Appleton, 1912.
Windolph, Charles. *I Fought with Custer: The Story of Sergeant Windolph, Last Survivor of the Battle of the Little Bighorn as Told to Frazier and Robert Hunt*. Lincoln: University of Nebraska Press, 1987; orig. pub. 1947.
Wineapple, Brenda. *Ecstatic Nation: Confidence, Crisis, and Compromise, 1848–1877*. New York: Harper, 2013.
Wittenberg, Eric J. *The Battle of Brandy Station: North America's Largest Cavalry Battle*. Charleston, SC: History Press, 2011.
———. *Like a Meteor Blazing Brightly: The Short but Controversial Life of Colonel Ulrich Dahlgren*. Roseville, MN: Edinborough Press, 2009.
———. *Protecting the Flank at Gettysburg: The Battles for Brinkerhoff's Ridge and East Cavalry Field, July 2–3, 1863*. El Dorado Hills, CA: Savas Beatie, 2013.
Woodworth, Steven E. *Beneath a Northern Sky: A Short History of the Gettysburg Campaign*. Wilmington, DE: Scholarly Resources, 2003.

NEWSPAPERS AND PERIODICALS

Bismarck Weekly Tribune, 1876.
Chicago Inter-Ocean, 1874.
Confederate Veteran 7, 1899.
Daily National Intelligencer, 1865.
Detroit Advertiser, 1865.
Elizabethtown News, 1921.
Frank Leslie's Popular Monthly, 1888.
Galaxy, 1876.
Harper's Weekly, 1864.
Helena Daily Herald, 1876.
Montana: The Magazine of Western History, 1971, 1976.
New York Herald, 1876.
New York Times, 1863, 1876, 2012.
New York Tribune, 1874, 1910.
Richmond Times, 1899.
Southern Historical Society Papers, 1899.
Time Magazine, 1968.

ARTICLES AND CHAPTERS

Ambrose, Stephen E. "William T. Sherman: A Personality Profile." *American History Illustrated* 1 (January 1967): 5–12, 54–57.

Bjork, Ulf Jonas. "The Swedish-American Press and the Sioux." *Swedish-American Historical Quarterly* 60, no. 2 (April 2009): 72–90.

Coward, John M. "Explaining the Little Bighorn: Race and Progress in the Native Press." *Journalism and Mass Communication Quarterly* 71, no. 3 (Autumn 1994): 540–49.

Custer, George A. "The Red Man." *The Harrisonian: Journal of the Harrison County*, no. 2 (1989); reprint of May 5, 1858, article.

Dippie, Brian W. Introduction to *Custer and the Great Controversy: The Origin and Development of a Legend* by Robert M. Utley. Lincoln: University of Nebraska Press, 1992.

———. "The Southern Response to Custer's Last Stand." *Montana: The Magazine of Western History* 21, no. 2 (April 1971): 18–31.

Dustin, Fred. "George Armstrong Custer." *Michigan History Journal* 30 (April–June 1946): 227–54.

Ehrlich, Matthew C. "Myth in Charles Kuralt's 'On the Road.'" *Journalism and Mass Communication Quarterly* 79, no. 2 (Summer 2002): 327–38.

Frost, Lawrence. "The Beginnings of the LBHA." *Little Bighorn Associates Newsletter* 20, no. 1 (1987): 3–4.

Gallagher, Gary W. "Two Generals and a Valley: Philip H. Sheridan and Jubal A. Early in the Shenandoah." In *The Shenandoah Valley Campaign of 1864*, edited by Gary W. Gallagher. Chapel Hill: University of North Carolina Press, 2006.

Gates, Arnold. "Galusha Pennypacker." In *Historical Times Illustrated Encyclopedia of the Civil War*, edited by Patricia L. Faust, 574. New York: HarperCollins, 1991.

Ghaemi, Nassir. "Sherman's Demons." *Atlanta* (November 2006): 76–82.

Gompert, David C., and Richard L. Kugler. "Custer and Cognition." *Joint Force Quarterly* 41, no. 2 (2006): 87–93.

Hill, D. H. "McClellan's Change of Base and Malvern Hill." In *Battles and Leaders of the Civil War*, Vol. 2, edited by Robert Underwood Johnson and Clarence Clough Buel, 383–95. New York: Century, 1887–1888.

Hofling, Charles K. "General Custer and the Battle of the Little Big Horn." *Psychoanalytic Review* 54, no. 2 (Summer 1967): 303–28.

————. "George Armstrong Custer: A Psychoanalytic Approach." *Montana: The Magazine of Western History* 21, no. 2 (1971): 32–43.

Hutton, Paul Andrew. "Could Custer Have Won?" *Quarterly Journal of Military History* 25, no. 2 (Winter 2013): 35.

Law, E. M. "From the Wilderness to Cold Harbor." *Century* (June 1887): 227–300.

Mangun, V. Foreword to *I Fought with Custer: The Story of Sergeant Windolph, Last Survivor of the Battle of the Little Big Horn as Told to Frazier and Robert Hunt.* Lincoln: University of Nebraska Press, 1987.

McBlain, John F. "With Gibbon on the Sioux Campaign of 1876." *Journal of the U.S. Cavalry Association* 9, no. 33 (1896).

McClellan, David. "The Battle of the Little Big Horn in Hemingway's Later Fiction." In *Fitzgerald/Hemingway Annual 1976*, edited by Matthew J. Bruccoli, 245–48. Englewood, CO: Information Handling Services, 1978.

————. "Is Custer a Model for the Fascist Captain in *For Whom the Bell Tolls*?" In *Fitzgerald/ Hemingway Annual 1974*, edited by Matthew J. Bruccoli and C. E. Frazer Clark Jr., 239–40. Englewood, CO: Information Handling Services, 1975.

Miller, William E. "The Cavalry Battle Near Gettysburg." In *Battles and Leaders of the Civil War*, Vol. 3, edited by Robert Underwood Johnson and Clarence Clough Buell, 401, 404–5. New York: Century, 1887–1888.

Moore, Charles. "The Days of Fife and Drum." In *Collections and Researches Made by the Michigan Pioneer and Historical Society*, Vol. 28, 450. Lansing: Michigan Pioneer and Historical Society, 1900.

Moore, Robert. "Custer and the Shadow Soldiers." *Civil War Times* 39, no. 1 (March 2000): 29–34, 58.

Myers, Rex C. "Montana Editors and the Custer Battle." *Montana: The Magazine of Western History* 26, no. 2 (Spring 1976): 18–31.

Patchen, Scott C. "The Battle of Crooked Run: George Custer's Opening Act in the Shenandoah Valley." *North and South* 11, no. 2 (December 2008): 76–82.

Rosenberg, Bruce A. "How Custer's 'Last Stand' Got Its Name." *Georgia Review* 26, no. 3 (Fall 1972): 279–96.

Russell, Don. "Custer's First Charge." *By Valor & Arms: The Journal of American Military History* 1, no. 1 (October 1974): 20.

Russell, Karen Miller, Janice Hume, and Karen Sichler. "Libbie Custer's 'Last Stand': Image Restoration, the Press, and Public Memory." *Journalism and Mass Communication Quarterly* (September 2007): 582–99.

Sabine, David B. "Philip Kearny." In *Historical Times Illustrated Encyclopedia of the Civil War*, edited by Patricia L. Faust, 408–9. New York: HarperCollins, 1991.

Showalter, Dennis. "The U.S. Cavalry: Soldiers of a Nation, Policeman of an Empire." *Army History* 8 (Fall 2001): 6–24.

Steckmesser, Kent L. "Custer in Fiction: George Custer, Hero or Villain?" *American West* 1, no. 4 (Fall 1964): 47–52, 63–64.

Stewart, Edgar Irving. Introduction to *My Life on the Plains: or, Personal Experiences with Indians* by George Armstrong Custer. Norman: University of Oklahoma Press, 1962.

————. "A Psychoanalytic Approach to Custer: Some Reflections." *Montana: The Magazine of Western History* 21, no. 3 (1971): 74–77.

Thompson, Mark. "The Enduring Custer Legend." *American History Illustrated* 11, no. 3 (June 1976): 18–31.

————. "Guns of the Revolution: Henry Knox, George Washington, and the War of American Independence." In *Sons of the Father: George Washington and His Protégés*, edited by Robert M. S. McDonald, 121–48. Charlottesville: University of Virginia Press, 2013.

Utley, Robert M. Introduction to *A Complete Life of General George A. Custer*, Vol. 2: *From Appomattox to the Little Big Horn*, by Frederick Whittaker. Lincoln: University of Nebraska Press, 1993.

Wert, Jeffry D. "Battle of Brandy Station, VA." In *Historical Times Illustrated Encyclopedia of the Civil War*, edited by Patricia L. Faust, 76. New York: HarperCollins, 1991.

―――. "Edmund Kirby." In *Historical Times Illustrated Encyclopedia of the Civil War*, edited by Patricia L. Faust, 419. New York: HarperCollins, 1991.

―――. "William Paul Roberts." In *Historical Times Illustrated Encyclopedia of the Civil War*, edited by Patricia L. Faust, 636–37. New York: HarperCollins, 1991.

White, Richard. "Frederick Jackson Turner and Buffalo Bill." In *The Frontier in American Culture*, edited by James R. Grossman, 29. Berkeley: University of California Press, 1994.

Whittaker, Frederick. "The Dashing Dragoon." *Beadle's Boy's Library of Sport, Story and Adventure* 1, no. 98 (April 26, 1982).

WEB PAGES

Davis, Daniel. "Brothers at Bassett Hall." *Emerging Civil War*, October 25, 2011, http://emergingcivilwar.com/2011/10/25/brothers-at-bassett-hall (accessed April 17, 2014).

Gray, Michael P. "The Wilderness during the Civil War." *Encyclopedia Virginia*, Virginia Foundation for the Humanities, April 15, 2011, www.encyclopediavirginia.org/Wilderness_During_the_Civil_War_The (accessed May 8, 2014).

Hardy, John W. "Tales from a Civil War Prison." *Archeology*, August 30, 1999, archive.archaeology.org/online/features/civil/words/hardy.html (accessed April 17, 2014).

Jones, Evan C. "The Macabre Fate of a Civil War Major." Historynet.com, June 12, 2006, www.historynet.com/sullivan-ballou-the-macabre-fate-of-a-american-civil-war-major.htm (accessed April 26, 2014); orig. pub. in *America's Civil War* (November 2004).

Marvel, William E. "Who Was the Youngest Civil War General?" Historynet.com, June 13, 2011, www.historynet.com/who-was-the-youngest-civil-war-general.htm (accessed April 19, 2014).

West, Elliott. "The Civil War and Reconstruction in the American West." Gilder Lehrman Institute of American History, 2014, www.gilderlehrman.org/history-by-era/reconstruction/essays/civil-war-and-reconstruction-american-west (accessed May 14, 2014).

INDEX

ABOUT THE AUTHORS

Edward Caudill is professor of journalism and electronic media at the University of Tennessee. His research interest is history, myth, and popular culture.

Paul Ashdown is professor emeritus of journalism and electronic media at the University of Tennessee. His research interests are nineteenth- and twentieth-century media and cultural history, literary journalism, and war, memory, and society.

They are coauthors of *The Mosby Myth: A Confederate Hero in Life and Legend*; *The Myth of Nathan Bedford Forrest*; and *Sherman's March in Myth and Memory*.